— Empire in Question —

— *Empire in Question* —

READING, WRITING, AND
TEACHING BRITISH IMPERIALISM

Antoinette Burton

with a foreword by Mrinalini Sinha
and an afterword by C. A. Bayly

Duke University Press   Durham and London   2011

For G. F. B.
with love

A WOMAN SELDOM RUNS WILD AFTER AN ABSTRACTION.
—John Stuart Mill, *The Subjection of Women* (1851)

Contents

Foreword   MRINALINI SINHA

Antoinette Burton is associated more closely than most with what today passes under the sign of the "new" imperial history. This identification is both a fitting and yet an inadequate tribute to Burton's extraordinarily rich and generative scholarly oeuvre. It is fitting because there are few who can match Burton in the quantity or in the quality of her scholarly interventions on the state of British and of British imperial historiography. She, along with a handful of scholars, has produced a body of work whose impact has been nothing short of transformative as regards the ways in which scholars study empires and imperialism. This body of work, new in itself, has rejuvenated several subfields. Consequently, she has often been on the front lines of battles that have periodically erupted over the changes in the contours of imperial historiography. Yet the equation of Burton's oeuvre with the "new" imperial history is also incomplete and inadequate. One of the hallmarks of Burton's scholarship has always been a persistent questioning that refuses to settle comfortably within the congealed boundaries of a stable field. She should not be reduced to the poster child for the demarcation of a circumscribed field of study or noted mainly for an allegiance to an a priori approach to the subject under study. This volume, more than any of Burton's numerous individual contributions, and certainly more than the polemical pieces among them, is unique precisely because it brings out this particular, and often overlooked, element of her multidimensional oeuvre.

In this sense, then, *Empire in Question* reintroduces Burton as a scholar and frames her scholarship anew. To be sure, the specialist as well as the neophyte is likely to be familiar with—or, at least, to have heard of—many of the previously published essays in this volume. Several of them, after all, have acquired the status of "classics," appearing with almost unfailing regularity in footnotes and in syllabi covering such subjects as British history, imperial history, South Asian history, women's history, gender studies, cultural studies, and postcolonial studies, as well as contemporary theory, methodology, and historiography. These mostly well-known essays come sandwiched strategically between a characteristically brilliant stocktaking of the contemporary state of imperial history in an introduction written specifically for this volume and a provocative call to arms in a new concluding essay that points toward a future agenda for imperial history. The total experience is something more than a sum of its parts. Between the covers of this book, the essays work both cumulatively and in conversation with one another to produce something unforeseen: what at first may have seemed familiar becomes unexpected and contains an element of "discovery." Even those who know the body of Burton's work well will welcome the chance to view it whole, freed of the burden as representative of a particular side in the battles over imperial history.

There will, of course, be as many ways to read this substantial volume as there will be readers. On one level, the volume, both in the choice of the material included and in its arrangement, has all the elements of a retrospective. Part I contains the more ambitious programmatic and diagnostic of Burton's contributions, while part II consists of finely crafted individual studies that put these ideas to work. Students of imperial history, apart from appreciating the convenience of having many of these scattered essays in one handy volume, will delight at the opportunity to see the sheer ambition of Burton's choice of canvas on which to work. Here are to be found many of the themes that Burton has over the years helped to make de rigueur in contemporary imperial historiography: the expansion of the narrative of British history as an isolated "island story"; the incorporation of the cultural domain in assessing the workings and legacies of imperialism; the use of gender as a tool of analysis to complicate both homogenous group identities and unidirectional relations of power; the engagement with the histories, as well as the historiographies, of regions beyond Europe; and attention to the politics of archives and of the discipline of History itself. Burton, as this volume amply demonstrates, has been there from the very beginning, and at every step of the way, in the seismic transformations that we now take so much for granted —the historiographical developments, for example, that have brought together, on the one hand, the field of British history with that of British imperial history and, on the other, imperial history with a broader interdisciplinary scholarship on imperialism. If these developments have become routine now, it is still useful to be reminded of the struggles, successful and otherwise, that were involved. It would be easy to underestimate a contribution so influential as to have become normative. As Samuel Johnson wrote in *Life of Dryden* (1784), "Learning once made popular is no longer learning; it has the appearance of something which we have bestowed upon ourselves, as the dew appears to rise from the field which it refreshes."

This volume, on yet another level, invites reflection precisely on the stakes of these past battles by drawing attention to the uneven, often contrary, development of imperial historiography over the past decade or so. The volume is not, from this perspective, just another salvo in the process that led to the consolidation, however gradual and contentious, of a new field's formation, whether under the sign of the "new" imperial history or that of postcolonial studies. Rather, it provides a way to open up the field of study once again and, as such, to re-evaluate Burton's own, earlier contributions in this light.

Empire in Question invites such a reading not only through the contents of the introduction and the coda that bookend the more familiar essays, but also through the decision to arrange the essays in each of the two sections chronologically. Even if much in the volume suggests the current interest in the spatial, the structure and the spirit of the book's contribution—and, I would submit, its most interesting intervention—lies, in fact, in the realm of the temporal. Here for the first time we see the full import of Burton's agonistic relationship to imperial history or imperial studies as a "field." The "field" that Burton has helped bring into being for over a decade now was never meant, as this volume reveals—perhaps only retroactively—to be a fixed "space" that is created by the erection of determinate, and eventually calcified, boundaries but, to borrow Gail Hershatter's insightful observation about a different field, was imagined always as a "conjuncture."[1] The latter highlights notions of flux and of multiple determinants; and, as such, it serves as a reminder of the entanglements of imperial history / imperial studies as field formations in a variety of processes and politics that are ongoing. The book, by my reading, is thus not a retrospective that demonstrates where imperial history has been. It is, instead, through a combination of the familiar and the new essays, a guide both to where it could have been and to where it still could be.

The book serves a ground-clearing function, now that some of the earlier passions on the state of imperial history have cooled somewhat, by correcting for partisan distortions and repositioning Burton historiographically. She emerges neither as the vampire slayer of an "old" imperial history nor as the high priest of a "new" imperial history. Her allegiances, as they emerge from these pages, have had little to do with any a priori commitments to this or that topic, approach, or methodology. Her allegiances seem to belong most broadly with a form of *critical* history that is ever alert to the implications of the unanalyzed and the underanalyzed elements of one's own and of others' thinking. The fifteen previously published essays, in their eclectic form and content, as well as in their functioning as historiographical snapshots of particular times and of particular places, support this view. The essays demonstrate, for example, Burton's contributions to the thrust-and-parry of a process that has led— sometimes wittingly but also, more often then not, unwittingly—to the considerably redrawn contours of contemporary imperial history. However, the essays quickly demonstrate that only a single unifying element runs through all of them: the practice of history as *critique.* The heat and dust of battle have sometimes eclipsed this most illuminating and, arguably, the longest-lasting dimension of her contribution.

Consider some of the following examples. If the case for registering the impact of Britain's empire "overseas" on Britain "at home" in the early essays from the '90s is made largely on the strength of what some would dismiss as the "merely cultural," subsequent essays extend the argument to the very heart of "domestic" British politics. Likewise, while earlier essays lament the narrowness of many a "national" history of Britain, others lament the ways in which a newly expanded British history can simply re-center the obsession with the nation. Then, again, just when gender history appears to be in danger of being confined within a room of its own, Burton uses gender and feminist historiography to enter into debates about the fate of social history or about the status of the imperial archives. By adopting a chronological order for the essays, Burton has allowed the traces of her own intellectual development to remain visible. The unfolding of her practices of history as critique, moreover, reveals a formidable coherence at the heart of her intellectual project. The shifting targets in Burton's scholarly essays, no less than the co-written meditation on collaborative pedagogy as a substantive and practical intervention in arguments about the contours of imperial history, do not bespeak attempts either to establish or to follow any particular "school." They are the products of a scholarly mind that is wide ranging and of a scholarship self-consciously "worldly" precisely in the sense of Edward Said's use of the term.

Having freed herself from the burden of bearing the torch for a particular version of imperial history, Burton can train her considerable acumen, as she does in the introduction and, most notably, in the coda, on the current impasse in British imperial history. More recently, indeed, the "field" is gamely shared by routinized new imperial histories and "revisionist" British-empire histories that are fast becoming the rage. Incorporating, as well as blunting the edge of, many of the challenges thrown up by a different moment in the debates over imperial historiography, these histories too often trade on a largely stylistic, and often belated, sense of their own "newness." These include the recasting of British imperial history as global history *tout court*—a critique raised to great effect in Burton's coda to this volume—as well as the recycling of many of the perennial apologetic topoi from the study of empires and imperialism. To wit: the extent to which the inherent complexity of empires resist any generalization about the exploitative character of imperial relations; the degree to which the "agency" of the colonized lets imperial power off the hook; the relative weight of the "trauma" of imperialism on the agents of imperialism and on those subject to imperialism; and, most questionably, the balance between the "benign" (read, good) and more problematic aspects of empire. This, as Burton, quoting Yogi Berra, puts it, is in many ways indeed "déjà vu all over again." Burton's own mode of critical histories of empire, however, reminds us of both what has changed and what remains the same. Whether the way forward for British empire history lies, as she suggests, in greater engagement with the histories and historiographies of other coeval empires and of empires in other historical periods or in something else, the most important lesson that I take away from her work is precisely this: the openness to revision so as to be constantly vigilant against the drift toward calcified banalities of what were once radical propositions.

Preface

A Note on the Logic of the Volume

I intend this volume to serve less as a theoretical white paper on imperial history than as a set of accumulated reflections on the state of British imperial history over two decades. The collection is divided into theory and practice, not to draw false distinctions between those two domains, but to signal the relationship, and sometimes the tension, between different genres of thinking and writing. Essays in each section are arranged in the order of original publication to give a sense of how issues in the field developed over time. I have not altered the original essays (except for stylistic consistency) in the hopes that what eventuates is a kind of historiographical freeze frame (from my vantage point, of course). My introductory essay does not rehearse each essay but provides an overarching autobiographical context, with an emphasis on the contingencies of my own location(s). I think, I hope, that the final essay of the volume works as self-critique, a call for polyphony that moves beyond the binaries I began my career with, which have characterized a variety of imperial histories in the last two centuries—my own included—and which remain challenging to get beyond.

Acknowledgments

When I was a child, my parents had an intriguing title on one of their bookshelves: *These Ruins Are Inhabited*, by Muriel Beadle. Published in 1961, the year I was born, the book described the sabbatical the Beadle family—husband George, wife Muriel, and son Redmond, all from Pasadena—took in Oxford in the late 1950s, chronicling many postwar English curiosities such as the greengrocer who was closed every day of the week but Thursday, the bathroom without the toilet, the free medical services of the local general practitioner. I read the book with great interest as a teenager as my own parents had dragged us—my two sisters and me—off on sabbatical to Britain not once but twice, in 1968 and 1972, submitting us to the rigors of the coal-heated house and the seemingly heatless interiors of the local state school. My friends and family have indulged my subsequent Anglo-skepticism with varying degrees of appreciation, patience, and exasperation. Thanks go to my parents and sisters and David, to Deb and Emie, to George and Laura, to Philippa and Dane, to Ania and Minnie, to Hannah and Madhavi, to Mahua and Lara, to Jennifer and Herman, to Barbara and Gerry, to Catherine and Stuart, to Fiona and Ann and Marilyn, to Jean, to Augusto, to Jed, to Dana and Kathy and Clare, to Gary and Susie, and to Tony and Sally as well. Paul and Nick and Olivia are so good, too good, to me. Debbie, Jamie, Danielle, Melissa, Karen, Emily, Nathan, Anna, T.J., Zack, Rachel, Ashley, Joel, Ian, Brandon, David, Eileen, Becky, Rebecca, Kerry, Mickey, Susan, Jin, Julie, and Irina know, I hope, how much I owe them. Tom and Jan have made many things possible. So have Mina and Nagwa and Danielle; I will long be in their debt. Miriam Angress is as warm and wonderful an editor as anyone could wish for; I am deeply grateful for her insight and her friendship. Finally, this book belongs to

Gerri, in ways I understand and in ways I don't. It always has, and it always will.

Chapters earlier published in the following venues:

"Rules of Thumb: British History and Imperial Culture in 19th- and 20th-Century Britain," *Women's History Review* 3, no. 4 (December 1994), 483–500.

"Who Needs the Nation?: Interrogating 'British' History," *Journal of Historical Sociology* 10, no. 3 (1997), 227–48.

"Thinking beyond the Boundaries: Empire, Feminism, and the Domains of History," *Social History* 26, no. 1 (2001), 60–71.

"Déjà Vu All over Again," *Journal of Colonialism and Colonial History* 3, no. 1 (April 2002), available online at http://muse.jhu.edu/journals/cch.

"When Was Britain? Nostalgia for the Nation at the End of the 'American Century,'" *Journal of Modern History* 75 (June 2003), 359–74.

"Archive Stories: Gender and the Making of Imperial and Colonial Histories," *Gender and Empire*, ed. Philippa Levine (Oxford: Oxford University Press, 2004), 281–93.

"Gender, Colonialism and Feminist Collaboration," *Radical History Review* 101 (Spring 2008), 198–222 (with Jean Allman).

"Fearful Bodies into Disciplined Subjects: Pleasure, Romance, and the Family Drama of Colonial Reform in Mary Carpenter's *Six Months in India*," *Signs* 20, no. 3 (1995), 545–74.

"Contesting the Zenana: The Mission to Make 'Lady Doctors for India,' 1874–1885," *Journal of British Studies* 35 (July 1996), 368–97.

"Recapturing *Jane Eyre*: Reflections on Historicizing the Colonial Encounter in Victorian Britain," *Radical History Review* 64 (Winter 1996), 58–72.

"From 'Child-Bride' to 'Hindoo Lady': Rukhmabai and the Debate about Sexual Respectability in Imperial Britain," *American Historical Review* 104, no. 4 (October 1998), 1119–46.

"Tongues Untied: Lord Salisbury's 'Black Man' and the Boundaries of

Imperial Democracy," *Comparative Studies in Society and History* 42, no. 3 (2000), 632–59.

"India, Inc.? Nostalgia, Memory, and the Empire of Things," *British Culture and the End of Empire*, ed. Stuart Ward (Manchester: Manchester University Press, 2001), 217–32.

"New Narratives of Imperial Politics in the 19th Century," *At Home with the Empire: Metropolitan Culture and the Imperial World*, ed. Catherine Hall and Sonya Rose (Cambridge: Cambridge University Press, 2006), 212–29.

Imperial Optics

Empire Histories, Interpretive Methods

I promised to show you a map you say but this is a mural
then yes let it be   these are small distinctions
where do we see it from is the question.
—Adrienne Rich, *Atlas of the Difficult World* (1991)

The sentiment of empire is innate in every Briton.
—William Ewart Gladstone, "England's Mission" (1878)

The trouble with the Engenglish is that their hiss hiss history happened
overseas, so they dodo don't know what it means.
—Salman Rushdie, *The Satanic Verses* (1988)

For the better part of two decades, I have taught an upper-level undergraduate history course, "Victorian Britain," with a syllabus that has
featured—or operated under the sign of—the quotes by William Ewart
Gladstone and Salman Rushdie. Their juxtaposition is emblematic of the
version of "Victorian Britain" I have staged in the course, laying primary
documents from the period alongside historiographical interpretations
that derive largely, if not exclusively, from a postcolonially inflected imperial history: one that takes "imperial culture at home" as both object of
inquiry and vantage point. So we have read conventional, "domestic"
high politics alongside imperial events and phenomena; parliamentary
speeches alongside various forms of literary expression and print culture;
war diaries alongside accounts of imperial museum spectacle. And while
Edward Said is not on the syllabus, it does feature a number of secondary
works that reflect modern British history writing "after the imperial turn"

—which I take to mean the accelerated attention to the impact of histories of imperialism on metropolitan societies that has occurred in the wake of decolonization, pre- and post-1968 racial struggle and feminism in the past quarter of the twentieth century.[1] The chief pedagogical impulse of the course has been to understand nineteenth-century domestic politics and society as profoundly shaped by British imperial encounters and experiences abroad—and, more ambitiously, to suggest that what we in the post–1945 period have come to know as Victorian was in many respects the effect of such encounters, large and small. As with modernity, which postcolonial critics have argued was perforce colonial, so, too, with Victorian culture—which, my syllabus suggests, cannot be understood outside the ambit of empire, imperial power, and its constitutive impact.

I will return to that question of "we" in due course. Meanwhile, the stakes of undertaking such an interpretive method in fin-de-siècle North American classrooms have been high in the past two decades. Many undergraduate students come to modern British history in the U.S. in search of "corsets and crinoline" (as a student once told me) and, as fervently, in search of islands of whiteness in what they often perceive of as a sea of ethnic and area studies / history in the North American higher-education curriculum. For them, even now, Britain represents whiteness in ways that the history of the U.S. perhaps cannot—though often in unpredictable ways. Teaching Victorian culture as a racialized landscape shaped by decades, if not centuries, of colonial peoples, goods, and ideas coursing through its highways and byways typically startles expectations and generates engaged and sometimes heated debate, especially, though by no means exclusively, about the question of Ireland's relationship to nineteenth-century colonialism. Teaching the Victorian period as always already imperial not just implicitly but as part of a pedagogical meta-narrative about the relationship of modernity to the world-historical phenomenon of colonialism in world history is an ongoing challenge, and never more so than after the events set in train by September 11, 2001. In 9 / 11's immediate and extended aftermath, interest in British imperialism was piqued, so that many students began to seek out the course as a kind of palimpsest of, if not a primer for, an emergent American imperial hegemony of the twenty-first-century kind. In this context, teaching Victorian Britain as I have done provides an occasion for students to think through, in potentially quite concrete terms, what it means to be a globally conscious North American citizen in an increasingly and aggressively imperialized world. As Heather Streets has written with reference to the pedagogy of imperialism in her own classroom, to say that re-casting Britain itself as an imperial landscape—and the recognition of racial hierarchy, social exclusion, and complexity of colonial rule that that entails—means coming to terms with what is often American students' own sense of identification with all that is benevolent and emancipatory in the Anglo-American world is no mere hyperbole.[2] Ideally, what is at risk, for students as well as for scholars, is the certainty of the nation as an analytical category, as a cherished ideal, and as a guarantor of the sovereign Western self as well.

I open with this curricular genealogy in order to underscore how much of the work collected in the pages that follow grew directly from an effort to think through the British empire with and for students living in North America whose images of imperialism have emanated from popular video games (Microsoft's *Age of Empires I–III*), blogosphere accounts of ongoing conflicts in the Middle East, and (though admittedly less so) Victorian novels and Masterpiece Theatre. This does not, of course, exhaust the contemporary archive of imperial Victoriana, but it captures, I think, some of its lineaments. I have taught my course in three different institutional settings since 1990—a third-tier Midwestern university, a private university on the East Coast, and a big-ten public research university. Each of these has had a predominantly white, aspirant middle-class student body, and almost regardless of class origin, gender, or color, those who make their way to the course I call "Victorian Britain" have brought some version of *The Jewel in the Crown* as the embodiment of British imperialism with them. Nuancing the images of the British empire that flow from various outlets of print, musical, and virtual culture has been a major pedagogical project—as has rigorously historicizing students' identification with the civilizing mission *and* their investment in viewing the Victorian empire as a kind of blueprint for current imperial forms and projects. The impact of 9 / 11 on these preoccupations has, of course, been acute. But the preoccupations predate that fateful day, having emerged from my dissertation research—which focused on the ideological work of empire and the image of the Indian woman in feminist and suffrage writing from 1865 to 1915—and they have fed my teaching from the start. As is true for many professional historians, the work I have done since the Ph.D. was produced at the boundary of the archive and the classroom. My work has been shaped, in turn, by a conviction that was fairly marginal in the late 1980s but has gained more credence in the past two decades—namely, that histories of Victorian national / domestic politics and culture should be thought of in dynamic tension with histories of British imperial ambition, ideology, and territorial expansion. Although there are a variety of explanations for why this claim about the impact of empire on the "home front" has begun to shape apprehensions of Victorian history—and for how challenges to the separation between imperial and national histories have been met—my own intellectual pathway toward the imperial turn was marked by the conjuncture of feminist history and postcolonial studies, a conjuncture epitomized for me by the work of Gayatri Spivak.

Spivak's most influential essay, "Can the Subaltern Speak?," is nothing less than canonical now, a touchstone for both feminist history and postcolonial theory.[3] Yet I first encountered the ideas in this infamous essay not through the thing itself but via what looks now like a draft version, an article titled, "The Rani of Sirmur: An Essay in Reading the Archives," which appeared in the journal *History and Theory* in October 1985.[4] "The Rani of Sirmur" was literally put into my hands by a French historian at the University of Chicago, where I was a graduate student studying for prelims. She effectively said, "Here—you're interested in women and India. Read this." I hope I do not do her a disservice when I say I suspect that she had no idea what "this" would mean to me. Despite the presence of a strong South Asian studies program (including one of my advisers, Bernard S. Cohn), the University of Chicago was awash in Michel Foucault in those days, but not in Said or Spivak or Homi Bhabha. She handed me "The Rani of Sirmur" as if it were a curiosity, an access point into a world she was aware existed and had little interest in herself but had gathered from afar might be useful to this curious graduate student hoping against hope to write a dissertation on feminism and imperialism in a department utterly unconvinced of either the legitimacy of women's history or the possibility of postcolonial studies.

Like Said's book *Orientalism* (1978), which I had read just the previous year, "The Rani of Sirmur" went off like a bomb in my head. It is interesting, twenty-plus years on, to think about why. In many respects, the arguments Spivak was making in that essay are old chestnuts now. The history of Third Worlding through the creation of Europe as a sovereign subject, the work of Orientalism in hallowing out women and other gendered subjects, the complicity of dominant Western feminisms in both the fetishization and the erasure of disappeared subjects like the Rani, and, of course, the illegitimate efforts of an effectively imperial discipline such as history even to imagine it could retrieve archival "remnants" like her—all of these gave shape to critiques that my own preparation for examinations and preliminary research were together beginning to make visible but that were not recognized by most of the interlocutors I had at hand. Said's *Orientalism* was of course hugely consequential to my intellectual and political formation. But as feminist scholars of many stripes have since noted, with varying degrees of acrimony and regret, his engagement with women and gender or feminist analysis was woeful. As bell hooks has said about the inattention to gender in Paolo Freire's *Pedagogy of the Oppressed*, when you are thirsty, you drink water with dirt in it.[5] By comparison, Spivak's essay was like spring water, operating as it did from a presumptively feminist position that challenged at once the very basis of history's universalist claims to recognize all subjects and, of course, liberal imperial feminism's willful disavowal of its own methodological and ideological investments in an emancipatory recovery practice. She did so with a determination to expose what Kumkum Sangari calls the pressure of historical placement on the contemporary theoretical moment.[6] I will quote from the start of the essay:

> One of the major difficulties with consolidating a figure from the British nineteenth century in India as an object of knowledge is that British India is now being painstakingly constructed as a cultural commodity with a dubious function. The deepening of the international division of labor as a result of the new micro-electronic capitalism, the proliferation of worldwide neocolonial aggression, and the possibility of nuclear holocaust encroach upon the constitution of the everyday life of the Anglo–US. The era of *Pax Britannica*, caught in a superrealistic grandeur on television and on film, provide that audience at the same time with a justification of imperialism dissimulated under the lineaments of a manageable and benevolent self-criticism.[7]

This passage reminds us that Spivak's work—and, indeed, the narrative and discursive and institutional momentum of postcolonial studies in the North American academy more generally—occurred at a very dense moment of Raj nostalgia in the U.S. Richard Attenborough's *Gandhi* and *A Passage to India*, *The Jewel in the Crown*, and all manner of *Masterpiece Theatre* knockoffs were flooding the markets in the U.S., shaping the character of Anglo-American apprehensions about the East and about the power and possibility of Anglophone empires for decades to come. To watch the fragmented political biography of the Rani of Sirmur, mother-guardian of the minor king, Fatteh Prakash, in the context of British India who, awkwardly for the Raj and for the congeries of Hindu pundits (who also have a stake in her fate) declares her intention to be Sati, become the platform for a wholesale, though characteristically subtle and nuanced, assault on the disciplinary apparatus of history was, frankly, a breathtaking experience in 1985. So was Spivak's conclusion that there is no Rani to be found here, a statement not just about the inaudibility of the Rani's "voice" in imperial history but also, of course, about the preternatural impossibility that history would ever recognize, let alone capture, the Rani as more than an archival, indexical trace of the convergence of imperial British and indigenous religious patriarchal power in the will to domination over gendered colonized subjects. As Spivak puts it, not only is there no Rani to be found here, but "there is no romance to be found here. Caught between patriarchy and imperialism, [the Rani] is almost an allegorical predicament."[8]

It is tempting to think of this encounter with Spivak's form of feminist postcolonial critique as conjunctural in the way that Stuart Hall intends that term—that is, as "a contingent historical moment defined by a reorganization of an . . . existing cognitive-political problem-space" that requires not simply recognition but "strategic intervention."[9] In many respects, "domestic imperial culture" became for me, as for a number of others in the late 1980s and early 1990s, just such a problem space: one that had existed historically and to some degree historiographically, however marginally, but came into view for a generation of scholars precisely as a site of intellectual and political intervention most urgently in the last two decades of the twentieth century.[10] We await a comprehensive account of why this was so. In my case, it was enabled by feminism as both a contemporary political movement and a subject of historical inquiry, for my apprehensions of anti-imperialist critique came especially through the work of black British feminists such as Pratibha Parmar, Hazel Carby, and, ultimately, the collective enterprise based in London known as the journal *Feminist Review*.[11] Carby was herself connected to Hall's Birmingham Black British Cultural Studies project, and her essay "White Women Listen!" (1982) was as much a clarion call as Spivak's early subaltern thinking.[12] I read Carby's work for the first time alongside North American feminist-of-color classics such as Audre Lorde's *Sister / Outsider* and Gloria Anzaldúa's and Cherríe Moraga's edited collection *This Bridge Called My Back*, texts I also taught in an "Introduction to Women's Studies" course at Indiana State University and then at Johns Hopkins University.[13] This corpus of feminist thinking, together with histories of the women's movement in the U.S. such as Ellen Dubois's *Feminism and Suffrage* (1978) and Angela Davis's *Women, Race, and Class* (1982), formed the theoretical and empirical basis for my own attempts to intervene strategically in British national and imperial history—an intervention I was simultaneously endeavoring to put into practice in concrete terms in my undergraduate class in Victorian history, first tested while still a graduate student in Chicago and later refined at Indiana State and the University of Illinois.[14] The pressure of these pedagogical contexts cannot be gainsaid. The "local" audiences I aimed to address in those classroom settings required a clarity of argumentation and a set of translational skills I believe we are always in the process of perfecting as we move from our own research and writing to the space of the college or university classroom and back again. The problem space of domestic imperial culture—a site always already constructed by and through regimes of race, class, and gender—was always public and presumptively political for me, linked as it was not only to contemporary theory but also to the unfolding of contemporaneous postcolonial British history in the last decades of the twentieth century and the first years of the twenty-first century, however removed I was from the lived experience of daily life in the once and future imperial metropole.

As this highly personalized account illustrates, the combination of feminist and postcolonial critique nurtured a conviction—admittedly not widely shared among professional historians even now—about the impact of the present on the project of writing about the past. It is a critique that clearly entails a suspicion of the claims to objectivity that shape much modern history writing, especially in and about Britain, where an empirical tradition continues strong in ways that have left their mark on the debate about the "new imperial history"—and where a curious aversion to the politics of the personal remains, the recent autobiographical essays by Catherine Hall and David Cannadine (and the vast differences between them) notwithstanding.[15] Tellingly, perhaps, our counterparts in French history show no such aversion, as the recent collection *Why France?*—which features highly personal reflections on the practice of French history by Americans—testifies.[16] Also noteworthy is Geoff Eley's foray into intellectual autobiography, which recaptures the interlacing of twentieth-century politics with the professional formation of an Englishman who has worked the majority of his professional life in the U.S. as a historian of Europe and whose primary research orientation has been Germany rather than Britain.[17]

For some, this pattern may suggest a distinctive preoccupation with the self, that notorious and enduring core of American cultural modernism to which even those like Eley (a grammar-school boy, British born and bred) evidently eventually succumb. And yet in ways yet to be fully examined, the autobiographical does exercise an influence on the writing of history. What Jeremy Popkin calls "speaking of careers" and hearing how they affect history writing is as important to do while historians are alive as it is after they die.[18] In my case, the convergence of my training as a historian with late-twentieth-century history tells a small story about how British and imperial history was written in America, where America represents a set of enunciative spaces with specific temporal, regional, and institutional pressure points that this collection, again, is a minor attempt to countenance. The grip of theoretical critique that insisted on the impact of present politics and autobiography on writing about the past was strengthened by my experiences in Britain as a graduate student doing research and later as a full-time teacher and scholar in the U.S. It was also aided by being the oldest daughter of Anglophilic parents and of a father, in particular, whose wartime experiences in England (he was wounded in Belgium in 1944 and transported to the 216th Station Hospital in Warminster) generated a lifelong love of Britain that include two sabbaticals, during which (at six and eleven) I attended school in suburban London.[19] Though they are particular to me, and difficult to assess in terms of their precise impact on my various trajectories, these experiences shaped how I encountered British imperial archives and how I have written about what I saw there.

Living in London and doing pre-dissertation research there in the summer of 1986, at twenty-five, I was confronted, in the wake of the bombing of Libya by the United States, by anti–Americanism of a kind I had never imagined. Although I went to the Fawcett Library (now the Women's Library) looking for evidence of Josephine Butler's anti–Contagious Disease Acts campaign in India on the basis of a bibliographical tip, when I found it, the overlapping of national and imperial discourses echoed what I was reading in the newspaper at the end of every day amid the damp and dusty shelves.[20] I spent part of my Fulbright year in Britain in 1987–88 making a case, via presentations at the Institute for Commonwealth Studies and the Institute for Historical Research in London, about the centrality of women to empire and of empire to the Victorian women's suffrage movement. I met a combination of indifference, contempt, and outrage that, for better or worse, has left indelible marks on my style of argumentation and my choice of subjects ever since. For what it is worth, that response—which might usefully be thought of as the "no fatal impact" line of argument—was similar at early presentations at meetings of the American Historical Association and the North American Conference of British Studies.[21] Citing these professional experiences is one way to signal the particular, and historically dynamic, brand of Anglophilia—embedded in assumptions about the racial homogeneity of modern Britain and, more often than not, untutored in its long history of black settlement—that operates in some spaces of the Anglo-American academy, especially, though not necessarily exclusively, among a certain generation of American historians of Britain. Doing so also draws attention to the skepticism of most practicing British historians —their location notwithstanding—with respect to feminist and postcolonial readings of history as well. This is not to discount intellectual or methodological debates or disagreements, of course, but rather to suggest that there are cultures of British and empire history writing shaped by the micro- and macro-events of the past quarter of a century, at least. Recalling these experiences, making them part of a historiographical record, contributes to an archive of the structures of feeling that have gone into the writing, reading, and teaching of British imperial history in the late twentieth century.

Perhaps most significant, I lived part of that Fulbright year in the company of a fellow University of Chicago graduate student who was African American—and who spent the year coming to terms with racism both in the hallowed halls of British academe and on the streets of the metropole. To be sure, she also found racism on the streets of the South Side of Chicago and on the quad of the University of Chicago, where she arrived prepared to study Irish history with a supervisor (also mine, the self-styled Irish patriarch Emmet Larkin) who simply could not countenance an African American woman wanting to study Irish history. Despite this, her experiences in London—where she was hailed (in Stuart Hall's sense of the term) as a Jamaican, a Barbadian, and always as an alien—shocked and traumatized her. To the extent that I was capable of sharing in that experience, it calcified for me the link between the imperial past and the postcolonial present in ways I am sure I still cannot appreciate fully, in part because I know I do not have a panoptical sense of my own historicity, let alone of postcolonial British history or history writing. I take this occlusion to be one consequence of the critique of "the evidence of experience" that Joan Scott so skillfully has elaborated and that in many respects is the basis of the anti-foundationalism of some feminist and postcolonial practice.[22] Being a white, middle-class American woman of a certain age, doing British imperial history made a difference to the kinds of histories I have found, let alone written, and to the interpretive frameworks through which I have struggled with the historical phenomenon of empire. Research, writing, teaching—all, in other words, are embodied experiences in ways that belie claims to total objectivity for the historian even as they require, of course, responsible, self-aware interpretive methods.[23] As must be clear by now, an appreciation for the politics of my own location and for that of others writing about British empire and imperial culture derives from having grown up professionally at the intersection of specific iterations of feminism and postcoloniality in the U.S., in Britain, and in the imaginative spaces—personal and familial included—in between.

Exposure to historians of Indian women and Indian feminism in Britain and the U.S. and in India was also instrumental to my formation as a feminist scholar of imperial culture. Here I credit the work, mentorship, and collegiality of Urvashi Butalia, Geraldine Forbes, Madhavi Kale, Meera Kosambi, Veena Oldenburg, Barbara Ramusack, Tanika Sarkar, and Mrinalini Sinha, as well as the feminist community nurtured by the triennial Berkshire Conference of Women Historians, which has been a critical, if not unproblematic, space for intellectual exchange and professional and political dialogue between and among scholars working on subjects outside the West and thrown up by the history of British and other national empires. As the call for transnational research has gained velocity, the exclusionary apparatus of the U.S. state has made travel to the Berks by "international" scholars more and more difficult. A chapter in the history of imperial historiography yet to be written, this paradox also underscores the worldwide asymmetry of resources, academic and otherwise, that enables North America to continue to be a central meeting place for such large international feminist gatherings such as the Berks—

and that makes the cost of travel there for scholars in India, Africa, Latin America, and the Middle East prohibitively, if not impossibly, high. For all the talk of de-centering empire even among feminist and postcolonial scholars, and despite even the virtual access of scholarship via e-journals and other electronic forms, the terrain of that work and the circuits of its dissemination remain instructively rooted in older geographies of imperialism whose superstructural realities are not likely to be displaced any time soon by the promise of "global" connectivity.

In spite of these limitations—and, of course, because of them—the research and teaching agendas that eventuated from these cumulative experiences and the vantage points they provided were organized in the first instance around remapping the boundaries between home and empire in the Victorian period to make visible the constitutive effects of empire in all its dimensions on Britain "proper." This involved calling into question the presumptive core-to-periphery flow of ideas, people, and even policies by emphasizing colonial encounters "at the heart of the empire" and arguing for a view of Victorian Britain as the effect of the colonial encounter rather than as an exclusive point of origin. That challenge was supported, in turn, by the emergence of research by scholars of the British empire such as Mrinalini Sinha, whose book *Colonial Masculinity* (1995) argued for gender as a site on which English domestic ideals and colonial Bengali ideals of manliness could be seen to be working in concert rather than in separate domains. In the process, she coined the term "imperial social formation" to capture a terrain that was neither domestic nor imperial, offering a crucial feminist model for rethinking how Victorian imperial power circulated.[24] The work of Ann Stoler, both alone and in collaboration with Frederick Cooper in the collection *Tensions of Empire*, was equally critical. Following Frantz Fanon's claim that Europe was made in the Third World, the case studies Cooper and Stoler collected ranged well beyond the British empire, arguing for the colonial encounter as foundational to European metropolitan bourgeois social and sexual orders—which, by implication, were among the effects of such an encounter rather than strictly antecedent to it.[25] Any scholar of the Victorian period who has read Henry Mayhew's *London Labour and the Labouring Poor* (1861)—a dense and complex text that maps the urban underworld in decidedly racialized and ethnographic terms—would surely entertain the legitimacy of such a claim.[26] Remapping imperial culture also involved asking who was a right and proper subject of British imperial history—part of a larger project, shared by feminists, social historians, and a variety of interdisciplinary practitioners, of expanding the landscape of history to include a variety of players beyond the high political. These included women, the enslaved and freed, colonial peoples, and a host of "others" who peopled Victorian imperial culture, moved across its multiple boundaries, and, in the process, made clear the permeability of the domestic to the imperial. Last but certainly not least, remapping the imperial onto the domestic involved acknowledging that empire and imperial ideology did not typically operate as juggernauts, razing everything in their path. What John Darwin calls Victorian imperialism's "chaotic pluralism" is akin to what Stoler insists on as the "precarious vulnerability" of modern colonial regimes—interpretive postures that make the work of reimagining imperial culture hopeful, if not exactly utopic, when it comes to thinking about the functions of agency and resistance in the shadow of empire's indubitable power to define, to manage, to know, to coerce, to appropriate, and to destroy.[27]

As must be clear by now, my own work was greatly shaped by what feminists call, after Adrienne Rich, the politics of location—a kind of standpoint theory best evoked by the quote by Rich ("Where do we see it from is the question") that serves as an epigraph to this chapter. With its evocations of maps and its anticipation of the idea of "positioning system" that has become common in the technology of the GPS, Rich's question centers space and cartography at the heart of feminist interpretive approaches. The work of Catherine Hall has been absolutely consequential to this project of feminist remapping in the British and imperial context, not least because of the ways in which it epitomizes the link between the feminist critique of public and private spheres and that of the home and empire binary. Perhaps most powerfully, and in partial collaboration with Keith McClelland and Jane Rendall, Hall took direct aim at the putatively insular character of the Whig political narrative by resituating the Reforms Acts of 1832 and 1867 in their gendered, imperial contexts, thereby demonstrating that the impact of empire at home was not limited to low culture or the domain of the social; it affected the very highest levels of the political nation, as well.[28] The accomplishments of her monograph *Civilizing Subjects* (2002), which plots metropole and colony in the same problem space, have been as significant to the shape and direction of the new imperial history.[29] As the eponymous title of one of her collections, *White, Male, and Middle Class*, suggests, for Hall, as for other feminist historians, race and gender and class were not only identity categories; they were, to borrow from Paul Gilroy, among the interdependent modalities in which imperial Englishness was lived.[30] That these attempts to redirect British history toward its imperial past to make a case for historicizing that past as deeply imperial at the center, as well as in the "far-flung" reaches of empire, occurred during an extended historical moment that witnessed debates about the scope and character of the national curriculum, the murder of Stephen Lawrence and the quest to bring his killers to justice, and the Bradford riots, reminds us of the stakes of national-imperial history in a postcolonial frame. In more than merely theoretical terms, it is no longer possible to teach British history of the nineteenth century as if empire was off-center, over there, inconsequential to the operation of politics and culture in the metropole and throughout its fissiparous spaces. However risible Jack Straw's public pronouncements about a "rising sense of Englishness" seemed only a few months before September 2001, the debate about the relationship between whiteness and belonging has only intensified under the pressures of 7 / 7 — a traumatic event that contributed to an already tense sociopolitical landscape in which postcolonial identity and post–9 / 11 anxieties play out in patently brutal and fatal forms.

Debates about what proportionality to accord to empire in the making of Victorian history abound, even rage.[31] I am by no means the only one to wonder what British history would be in institutional terms outside Britain were it not for a revival of interest in empire to save tenure-track positions in the field—positions often recast as "British empire and the world" or "British empire with a specialty in Africa" or "British empire with a specialty in South Asia"—from the administrative chopping block in an era of shrinking employment in higher education in the U.S. Beyond the Stansky Report, issued by the North American Conference of British Studies in 1999 to address "the state and future of British Studies in America," such speculation occurs more often in the relative safety of conference panels and the quiet anonymity of informal conversations than in print.[32] Yet it would be a mistake to imagine that what is at risk from feminist and postcolonial challenges is simply the purity of the national narrative. At issue, and vitally, is also the question of method: by what interpretive and conceptual means should we write new imperial histories? For me, feminist theory and postcolonial studies have been not just reorientation devices, drawing our attention to heretofore unseen subjects and histories, but equally carriers of methodological procedure—rooted most famously, or infamously, in poststructuralism and its analytical presuppositions. Among those is a rigorous and highly principled skepticism about the possibility of a sovereign subject, whether self or nation, subaltern or empire. It is a skepticism born in part out of a conviction about the epistemic (and very real) violence of a priori categories and in part out of a commitment to foregrounding the performative character of identity and hegemony both. So to borrow from Joan Scott, gender is not simply an identity; it is the result of the collision of power with historically contingent forms of embodiment, sociality, and political economy. It is, in other words, itself *the effect* of specific configurations of power, and highly kinetic ones at that. Refracting these insights through the work of the feminist philosopher Judith Butler and, as instructively, through the anthropologically informed historical work of Bernard Cohn, I came to appreciate articulations of nation and empire as being achieved performatively—that is, produced through the collision of specific power-laden forms with historically specific events (such as Cohn's famous durbar example) that reveal the invention of tradition, of claims to authority, of politics as such.[33] To see gender as a regime of power is to interrupt its naturalized association with "male" and "female" and to render those binaries visible as consequences of, rather than as antecedents to, ideological interests in the same way that the home–empire binary can be thought of as the effect of equally interested forces on the Victorian scene (and beyond, of course). That home and away were themselves complexly gendered terrains, in ways at once imaginative and material, ratifies claims not just that they must be understood as implicated in the discourses of colonial modernity but also that failing to do so implicates us in the reproduction of the very forms of colonial knowledge we seek to historicize.

The question of method in imperial history is obviously not bound only to these concerns. Indeed, what I have just described represents a peculiar, though not entirely idiosyncratic, account of early work in what has come to be called the new imperial studies. That work was and continues to be highly interdisciplinary, drawing on scholarship in literary studies, anthropology, and geography—geography being perhaps the most influential in the long run for recourse to spatial ways of thinking and interpreting. Through historians' borrowing of geographers' vocabulary and geographers' attention to histories of space and place, we have ended up with maps and webs and networks—not just as descriptive terms, but as the basis for methodological and even prescriptive theories of empire as well.[34] In many respects, creative appropriation from quarters of the academy beyond history per se has given historians of empire critical tools for locating imperialism in transnational and world history, thus answering the implicit and sometimes explicit call of "globalization" to make the history of empire applicable to contemporary political theory, economic analysis, and foreign policy in the context of the war on terror in the new millennium. Innovative methods that insist on the spatiality of imperial power have aimed to move beyond the core–periphery binary, raising doubts in the process about whether prizing open the "domestic" spaces of Victorian culture at home remains the most important task of the new imperial history—or whether it even constitutes a critique of imperial history at all, serving perhaps instead to reinscribe the metropole as the heart of the empire via a very liberal notion of flows and counterflows. I admit to having mixed feelings on this score. On the one hand, enlarging the boundaries of empire to include, and to implicate, Britons at home in the imperial project has clearly been a major preoccupation of my career as a Victorianist; on the other hand, I am alive to the need to de-center Britain, and India with it, as "the" subjects of imperial studies. On a third hand, and as a more than occasional visitor to and student of Britain today, I remain persuaded that much work remains to be done in curricular terms and in public discourse to loosen the binary of home and away and to sediment a deeply felt conviction about the permeability of "native" culture in Britain to imperial ideas, forces, culture. For want of space to examine the full range of possible examples of how this might occur, the spate of museum exhibits in London and elsewhere in the past decade will have to serve as an abbreviated case in point. The theme of the British Empire and Commonwealth Museum in Bristol may be "Empire and Us," but whether it enables schoolchildren and other viewers to come away with a sense of empire's centrality, its indispensability, to the making of "us" at home remains an open question. As an exhibitionary complex, it does more to document empire "over there" than to trace imperial impact on the "national" scene, with the possible exception of the moment when colonialism came most dramatically home to roost, as in the post–1945 "Empire Windrush" period.

Numerous constituencies and agents are, of course, at work in such a project, many of them of Asian and African descent and many of them using the visual and the virtual to rematerialize the historical presence of colonial peoples, their labor, and their lives in contemporary Britain.[35]

Indeed, the role of spectacle in shaping domestic apprehensions of imperial citizenship has a deep history in the nineteenth century, and recent scholarship on visual and material culture from 1851 onward has done much to enhance our understanding of how and under what circumstances Victorians of different walks of life encountered and consumed empire at home.[36] A propos, I think we must take more seriously the prospect that the writing of imperial history—and, indeed, whatever generic forms through which "history" is deployed—are spectacular performances on which the imperial past has left its footprint. These traces cannot but imprint, in turn, the production of empire history and in the process stage its dramas in often spectacular ways, as the television careers of Niall Ferguson and Simon Schama remind us. Unsurprisingly, what gets bundled up as imperial history for transatlantic and global consumers is highly, if unselfconsciously, selective.

Thanks in part to the work of the first five volumes of the new *Oxford History of Empire*, the role of literary studies and, especially, of postcolonial theory in recasting the imperial history of the long nineteenth century is only too well known, though arguably distortedly so.[37] The impact of what the North American academy calls area studies—South Asian, African, Middle East, and East Asian interdisciplinary work that may or may not be supported by government-supported (Title VI) centers at research universities—is perhaps less directly visible beyond the U.S., but it has been instrumental in shaping my thinking about empire partly because of my interest in South Asia. Beginning with my training at the University of Chicago, which has a well-developed, serious, and influential South Asian studies program, I defined myself as a historian of empire in contradistinction to those enrolled in that program. I did not have vernacular languages, and India per se—as opposed to British India or Britain proper—was not my object of study. Despite this, I always identified strongly as a historian of colonial India—an identification fortified, in ways I have only recently begun to appreciate, by my reliance on postcolonial theory, a body of work produced by diasporic South Asians but also derivative in many ways of the career of British imperialism itself.[38]

It was not until I lived and worked at a university where African studies was a powerful institutional force—and until I collaborated in teaching and writing with a leading feminist historian of Africa, Jean Allman—that I realized the doubly imperial character of a British imperial history in which the Raj is the presumed center. For many Africanists in the U.S., as for area specialists working outside the West in regions formerly colonized by Europeans, even a "reformed" imperial history is still imperial history because it does not imagine non–Western subjects except as colonial subjects. For Africanists and some East Asianists, postcolonial theory is also suspect because of the comparatively unselfconscious Indo-centricity of its leading lights and its semi-colonizing posture toward scholarly practices outside Euro-America. For some who identify as Africanists, global and transnational studies represent extensions of the kind of imperial history area studies scholarship has aimed to displace, even discredit. For someone who had long taken the politics of location as a first principle, this view from African studies was especially unsettling, a hard lesson about the enduring power of racial hierarchy (brown over black as well as white over non-white, for instance) of the kind I had written about via the political career of Dadabhai Naoroji (a light-skinned Parsi discredited as a "black man" when he ran for Parliament in the late Victorian period) but whose ongoing ideological work I frankly understood too belatedly. Watching graduate students in British history struggle with this conundrum as they have tried to envision a transnational imperial history has also been transformative in unlooked-for ways. What I came to appreciate with particular vividness is that the problem of "we" is thus bound up inextricably with the question of audience: to whom do we direct our histories, who interpolates us, whom do we want to be read by? (How) do we construct our topics, our research plans, our archival and extra-archival pathways and our narratives accordingly? What "world" do we call into being when we credit British imperialism with achieving global power, and what worlds do we reproduce as abject or exclude from consideration as "sovereign" subjects when we do so? And where do these maneuvers position the students we teach in British and imperial and world history classrooms as we encourage them to reach for critically engaged interpretive frameworks as well as "global" knowledge sets?

To be sure, not all postcolonial scholarship is Indocentric.[39] Yet the pull of India and especially of Raj histories in the North American academy and popular culture means that for many Americans, the British empire *is* India, a conflation too easily reproduced in syllabi and even in scholarly work, despite the availability of research on empire in and around the Pacific, Africa, and the Caribbean as well. This speaks to the asymmetry of "global" distributions of all kinds of knowledge, where "global" is merely shorthand for Americanization at the site of production and consumption: Americanization as the sign of academic market capitalism, in short. Nor are Africanists the only ones to press the question of who exactly the audience is for even a critical imperial history. Engagement with scholarship produced by historians working in and writing about the former white settler colonies has been instructively disorienting in this regard. In response to my recurrent interrogative, who needs the nation?, feminist historians in Australia like Ann Curthoys countered with an equally challenging one: now that we have the nation as a legitimate framework, you are telling us we should disavow it?[40] Not surprisingly, some of the most interesting transnational work—work that de-centers the British empire by relocating it in a congeries of imperial and global force fields—has come from the antipodes, reminding us of the circuitous intra-colonial routes and unlooked-for intra-imperial borrowings that shape much of what we recognize as the basis for modern law and citizenship.[41] At best, such reorientations require us to be constantly vigilant about our own politics of location; at worst, they throw the very legitimacy of the enterprise of imperial history into question. At the very least, they point to the necessity of acknowledging that the U.S. is not the only formerly colonial axis on which imperial histories pivot and that subjects thrown up by the view from Vancouver and Suva, Wellington and Shanghai, are as variegated as the methods by which historians have brought them to the sightlines of history. My collaborations with Tony Ballantyne, together with the pressures of world history's reinvigoration as subject and method in recent years, have brought home to me the urgency of recognizing the multiplicity of views beyond the metropole and British India both. This kind of ex-centricity, and the webs of connection it has the capacity to materialize, is notoriously hard to enact and sustain across a complex of sites that may or may not include Britain proper. But it is arguably one of the most exciting directions for the newest of the new imperial histories—histories that often are as much the result of a concern with genealogies of a "global" that was sponsored by terrains (such as the oceanic or the littoral) preceding modern empire, whose impact in turn has been secondary to inter-regional currents and translocal forces in specific times and places.[42]

Such ex-centric locations and the methods they enable are no less implicated in the dialectical relationship between imperial history and the imperial and imperializing present, a kind of occupational hazard to which even critics of empire are susceptible. We must, it is true, be wary about "switching too easily between the past and the present tense of empire," not least because this is a solipsistic dimension of influential contemporary argument that aims to trade in the cultural capital of an unbroken history of modern Anglophone empires; an empire-by-analogy argument that aims to make a case, in effect, for the teleology, the inevitability, of a twentieth-century and twenty-first-century American empire as the legacy of the nineteenth-century British one.[43] To return to my opening pedagogical concerns, my undergraduate students are most eager to understand the former British empire as a retrospective projection of contemporary U.S. imperialism. How typical they are is hard to say, and certainly experiences of teaching an imperialized British history in North America vary widely, not only according to regional location, but also according to the point of origin—and accent, if they are English—of "British" historians in any given classroom. Nonetheless, I try to capitalize on students' anticipation of Anglo-American connections to make them aware of their own locations in time and space—of their own historicity, in short. Among the purposes of my course is to suggest that if locative positions and interpretive methods are invariably co-produced— if, in other words, we are imperial historians in ways that are subject to contingencies of time and place without being fully determined by them —then empire history is never disinterested and is only ever partial and provisional as well. Its teleologies are hubristic fictions; its predictive ambitions are equally so, for feminist and postcolonial histories of empire as for all others. What this tells us as scholars about the possibility of thinking or writing or teaching a genuinely principled and self-critical anti-imperial history remains a compelling, if bedeviling, intellectual, political, and epistemological provocation.

By far, the most provincializing experience has been my encounter with graduate students *outside* British studies who are interested in empire and, more specifically, in gender and colonialism, for how it can help them in their dissertation projects in Russian, East Asian, Ottoman, and American history. In this respect, I have been enormously privileged to work for ten years in a department at a public university with rich traditions and deep faculty numbers in those fields. These faculty members draw talented students determined to understand British imperialism as a model, if not *the* model, for modern imperial power alongside which and increasingly against which they come to measure the histories of those formerly imperial (though unevenly postcolonial) regions. To recognize the impact of a public university in the pedagogical project of unmaking empire at this particular historical juncture is surely ironic, for as I write, public education is in a catastrophic crisis that is not unrelated to late-imperial decline in the U.S. All the more reason to underscore that it is these encounters, in the graduate program at the University of Illinois that have compelled me to identify what, for me, is still the core commitment of the kinds of empire history I want to write and read and teach. These include works that are vigorously and rigorously skeptical of the British empire's triumphalist account of itself—and that enact such a point of view either by subjecting the evidence of empire to cultural critique or by seeking to relocate it alongside, in competition with, or in collusion with that of other, contemporaneous Victorian empires. In addition to provincializing Europe, the work of a critically engaged, self-consciously "British" imperial history can, and surely also should, entail provincializing itself.[44]

The triumphalism of which I speak is particular, it should be said, to the Victorian period: it encodes very specifically nineteenth-century *English* (as opposed to British) presumptions and values at its heart and can have legs only if one stays within the geographical and historiographical confines of the British empire itself. It is an account that routinely and often unselfconsciously embeds colonial India at its center and proceeds from the, again, often unspoken assumption that the Raj is the grounds of comparison, the yardstick, against which the "colonialism" of other British imperial possessions and the "imperialism" of other European and non–European empires should be measured. To the extent that my work has forwarded India as the heart of the Victorian empire, I have contributed to this tendency—though primarily in my work as a Victorianist, I think, and not as I have moved into thinking about the twentieth century or beyond the bounds of the British empire per se. Regardless, Indo-centric imperial history, in the end, is a history that elites and would-be elites in America and Britain—equally, if differently—have inherited from the Victorians and that scholars too numerous to mention here have been at pains to critique by all manner of optics and methods.[45] That inheritance is arguably easier to see and to appreciate, perhaps from any vantage point, in the penumbral shadow of American empire, a problem space that has become visible at an accelerating rate in the U.S. (Although where it exists, such a clear-sighted view is as arguably belated with respect to the actual history of American imperialism, however we parse that phenomenon.) The recurrent presumption of whiteness as the shared terrain of Anglo-global imperialism—what Radhika Mohanram has called "imperial white"—also requires vigilant attention, as do the recurrent, if historically and generically specific, manifestations of the spectral other, whether in the form of allegedly gormless, indisputably suffering brown bodies at Abu Ghraib as rationales for the war on terror or in the images of Afghani and Iraqi women who serve as pretexts for Western military occupation.[46] Nor is this simply an "academic" empire question. Evidence of the ongoing purchase of the "special relationship" and of the prestige of shared "Anglo-Saxon" virtues and values in public discourse and international diplomacy gives these matters the utmost urgency, even as it reveals the long reach of Victorian presumptions about which nations constitute the foundations of the global and the persistence of ethnic whiteness as a criterion for world leadership.[47]

As important as a critique of such maneuvers is, it is also in danger of re-treading the old, familiar, commodifiable imperial terrain (India as a precursor to and model for Iraq, for example) and of occluding not just the histories of empire elsewhere but also the *aftermath* of empires beyond the jewel in the crown: in Alice Springs, in the Ureweras, in Harare, on Vancouver Island, in Hawaii, in the Philippines, in Puerto Rico, in Marseilles, in Berlin, in Amsterdam, in Seoul, in Oaxaca, in Tashkent.[48] What is urgently required is a critical recognition of, and a well-developed set of arguments about, the imperial, the colonial, and the global not as givens, but as positioning systems (*pace* Rich) and even (re-)orientation devices (*pace* Sarah Ahmed): as interpretive mechanisms that identify objects of inquiry by locating them in spatial, racial, and gendered grids of intelligibility that, in turn, do not and cannot exist outside power in all its scalar variety.[49] Like transnational studies and world history, imperial history is as much a method as a subject of inquiry, if not more so, and that which it consolidates as a subject or as a terrain of inquiry is embedded in optics that are likely to have some relationship to past or present empires.[50] Imperial history is not, in other words, the view from nowhere. There is a politics to its location(s), and where we see it from is the question. *Whence* we see it shapes the "it" that we bring into view. This may be the proverbial cliff from which many will refuse to leap, but it remains for me a sine qua non of feminist, postcolonial, and, indeed, anti-imperial practice. For we, too, however variously and recalcitrantly, are effectively the consequence of our own collisions with imperial historicity.

Or, as one scholar of indigeneity has put it, all of our work "rests on empire."[51] In this sense, whether "we" are imperial citizens or imperial historians or both, we are not innocent of empire and all that it entails. This is so not only because we cannot afford to be innocent, but because whether we like it or not, this complicity *is* the effect of historical placement; this complicity is *the effect* of what, in 1982, Adrienne Rich bitterly and prophetically called "North American time"—for those of us who live in the U.S. and, because empire is about the attempt to temporalize as well as to territorialize and moralize, for some who do not.[52] I do not dispute or deny the power of anti-imperial politics, coalition, alliance, or even intention. Nor do I necessarily give up on the possibility of spaces outside the ambit of empire. But I do want to acknowledge the material reality of living "among empires" and amid the multiple and uneven traces of their predecessors.[53]

In view of this facticity, this imperial facticity, I want above all to register the power of postcolonial feminist criticism to move beyond self-evidently gendered subjects and offer self-critically engaged alternatives to politics and history, if not to empire per se. I do so even as I recognize the fugitive character of that species of criticism that may well have had its day.[54] I say this not because feminist history or postcolonial studies is over, but because of the rising power of new interpretive forms congealing around a kind of academic global cosmopolitanism—one that dismisses a caricatured version of those projects even as it seeks company with emergent neo-imperial elites.[55] In light of this phenomenon, and in keeping with the radical promise of earlier and ongoing feminist postcolonial work, I seek distance from the entanglement of liberal cosmopolitanism with liberal internationalism and, in the end, with the kind of redemptivist America-centered globality masquerading as a critique of imperialism that debuted at the beginning of the twentieth century at Versailles, well before the British empire officially ended.[56] In many ways, the triumphalism of historical recovery, whether feminist or postcolonial or anti-imperial, is one legacy of such a liberal redemptivist vision that I have never been interested in reproducing, preferring instead the kind of interpretive agnosticism about the capacity of history to completely retrieve the past that is on display in Spivak's analysis in "The Rani of Sirmur."[57] Far from disabling, a commitment to the anti-hubristic potential of anti-imperial history and a correlative acknowledgment of the perennial present-ness—and the ineluctable embodiedness—of empire then and now enables my conviction that these perspectives must inform the subjects we teach and the objects we consolidate *as imperial* when we aspire to produce histories of empire in the twenty-first century. Precisely how we do that, and which "we" we are after, will undoubtedly remain a subject of intense debate—debate that is as crucial to the fate of imperial history as anything else. *Empire in Question* provides, I hope, one critical feminist genealogy of this contemporary challenge. I offer it as much in order to continue to interrogate my own ongoing investments in the intellectual and political possibilities of imperial studies as in the service of capturing the shifting, fractious, and ultimately unfinished business of empire's histories.

Part I

HOME AND AWAY

Mapping Imperial Cultures

Rules of Thumb

British History and "Imperial Culture" in Nineteenth-Century
and Twentieth-Century Britain

I cannot help thinking that in discussions of this kind, a great deal of misapprehension arises from the popular use of maps on a small scale. As with such maps you are able to put a thumb on India and a finger on Russia, some persons at once think that the political situation is alarming and that India must be looked to. If the noble Lord would use a larger map—say one on the scale of the Ordnance Map of England—he would find that the distance between Russia and British India is not to be measured by the finger and thumb, but by a rule.
—Lord Salisbury (1877)

Historians have always been concerned with maps and mapping and British historians are certainly no exception. Because history writing in the West has been instrumental to the building of nation-states, historiography itself has become an institutionalized expression not just of national identity, but also of the geographical reach of national power. In the British context—where the very use of the term "British" denotes the coercive power of the English state to create a Greater Britain out of itself and the Celtic fringe—doing modern British history has implicitly meant accounting for what constituted Britain territorially and, not coincidentally, elaborating the territorial extent of British influence.[1] While this preoccupation with geographical parameters may be attributed to Britain's insularity, it was also, from the mid-nineteenth century onward, a consequence of British imperial conquest and of the sense of historical mission that both motivated and sustained it. J. R. Seeler's *The Expansion of England* (1883) not only gave imperial history its "institutional life . . . [and] respectability," but it helped to guarantee that the boundaries between the history of Great Britain and that of Greater Britain were clearly drawn.[2]

Despite the fact that empire was believed to be "a determining fact in the life of both the metropolis and its dependencies," for almost a century the history of empire was treated as if it occurred on another planet, far away from England's "green and pleasant lands," disconnected in time and space from "the Mother Country"—that saccharine, stolid, and basically static imperial referent. It was not routinely the purview of conventional British historians; instead, it remained the territory of self-styled "imperial historians," the *burra sahibs* of the British historical establishment. It was often examined and interpreted from the vantage point of established university chairs in "imperial history," giving armchair imperialism a whole new meaning. Imperial history has historically been a kind of national subfield, albeit an important one, into which scholars who are not of the British Isles, and even some who are, wander at their peril.[3] A. P. Thornton likened American students of Victorian imperialism to "tourists in an unfamiliar terrain," adding that "their academic forebears would as willingly have become Mexican citizens as have written books on the British Empire."[4]

Until recently in historical terms, then, the rule of thumb in British history has been to map a set of quite differently imagined communities: "home," on the one hand, and "empire," on the other. "Home" itself was, of course, as falsely unitary as "empire," with England as the symbolic center and Wales, Scotland, and Ireland its "internal others."[5] It is a testament to the power of a common racial heritage—and to the forces that invent it—that in nineteenth-century and early-twentieth-century Britain, the domestic underclasses and white ethnic minorities who were prominent in the colonial enterprise could and did become the imperial "overclasses" by virtue of their essential Britishness.[6] Home and empire have nonetheless traditionally been constituted as separate and distinct spheres: one, the source of Britishness, progress, and civilization; the other, precisely that—the other side of the world, the "dark continent," the as yet undomesticated space of cultural backwardness. For all Britain's claims to be the "mother country," there was no doubt among Seeley's contemporaries—or, for that matter, among generations of imperial historians after him—about where the "heart of darkness" lay on the map of Greater Britain. Staging Britain and its empire as dichotomous rather than as dialectic spaces was itself a technology of imperial rule—one of many "grandiloquent displays"—that called on Britons and others to recognize and, hence, to legitimate Britain's role as a world imperial power.[7]

Generations of historians of the Victorian empire, more typically than not, have maintained these artificial distinctions, focusing on the geopolitical hows and whys of European imperial formations rather than on the domestic sociopolitical forces that enabled Britain's imperial projects in India and Africa and throughout the white settler colonies or, more subversively, on the extent to which neither society was purely, homogeneously either "home" or "empire." Historians of conventionally domestic British history, for their part, have been remarkably insular, so much so that "British historians have largely failed to ask what empire has done to 'us.' "[8] Cecil Rhodes's conviction that the working classes' support for empire at home prevented civil war is an important clue to the centrality of empire to domestic social attitudes and domestic political ideologies, but his was an observation not much heeded by his contemporaries writing imperial history. The first modern imperial historians (J. R. Seeley, E. A. Freeman, Lord Acton) were more concerned with articulating the historical racial connections between Anglo-Saxons, Teutons, and Greeks to promote Britain's imperial greatness to the world than with examining popular manifestations of that racialism in their own historical present.[9] History from the bottom up had yet to be invented, and in the meantime, imperial history, like "domestic" historiography, operated not just from the top down but also from the center outward. The Anglocentricity of the combined enterprise can hardly be in doubt. As J. G. A. Pocock observed more than a decade ago, it is largely as "English history" that the history of Britain and its settler colonies was, and to some extent still is, "historically intelligible."[10]

That practitioners of imperial history ultimately have been concerned with the imperial nation at home there can be equally little doubt. Understanding how a small metropolitan state like Britain grew into a global empire was instrumental for sustaining those quintessentially Victorian myths of cultural and racial superiority that, after 1900 and especially after 1945, did not seem as historically guaranteed or as unshakable as they once had.[11] But even when the security of the nation was a motive force behind the production of imperial history, it did not necessarily entail working to understand or to historicize the interactions between metropole and empire. This was ironic, since much of the business of colonial India was run from Whitehall, while the Office of the Secretary for India was known as

"India in England."[12] Failure to think and to write dialectically also tended to foreclose the role of the colonial dependencies in the historical development of British imperial power. Although the colonies-as-agent approach did find expression in the later work of Ronald Robinson and John Gallagher, tracing its particular was a task claimed largely by colonial nationalists.[13] As Partha Chatterjee and others have insisted, interpretations of colonial agency have proved to be as influenced by Western imperial paradigms as by traditional "imperial history," though in significantly different ways.[14] And in keeping with Whigs' historical notions of progress, the movement of ideas, culture, and "improvement" was presumed to flow in one direction: from home to away. P. J. Marshall rightly reminds us that British models—from utilitarianism to the welfare state—historically have been projected onto the empire, much as Lord Salisbury advised that the Ordnance Map of England be used to assess the true scope of territorial possession and any external threat to it.[15] Historiographical practice to the 1950s neatly replicated the Orientalist frame out of which it distantly originated, so that the Otherness of empire became the natural possession of British national identity at the site of academic institutionalization, as well as at other institutional sites throughout the culture. All of this has led Salman Rushdie to remark, with his usual flippant accuracy, that "the trouble with the English is that their history happened overseas, so they don't know what it means."[16]

Rushdie is correct in at least one important respect: empire still occupies a basically marginal place on the map of traditional British history. This is perhaps paradoxical, especially in light of the flurry of Raj memorabilia—the making of the film *A Passage to India*, the production of *The Raj Quartet* by British television, the re-release of *Lawrence of Arabia*—that emerged in the 1980s and that has been critiqued so effectively by Indian scholars and others who insist on its function as nostalgia and its uncritical reproduction of Victorian racialism, Orientalism, and convictions of cultural superiority.[17] It may also seem an odd claim to make, in light of the volume of scholarship currently being produced on race and imperialism in the North American academy—a trend of which the conference in Cincinnati whence this collection emerged is self-consciously a part. But Rushdie's observation misses an important point. What both popular-culture productions and some of the recent scholarship (especially when it is concerned with European imperialist ideologies) have failed to recognize is that empire was not a phenomenon "out there." The consequences of empire—its attendant enterprises (such as the slave trade), its socio-cultural appendages (foreign missions, *zenana* teacher-training societies), and, most important, its colonial subjects—were everywhere in European culture *at home*. Empire was not a singular place but a set of geographical and cultural spaces. To borrow from Gyan Prakash's definition of the Third World, empire can be understood as "a variety of shifting positions which have been discursively articulated."[18] Its history, therefore, is neither a distant cousin to that of Britain proper, nor a discrete dimension of the British historical experience. It is an integral part of "British" social, political, and cultural history because empire itself was the product of British national institutions and because "domestic" British culture was so thoroughly influenced by its apparently external empire. We can, and perhaps should, speak, as Helen Callaway does in her study of colonial Nigeria, of "imperial culture" at home.[19] For if, as Shula Marks has argued, it is impossible to understand histories of Britain or historical notions of Britishness "outside of the imperial and post-imperial experience," it is equally impossible to conceptualize the map of Great Britain without appreciating that the cultural effects of imperialism historically have been inscribed on it.[20]

There is much recent historical work suggesting that the nature and extent of imperial culture in the British Isles require the attention of British historians, whether their "field" is Great Britain or Greater Britain. Bernard Semmel's *Imperialism and Social Reform* was a breakthrough in 1960, insisting, as Benjamin Disraeli, the Webbs, and other less-well-known Victorians had, on the connections between domestic social reform and imperial ideologies, especially after 1895.[21] While they echo many of the concerns raised by Semmel, John Mackenzie's *Propaganda and Empire* (1984) and *Imperialism and Popular Culture* (1986) have taken a different methodological tack, arguing for the notion of imperialism as a core ideology that could mediate class differences and thus worked to produce a unifying imperial British identity.[22] By enumerating the ways in which empire and its signifiers were produced and manipulated at home—in music halls, on biscuit tins, through film and other avenues of popular culture—Mackenzie and his collaborators point to the artificiality of empire conceived of as exclusively "over there" and effectively refute the notion, so central to traditional imperial history, that "the man in the street cares more about the Australian cricket matches" than about imperial affairs.[23] Indeed, the British culture of sport, as C. L. R. James clearly understood, has provided one of the most revealing arenas for analyses of imperial ideologies and practices during particular historical moments, down to and including the present day.²⁴

Historical work on white women active in the imperial enterprise has helped break down anther kind of separate spherism inherent in traditional imperial history by demolishing the assumptions that empire was "no place for a white woman" and was acquired "in a fit of absence of wives"—both convictions that were practically axiomatic among a certain generation of imperial historians. Jane Hunter's *The Gospel of Gentility* (1984), Claudia Knapman's *White Women in Fiji* (1986), and Helen Callaway's *Gender, Culture, and Empire* (1987) are each concerned with demonstrating that empire was not an exclusively white masculine space and that the export of both Victorian gender ideology and European women affected European communities and indigenous populations in colonial societies. As critics have pointed out, such attempts to re-map the colonial landscape can observe their own rules of thumb, privileging gender over race and, at times, failing to understand the cooperation of race, class, and gender systems in the production of culturally imperial ideologies and practices.²⁵ They can also, by centralizing the experience of white women, marginalize Third World women (again) right off the proverbial map, thus "re-enacting their historical disenfranchisement" and illustrating that discourses in Western feminist studies and women's studies are no more exempt from the political impact of the locations that produce, without finally determining, them than those of traditional imperial historians have been.²⁶

Although it remains peripheral to the production of conventional British history, the influence both of empire at home and of gender on empire is beginning to be acknowledged and written into the historiography of Britain "at home." Suvendrini Perera has argued that the very form of the "English novel" was constituted with reference to imperial ideologies, while Jenny Sharpe demonstrates that the "colonial scene" shaped apprehensions of the sexual politics of empire in ways that were fundamental to the constitution of that "domestic" genre.²⁷ Using other kinds of historical evidence, Catherine Hall, Leonore Davidoff, and Mary Poovey have examined the links between gender, race, and class in part by foregrounding the imperial context in which domestic gender ideologies have been articulated, so that empire is not simply the backdrop for, but also an active agent in, the construction of cultural and especially social-reform discourses.²⁸ For Poovey in particular, race and empire played a crucial role in the ideological work of gender in mid–Victorian England.[29] Clare Midgley's *Women against Slavery: The British Campaigns, 1780–1870*, continues in this direction, re-materializing the ways in which antislavery politics shaped both high politics and feminist discourses in Victorian Britain.[30] Susan Pedersen's study of the sexual politics of colonial policymaking by feminists in the twentieth century and the essays in Michael Roper's and John Tosh's edited collection *Manful Assertions* are two more excellent examples of the ways in which British historians are working to understand the impact of imperialism on both dominant and oppositional discourses and to shed a longstanding cultural amnesia about the impact of whiteness on English / British history and, in turn, on its historiography.[31]

The ramifications of this for traditional political history in Britain are enormous, since these scholarly analyses taken together demonstrate how thoroughly political subjectivity was dependent on the exercise of authority over "Others," thus revealing more concretely the ways in which empire was fundamental, if not central, to the histories of Western democratic, humanitarian, and liberal traditions. What scholars of British literary traditions take for granted, British historians seem loath fully to countenance—namely that, in the words of Gayatri Spivak, it is not possible to read modern British literature or history "without remembering that imperialism, understood as England's social mission, was a crucial part of the representation of England to the English."[32] It was crucial, we might add, to British, European, and colonial native audiences, as well. Even if we acknowledge—as, for example Nigel Leask insists in his recent book on British Romantic writers and the East—that such representations were directed at a European audience and hence were "saturated by the nationalist and proto-nationalist claims of rival European states," we are still obliged to engage the premise that "national" culture was as much a product of imperial expansion as imperialism was an . . . exportation of that culture."[33] There *will* be disagreement over the relationships between "national" culture and "imperial" culture and about the role of historians and cultural critics in perpetuating misapprehensions about the dynamics of their interaction. As Gauri Viswanathan has suggested, the stakes are high, since the political culture of entire historiographical traditions are invested in not just the marginalization of colonialism, but also in the ways in which its relation to metropolitan cultural formations has been underexamined and, above all, undertheorized.[34]

For all their innovativeness, these new cartographies are problematic, as well. The danger here is to continue to polarize: to view home as the original mother to which empire was "beamed back" and to conceptualize empire as a "dark continent" that European women (the Western cultural Other) actually did miraculously "penetrate" and "uplift." Even Freda Harcourt, whose important and often overlooked essay on the linkages that Benjamin Disraeli self-consciously forged between the political reform of 1866–68 (which created a host of new national / political subjects at home) and Britain's almost simultaneous involvement in the war in Abyssinia (which provided "a conspicuous site where British imperial strength could be . . . paraded" before the newly enfranchised, thus generating their commitment to an imperial nation), tends toward reifying the very same polarities of empire versus home that Victorians themselves seemed determined to articulate.[35] In reality, there was so much movement back and forth between Britain and its imperial possessions that the imperial culture cannot be located exclusively in the metropole or in the colonies. The fact that E. M. Forster wrote *A Passage to India* in Weybridge is an ironic reminder of the proximity of empire to home and of how little fixity the distant parts of empire had.[36] Judith R. Walkowitz's recent study of narratives of sexual danger in Victorian London also underscores the portability of imperial referents: the division of the capital into East and West occurred along racial, if not imperial, lines and mapped an urban space where ostensibly domestic Others were not without their imperial signifiers.[37] But even the term "imperial culture" (with its implicitly hegemonic whiteness) is at risk, since British culture at home at home was shaped, and had been at least since the fifteenth century, by non-white populations living in Britain—the result of slavery and of early modern imperial expansion. Peter Fryer's work on black Britons, Rozina Visram's work on Indians throughout the British Isles, Bhikhu Parekh's collection on immigrant intellectuals—these histories, and many others, do more than reaffirm the fact that multicultural diversity has always been at the heart of self-styled Anglo-Saxon culture.[38] They require that we reject the traditional binaries of home and empire, Britain and the colonies, to account for the geographic dispersal of "imperial" culture and "colonial" power relations. In the wake of 1492 / 1992, it is particularly urgent that we understand modern British imperialism in particular and European colonialism in general not just as acts of conquest, but as a significant new phase in the history of intercultural discovery, negotiation, and contest.

This is not to obscure the violence with which European conquistadors "explored" their new world, for it is undeniable that, "at its most powerful, colonialism is a process of radical dispossession."[39] Nor is it my intention to erase the exercise of imperial power to which all colonial subjects could finally be subject. Jamaicans and Trinidadians did not voluntarily "discover" the cities and seaports of the metropole, and the conditions under which they negotiated the dominant culture in Britain were not completely of their own making. Even for someone like C. L. R. James, who claimed to feel British "not merely in historical facts but in the instinctive responses," living in Britain always felt like being "transplanted as a hot-house flower."[40] And yet residence in Britain certainly meant living in the "empire" for men and women like James, even as many of them came to make it their home and, by doing so, to contest and transform what constituted Britain and Britishness.[41] As Thomas Holt's recent book, *The Problem of Freedom: Race, Labor, and Politics in Jamaica and Britain, 1832–1938*, bears out, the very term "British Isles" meant more than simply England, Ireland, Scotland, and Wales from the vantage point of black Britons for whom the Caribbean was also "home"—an insight that suggests once again how multivalent and politically powerful the geographical referents in "British" history remain in the construction of national identities.[42] These historical circumstances (to which I have done little more than allude, despite the volume of historical work that testifies to them) point to the heterogeneity of "imperial" experiences and the multiplicity of "colonial" spaces that were among the historical consequences of British imperialism. Needless to say, it is the historical condition of postcolonialism that makes an appreciation of them possible. Those who wish to map histories of "Britain" therefore cannot continue to anchor their work either at home or in the empire, but must seriously consider situating it in the multiple Euro-colonial locations produced by the historical projects of imperialism. To borrow from Anna Davin, it is imperative to develop a more expansive sense of "where," as well as of when and of how, while doing British history.[43]

To achieve this, historians of Britain must heed C. A. Bayly's admonition that traditional imperial history, traditional "British" history, and, especially, nationalist histories all belong in the same field of debate.[44] To these I would add women's histories and feminist histories. British imperial expansion and its ideological practices must be understood in the context of the farthest-reaching discursive fields possible—fields in which imperialist attitudes at home and anti-imperial movements in the colonies played influential, and interdependent, roles. The rise of Liberal Union-ism, typically seen as part of the "English–Irish question," occurred if not in conjunction with the institutionalization of Indian nationalism, then certainly in relation to it. British women's movements and domestic oppo-sition to them were equally enmeshed in imperial discourses and the na-tionalist ideologies that animated them.[45] Colonialized men and women simultaneously borrowed and rejected the terms of both Western femi-nism and colonial nationalism as they sought to fashion their own political subjectivities.[46] And the activities of the British Committee of the Indian National Congress, as well as of a variety of Indian and African statesmen and male and female students and intellectuals who traveled and worked in Britain from the mid–Victorian period forward, place much of what has been considered "colonial" politics and culture "at home." These kinds of interrelationships add legitimacy to Edward Said's claim that "no country on earth is made up of homogeneous natives; each has its immigrants, its internal 'Others', and each society . . . is a hybrid."[47] The geopolitical effects of this hybridization should not be underestimated. Gandhi's expe-riences in South Africa and in London—two differently imperial / colonial locations—shaped his nationalism and his political strategies and, with them, the whole direction of the British empire.[48]

Such emigrations and the variety of colonial / imperial identities they created disrupt the kind of historiographical boundary keeping that I have been describing. And as if Gandhi's attitudes toward Indian women were not enough proof of the need for continued attention to the historical operations of gender in national and imperial histories, his admiration for some British suffrage women, acquired during one of his visits to Britain, suggests how his "nationalist" views were partly shaped by his experience of "imperial women."[49] British feminists' associations with Indian na-tionalists, with the campaign to repeal the Contagious Diseases Acts in India after 1886, and with Indian feminists in India and Britain point in turn to the impact that colonial nationalism had on the cause of women's emancipation in the West—a cause that, at least in the United Kingdom, took the empire as its proper sphere of action.[50] Historians of Britain clearly cannot afford to see imperialism, colonial responses, or women as marginal to their concerns. Because of what we know to be the interlock-ing operations of race, gender, and class systems in the constitution of Englishness, Britishness, and "Otherness," we need to structure analyses of these cultural paradigms into our understanding of what constituted

Britain in the nineteenth century and twentieth century. Attention to the "intermixture" that characterized Britain and the world, particularly in the nineteenth century and after, may endanger the production of "national" histories, but not without first revealing the ways in which those histories have been unfaithful to the fragmentary bases out of which they, like modern nations themselves, have been consolidated.[51]

Although reading practices are rarely examined or talked about as constitutive of historiographical production, they are, as every practicing historian knows, fundamental to the construction of methodologies, fields of historical research, and analytical and theoretical positions.[52] The historiographical divide that I have described in the British tradition can and should be remedied by a shift in reading habits, particularly among practitioners and teachers of conventionally "domestic" Victorian history. In this respect, Kumkum Sangari's and Sudesh Vaid's collection *Recasting Women: Essays in Colonial History* is a must-read for British historians, precisely because its contributors take as "the social" the wide spectrum of colonial / imperial relations. It has much to tell us about the ways in which gender was used to define dominant ideologies in India *and* in Britain, and the conversations it has generated suggest how both colonizer and colonized relied on notions of Indian tradition as a strategy for political and cultural containment.[53] Mrinalini Sinha's work on the Ilbert Bill controversy, Janaki Nair's research on Englishwomen's representations of the zenana, Barbara Ramusack's essays on twentieth-century British women involved in Indian campaigns about women, and Catherine Candy's study of Margaret Cousins are recommended reading for historians of modern Britain because they demonstrate some of the ways in which imperial and colonial discourses meshed and clashed, and, most significantly, how they spilled over traditional imperial–colonial boundaries.[54] My own work, and that of Vron Ware and others on "imperial feminism," indicates that British feminists, Indian nationalists, and Indian feminists shared a set of discourses that orbited around many of the same assumptions. When conflicts occurred among them, it was not always along an imperial–colonial axis; relationships could also be fragmented or cemented around gender, class / caste, or the terms of political self-determination. In this political and cultural diaspora, Britain was no more or less the center of empire than India was, geographically speaking. Though the dominant discourses of the time may have invented these polarities, and certain historically specific generations of British / imperial historians reproduced them, we need not accept them as signifiers of historical truth. Re-materializing "imperial culture" in fact not only radically de-centers the narrative of traditional British history; it continuously destabilizes the binaries that have underwritten it.[55] Ideological encounters did not occur *between* East and West or between the "mother country" and her "colonial sons." They were dispersed through the various mappings of imperial power, colonial resistance, and political collaboration that individuals, groups, and institutions proliferated in the pre-postcolonial period and beyond. To be a "British" historian in the late twentieth century requires doing more than simply acknowledging the importance of such cartographies; it means continually interrogating the ways in which they structure the very ground of one's historical research, reading, and teaching. It means, in short, transforming the very foundations of what has traditionally been "British" history. And it means, finally, taking seriously the ways in which feminist and postcolonialist histories themselves have made possible and, indeed—as Sangari and Vaid have recently argued—continue to make imperative such critical re-mappings.[56]

To argue that Britain itself has become a foundational concept, a totalizing unitary subject of historical practice, is not, as some will surely argue, simply to taint pure British history with critical theory—whether postmodern or feminist or both. Rather, this maneuver throws into question the sacral character with which many British historians have invested Britain itself. The point is not necessarily to do away with foundations. By critiquing the ways in which "Britain" has been deployed in British history, I am not suggesting that we repudiate it but that we problematize it by revealing its fundamentally politicized nature, particularly when it comes to the subjects of women / feminism and colonialism. The task, as Judith Butler has recently written, is "to interrogate what the theoretical move that establishes foundations authorizes, and what precisely it excludes or forecloses."[57] Our own re-mappings are, needless to say, subject to the same interrogations because they cannot but be as historically and politically contingent as the cartographies that came before.

In keeping with this concern, I am acutely aware of the fact that the alternative cartography I propose is rooted, as Chandra Mohanty has written about her own mappings, "in my own discontinuous locations."[58] I foreground my whiteness, my gender, and my class position inside the North American academy not as any kind of disclaimer, but as a recognition of my own accountability and the ways in which it is shaped, without being fully determined, by the situations I occupy. I understand, too, that our perspectives as historians are shaped, again without ultimately being dictated, by the way we become "professionalized" and by the way the discipline of history is institutionalized in Western university settings. The nation-state may no longer be an appropriate unit of historical analysis,[59] but historians in North America are still trained largely in accordance with its boundaries, not to mention at the heart of many of its nation-building structures (Anglo-American graduate programs, national libraries and archives, multinational corporations' publishing houses). I am equally concerned about being mistaken for someone endorsing what Dipesh Chakrabarty has recently called the "artifice of History"—by which he means the tendency to read every history produced in the academy as if it were a history of Europe, even when it is properly "about" China, India, or Africa.[60] Nor, finally, do I wish to be confused with those who have a romantic longing for "home" and therefore want to extend its reach by domesticating all of the spaces of, in this case, "imperial" culture. How "India," "Britain," "home," and "empire" are configured is a set of historically specific processes of interest to many of us engaged with the politics of history writing in the West, articulating as they do not just historical realities but also the contingency of all historiographical productions. We are vigilant against investing any of these places with essentialized meanings, we hope, because we understand them as discursive terrains that shift and change shape depending on their—and our—historical specificity.[61] This is more than just a throwaway line or a one-off "decolonizing" gesture. As Jane Haggis reminds us, our voices as historians are a part of the colonial and imperial relationships that we seek to describe, and we must not neglect to map our own shifting locations as we set about reimagining specific historical traditions.[62]

What brings together these heretofore discontinuous "fields" of history is not spatial connectedness, or even disconnectedness. Lord Salisbury's comments reveal how that kind of approach is in itself a product of imperial mappings and, as I have suggested, of historiographical overmappings, as well. It is, rather, the fact that they share a temporal—and hence, a historical—space, a coincidence of place in time, that warrants our attention and our intervention. Recognizing this, and reconstituting British history accordingly, requires that we rethink what Ann Stoler has identified as "colonial categories . . . [and] the boundaries of rule."[63] We must also confront and reject the post–Enlightenment conviction that still underlies much of the practice of Western history writing today—

namely, that "the time of European modernity . . . [is] the time of the globe"; that the West is the future that its Others eventually will encounter.[64] Until we dis-embed our own historical practices from that unwritten assumption, we will continue to stage what Johannes Fabian calls "the scandal of domination" and to map home and empire, Britain and the colonies, as territories separated in time and space whose distances can be measured only by the traditional rules of thumb.[65]

2

Who Needs the Nation?

Interrogating "British" History

In his essay "Origins of the Present Crisis" (1964), Perry Anderson argued that British colonialism had made "a lasting imprint" on English life because of the historically imperial basis of mercantile capitalism.[1] As interlocutors of capitalism from J. A. Hobson to E. P. Thompson have done (on those rare occasions when they have addressed the impact of empire on domestic English culture at all), Anderson focused his attention on the working classes. They were "undeniably deflected *from* undistracted engagement with the class exploiting them. This was the real—negative—achievement of social-imperialism," according to Anderson. "It created a powerful 'national' framework which in normal periods insensibly mitigated social contradictions and at moments of crisis transcended them."[2]

Although Anderson touched but briefly on empire, he was rare among his left academic contemporaries in suggesting that Britain's colonial enterprises had a constitutive effect on working-class and, indeed, on English life as a whole in the modern period, despite the fact that the expropriation of colonial rent and resources was, historically, one of the two major pillars of primary capital accumulation in the West.[3] Eric Williams's *Capitalism and Slavery* (1944) had posited both empirical and ideological connections between the plantocratic practices of empire and domestic British politics and society, though its impact outside Caribbean history and slavery / emancipation studies was arguably limited for decades.[4] It is tempting to stop here and talk about the relative invisibility of empire in British Marxist analyses, at least in the 1960s and 1970s. Eric Hobsbawm's *Industry and Empire* (1968) is an important exception, though it does not deal with the cultural or even the political ramifications of empire for "domestic" culture and society. The consequences of historical amnesia in British historiographical traditions have been variously explored by Gauri Viswanathan's critique of Raymond Williams, E. P. Thompson's remarkable monograph *Alien Homage*, and the introduction to Catherine Hall's *White, Male, and Middle Class*, all of which grapple with the ramifications of such willful blindness in different ways and for different ends.[5] What I want to focus on here is Anderson's observation about the "national" framework created through the appropriation of imperial discourses and politics by elites and populists, because it signals, I think, a nostalgia for the nation that is often articulated even, and perhaps especially, by ostensible critics of empire. For Anderson, as for others interested in the relationship of imperial culture to British history, what was regrettable about empire was in many respects enabling for the nation, insofar as the fact of colonialism provided what, in Anderson's own estimation, was the very grounds for "national culture." In light of Anderson's essay "Components of the National Culture," which argues that Britain produced no "overall account of itself because a classical sociology originating "at home" failed to emerge, what empire achieved for the nation is hardly insignificant. Taken together, Anderson's two essays imply that it was colonialism that provided the opportunity for Britons of all classes to conceive of the nation and to experience themselves as members of a "national culture."[6]

Such an observation runs the risk of seeming almost pedestrian, especially given the burgeoning of work in the past ten years on the imperial dimensions of Victorian and, to a lesser degree, twentieth-century British society. As a participant in and critic of these developments, I want to register my unease at some of the conservative effects of this re-mapping of Britishness, historically conceived. I want to suggest that among the subjects being implicitly and perhaps unconsciously conserved in current debates is the nation and its integrity, in part because there is nothing inherently destabilizing to the nation in critical attention to empire as a constitutive part of "British" history and society—either in Anderson's time or now. Moreover, I want to argue here that one tendency in current responses to "imperial studies" is to shore up the nation and reconstitute its centrality, even as the legitimacy of Great Britain's national boundaries are apparently under question. What is at stake in these debates is not just the nation per se, but the territorialized domains of the social versus the cultural, and with them the complicity of history writing itself in narratives of the "national" citizen-subject. Despite traditional British historians' almost pathological fear of contamination by literary studies via the linguistic turn, it is actually anthropology and the "ethnographic" turn that places the sovereignty of British history at risk.[7]

It would have required a Herculean effort in 1996 to gainsay Edward Said's claim, "We are at a point in our work when we can no longer ignore empires and the imperial context in our studies."[8] As Peter Hulme has pointed out, the enduring purchase of Said's work—its "irritative process of critique"—lies in its insistence that what is at risk from attention to Orientalism is the integrity of the European "heartland" itself, because "the principal motifs and tropes of . . . European cultural tradition, far from being self-generated, were the product of constant, intricate, but mostly unacknowledged traffic with the non–European world."[9]

Recent scholarship in British history has documented the traces of empire that were everywhere to be found "at home" before the First World War—in spaces as diverse as the Boy Scouts, in advertisements for Bovril, and on biscuit tins; in productions as varied as novels, feminist pamphlets, and music halls; and in cartographies as particular as Oxbridge, London, and the Franco-British Exhibition.[10] Either because they were part of permanent communities with long histories and traditions in the British Isles or because they were travelers or temporary residents in various metropoles and regions throughout the United Kingdom, a variety of colonial "Others" circulated at the very heart of the British empire before the twentieth century. They were, as Gretchen Gerzina has recently noted, a "continual and very English presence" from the Elizabethan settlement onward.[11] If there is little consensus about the significance of empire's impact on Britain's domestic cultural formations, primary evidence of its constitutive role nonetheless abounds, and scholars of the Georgian, Victorian, and Edwardian periods are at work to re-map Greater Britain as an imperial landscape using a variety of evidentiary bases and techniques.[12] Empire was, in short, not just a phenomenon "out there," but a fundamental part of English culture and national identity at home, where "the fact of empire was registered not only in political debate . . . but entered the social fabric, the intellectual discourse and the life of the imagination."[13]

If these claims would seem to make good historical sense, they have met with an opposition so determined that it would be easy to imagine that they pose some kind of threat to national security. While it is undoubtedly true that there are important recent voices—Catherine Hall's,

Bill Schwarz's, Laura Tabili's, and Mrinalini Sinha's among them—taking issue with the siege mentality of British history, I have chosen to focus here on the battlements and, more specifically, on how and through what kinds of referents they have been drawn and defended. Studies that seek to rematerialize the presence of non-white Britons in the United Kingdom before 1945 have attracted the most censure, in part because, as Paul Gilroy has argued with regard to the emergence of black history in Britain, they are perceived as "an illegitimate intrusion into a vision of authentic national life that, prior to their arrival, was as stable and peaceful as it was ethnically undifferentiated."[14] Accusations by a British government minister in 1995 that the elevation of historical figures such as Olaudah Equiano and Mary Seacole to the status of British heroes constituted a "betrayal" of true British history and "national identity" certainly testify to the political contests that representation has the power to set in motion.[15] But recent attention to empire's influences at home has provoked a response even when the topics are commodities and aesthetics, ideologies, and politics, rather than an "alien" presence. Whether by a calm, cool refutation of claims about empire's centrality (as shown by Peter Marshall's essay in the *Times Literary Supplement*, "No Fatal Impact?") or via the impassioned denunciations of Said (articulated in John MacKenzie's recent monograph *Orientalism: History, Theory, and the Arts*), those in charge of safeguarding Britain's national heritage, from Whitehall to the Senior Common Room, have raised the standard in defense of the nation's impenetrability to outside forces. Although a number of scholars are beginning to track empire's constitutive impact on metropolitan society as the starting point for new critical geographies of British imperial culture, empire cannot be viewed as having made Britain "what it was" for Marshall because it was so centrifugal and uneven—and by implication, perhaps, untraceable—in its impact.[16] This kind of response worries me because it seems to echo J. R. Seeley's infamous quip that the British empire was acquired in "a fit of absence of mind" (a phrase later amended to "a fit of absence of wives" by Ronald Hyam). John MacKenzie's role in this debate is perhaps the most puzzling and intriguing, since his series "Studies in Imperialism," now numbering more than twenty volumes, has arguably advanced our understanding of the myriad ways in which empire, to quote his monograph, was "a core ideology" of national culture.[17]

Clearly, the persistent conviction that home and empire were separate spheres cannot be dismissed as just any other fiction.[18] Because history writing is one terrain on which political battles are fought out, the quest currently being undertaken by historians and literary critics to recast the nation as an imperialized space—a political territory that could not, and still cannot, escape the imprint of empire—is an important political project. It strikes at the heart of Britain's long ideological attachment to the narratives of the island story, of splendid isolation, and of European exceptionalism. It materializes the traffic of colonial goods, ideas, and people across metropolitan borders and, indeed, throws into question the very Victorian distinctions between "home" and "away" that defined the imagined geography of empire in the nineteenth century—helping to challenge the equally Victorian conviction that "England possesses an unbroken history of cultural homogeneity and territorial integrity."[19] Yet what it potentially leaves intact is the sanctity of the nation itself as the right and proper subject of history. It runs the risk, in other words, of remaking Britain (itself a falsely homogeneous whole) as the centripetal origin of empire rather than insisting on the interdependence, the "uneven development," as Mrinalini Sinha calls it, of national and imperial formations in any given historical moment.[20] And—perhaps most significantly—it leaves untouched the conviction that "national" history can be tracked through a linear chronological development (with empire added in) rather than as "a set of relations that are constantly being made and remade, contested and refigured, [and] that nonetheless produce among their contemporaneous witnesses the conviction of historical *difference*."[21] In *Imperial Leather*, for example, Anne McClintock tends to see empire and nation precisely as *two*, and in a sequential relationship at that. "As domestic space became racialized," she writes, "colonial space became domesticated."[22] Here not only is the binary reinstantiated, not only is the "nation" represented as a privileged and cohesive subject, but empire follows nation in a fairly conventional linearity.[23] The fact that this relationship is a classically *imperial* concept of nation–empire relations should be our first clue to the limits of its critical usefulness (not to mention its historically specific constructedness). Rather than emerging as an unstable subject in the making, the nation is in danger of functioning as a pretext for postmodern narrative in the same way it functioned as the foundation for post–Enlightenment historicism. Such a coincidence implicates them both, though differently, in the meta-narrative(s) of Western imperial discourse, where the nation historically *has* served as the sovereign ontological subject.[24]

Despite the veritable explosion of work in the field, few have been willing to embrace or even engage the notion of deracinated, mobile subjects posed by Gilroy's *Black Atlantic* (a text that has been woefully under-engaged by British historians, at any rate). Britain—and England within it—tends to remain the fixed referent, the a priori body on which empire is inscribed. Even when it is shown to be remade by colonialism and its subjects, "the nation" often stands as the mirror to which imperial identities are reflected *back*.[25] This is so because not many historians are willing to countenance fully the notion that the nation is not only *not* antecedent to empire, but that as both a symbolic and a material site the nation—as Judith Butler has argued for identity and Joan Scott for gender and experience—has no originary moment, no fixity outside the various discourses of which it is itself an effect. So, to paraphrase Anna Marie Smith, the fiction of a pre-existing England is left largely unchallenged.[26] Rarely is the starting point of the newly imperialized British history the "precarious vulnerability" of imperial systems, as Ann Stoler has strenuously argued for the context of the Dutch East Indies.[27] Indeed, the very concept of Britain, and of England within it, seems to have a "fantasy structure" that is more resilient and more resistant to its own displacement than almost any other "national" imaginary today.[28] Even the naming of Britain as an imperial space—a maneuver that challenges the colonial status quo by implying that "home" was not hermetically sealed from the colonies—potentially works to naturalize the distinctions between "home" and "empire," when it seems clear that the nineteenth century is one particular historical moment during which such discursive categories were being affirmed (if not invented) and circulated as evidence of "modernity" and civilization in the first place. Perhaps this is a question of emphasis. In the case of McClintock, at any rate, I think the emphasis is not placed carefully enough.

One of the many queries that follows from such observations is this: if the fixity of nation is in fact being conserved in some new imperial studies projects, why has opposition to them been so fierce? I think this is a matter for discussion and debate. For my part, I believe that the terms in which such critiques are articulated—both in print and in public—reveal a lot about the stakes involved. John MacKenzie, for example, takes Said and all those who have ever footnoted him to task because their work is not sufficiently historical. Here "History" (with a capital H) is a convenient stick with which to berate the un- or under-disciplined and the great "unwashed"—literary critics, yes, but feminists and postmodern sympathizers, as well.[29] Rarely is the disciplinary power of history so blatantly on display—though other examples may be gleaned from a perusal of the pages of the book review section of the *American Historical Review* for the past decade, where the "Real History" stick is routinely used to discipline authors of postmodern or cultural studies works, especially those interested in "discourse" or textual analysis.[30] It might be argued that this is evidence that traditionalists are fighting a losing battle, since the book review is not a particularly effective or enduring site of protest.[31] Yet it also suggests that the refashioning of Britain's conceptual borders—and, indeed, of British history's "mission" itself—is by no means a fait accompli. Clearly, one of the purposes of a discipline is to discipline. The necessity of disciplinary action may seem especially urgent in a historical moment such as this one, when disciplinary boundaries are said to be dissolving—and their perceived dissolution is producing what Judith Allen aptly calls historically unprecedented "spatial anxieties," as well.[32] The impulse to discipline may also be an indication of how invested some professionals in Britain and the U.S. are in the historicist (and implicitly empiricist) models that are at least partly responsible for their material and political hegemony, historically if not also today.[33] But an equally powerful purpose of disciplinary action is also, surely, to enculturate—a project historically bound up with the mission to produce a certain sort of cosmopolitan liberal subject among educated citizens and, especially, among university students. If disciplinarity is in fact a kind of cultural artifact, historians' attempts to patrol their own shifting boundaries may be read as a historically intelligible fear that literary studies and cultural studies more generally are in the process of stealing "culture" itself.[34]

I want to be clear here that I am not unappreciative of Said's limits, oversights, or glosses, and that I find the materialist critique of *Orientalism* articulated by Mrinalini Sinha, Benita Parry, and others to be helpful guides to a more politically engaged, rigorously historical approach to texts and contexts. Nor would I deny that the emergence of a "new, multivocal historical discourse" may serve in part "to hide stasis or even further segregation at the level of social relations."[35] But I do think that recourse to arguments about the truest, "most historically" historical method such as those invoked by MacKenzie runs parallel to the desire for a return to the truest, purest nation—one not entirely untouched but certainly not centrally defined by empire, its institutional practices and its political legacies.

"Why the need for nation?"—posed, significantly, by the contemporary black British cultural critic Kobena Mercer—is not, therefore, a rhetorical question.[36] Those who need it tend to require that their historical subjects be national at heart—not only fixed by borders, but equally unfragmented and coherent, as stable as the rational post–Enlightenment subjects that postcolonial studies, feminist theory, and postmodernism together have revealed as a kind of self-interested, if historically intelligible, modernist Western fantasy. Nostalgia for and attachment to the nation are thus connected with regret for the passage of that historical moment when the subjects of history were as yet uncontaminated by the critical apparatus set in motion by decolonization, the women's and other social movements, and the gradual, if glacial, democratization of the Western academy over the past quarter-century.[37] As historians of American women in the 1950s have argued, one historically engaged response to such nostalgia is to remind its advocates that the power of her image notwithstanding, there never was a June Cleaver (the famous postwar television mom)—or, rather, that she was a fiction, the invention of a cultural moment that has continued to displace and obscure the material conditions under which such iconography (like that of the nation) emerged.[38] This is not to say that we should disregard the historical "fact" of nation. It is, rather, to suggest that in our attempt to understand its historical significance, we need to pay more attention to the question of who needs it, who manufactures the "need" for it, and whose interests it serves. In this sense, my initial interrogatory, "Who needs the nation?," might profitably be imagined as the question, "Who can afford to be sanguine about (or oblivious to) needing the nation?"—thus guaranteeing that social class, material dispossession, and political disenfranchisement will inform historical narratives about imperial culture.[39] If, as Homi Bhabha claims, "The western metropole must confront its postcolonial history . . . as an indigenous or native narrative internal to its national identity," then this kind of refiguring requires us to ask how—that is, through what kinds of practices—is it possible to practice "British" history so that it does not continue to act as a colonial form of knowledge.[40]

The fact that arguments about the boundaries of the nation and the integrity of the citizen-subject are increasingly advanced by *social* historians who are simultaneously enmeshed in debates about the merits of *cultural* history and cultural studies is surely significant. The coincidence of debates about empire with debates about the legitimacy of both culture as an object of historical inquiry and the tools used to unpack it (i.e., deconstruction) suggests that History, the Nation, and the category of the Social are being recuperated as endangered species in need of protection from a variety of "others." Susan Pederson, who gave a keynote address on gender and imperial history at the Anglo-American Conference in London in the summer of 1995, constructed just such an identity of interests when she asserted that practitioners of history are, have been, and always will be interested in "political outcomes" and that, as a result, the kinds of textual analyses performed by feminists and others in the field of gender and cultural history are not finally useful to Historians (capital H). A similar kind of argument, offered as a lament in the context of an essay basically sympathetic to new narrative forms in history writing, was articulated recently by Dorothy Ross, who claimed that the contributions of cultural history are limited because cultural history cannot address what, for her, represents historians' "real" concern: change over time.[41] Nor is this debate limited to the West, as animated discussions of the way subaltern studies has been corrupted into "bhadralok" and "Bankim" studies in India testify.[42] On offer in cultural history, of course, is the promise of new possibilities for the "political narrative," through a set of analytical techniques that juxtaposes social history's commitment to history from the bottom up with a commitment to history from the side in, if you will—this is the turn to the ethnographic to which I alluded at the start, where the ethnographic allows for a vertical rather than an exclusively horizontal vision.[43] Projects concerned with public representation, material culture, and historical memory—such as Raphael Samuel's *Theatres of Memory*, James Vernon's *Politics and the People,* Judith Walkowitz's *City of Dreadful Delight*, Patrick Joyce's *Democratic Subjects*, or Laura Mayhall's work on the Suffragette Fellowship—are good examples of how insights drawn from anthropology can give historical thickness to cultural forms and reshape our notion of the domains of the political, the social, and the cultural—as well as challenge our convictions about their separability—in the process.[44] They also interrogate the convention that change over long periods of time is the "real" interest of historians by emphasizing the local and the quotidian (two characteristics of ethnographic work). Despite the fact that this kind of scholarship remains largely bounded by traditional conceptions of the nation, hardly touching on imperial culture at all, its success is due in part to the fact that its authors do not insist that one historical technique must displace another, or even that one technique for recovering the past is more properly historical than the other. With the possible exception of Joyce, these authors do not operate as if the Whig interpretation of progressive evolution—and extinction—really obtained.[45] In fact, crucial to their approach is a critique of the very self-fulfilling, liberal narrative of progress that gave rise to, and continues to sustain, the idea of the autonomous, originary nation to begin with. In this sense, in the British context at least, such work threatens the sovereignty of a nation whose very sanctity, historically and culturally, is bound up with Victorian notions of progress, mission, and historical destiny—the very hallmarks of nineteenth-century imperial ideology itself—because it questions claims about the primacy of temporality that are at the heart of modern historical narrative practices.

As Elizabeth Ermarth has so persuasively argued, these claims appear to be so commonsensical that they continue to masquerade as "a condition of nature" rather than as "a convention and a collective act of faith," not just among historians, but throughout Western culture.[46] Britain, therefore, is not an exceptional case—though, as a French observer has remarked, "No country [is] more consistently bent upon differing from others" than Britain, and England within it.[47] The tenacity of the nation in debates about remaking British history signals a historically and culturally specific kind of attachment to the project of linear progress, even as it dramatizes how imperial traditions have shaped that investment and, finally, how tenuous the stability of "national" culture really is. That these debates occur while a post–Margaret Thatcher Tory government tries to negotiate a place in the postcolonial European Union indicates how crucial it is to see imperial and continental histories as equally implicated in the uneven development of "British" history and society.[48] I hasten to add that the aim of such multi-perspectival practices is not identical to liberal multicultural inclusion, which can tend to reinscribe identities in the process of politicizing them. Nor is its end "a more cosmopolitan and sophisticated parochialism," unless it is a less geographically fixed and, by implication, less permanently realized version than the kind of parochialism to which we have become accustomed.[49] The kinds of new practices that are being resisted help to make this kind of imaginary possible by unmasking the fictionality of conventional historical narrative and exposing the fictions of an apparently insular "British" culture—by insisting, in other words, that narratives of the nation (like all stories) are never "found" in nature but are always construed by historians for implicit and explicit political purposes and in discrete historical circumstances.[50] Yet this remains the intriguing and unsettling paradox of the "new" imperial history and studies, for the work of unmasking, however valuable, can, and often still does, leave the nation in pride of place rather than staging it as precarious, unmoored, and, in the end, finally unrealizable.

It would be fair to say that the model of a performative, rather than a prescriptive, nation is one that has scarcely been explored in any national history.[51] Following Carlo Ginzburg and Emmanuel Le Roy Ladurie in the late 1970s, there seemed to be a moment when some European historians were willing to recognize the historical precariousness of nation-state formation.[52] But a monograph such as Eugen Weber's *Peasants into Frenchmen* (1976) looks now like a kind of one-off production rather than the beginning of a revisionist trend that took the artificiality of national categories and the coercive power of their normalizing regimes as its point of departure.[53] In the English case, Philip Corrigan's and Derek Sayer's *The Great Arch* (1985)—subtitled, significantly, "English State Formation as *Cultural Revolution*"—posited the state itself as a cultural effect in a series of essays which, in retrospect, look not just way ahead of their time, but like a model still waiting to be fully utilized, at least by British historians.[54] The combination of historical analysis and politically engaged skepticism about the naturalness of the modern state that their book enacts represents a model to which we might profitably return, not least because of its emphasis on the state, and with it the nation, as something *always* in the process of becoming. Or, to use language that draws as much on Bernard S. Cohn as it does on Greg Dening and Judith Butler, they managed to stage the state as a historically pliable ideal always being performed through repetitive and ritualized acts, but never fully achieved.[55] Here I want to note that historians of the early modern and early Victorian periods have been more interested in exploring how the nation was as such "forged," a phenomenon that suggests how much work is yet to be done to subject the later nineteenth-century state to scrutiny in order to understand that it also was by no means a fait accompli but was also always in the making.[56] Yet it is equally important to underscore that the burden of representing fragmentation, diaspora, and community making as operations of nation building would seem to have fallen disproportionately on former colonies and postcolonial nations, the U.S. included. Significantly, when national history is challenged there, it tends to be by those interested in the anti-citizens of modernity—slaves, African American freed men and women, white suffragists, Native Americans, and, most recently, gays and lesbians—many of whom are said to inhabit, à la George Chauncey's *Gay New York*, a kind of anti-national subculture, *even* (and perhaps especially) when they aspire to national belonging.[57] Not incidentally, this unequal burden is one of the lingering effects of the kind of asymmetry that is foundational to colonialism and its cultural productions. At the same time, concern about the disciplinary regimes imposed by history is articulated rarely enough, even as interdisciplinary work abounds and threatens, in quite concrete and salutary ways, to remake epistemologies at the heart of the liberal tradition—especially where "discipline" works in opposition to the "playfulness" of subjects when they end up exceeding conventional boundaries. Clearly, the politics of who or what is the subject of a "national" history begs the question of how such a subject becomes national-ized, as well as what kind of disciplinary action such a process requires.

I am not sure that I would go as far as Catherine Hall does in calling for Britain to be conceptualized as a "post-nation"—one that is not ethnically pure but "inclusive and culturally diverse."[58] This is not because there is something inherently destabilizing to civil society in going "beyond the nation," as Partha Chatterjee fears, but because I am keenly aware of the persistent operations of the "citizenship machinery" deployed by the con-temporary transnational state (as I am sure Hall is, as well).[59] Nor do I want to suggest that critics of national history are always or completely impervious to the romance of nation building that seems to haunt all of the modern disciplines. Historians of women, of blacks, and of other "Others" often have sought inclusion for their subjects in the narrative of the nation-state—trying to make them, in W. E. B. Dubois's wonderfully ambivalent phrase, "The ward[s] of the nation."[60] Even Ruth Behar and Deborah Gordon, the feminist anthropologists who recently edited *Women Writing Culture*, ground their attempt to remake the discipline in the hope that the new feminist anthropology would have "no exiles."[61] It is admittedly possible to read their call as an attempt to frustrate tradi-tional structures of the nation-state—to argue that no one should have to be an exile in the sense of being prohibited from a place.[62] Yet even this generous reading tends to obscure the question of why critics of the regulatory power of their own discipline seek to reformulate it as some kind of idealized nation—that is, one with no exiles. Who writes—who even sees—the histories of subjects exiled from the "national body," those refugees (deliberate or otherwise) from national history and its disciplinary regimes, especially before the twentieth century?[63] Feminist historiography, which works at the boundaries of a variety of disciplines, as well as at the intersection of the academy and the community, should be one site for this kind of interrogatory work. But as Ien Ang has observed, feminism, no less than the discipline of history, "must stop conceiving itself as a nation, a 'natural' political destination for all women, no matter how multicultural."[64] Indeed, the rhetorics of destination, of arrival, and of home itself have provided "sentimental story lines" not just for women's national imaginaries, but for nation-states operating via transnational capital, as well.[65] What we need is conceptual work that turns "on a pivot" rather than on the axis of inside and outside—an image that suggests not just a balancing act, but the kind of counter-clockwise historicizing maneuver such "subjects" require in an era when national histories, unlike the pivot, seem unwilling or unable to budge.[66]

Why social history and cultural studies must necessarily do battle is, frankly, a puzzlement—except that this is an age when resources are scarce, when all histories can evidently lay claim with equal success to the notion that they are embattled, and when the social Darwinist presumptions of the social-science disciplines still apparently have some appeal for those who would have the strong triumph over the weak. Read in this context, Sherry Ortner's "Theory in Anthropology since the 1960s," which traces the clearly national divisions between American attachment to explanatory frameworks that privilege culture versus British insistence on "society" as the crucial analytical component, suggests that the contest for British history may well be about who should be permitted to write it, and from what ideological perspectives.[67] Clearly, this is an age-old battle with historically specific meanings that tell us as much about the political economy of the Western academy as they do about the crisis of Britishness, in cultural terms. The brouhaha in Britain over Roger Louis (an American) being chosen as the editor of the new *Oxford History of the British Empire* is more indication of how easily these (again highly naturalized) nationalistic lines can be drawn in the sand.[68] Yet if we revisit Stuart Hall's equally compelling account of the rise of cultural-studies paradigms in Britain, we see that the tensions between culture and the social as analytical premises are not merely lineaments of national difference; they have long and fraught legacies not just inside modern disciplinary practices such as history writing and anthropology but also at the heart of interdisciplinary projects.[69] The fact that the category of "culture" traditionally has been used to legitimate imagined communities either on the move or outside the West (as a substitute for nation-ness, if you will) may in part explain why metropolitan historians are loath to see that category applied to the center. In many ways, using culture rather than the nation or even the social as a primary historical tool means exoticizing the grand narratives of British history and de-familiarizing the naturalness of its ideological corollary, imperial greatness. Indeed, given its historic relationship to colonialism,[70] the analytic of culture may threaten to de-naturalize, if not corrupt, the apparent coherence and purity of nation-ness of an always already fragmented and multicultural entity such as the "United Kingdom," although cultural studies of the Celtic fringe in op-position to Englishness have not proved much more successful than colo-nial histories in challenging the presumptive originality of "Britain," and with it "England," as the heart of the empire, except perhaps to revive the "four nations" impulse in domestic British historiography. This is an ex-ception that is often as frustrating as it is interesting, insofar as it repre-sents more of an additive than a reconstitutive position with regard to the construction of ideas about nation and national cultures.[71]

That social history is characterized as the strong and cultural history as the weak "historical" approach bears some scrutiny. The fact that the struggle between the social and the cultural is being played out on the terrain of empire should command our attention no less actively than the flowering of production on empire and imperial culture itself. Although the struggle is often framed as a Manichean battle between the empiricists and the deconstructionists—those who believe in coherent nations, sub-jects, and histories versus those who don't—this is a red herring designed to throw us off the scent of other compelling issues. Chief among these is the fact that modern history writing (and not just in the West) historically has been a "narrative contract" with the territorially bounded nation-state.[72] Prying the nation from that contract is nothing less than a struggle to reorganize and reconstitute the spatial bases of power.[73] Few can escape the struggle over geography, and British history in an age of postcolo-niality is no exception. If narratives of geography are at stake in narratives of history,[74] then undoing the narrative contract may mean displacing nation-states such as Britain from center stage. It may call for an analytic frame that recognizes that "the imperium at the heart of the nation-state" was "not an entity *sui generis*."[75] It may even require a cultural map that is "all border," as well—especially since the nation itself historically has served as "the ideological alibi of the territorial state."[76] This work involves more than just challenging the parameters of "British" history or studies. It means unmasking the complicity of history writing in patrolling the borders of national identity.

Casting the project of an unstable "British" history may well end up letting let the nation in through the back door, although that is not my intention. Such a result may, in the last analysis, be testimony to how difficult it is to escape the grasp of national investigative frameworks even when one attempts a highly self-conscious and, one hopes, principled critique of the allure of nation-ness for "British" historians. Admittedly, in this essay I offer more of a diagnosis than a prognosis, in part because I think that the question "Who needs the nation?" still rings hollow for many. The extent to which we will succeed in displacing the nation from center stage depends in the end on our willingness to take seriously the ramifications of the claim that a nation is never fully realized but always in the making—and to interrogate the ways in which our own narrative strategies may help fetishize one of history's most common explanatory frameworks, if not its most seductive investigative modality. This is, I hope, a practice worth imagining, for it suggests that one does not have to give up on history to interrogate the narrative strategies of its practitioners or to fight for (and about) its unstable meanings.

3

Thinking beyond the Boundaries

Empire, Feminism, and the Domains of History

The "new imperial history" has been nothing if not controversial. Followers of its career in recent years can recall with amusement (or despair) a variety of transatlantic rantings about its impact on national curriculum standards, its failure as History (capital H), its hegemonic aspirations in the field of British studies—not to mention the unsuitability of Americans and other former colonials for the task of writing histories of British imperialism in such august venues as the new issue of the *Oxford History of the British Empire*.[1] In all of the excitement, one of the most interesting and provocative issues raised by this emergent body of scholarship—namely, the relationship between the social and the cultural as both historical and historiographical domains—has been routinely unexamined, if not overlooked altogether. Concern about the fate of the social in the wake of cultural history and cultural studies has, arguably, been a characteristic preoccupation of the profession in the West in the fin de siècle.[2] As Victoria E. Bonnell and Lynn Hunt observe in their introduction to *Beyond the Cultural Turn*, what has been unsettling to many about the move toward culture as a site of intellectual enquiry is that it "threatened to efface all reference to social context or causes and offered no particular standard of judgment to replace the seemingly more rigorous approaches that had predominated during the 1960s and 1970s." The cultural turn, in other words, has been held responsible for "the collapse of explanatory paradigms"—even though, as they acknowledge, it could easily be seen as an effect of that collapse, as well.[3]

Anxiety about the future of the social has gained ground in recent work on empire in part because attention to imperialism as a historical and cultural phenomenon is often assumed to have given legitimacy, if not birth, to recent interest in culture as a category of intellectual investigation. A certain historical amnesia is at work in such equivalences, of course. For although Edward Said's monograph *Orientalism* and his book *Culture and Imperialism* have done, and continue to do, much to promote the idea that culture is a compelling as well as a legitimate site of analysis, both cultural anthropologists and the first advocates of cultural history could persuasively claim that their early work was, at the very least, historically coincidental with Said's oeuvre.[4] And they might even reasonably argue, as Benita Parry has done in the reissue of her study *Delusions and Discoveries*, that Said himself was part of a larger trend that embraced culture not just as an analytic category but also as a methodological tool.[5] Clearly, the way that imperial history and imperial studies were undertaken in the last two decades of the twentieth century—in their weakest revisionary modes, as well as in their most forceful transformative incarnations—has much to do with the shape of this fierce debate over origins. What is more, the proprietary tone adopted by many people, such as Parry, who refuse to embrace postcolonialism and all that it entails, can tell us much about what is at stake, and for whom, as culture has become democratized as a subject of contemporary enquiry. If in the quest for a reliable genealogy of postcolonialism and its relationship to cultural studies, the new imperial history and (more recently) academic discourses about globalism and cosmopolitanism have verged on fetishism, they have also revealed the possessive individualism at the heart of desires for "truthful" narratives about the recent past—not to mention the unbecoming sight of intellectuals turning on each other "over the failure to formulate vanguard practices of resistance."[6]

As compelling as they are, such spectacles are in danger of distracting from the issue that concerns me here—that is, to enquire into the use to which the categories of the social and the cultural are put in contemporary historiography and, in a related query, to ask what definitions of social and cultural history tend to flow from those usages. I submit that, in addition to being questions of general intellectual interest, these are issues of particular political interest to feminism and to feminists in the twenty-first century. This is so not only because the category "woman" and the analytics of gender have contributed in large measure to shaping these distinctions and debates, but because the work of feminist historiography has been critical in setting up the social and the cultural both relationally

—and at times, competitively—in the scholarship that has emerged under the rubric of the "new imperial history."[7] Thinking through these questions and beyond the boundaries they delimit is itself a recognition of the historical fact of postcoloniality and its contemporary conditions. I hope my reflections will be read as a principled response to what David Scott calls the "demand of criticism in the post-colonial present," especially where criticism is understood as the kind of engaged political practice for which feminist history historically has striven.[8]

"Culture" is probably one of the most commonly invoked and least theorized concepts in history writing and feminist studies today. This is not to say that *definitions* of the term do not abound. If one were to do an ethnography of the word over the past decade, one would no doubt find a general consensus about its status as a set of practices, a site of knowledge production, a domain whose boundaries are most often in flux but routinely agonized and argued over. Many scholars who use the term "culture" recognize what Bill Readings called its doubleness, the way it names both an identity and a process of development.[9] Those of us who draw on anthropological work tend to understand it not as "entrapment"—that is, the effect of determinant historical conditions—but, rather, as "the givenness of circumstances within which individuals make their choices, their lives, their histories."[10] The field of culture is, in other words, a terrain of ongoing struggle as well as of practice—"a realm where one engages with and elaborates a politics"[11]—in part because culture is understood to represent "the production, interpretation and contestation of meaning" itself.[12] For feminists, whether historians by training or not, culture has come increasingly to mean that which makes the boundaries of domains seem natural, that which gives ideologies power, and that which makes hegemonies appear seamless. This is an idea which is intriguing since it would seem to suggest that culture itself is not a domain capable of being naturalized or naturalizing others in the process.[13] Perhaps especially for historians of women and gender and sexuality, culture has become an essential critical tool because of the space it—often literally—opens up for analyzing the margins, the intersections of historically marginal identities, and even, in some cases, the operations of dominant and would-be hegemonic systems of power.

Yet as commonplace and apparently ready-made as the term has become, the genealogies of culture as a concept—by which I mean not just its origins or history but the ongoing conditions of its production—are rarely attended to. First, I want to argue not simply that culture comes with the baggage of colonialism—for Nicholas Dirks's idea that emergence of culture itself is historically coincidental with the rise of imperial ideologies in the latter half of the nineteenth century is by now widely agreed on—but that historians are apt to use it unproblematically, sometimes in ways that naturalize the associations between women, people of color, "natives," and other subjects of ethnicity and race, on the one hand, and "the cultural," on the other.[14] These extravagantly marked bodies are, in other words, often consigned to what has been aptly called "the savage slot"—a space that, for all intents and purposes, is equivalent to "the cultural" in much current usage.[15] Despite the publications of excellent new research on the cultural dimensions of high politics and masculinity—Catherine Hall's work on Governor Eyre, Gail Bederman's counter-reading of Theodore Roosevelt, and Maura O'Connor's analysis of Garibaldi and Italian nationalism come to mind[16]—women, "black" people, and gays and lesbians in history remain all too readily available as the apparently self-evident representatives of culture, and hence as the primary objects of cultural history, in ways that can banish gender, race, and the material conditions of sexual practice from politics, whether high or low, whether institutional or otherwise. As Laura Mayhall has shown in the case of the historiography of British women's suffrage, the segregation of certain historical identities from certain historiographical domains has resulted in scholars' resolutely fixing a historical subject such as feminism outside the realm of the political.[17] For those interested in excavating the histories of people of color, such segregation is even starker, and can even place them outside the pale of History proper—as when Paul Gilroy's *The Black Atlantic* was characterized in an essay in the *American Historical Review* as an example of a transcontinental study that requires proper historical work to fill in its gaps.[18]

If the cultural has become implicitly identified with bodies black, brown, and sexualized—dwelling, by extension, on the cusp of history itself—the concept of the social is apt to become similarly naturalized: misrecognized and distorted as the stable, contained, "knowable" opposite of culture. In this sense, culture is not merely the social's Other in current usage; it works as the kind of messy, inchoate, and fundamentally dependent category alongside which the social can be measured, appreciated, and reconsolidated in new historical and historiographical forms. In fact, of course, "the social" of social history has a history of its own, emerging out of the struggle to gain visibility and authority only a few decades ago, in the memory and through the work of many now established historians. What helped to legitimate the social as a historiographical terrain (against high politics and intellectual history) was in part its claim to be a site for problem solving, a vehicle for testing political outcomes against political fantasies, promises, and even utopias. Social history also came indubitably out of the long nineteenth-century tradition of social science; whence, its practical imperative. Social historians often rely on that tradition and that pragmatism to call into question the groundedness and "reality" of cultural studies and other related practices.[19]

Significantly, perhaps, the hegemony of social history in its original, quantitative, empirical form has been relatively short-lived in historical terms.[20] That the battle between the social and the cultural should be occurring at a historical moment in which the social and, with it, social history are believed to be under attack—or, at the very least, at risk—from postmodernism and postcolonialism is surely equally significant.[21] I would like to suggest that instead of understanding culture primarily or even exclusively as the latecomer to modern Western traditions of history writing and historical thinking—a kind of inauthentic and therefore lesser ideological actor—culture has actually become the sine qua non against which the social is often reappropriated and reclaimed as the truly legitimate site of history. This is the tendency of Bonnell's and Hunt's *Beyond the Cultural Turn*, which, among other things, aims to rehabilitate "the social" of social history through new empirical approaches, though without significant reference to either the fact of colonialism or the historical impact of decolonization on the social sciences from the 1960s onward.[22]

What is striking to me is how pervasive the polarization of the social and the cultural is, and how complicit historians can be in constructing—and in the process, reproducing—the alleged differences between social and cultural history on it. For it would seem that the pathologization of culture and the concomitant embrace of the social-as-savior is at work in a variety of professional venues, some more visible and permanent than others: as throwaway lines in conference papers, book reviews, monographs, articles, and review essays. Such is also the subtext of much contemporary anxiety and debate about the future of history departments that "go cultural"—the fin-de-siècle equivalent of "going native"—in hallway conversations, regional and national meetings, and, of course, job-search committees. I do not wish to be read as saying that critiques of cultural history or studies should be dismissed out of hand or that they have no pedagogical or political value, let alone historical worth. Susan Thorne's *Congregational Missions and the Making of an Imperial Culture in Nineteenth-Century England* is an excellent example of what a principled engagement with these issues can do for the debate about the social and cultural in the field of British history and empire studies. Her thoughtful study also, perhaps inevitably, bears traces of the effects of the linguistic, cultural, and feminist turns that British history has taken since the 1980s—all the more intriguing since it was her salvo (with David Mayfield) about language, politics, and the working class that launched an ongoing series of spirited discussions in *Social History* about the fate of social history as a historiographical practice in the late twentieth century.[23]

Clearly not all scholars working with, in, or through the domain of the social wish to discount the cultural as a historical subject or a historiographical method. Indeed, Geoff Eley and Keith Nield have recently plead for a kind of truce—"a pause for breath"—in the war between "discursivity" and "reality" precisely because these terms are excessively reductive and do not begin to capture the methodological flexibility with which many historians approach a given problem or work with a given set of sources. Eley and Nield wish, moreover, to de-polemicize the debate to re-politicize it, specifically to appreciate more fully what impact Thatcherite and Blairite Britain have had on the deployment of such terms and methods in the United Kingdom and beyond.[24] Yet recourse to the apparently redeeming power of the social is a common enough reflex in today's disciplinary culture. What is most interesting to me is when and how the social in social history gets ascribed to "the archive," by which historians tend to mean "hard data," whether in the form of national repositories, institutional records, or some kind of "documentary" evidence, while the cultural is identified in very general terms with the linguistic turn, which is taken to mean the realm of language or the symbolic.[25] The fact that the archive and the linguistic turn are presumed to be antithetical points to the considerable limitations of this debate, as well as to a certain fashionable willingness to use postmodernism as the whipping post for all that is allegedly "wrong" with contemporary scholarship. More to the point, as Florencia Mallon has noted, confining discourse to the linguistic or symbolic realm casts doubt on the possibility of using "discursive / textual / linguistic analytical techniques" to scrutinize subaltern practices "as contested and constructed arenas of struggle over *power*" in its most material embodiments and institutionalizations.[26] What is more, such a move leaves the social in place as a kind of stolid referent, a domain whose boundaries are not in flux (since that is the nature of the culture, as it were; its characteristic feature) and therefore one whose contingencies need not be worried over. In some cases, it has also allowed social historians to lament the evacuation of politics from the recent imperial turn in European and, especially, British history and consequently to leave in place an often unreconstructed notion of the political domain, as well— and in the process, to neglect the analytical possibilities that culture *as* politics offers to historians and feminists alike.[27]

Given the role of literary critics in both cultural studies and the direction the new imperial history has taken, the association of culture with language and the social and political with the empiricism of a certain form of history is not all that surprising. These facile ascriptions gloss over, among other things, the debt that cultural historians owe—and, indeed, continue to recognize—to anthropologists, for whom, ironically, the very concept of culture is under interrogation and who consistently in the past decade and a half have turned toward the historical as a necessary and often legitimating category.[28] Such equivalences also enable social historians not just to take refuge in a unified subject, as against the fragmentation threatened by culture or a cultural reading of evidence, but also to claim that because culture and cultural history need not necessarily be grounded in "real" life or materiality, they are somehow politically and ideologically suspect.

The history of the archive is a history of loss, which may begin to explain why many social historians, patently aware of their own shifting fortunes in the past decade, are so eager to place it under "protective custody."[29] I would argue, as Madhavi Kale does so provocatively in *Fragments of Empire*, that it is the archive itself that should be subjected to continuous suspicion and radical doubt, serving as it often does to normalize, through classification and re-presentation, what are invariably "fragmented, fractured and disassembled" strands of historical evidence and experience.[30] If we fail to recognize how historical practice (or, indeed, any practice of looking) is in danger of reassembling and recalcifying what counts as evidence—and, in turn, what "looks" like it belongs to the domain of the social or the cultural or the political—we miss a valuable opportunity to interrogate our own investments in those domains. As Foucault would have it, any given archive acts as "a reflection that shows us quite simply, and in shadow, what all those in the foreground are looking at. It restores, as if by magic, what is lacking in every gaze."[31] In the spirit of feminist historiography, I would go as far as to say that if we fail to recognize this dynamic, we neglect an obligation to investigate our sense of identification with the archive itself, as well as to ask questions about its capability (and ours) fully to know the subjects it claims to represent. In this sense, I think there is, and must be, a fundamental humility at the heart of feminist, and no doubt all intellectual work, that recognizes the unknowability of history, the chimera of all claims to total knowledge, the radical inaccessibility of the truth of the past. And contrary to what some critics of poststructuralism and postcolonialism have suggested, it *is* possible to embrace this unknowability not in a spirit of "hip defeatism" or ludic irresponsibility, but from a posture of utopian possibility—born of the promise that pluralism in its most vigorous, contentious forms can and does offer.[32]

At this juncture it behooves me to underscore that my remarks—indeed, my very vantage points—are both enabled and constrained by my training as a British historian and my engagement with what are largely British traditions of social history, with E. P. Thompson and his complicated legacies at the heart of that trajectory—imperialism not least among them. I must also acknowledge that the debate in this field has been influenced by rigorous discussions of British social history's vexed relationship to poststructuralism.[33] Yet because of the profound and, indeed, thoroughgoing impact of Thompson on American social history as a project—a topic taken up in exemplary fashion by Robert Gregg in *Inside Out, Outside In: Essays in Comparative History*—the story of *The Making of the English Working Class* and its role in shaping an Anglo-American tradition means that this is not simply a *British* story.[34] And if only because of Thompson's relationship with India, on the one hand, and the political issues of imperialism and decolonization, on the other (relationships tracked by Gregg and Madhavi Kale in their germinal "The Empire and Mr. Thompson"), the ways in which colonialism has cast a long and largely unrecognized shadow across the history of social history as a whole simply cannot be gainsaid.[35] Nor can these questions be relegated to European history, however cosmopolitan. Historians of American imperialism (especially of the Philippines and Puerto Rico) have begun to address these challenges. For the most part, and at least for now, in the early, heady days of this new work, they seem as yet untroubled by the social–cultural distinction, choosing instead to locate their work squarely inside a cultural tradition—a tradition that, apparently, sees not cultural history as a kind of failed social-history project, but as a legitimate, if eminently contestable, domain.[36]

This is a point worth underscoring for several reasons—prime among them being that women's gender and feminist history have been instrumental in interrogating the limits of the official historical archive and in insisting on a consideration of a variety of sources as legitimate evidentiary material for history writing. The "new women's history" itself grew partly out of quarrels with social history, it is true. And compared with what has occurred in Britain and Europe, the explosion of scholarship by and about people of color, women, and those of diverse sexualities, as well as their relatively high numerical presence in institutions of American higher education, must not be overlooked. This is especially important given the backlash against the putative liberalism of the American Historical Association (AHA) that is represented by the emergence of the new Historical Society—which views itself as the alternative to the cultural-history "bias" of the AHA—and its corporate sponsors.[37] But neither should these genealogies blind us to the tenacity with which some historians of women, gender, and feminism participate in caricatures of cultural history and cultural studies and take up a defense of "real" archival evidence—as against fiction, "the literary," or even the visual. The "archive hound" may be a white, male, and middle-class model, but it still has tremendous purchase as the standard against which many historians, men and women, measure the quality of historical research, award prizes, choose job candidates, and create powerful and often enduring narratives about the work of their fellow historians.[38]

Until we excavate and denaturalize the "archive logic" that dwells at the heart of what is generally accepted as professional historical practice, the ideological stakes in debates over the social and the cultural in the new imperial studies and elsewhere will remain obscure, and, I fear, the larger political significance of the new imperial studies may be lost. This is all the more urgent since, recent discussions of the archive as a conceptual problem notwithstanding, very little attention has been paid to the relationship between the emergence of archival work as the mark of history's professional status, on the one hand, and the high tide of Western colonial expansion, on the other.[39] This oversight persists despite the fact that the rise of scientific history and the age of empire coincided in the late nineteenth century, when rhetorics of data accumulation, revenue extraction, and (re)source management provided the foundations for disciplinary and colonial discourses equally. Anthropologists have been better than historians at noting the relationship between their archives (ethnographies), the history of colonialism, and the emergence of their discipline.[40] At any rate, making visible the historical coincidence of history as a discipline with the consolidation of European empires is a crucial task if we wish to countenance fully the ramifications of the new imperial history and interrogate its relationship to archival knowledge, traditional or otherwise.

Rematerializing that historical coincidence enables us, in turn, to challenge history's claims to objectivity in new, more historically nuanced ways. It also requires us to remember that the domains of the social and the cultural—and, indeed, of the political—are not simply *found* in history but are always produced through and by historiography and its authors. In other words, just as history creates the nation by narrativizing it (as Sanjay Seth has observed in the context of Indian nationalism), so, too, do historians create and reproduce these domains both in and through their protocols of research and writing.[41] Homi Bhabha's observation is especially useful here: "The thing we name as culture . . . is always a naming in response to a crisis, a crisis of survival," then as now.[42] As Mary Poovey's work illustrates, the social in the nineteenth-century English "social body" was the function of the emergence of the early Victorian state, especially in response to the crises of poverty and disease. And as Tony Bennett has suggested, "culture" became a visible domain ("the science of the reformer," to echo the subtitle of his book) in Britain precisely at the moment when the mid– to late Victorian state began to discipline a variety of others—women, "natives," the working classes—or, at the very least, to bring them into its sightlines.[43] Indeed, as Matthew Arnold remarked in 1867, "Culture suggests the idea of the state."[44] In light of these historical claims, we need perhaps to be reminded that there is not as much of a dichotomy between political economy and the so-called cultural sphere as recent critics of postmodernism have tended to read from the new cultural history and studies (or that that dichotomy is unstable because it is always historically produced and historically contingent).[45] If that is the case, we might consider the ways in which it is possible to do a cultural reading of "the social" or a social reading of "the cultural"—

procedures that underscore the dialectical relationship between the two categories as epistemological domains *and* historiographical practices.[46]

Such convictions have arisen in part in the context of my research, mostly recently around the Indian National Congress (INC) and its activities in Britain in the 1880s and 1890s.[47] A variety of audiences have presumed this to be a project of recovering a diasporic nationalist culture, despite my attempts to be heard as saying that the debate in the late nineteenth century was partly over whether the INC should be labeled a social or a political movement. Significantly, perhaps, many INC members strove to be taken seriously in the metropole as a *political* movement, while their metropolitan critics and detractors, and even some sympathizers, insisted on seeing them as a *social* movement—not least because the question of conjugality and, with it, definitions of "the authentic Indian woman" were at the heart of many of the nationalist debates that reached British readers and officials "at home." In that historical context, to be considered political was to be seen as simultaneously free-moving or autonomous *and* as part of a tradition of legitimate engagement with and protest against the state. To be considered a "social" group was to be thought of as that which needed to be controlled, policed, and regulated *by* the state.[48] The presumption I have encountered in a number of venues that Indian nationalism is necessarily or self-evidently a cultural subject is frankly insidious. The possibility that I might be interested in doing a *cultural* history of this debate over the socio-political character of the INC *without* characterizing the INC as a cultural movement is a point I have had some difficulty making, perhaps because we are not paying enough attention to the differences between domains and practices, or categories and methodologies, in our conversations and debates about the social and the cultural.

Nor am I alone in finding such boxes so carefully cut out. As Laura Mayhall has suggested, attempts to reorient British suffrage historiography away from the "social movement" arena and back into the domain of politics in which many suffrage women, arguably, viewed their struggles produces bafflement, if not resistance.[49] Let me be clear that I am not pressing a naïvely historicist agenda, one that claims we should assign the historical subjects we are studying to those domains that they themselves might have recognized or identified with. What I am suggesting is that, as we write and as we read, we ought continually to be mindful of the fact that historians play an active role in deciding what or who gets read as the embodiment of culture, often for legitimate reasons and always, of course, for political purposes, whether acknowledged as such or not. I take this to be a profoundly, though by no means exclusively, feminist insight—one that recognizes the dialectic relationship between past and present and that takes seriously both the historicity of the contemporary moment *and* the accountability of the historian for working out his or her relationship to it.[50]

Embracing such a feminist reading also means taking seriously the proposition that, in addition to women and men, subjects such as the nation, the empire, and history itself are right and proper objects of feminist enquiry and that feminism has played a historical role in determining what counts *as* history—whether social, cultural, or political. Otherwise feminists are in danger of merely reflecting back to the discipline what it has traditionally seen—that is, gendered, raced, and sexualized bodies serving as alibis in the "fraternal struggles" of history rather than acting as agents in the struggle *for* History, its cultural meanings, its political economies, and its social formations.[51] Why imperial history and the new imperial studies should be the glass through which we can see these questions so darkly on the threshold of the millennium is a question we need to continue to think through. Perhaps it is because studying colonialism in the postcolonial present offers such a historically compelling opportunity to see how history's "dream of perfect order is disturbed by the nightmare of its random, heterogeneous and often unruly" subjects—women and "natives" among them.[52] Clearly, it is not only the imperial / colonial archive in its narrowest sense that casts up and keeps in place potentially hegemonic histories. But since hegemonies are always unfinished business, the struggle against them is simply, and often joyfully, a feature of everyday life and, by extension, of ordinary historical practice, as well.[53]

4

Déjà Vu All over Again

When I read David Cannadine's *Ornamentalism: How the British Saw Their Empire* late in the summer of 2001, I was overcome by a sense of déjà vu. Those who have followed the scholarship that has emerged under the rubric of "the new imperial history" in the past decade or so no doubt had much the same experience. The preface to the book rehearses the central themes of that scholarship—the importance of women and gender as analytical categories in imperial narratives, the role of race and of "native" peoples in imperial histories, the emphasis on archives other than those produced by the colonial state as sites of evidence for histories of empire in all its geographical diversity—in order to clear the way for what Professor Cannadine trumpets as a "new," more definitive agenda. This new history is, apparently, the tale of an "interactive system," a "vast interconnected world": a world in which Britain and its empire were "very much" a part of each other.[1] Cannadine acknowledges Philip Morgan's work as the source of this model of interconnectedness, and he is generally gracious about citing the variety of historians on whose research he has relied for this synthetic and highly derivative study. Hardly original in its suggestion that metropole and colony must be understood in relation to each other, *Ornamentalism* struggles to characterize that relationship without advancing a sustained analysis (let alone a theory) of how such dependence worked itself out in concrete or even symbolic terms. Never mind that an antipathy to theoretical engagement (as opposed to that highly preferable method, "a-theoretical" empiricism) has been the occasion for occupational pride and even defiance among imperial historians right across the twentieth century.[2] Continuities of methodological conviction aside, readers of P. J. Marshall's *Cambridge Illustrated History of the British*

Isles (to name just one of a number of such sweeping accounts published in recent years) will recognize in *Ornamentalism* the same unresolved tensions that beset that ambitious and equally synthetic book. There, as in *Ornamentalism*, an attempt is made to grapple with the long-term ramifications of a post–Robinson-and-Gallagher model of imperialism without sufficient acknowledgment—among other things—of the possibility that "domestic" Britain may not in fact have been merely historically dependent on empire, but may, indeed, have been significantly, if not fully, constituted by it.[3]

Astute readers will be alive to an astonishingly similar oversight within both projects. Marshall and Cannadine, each in his own way, mistake the scholarship of, say, Mrinalini Sinha and Catherine Hall, for an attempt merely to register the claims of gender and race on imperial experience, rather than seeing it as an argument, however controversial, about the constitutive nature of empire on the whole sphere of the "domestic"— whether the domestic is conceived as parliamentary politics, social relations, or cultural mores.[4] To read the likes of Sinha and Hall more accurately would be to grant colonialism—and, heaven forefend, "natives" of all status positions rather than just elites—an active, even at times a collaborative, role in the process of *nation* building (rather than *empire* building per se). It would be to interrogate, as well, the imperial historicity—us first, then them—that continues to undergird all manner of imperial history writing and to acknowledge what Gyan Prakash calls the "uncanny doubleness" of imperial / colonial processes.[5] Admittedly, such doubleness, and the terrain of imperial social formation that it presumes, is virtually unrecognizable territory for traditional imperial history in Britain. The reactionary character of *Ornamentalism*, meanwhile, is all too familiar to students of the third and fifth volumes of the recent *Oxford History of the British Isles* ("The Nineteenth Century" and "Historiography," edited by Andrew Porter and Robin Winks, respectively)—a massive project totaling more than six thousand pages, which was overseen by William Roger Louis and funded jointly by the National Endowment for the Humanities and the Rhodes Trust. There, Cannadine's skepticism about the enduring value, as well as the full explanatory capabilities, of the new imperial history was anticipated in far more dyspeptic and, it has to be said, spirited and provocative ways than the rather cursory dismissal to which *Ornamentalism* subjects recent innovations in the field of imperial history.[6]

Having accounted for this historiographical déjà vu, I was still left with an odd sense that I had seen it all before—"how the British saw their empire," that is, laid out with all the complexities and unevenness of historical interpretation reduced to (or, at least, attributed to) one rather straightforward causal explanation: hierarchy and status. Then it hit me: *Ornamentalism* is an unwitting companion piece to the exhibit at the Victoria and Albert Museum (v&A) in London called "The Victorian Vision: Inventing New Britain," which was put on in June–July 2001. To be sure, that exhibit had its own catalogue, edited by John MacKenzie, a historian of empire who, through his now twenty-five-plus-volume series from Manchester University Press, *Studies in Imperialism*, has done more to put empire on the map as an object of comprehensive historical study than any other contemporary academic, save perhaps the Cambridge don C. A. Bayly. As an edited collection, *The Victorian Vision: Inventing New Britain* (taking its title from the name of the exhibition) does important ideological work of its own, which, unfortunately, limits of space constrain me from describing here.[7] I want to focus instead on the exhibit itself, and more particularly on the guided audio tour and the written texts (placards, signage, and other directionals) that spectators could follow throughout the installation. I do so in order to explore the ways in which the claims of *Ornamentalism* had already been laid out—quite literally—in the space of this lavish and well-attended exhibition by the time Cannadine's book appeared. The exhibit and *Ornamentalism* share a commitment to centralizing empire in the story of Britain, to reveling in the rhetoric of rediscovering its aristocratic delights, and, above all, to writing its past as coterminous with the history of its sovereigns—Queen Victoria prime among them—even as they carefully stage manage empire's presence in the larger historical account of modern British history. In this sense, the exhibit and the book are not only reactions against the new imperial history. They are alarmingly—and, of course, instructively—at odds with contemporary debates about race, postcolonial citizenship, and post-imperial identity that suffuse not just British history but the very social and institutional fabric of life in the British Isles in the twenty-first century.

Like *Ornamentalism*, "The Victorian Vision" thrilled to the rhetoric of exploration. "You are about to embark on a voyage of discovery," intoned the anonymous voice of the general Acoustiguide narrator at the start of the tape. Listeners were advised to remember two things "as you travel"—

namely, that the "new Britain" of the nineteenth century was enabled by the battle of Waterloo and Queen Victoria herself. Having identified the military and the monarchy as the twin foundations of the Victorian century—foundations of which Cannadine would indubitably approve—the organizers continually reminded us that the exhibit "presents the Victorians as they saw themselves" and that traveling through new Britain was a chance for vicarious exploration. These gestures toward the possibility of a democratic appreciation for an essentially royal or aristocratic empire are also moves that *Ornamentalism* consistently makes. "The Victorian Vision" began in earnest with "Royalty," a section that featured marble-limbed royal children and contrasting visuals of gypsy families cast as the "other" side of Victorian domesticity. It was not long before empire made its appearance, first in the form of Abraham Solomon's painting "The Flight from Lucknow" (depicting an Anglo-Indian family on the run, with ayah in tow, during the Mutiny of 1857) and then in images of "settlement nations" (representations of emigration by whites to settler colonies such as Canada, Australia, and South Africa). There is much to be said, of course, about how the royal couple served as the explicit model for all domestic family formation, but we must press on past the section called "Nature" (would that there were time!) to "The World." To get to "The World," you literally had to leave the first sections behind, pass through a corridor and go through double doors labeled "Terra Firma"—at which point you were greeted with a sign quoting Lord Palmerston: "The sun never sets on the interests of this country." This, as the Acoustiguide voiceover reminded you that Queen Victoria was the embodiment of imperial ideals who became the universal mother of empire. "Welcome to the wider world, which is the next part of our voyage." Among the first objects to be seen was a bust of Queen Victoria in the form of a wooden "Yoruba (Nigerian)" statue—"Probably made for sale to the Europeans," remarked the guide. Moving to case number 41: "This case of jewelry is a perfect example of what the British empire was all about." Ornamentalism, in short.

At this point, the Acoustiguide announced that John MacKenzie (who was identified as a leading historian of empire) would now take over the narration: "He will guide you on a tour of the empire in seven cases." India, Japan, China, "The Orient," "The Pacific," "The Americas," Africa —all wonderfully self-contained, spilling over with "things" that produced too many narratives and counter-narratives of their own to go into here, alas. Predictable perhaps were the artifacts that made it into each curio cabinet: Bombay tea for India (which was, we were told, "an empire in and of itself"), a boomerang for Australia, *Arabian Nights* for "The Orient." I believe I am correct in saying that Ireland *qua Ireland* made nary an appearance in the entire exhibit. More remarkable still was the case devoted to "The Americas," where a Singer sewing machine, a Native American harpoon, and a "negro" money box each ornamentalized—albeit in a confused and confusing way—the complex colonial and postcolonial relationship of the nineteenth-century United States to the "mother country." Lest we forget, a quote from John Bright—"England is the Mother of Parliaments"—adorned an adjoining wall. From "The World" we headed to "Technology and Work," where empire and Victoria would seem to have dropped out of sight, except, of course, for a huge quote from the queen emblazoned on a far wall: "I touched an electric button, by which I started a message that was telegraphed throughout the whole empire." Here the exhibition rather suddenly ended, though as you walked out you could view a series of short films made in the 1890s, one of the elderly queen in her carriage and—to make the last, indelible point about the technologies of imperial power—another labeled "Tribal Dancing, Murray Island, South Pacific, 1898."

"The Victorian Vision" managed imperialism in important ways. Although exhibition organizers were at pains to dramatize its formative role in shaping "New Britain" and even to suggest that it helped to make Victoria's reign the geopolitical spectacle it became, empire was quite literally cordoned off from the rest of the nation, even as it made its way into various nooks and crannies of the exhibitionary space. Those who embodied empire visually and textually were royals, military officers (few if any British Other Ranks were in evidence), painters of the rich or would-be rich, and a variety of mostly aristocratic pundits. Like *Ornamentalism*, the V&A offered the view from above: a promontory perspective that privileged monarchy as the fount of social, aesthetic, and national values, as well as the source from which all imperial ideals emanated. Indeed, it was difficult to escape the conclusion that "the Victorian vision" was also fundamentally an "imperial vision": a species of the benign, naturalized, and, of course, completely depoliticized interconnectedness that Cannadine's book seeks to make visible, if not triumphant.[8] The political—by which I mean not simply the domain of party or parliamentary politics but, more expressly, the struggle over power, over the bloody spoils of empire—was as absent from "The Victorian Vision" as it is from *Ornamentalism*, except possibly as an implied component of monarchical rule. And even this was leavened by the persistent bourgeoisification of Victoria at the v&a, chiefly through her identification with benevolent maternalism.

The absence of attention to power dynamics can hardly be surprising in a museum exhibit, yet it is nothing short of amazing in a scholarly book aimed directly at a new imperial history, one of whose sins allegedly has been the evacuation of politics from the story of empire. More unsettling still is the total lack of reference to the impact of imperialism at home in either book or exhibit. There is no indication of the flow of goods and people from empire to Britain; no evidence of the influence of colonial ideas on domestic politics; no attention to the grip empire had on the cultural imagination "at home" across two centuries. Empire, incredibly, remains as off-center in 2001 as it appeared to be in Victoria's time: a series of high-status spectacles that happened "over there" and were beamed back home but that had no lasting impact on the "national," let alone the regional or the local. In many respects, there is *only* the national in these accounts: an England masquerading as Great, if not Greater, Britain, propped up and sustained by the imperial, though not in anything but an ornamental way. Both the exhibit and the book thereby reproduce the traditional and oh-so-familiar geography of empire, despite a nod to the interconnectedness that "The World" foisted on "New Britain"—despite and, of course, because of the ways in which both the v&a and Cannadine manage empire's role in the long history of Britain's reinvention.

The stakes of this kind of management are incredibly high, for the practice of history no less than for contemporary politics. In addition to evacuating the prehistory of "the Victorian vision"—not just slavery but the ongoing violence of indentured labor and colonial economic and political regimes that continued well into the nineteenth century—it also fetishizes a kind of aseptic Victorianness for consumption in a racially fraught fin-de-siècle Britain. The fact that you could buy sheets of wrapping paper in the exhibit's gift shop imprinted with a colorful image of Britain's global empire from the *Illustrated London News* of the 1880s testifies to the ways in which such sanitized versions of Victorianness might make their way into the daily lives of twenty-first-century consumers, thereby naturalizing yet again the ornamentalism of the imperial experience. The paper shows a variety of "happy" natives submitting to the imperial yoke compliantly, even with gratitude: those were the days, if the gift shop is anything to go by. You do not have to be intimately familiar with the historical details of Empire Windrush (1948), the Notting Hill Riots (1958), the Brixton Riots (1981), the death of Stephen Lawrence (1993) and the subsequent police inquiries about racial profiling and racial prejudice in Britain throughout the 1990s—let alone the longer history of colonial and postcolonial migration to and struggle over "Britain" since the eighteenth century—to appreciate the kind of whitewashing that, together, "The Victorian Vision" and *Ornamentalism* tried to do in the year 2001.[9] That very summer, as visitors strolled through the V&A exhibit and Cannadine's book rolled off the press, Asian youths "rioted" in Oldham and various cities of the north of England, where they were quelled, sometimes quite brutally, by police. This eruption of violence should not be understood merely as a provocation. It needs to be made visible and (re)situated in both recent histories of racial violence *and* the larger narrative of post-imperial Britain—historical time that overlaps directly with Cannadine's lifetime. That time is exactly coincidental, in other words, with the childhood, adulthood, and professional career that he elucidates so evocatively and, it must be said, so bloodlessly, in the last rather curious chapter that is appended to *Ornamentalism.*

To suggest, as Cannadine and any number of reviewers on both sides of the Atlantic have, that Edward Said's *Orientalism* is the text with which his book should be paired is hubris, at best. It is painfully backward looking, as well. More apposite is the Runnymede Trust's report *The Future of Multi-Ethnic Britain* (2000)—a four-hundred-page primer that called for the establishment of a human-rights commission, an end to racially discriminatory search policies on the part of the police, and the abolition of the voucher system for asylum seekers.[10] The failure of the state-supported educational system to include the story of Britain's imperial dominance in school curricula also came under fire: the authors recommended that the history of the United Kingdom be revised to account for the impact of empire, ex-colonial migration, and non-white communities and constituencies on contemporary British life. In a section on "the future of Britishness," the report questioned the implicit equation of Englishness with whiteness and, in the process, argued that "Britishness" should be dispensed with because it was a "racially coded" identity that was no longer accurate (had it ever been) for describing Britain's multicultural character. A storm of protest followed from Tories and Labour leaders alike, as did calls for "native" Britons to defend their right to the integrity of the designation "British." Home Secretary Jack Straw announced that he was proud to be British. "Unlike the Runnymede Trust," he declared, "I firmly believe there is a future for Britain and a future for Britishness."[11] The Parekh Report (so-called because it was written by the Labour peer and South Asian political scientist Lord Parekh and others) affirms, above all, the relationship between critically engaged history and social justice: between antiracist teaching and the possibilities of a genuinely pluralist democracy. For Americans—many, if not most, of whom continue to view the United Kingdom as essentially white and empire as essentially a phenomenon "over there," and who were treated in the fall of 2001 to a number of laudatory reviews of *Ornamentalism* in the *New York Times*— this is a salutary reminder of the continued legacies of empire in and for Greater Britain.[12]

How does one reconcile the images of empire emerging so publicly and to such acclaim at this moment with the historical and contemporary events that inscribe a history of racial struggle and violence on a would-be ornamentalized imperial history?[13] Cannadine—former professor at Columbia University and now head of the Institute of Historical Research in London—fiddles while Bradford burns, perhaps. But equally compelling is the question of how we are to explain the gushing praise emanating from an imperial-history establishment that has reviled the new imperial studies for an absence of politics but that lavishes encomia on a self-confessed ornamentalist account of empire that bears no traces whatsoever of the "domestic" racial strife that was the legacy of the British empire to the twentieth century—and is, regrettably, scarcely more than a superficial gloss of the extant secondary literature on empire, with some photographs? Perhaps the emperor has no clothes after all. Which is not to say that the v&a exhibit and Cannadine's book have no politics, for surely they do. They are a particular incarnation of the politics of New Labour, which, as John MacKenzie insightfully observes in a generally positive review of *Ornamentalism* for the *Times Higher Education Supplement*, has witnessed "the continuing survival of strange forms of ornamentalism within Tony Blair's new Britain."[14] The significance of this historical convergence will have to await another forum, especially in the wake of the events of September 11, 2001, which propelled Tony Blair into the imperial world order in a newly invented, if historically familiar, Gladstonian role: that of liberal warrior in a revived special friendship with the United States. Suffice it to say for now that if, as George Dangerfield wrote more than half a century ago, "liberal" England was fated to die a strange death, "imperial Britain" seems destined for any number of "eternal returns" well into the new millennium.

5

When Was Britain?

Nostalgia for the Nation at the End of the "American Century"

By now it is practically axiomatic that rumors about the death of the nation in an age of postcolonialism and globalization are premature. Nowhere is this clearer than in the case of Britain. The transfer of Hong Kong to China, the devolution of Scotland, the moves toward abolishing hereditary peerage, and, on the very eve of the new millennium, the shift of power from London to Belfast—if these, taken either separately or together, do not signify the end of Britain as we have known it in its post–Victorian incarnations, it is hard to imagine what would.[1] To be sure, sterling persists as the "national" currency into 2003, while most of the rest of Europe went euro. There is still a monarchy and an established church. And neither the most reckless nor the most utopian among us can afford to be sanguine about the permanence of the recurrently "new" Irish situation or, for that matter, its long-term viability. Indeed, the very fact that national identities are repeatedly staged, ritualized performances designed to persuade subjects and citizens that the nation is above and beyond the vagaries of history, means that there have been many incarnations of "Britain" over time and across space. And yet, the thoroughgoing, if not radical, disjuncture with the past that the events of the last few years of the 1990s produced has yet to be recognized, let alone fully countenanced.

At the same time, it is difficult to ignore the ways in which the persistence, the endurance, and the longevity of Britain continue to be manufactured as evidence of its ongoing relevance in world politics and its ability to survive a putatively postnational future. Long after its demise in forms we have come to recognize in the twentieth century, "Britain" has a curious and instructive afterlife—one whose parameters and political stakes I want to sketch briefly here. In doing so, I want to consider how the U.S. has been and remains the audience perhaps ripest for performances of Britain's eternal Britishness. In the last three decades of the twentieth century, Britain emerged as a poignant, almost pathetic figure in American culture, a safe and utopian place where very little distinction between past and present could be discerned—a place untroubled, specifically, by the kind of racial strife that has torn at the fabric of modern American society, not least by intruding itself into twentieth-century American homes and the American psyche via television news and, later, commercial programming. I want to suggest above all that this persistent American image of Britain as a kind of Victorian and Edwardian oasis was possible because in its commercialized forms, both high and low, Britain has most often been stripped of its histories of blackness and imperial culture "at home"—even while, paradoxically, empire "over there" was (and remains) a central feature of Britain for export. Britain for export has in fact been a whitewashed Britain, a commodified balm for a certain segment of the American public seeking relief from racial tension and ugliness in the apparently racially harmonious past (and present) of the mother country.

Clearly, one of the most obvious public sites for the staging of Britain in America has been at the high political level: first in the Reagan–Thatcher revival of the special relationship, then in Clinton–Blair centrism, and, more ominously in recent days, in the Blair–Bush alliance. Without diminishing the importance of this domain, I want to dwell here instead on the ways in which the performance of Britain has also been visible in the American commercial appetite for British history, most spectacularly in forms available on PBS, in Merchant–Ivory films, or via the recent spate of Jane Austen mania—a craze that crossed both big screens and small and even made its way into regular network programming in the form of the weekly television show *Clueless*.[2] The extent to which this is an elite appetite in terms of class and race is a question worthy of more sustained discussion than I have space for here, especially if we wish to appreciate fully the tangled relationship between production and consumption, between representation and politics, and between politics and history in the modern "Atlantic world."[3] Regardless, the American media, in its various private and public incarnations, has certainly done its part to keep Britain before the eyes of the American public. This is in some respects a legacy of the post–Second World War period, though the monarchy and its accoutrements—routinely compressed as the sum total of Britishness—have been a source of interest, envy, and cultural critique for Americans since well before that, as Fred Leventhal's recent work has demonstrated.[4] Admiration for British pageantry, exceptionalism, and empire continues to be a theme of both network and cable news coverage, as the highly ceremonial passing of power in Hong Kong from Britain to China, the attention to fifty years of Indian independence, and the rhetoric around the Millennium Dome on New Year's Eve and day each testify. The relentless and prurient coverage of Lady Diana's life and death, and especially her funeral, paraded traditional Englishness before the American public at the very moment when Britons were trying (also with the help of the media) to understand whether such traditions still had purchase, why, and for whom.[5] The relative indifference with which many Britons in Britain viewed the televised ceremonies surrounding the death of the Queen Mother in April 2002 stands in stark contrast to the coverage of her passing on both cable and network television in the U.S., where (incredibly) one commentator for CNN actually claimed it was a story that was "emerging simultaneously" with accounts of escalating violence in the Middle East.[6]

Despite these contemporary images—and, of course, because of them —for many Americans Britain on TV looks consistently like history: like the past at work in the present.[7] Needless to say, there is plenty of American agency, even Yankee entrepreneurship, in this. Simon Schama's multi-part series on British history and the airing of the program *Victoria and Albert* in the fall of 2002 are only the most recent examples of what local PBS stations actively seek out and buy from British production companies. If Raphael Samuel and others have been right in thinking that the rise of the heritage industry means that all nations are destined to become theme parks, Americans get to see Britain as it was and is/as it is and was without ever having to go there—giving armchair imperialism a whole new meaning.[8] But we must not leave it at that, for the versions of British history most Americans get access to have a critically important, if complex, relationship to empire. British imperialism is never erased completely from sight; how could it be if we believe the claim of Edward Said and others that empire made its way into the very interstices of eighteenth-, nineteenth-, and twentieth-century British life? Here the subtle ways in which people of color and imperial commodities and trinkets make their way into the filmscapes of Austen movies provide interesting ethnographic opportunities, as well as for an uncanny reprise of Said's reading of Austen as classic text for the (re)discovery of empire at home.[9] In British-made programs—produced increasingly since the 1970s for export to the U.S.—empire is typically represented as a kind of agonistic moral dilemma (as in the critically acclaimed *Jewel in the Crown*), or as the quaint and exceptional ravings of a one-off egomaniac (as in the miniseries *Cecil Rhodes*), or, most recently, as the implied consequence of postwar immigration, which brought colonial people to Britain and left them with painful moral dilemmas about how to be black Britons or how to accommodate their blackness to British life and mores in the present (as in the multipart crime drama *Prime Suspect*).[10]

Such staging by now has a long television history, as Douglas Haynes's recent research on the relationship between discourses of white supremacy and British TV programming in the U.S. in the 1970s powerfully suggests.[11] Significantly, it is crime dramas and not historical programming per se that has brought race as a recognizably "domestic" British social issue into the livings rooms of a largely white, middle-class American audience in the 1980s and 1990s.[12] As such, it is a subject only dimly linked to empire, and, tellingly in the case of the Jane Tennison character of the *Prime Suspect* series, it is commonly connected (if not subordinated) to the story of a white woman's quest for professional recognition in the present day. In this way, empire and race are neatly and consistently segregated from each other at the same time that they are being refracted through the biography of a white woman. This maneuver is a continuation of narratives of Britain, empire, and home that originated with Victorian anti-slavery campaigns and have cast a long shadow on British fiction, from *Jane Eyre* to Virginia Woolf and beyond. Coded as a social issue equivalent to women's emancipation, Britain's racial "problem" appears to have little or no relationship to Britain's "real" history (whether of monarchy or empire). How many Americans, one wonders, have even heard of Stephen Lawrence—the black British youth beaten by a local white gang—let alone are aware of how his violent death in 1993 has been linked in public discourse to both legacies of the Empire Windrush (post-1945 immigration) or to longstanding questions of race relations in Britain?[13]

The PBS broadcast of "The Murder of Stephen Lawrence" in January 2002 arguably helped to redress this invisibility, though the conditions of its presentation tell us much about how the American media translates "blackness" in Britain to its viewers at the beginning of the new millennium. Screened on Martin Luther King Jr. Day, the program was introduced by Russell Baker as "highly unusual for *Masterpiece Theatre*"—not because it dealt with racism in contemporary Britain but because of the mix of genres (handheld camera / documentary technique combined with semifactual narrative) that the film featured. This astonishing declaration was followed by Baker's observation that "The Murder of Stephen Lawrence" allowed Americans to see racism in Britain today the way it had been in the U.S. during the era of the Civil Rights Movement.[14] With two brief strokes, Baker effectively whitewashed *Masterpiece Theatre*'s own historical preoccupation with upper-class England *and* reinscribed Britain as history in the present in a new and highly imaginative narrative—in addition, of course, to occluding empire yet again in the story of what was Britain. His introduction not only obscured connections between imperial history and the present; it also cast American racial problems as a thing of the past and Britain itself as a belated, if not a derivative, terrain of racial strife.[15] Moreover, the show was followed by a rerun of *Upstairs Downstairs*, and the publicity for the program was accompanied by advertisements for the next *Masterpiece Theatre* production of *Othello* (staged in contemporary Britain in a metropolitan setting).[16] Thus were Shakespeare and Edwardian Britain evoked as evidence of *Masterpiece Theatre*'s traditional commitments as well as its adaptability in the face of an ever evolving, ever modernizing transatlantic taste for Anglophilia.[17]

Perhaps this savvy packaging signals a departure for PBS with respect to its approach to British programming in America in the twenty-first century. In her review of "The Murder of Stephen Lawrence" for the *New York Times*, Caryn James hoped as much. At the same time, she reviewed the film and the *Othello* production in the same article and reminded readers that Othello was played by Eamon Damon, who had also played a character on HBO's popular prison series *Oz*—a contextualizing gesture that suggests that critics may continue to refract British television exports through a very particular kind of cultural lens, one that capitalizes on the drama racial struggles (and black actors) provide without attending to the political power that representations of "black Britain" at once reflect, produce, and contest.[18] Most if not all PBS watchers are still, I would argue, more likely to be aware of the effects of Salman Rushdie's *fatwa* on debates about multiculturalism in Britain than they are about the ongoing, daily impact of post-imperial history on British society.[19] Chances are that they understand those debates as "religious" or "fundamentalist" issues rather than as cultural and political manifestations of the demographic effects of postcolonial migration, labor conditions, and race relations in present-day Britain. This is a narrow, a-historical reading that the events of September 11, 2001, and after seem, unfortunately, only to confirm, at least as they are covered in the American media. It is also a reading that obscures the fact that British Muslims are largely Indian and Pakistani either by origin or descent and therefore represent, among other things, the after-effects of imperial rule in the contemporary metropole.[20] The image of the horseguard with a small tear in his eye that graced the cover of the *New Yorker* in September 1997, in the second of two issues in as many months devoted to commemorating fifty years of the end of empire, speaks as eloquently to the kind of American nostalgia for what Britain was as any PBS program—playing as it does on that classic London tourist experience, the changing of the guard.[21]

American nostalgia for Britain as an essentially white island of history is not, therefore, necessarily interrupted or challenged by the popularity of Raj fictions (where race happens "over there"); the occasional "real-life" crime episode where black Britons are involved (as policemen, suspects, or victims); or even actual events having to do with race, ethnicity, and postcolonialism in Britain, as the minimal coverage of the Bradford and Oldham race riots in the American news in the summer of 2001 testifies. Events in Ireland—which have historically had to do precisely with questions of race, ethnicity, and emergent postcolonialism—are an intriguing exception to which I can only allude here. Not unlike the Rushdie affair, they are typically understood in confessional terms rather than as indices of conditions of postcoloniality. What I want to explore for now is the ways in which nostalgia for Britain (Britain primarily as "England," it should be said) represents one expression of the contemporary desire for what America has not been in the twentieth century—that is, ordered, white, untouched by social upheaval, homogeneous, and polite, if not quaintly anachronistic.[22] And to appreciate this fully we must consider how and why the practice of British history in the U.S. has not only traditionally fulfilled this desire but also continues to do so by incorporating the challenges that postcolonial theory and history have to offer in a neatly repacked form of British studies, thereby attempting at once to neutralize the impact that the so-called new imperial studies has had on the "island story" *and* to make the imperial turn into a market advantage for upcoming professional historians (the next generation of purveyors of British history). In this sense, I want to suggest that, rather than an endangered species, British history both "high" (academic) and "low" (in its public culture varieties) is destined to survive well into the twenty-first century as a remarkably resilient cultural commodity.

I take as my historical evidence the report published in 1999 by the North American Conference of British Studies (NACBS), sometimes referred to as the Stansky Report because Peter Stansky, professor of history at Stanford University, was the presiding author.[23] The report was designed to assess the state of the field, evaluate the role of British history and British studies in the academy, and, especially, examine the prospects for students working primarily in history graduate programs. Compiled by committee, the report is, by its own admission, a response "to the widespread perception among the members of the profession that British Studies does not occupy the same position of importance within the academy [as it did]." Indeed, the authors of the report argue that "there is general agreement that British history no longer holds its traditional claim to attention in the American academy." Though they do not provide details about why this should be so, the implication is that the appreciation of things English in general has declined over the past few decades: "In future, rather than relying on a strong anglophilia among students and their families, the study of Britain must stand or fall on its broader significances for the history and present situation of humanity."[24] The question of how the democratization of undergraduate admissions has affected college and university life is completely sidestepped, thereby obscuring the ways in which the whiteness of the American university student body has been challenged since at least the 1960s. The authors of the report explain that British history courses "ought not, of course, be considered or planned solely on the basis of undergraduate appeal." But the authors of the report are not uninterested in addressing the question of audiences, which they believe are winnable by other means ("market trends are not our nemesis, but our opportunity").[25]

Chief among the report's preoccupations is an insistence on the fact that "the history of Britain is arguably the most important 'national' history precisely because it has been the most intertwined with, and influential upon, other histories worldwide, in all their dimensions—political, economic, social and cultural."[26] This linkage between British history and world history is then laid out in some detail, with sections devoted to (1) the interaction of the English state with its "nearest neighbors" (Scotland, Wales, Ireland); (2) Britain's relationship to "a great many countries and regions . . . most obviously South Asia, but also the Caribbean, Africa and even Latin America"; (3) "the huge diaspora of peoples from the British Isles," which has, it is claimed, "done much to[ward] making English the closest thing to a world language"; (4) "the Empire itself," which not only encompasses "the military and political 'expansion of England' and its ways," but is also "a story of complex relationships between the colonizing and the colonized, and of two-way flows of influence"; (5) "'globalization' in all its many dimensions—political, economic, social and cultural"; (6) other (mostly European) states and the process of state formation; (7) collaboration with English departments (where "the emergence of English as the second language of the world, where it is not already the first, only adds to the indispensability of British history"); and (8) the study of law and science.[27] Despite the fact that even contemporary Britons who are resistant to the Europeanization of Britain recognize the need to think of themselves "not as her Majesty's loyal subjects but as citizens of Europe," the economic realities of continental dependence and interrelationship are scarcely of concern in the report at all, raising questions about the scope of the global and the particular politics of American perspectives on the future past of Britain.[28]

At one level, the diagnoses and prognoses offered by the NACBS's report are not surprising. They are even admirable evidence of a principled awareness of the shifting place of Britain in the world and the academy and of the willingness of the body that is responsible for British history in North America to seize the moment and reimagine what a new, post-millennial British studies might look like. Like all useful historical evidence, the NACBS's report both reflects the historical moment in which it was written and produces a number of political and ideological claims worthy of further scrutiny if we are to appreciate more fully how nostalgia for Britain has worked, and continues to work, in the American context. Despite its recurrent emphasis on market opportunity, the report registers a profound ambivalence about the role of the new imperial studies in creating a climate where a new and improved British history is not just desirable but also, apparently, politically necessary and economically profitable. The authors of the report repeatedly reassure their readers that their text is not a prescription for a "postcolonial" British history. My sense is that they take up this position because they genuinely do not wish to be seen endorsing one method over another and because they understand (or misunderstand) postcolonialism as an "attack" on the nation.

According to the report, "No group has been more vocal in its condemnation of British Studies than those historians whose work focuses on the impact of imperialism on colonial subjects and who have had the most contact with colleagues in non-Western areas." And furthermore,

> New work in post-colonial theory, gender and empire, imperial legislation and indigenous resistance movements has helped formulate an attack on British studies from within and has been adopted—albeit in a caricatured form—by those wishing to argue against British replacement hires on political grounds. These demoralizing trends, along with the recent deaths of luminaries such as Edward Thompson, Raphael Samuel and Lawrence Stone, have cast a pall over British historians who have been more inclined to accept these criticisms and lament the end of an era than to mount a spirited defense of British Studies.[29]

The conflation of critiques of national history with attacks on the future of British studies is telling, especially since many interlocutors of the nation do not imagine that it is really in danger of disappearing, even and especially under the aegis of late-twentieth-century global capitalism.[30] The report's determination to link the narrative of attack with the death of British history's past "luminaries" is equally instructive, given the way in which Thompson became embroiled in debates about empire at the end of his life and the critiques of British history as usual in which Raphael Samuel was engaged—a project he called "unravelling Britain"—since at least the 1980s.[31]

Clearly, the positions articulated by the report are motivated in large measure by a concern for the waning appeal of British history as a subject in the American academy, as well as by its concomitant structural vulnerability in institutions of American higher education. These are not concerns to be dismissed lightly, if at all. What is significant, however, is the way British history is recast in the report, the way it is turned from unwitting casualty into a redemptive pedagogical and institutional, if not also a political, force. The right and proper place of empire in British history bears heavily on this redemptive possibility. Studies of the British empire in their most recent forms are represented in the report as a kind of corruption of "internal" national history rather than as projects that reveal the impact of empire on domestic relationships, economies, or imaginations. Imperial histories also emerge as the only politically motivated versions of British history on offer, as opposed to the "internal" version, which is apparently outside political considerations and immune, both in its origins and in its contemporary practices, from the impact of contemporary (let alone past) politics and history.[32] Even more striking is the way the "national" history of Britain is reinvented so that it becomes the best, most auspicious ground for doing imperial, world, global, and transnational histories. As the report notes, "British history is perhaps the best single avenue of inquiry into the large processes of 'globalization' in all its many dimensions—political, economic, social and cultural. As creators of the first true 'world system' and the first world market, and as the originators of industrialism, the British occupy a unique position in human history."[33] Again, these discussions are always connected to structural changes in the political economy of departments and universities, ever with an eye to the practical advantage that British history can bring. If this is the echo of a certain paradigm of "British" pragmatism—one that historically has pitted itself against the theoretical pretensions of the French—it also arguably approaches what might be called the stereotypically American quest for commodification and marketability, especially where that quest historically has invoked "human history" and universal values to ratify its self-interest.

The Americanization of British history that the NACBS's report offers circles invariably back through the nostalgia for (a certain version of) the "British" nation, which, as I have suggested, is characteristic of the American commercial appetite in the late twentieth century for things British more generally. That is to say, the report offers the possibility of a British history whose imperial past is the crucial, if also muted, foundation for the participation of British historians in shaping accounts of new global order as manufactured in the future American college classroom:

> Many of us believe that we must overcome the insularity that has too often afflicted British history. To remain viable, we need to demonstrate that *the history of Britain is not merely an "island story," but indeed a world story.* This group is not advocating imperial history per se: it, too, is susceptible to insularity in some of its preoccupations and practices. It is referring instead to an appreciation of British history as an avenue of inquiry into the larger processes that have transformed the globe and the relations among its inhabitants. *Though the term globalization strikes some as too triumphalist and trite to carry serious analytical weight, it does at least allude to the importance of an historical transformation that*

transcends national boundaries, a world-incorporating phenomenon that is at once political and social, economic and cultural, technological and intellectual. Historians of Britain—or more particularly of Britain in relation to the rest of the world—are as well prepared as anyone to understand the course and character of this global process.[34]

Here the "British" story becomes a world story, if not a stage for *the* world story—or, possibly, the lens through which other world stories are glimpsed. This might well be interpreted as a call for the British national story—which is, ineluctably, an imperial story—to be used as the basis for the kind of global or transnational history that looks out from the center to the periphery, taking in the latter without doing much to question the centrality of the former. This is especially true because the authors of the report do not expressly call for young British historians to be trained in anything other than the island story; at one point the report even suggests that "specialist" lecturers be "brought" into surveys and other courses to deal with other material or regions that arise in this new British-based model of world history. Many will recognize in this suggestion the "area studies" approach of the 1960s and 1970s in a new historical form, one that places disciplines such as English or programs such as South Asian studies in a subordinate position reminiscent of the status of "native informants" who made much of what counts as "colonial knowledge" possible in the first place.

The report concedes that "much of the most interesting scholarship in recent years has pursued lines of inquiry that . . . interrogate traditional conceptions of Britain and Britishness, rethinking the boundaries that have been drawn around these subjects." But the desire for a recentering of a nationalist agenda is difficult to ignore, even in its politically corrected, updated form, as when the authors remind us of the importance of the British diaspora. This, the authors claim, "has done much to[ward] making English the closest thing to a world language. This effect on world history is vast and largely unexplored, though its origins go back centuries in British history. A history of the English-speaking peoples, their similarities and differences, and their collective role in world history, would make a stimulating, and attractive, course (without having to carry Churchillian baggage)." Less obviously, but equally powerfully, the report's attempt to domesticate some of the new empire work is in danger of echoing an imperial attitude with regard to colonial peoples and encounters that reveals the neocolonial perils of such incorporationist gestures. To wit: "We have seen efforts to push the parameters of British history to the limits of its influence, incorporating the experiences of those peoples—Africans, Asians, and others—whose collision with this expansionist state transformed their societies and mentalities." The transformation of Britain itself by these "collisions" scarcely registers, though there is some recognition elsewhere in the report of the ways in which new scholarship has challenged the boundaries of Britain itself.

The fact that the report was written collectively may account for such contradictions and ambivalences in the text. Such unevenness is also evidence, I think, of the combination of paranoia and competition the authors convey in their quest to portray British history as an endangered species that, at the same time, promises to be a model for the salvation of national history, albeit only of the exceptional kind like Britain's. For example:

> British history increasingly must vie with African history and Latin American history and Chinese history and various other nationally or regionally-defined histories, not to mention thematically and ethnically-defined specialties such as women's history and Jewish history and military history. Whatever prospects exist for British history in this environment are less likely to be realized if its advocates insist on Britain's traditional place of privilege in the discipline than if they demonstrate that it remains a vital field of study that offers insights and connections that benefit students and colleagues in other areas. A British history that stresses its encounter with and significance to the rest of the world may be far better prepared to do this than one that accentuates its insularity.

As Bill Readings so persuasively argued in *The University in Ruins*, the language in which discussions about globalism and globalization are conducted is not that of culture but that of economic management.[35] This is a phenomenon that can be seen more starkly in the NACBS's report than perhaps the habits of American television-viewing audiences, unless we understand BBC productions and "British history" as it is taught in North America as "events which make audiences happen"—audiences that are curious about, and possibly seduced by, the romance of what was Britain. The fact that *Masterpiece Theatre* has long been funded by Mobil suggests important and heretofore unremarked connections between the corporate investments of public television and those of American universities. Some might argue that British history as it has been taught in this country can be read as a kind of competitive response to the likes of *Masterpiece Theatre* and its Russell Bakers: not as a way to interrogate Britain as history, but as a way to put a brake on the runaway American triumphalism (We are the future; you are the past) embedded in that publicly accessible and highly popular narrative. The fact that neither the NACBS nor the *Masterpiece Theatre* set appears to see or to care about the most statistically numerous constituency subject to commercial and artistic influences emanating from and through Great Britain—teenagers buying and listening to the kinds of music Paul Gilroy argues is the basis for a contemporary "black Atlantic"—reminds us of the ultimately limited reach of traditional British history (regardless of who its purveyors are), as well as of the equally limited purchase of the unproblematically "white nation" in an era of accelerated transnational commerce and racialized commodification.[36]

The most resistant, and perhaps most generous, reading of the NACBS's report is that it argues for British history as a local history, competing with other local histories in an age of globalization but with a historically new competitive disadvantage because of the material realities of late-twentieth-century capitalisms and their cultures—and that in doing so, it reproduces, consciously and unconsciously, some of the values and presumptions of British imperialism itself. Such a reading was anticipated twenty years ago by J. G. A. Pocock in the article "The Limits and Divisions of British History" for the *American Historical Review*. There he argued that British history is an ostensibly local history that "extends itself into Oceanic, American and global dimensions" on nothing less than a "planetary scale."[37] Pocock's location as an expatriate New Zealander practicing a particular brand of English history in the U.S. reminds us— among other things—of the peculiar circuitry of imperial and ostensibly national histories, as well as of the politics of location where historical interpretation is concerned.[38] Whether consciously or not, Pocock himself echoed modernist discourses of the interwar period, specifically those articulated by T. S. Eliot, who responded to Britain's imperial decline by advancing a robust English particularity that could reground Britain in a kind of self-contained (if not originary) national culture.[39] I would argue that the reach for the global that the NACBS's report articulates represents in many ways what globalization in its weakest forms can mean in practice in many American academic settings—that is, it can be a way to repackage existing national states and forms without either interrogating their location in geopolitical structures of power (what Mrinalini Sinha calls imperial social formation) or displacing the West as the originary site of knowledge, power, resources, history.[40] Clearly, numerous scholars are, and have been, at work countering the reinscription of an essentially British / European imperial worldview in narratives of the global—in monographs, textbooks, and well-established periodicals such as the *Journal of World History*.[41] But with its emphasis on state formation, world-systems theory, and economic empiricism, the race for the global in a time of economically straitened institutional circumstances may also signal a much coveted opportunity for those who feel threatened by the "cultural turn" to wrest the historiographical high ground away from representation toward a newly legitimated global "reality."[42]

The political implications of this kind of repackaging, as well as its consequences for commodity capital and the commercializing of virtually all domains of thought, practice, knowledge, and history, is a question one hopes the NACBS will continue to engage—especially given the appetite for British history that Americans of all kinds still have. My experience of teaching British history in a fairly wide variety of institutional settings (a former teacher's college, a small private university, a Big Ten setting) does not make me sanguine about the end of Anglophilia; quite the opposite. I have found that undergraduates of many different backgrounds and class positions come to British history classes hoping for the same kinds of relief from the combative subjects of racial strife and struggle they get in American history and literature courses that many white middle-class Americans seek when they turn on *Masterpiece Theatre*. The difference is that college students are more vociferous about their anger (and puzzlement) at the "corruption" of British history as they expected to receive it: they vote with their feet and on course evaluations, where they often pull no punches about the "excessive" attention to race and imperial subjects on my syllabi.

There may well be, in other words, more of an audience for an Anglophilic version of British history than the pundits imagine, even, perhaps, among unanticipated constituencies, since taste in history is correlated not directly or self-evidently to skin color or class position but, rather, to the complex matrix in which those signifiers create meaning and political consciousness. If indeed the face of Anglophilia is changing, that transformation runs parallel to the ways in which Britain, and British history, have not disappeared but are reappearing in "new," yet recognizable, cultural and political forms. As the reception in America of Cannadine's *Ornamentalism* suggests, even British imperial history is being repackaged and circulated without race, or with an attenuated account of it, thereby helping to guarantee that empire will remain user-friendly and unthreatening to the American fetish of Britain as whiteness.[43] The extent to which this kind of account whitewashes the racial strife at the heart of twentieth-century British history and naturalizes the vexed political contexts in which British history has been written in the past three decades is simply astonishing. For Enoch Powell (1912–98), a Tory member of Parliament for three decades, writing as recently as 1985, the specter of the empire taking revenge on the nation could be understood only in racialized terms: "What sort of country will England be when its capital, other cities and areas . . . consist of a population of which at least one-third is of African and Asian descent? My answer . . . is that it will be a Britain unimaginably wrecked by dissension and violent disorder, not recognizable as the same nation it had been, or perhaps as a nation at all."[44] In this view, Britain itself is in danger of being no longer recognizable as a nation because of the legacies of empire. Although it is tempting to ask it, the question is not so much why Americans—whether consumers of PBS or purveyors of British history—are so enamored of Powell's fantasy of Britain. Rather, it is how such whitewashed versions survive in an age of global communications, when it should be as easy to see reports of race riots in Britain as it is to see an ornamentalized British imperial history cross the sightline of an elite transnational readership. In this sense, the acclaim that has greeted Cannadine's book is in stark contrast to its real "Other"—not Said's *Orientalism* but the four-hundred-page Parekh Report, which underscored the fact of multicultural life in contemporary Britain and called for an end to "Englishness" as its signature national identity because of its equation with whiteness and the inaccuracy of that designation for a decidedly multiethnic population.[45]

Significantly, perhaps, I have found that many undergraduate students have less trouble accepting the "incursions" of race into the national narrative than they do those of gender and sexuality. This is more fruit for discussion, especially since in the NACBS's report the specter of empire appears to be much more threatening than that of gender or women or even "ethnicity," subjects the authors repeatedly acknowledge as "quite properly" a part of the story of national history. The report may have misread or overdetermined the cultural realities of the late-twentieth-century North American classroom, but its authors have their finger on the pulse of the late-twentieth-century university, which has come to recognize that it is no longer the citadel of national culture and has attempted to respond with corporate models of incorporation—primarily of "difference" and otherness but also, arguably, of those particular identities and politics that challenge the universals at the heart of globalization. In light of this shift, American universities have not just embraced globalization as the greatest good; they have also done so by simultaneously fetishizing and then absorbing the global: by incorporating "the world" as a utopian—and, one must say, fantastical—version of the nation-state and its "cultures." Nowhere is this more evident than in American engagements with Britain as history, the "when" that was Britain. In this sense, the much critiqued "return" of empire to British history is nothing compared with the eternal return of Britain in America, where British history is destined to live on as the longed-for savior of national history—and now, apparently, as the guarantor of transnational marketability, as well.

For many of us, the events of September 11 signaled a high-profile return of Britain to the world stage, with the old imperial power advising the new (though by no means unexperienced) American hegemon in what is perhaps the most dangerous moment in world history yet. Even the transfer of imperial power from one Anglophone empire to another—which historians interested in such geopolitical truisms have long recognized as having occurred in the immediate post-1945 era—appears to be newly visible in newly staged ways. In the same week that Blair's "foreign policy guru," Robert Cooper, argued in the *Observer* that "we still need empires," Emily Eakin opined in the *New York Times* that "today, America is no mere superpower or hegemon but a full-blown empire in the Roman and British sense."[46] The extent to which the news-watching American public knew about the tremendous popular opposition to Blair's support of the war against Afghanistan and, later, Iraq remains an open question, bound up in its own way with the comparative invisibility in the American media of racial disturbances in Britain in the summer of 2001. But claims about the new world apparently inaugurated by 9 / 11 should give us pause. It is worth noting here that Tony Blair's appreciation for the commodity value of a new script for the Anglo-American relationship was evident well before that terrible day. His gift to George W. Bush of a statue of Winston Churchill in the summer of 2001 is evidence of this, signaling as it does not just the reproduction of images of another historical moment in the Anglo-American relationship but also the desire for a new version of it, all of which helps to facilitate the recirculation of the British past in the present and, very possibly, in the future as well.

6

Archive Stories

Gender in the Making of Imperial and Colonial Histories

Historians who visit the Oriental and India Office Collections for the first time are often surprised by how powerfully the archival space itself evokes the Raj. Recently relocated in the new British Library in central London, the India Office produces the same promontory effect that Mary Louise Pratt argues was characteristic of modern European imperialism.[1] Portraits of "Oriental despots" who were courted and then displaced by the East India Company—painted mainly by European artists—grace the walls of the Reading Room, giving one the sense not just of being watched by figures from the past, but of being surveyed by the old colonial state and its minions, as well.[2] These spoils of rule give the place a residual clubland feel: they are a powerful reminder that the social worlds of imperial power, like those of imperial history, have been male-dominated for a very long time. If the Olympian perspective established by these images dominates visually, it does not necessarily shape the total archive experience, for despite the atmosphere of sepulchral hush that the company's paintings try to guarantee, conversations among patrons can reach such a whispered pitch that the Reading Room resembles "an Indian bazaar," especially as the hour of elevenses approaches, or so I have been told by more than one India Office *wallah.*

The genteel Orientalism of such a remark is matched only, perhaps, by the indelible imprint that imperial culture, metropolitan and colonial, continues to leave on the production of imperial histories well into the twenty-first century. To be sure, the ornamentalism of the India Office is in many respects sui generis, derivative of the peculiar place that India held in the British imperial imagination. Not all imperial archives are as conspicuously marked by the trappings of colonial rule and its comprador elites. Even when they are, they are still likely to have been the collaborative product, as the India Office collections themselves are, of "native" agency and state-sponsored information collection. They are hybrids rather than hegemons. What most if not all imperial archives surely contain, however, is the memory of imperial power in all its complexity and instability. Just as the decor of the India Office enacts a certain company drama, so, too, do imperial archives stage—organizationally and aesthetically—a variety of imperial stories that shape how historians of empire confront the "archival" evidence they find there.

By drawing attention to the lived experience of imperial archives, I want to address a dimension of imperial history rarely talked about: the role of such places in shaping the imaginations of historians who rely on them for the stories they tell, the (counter)narratives they craft, and the political interventions they make. I want to argue that archives, no less than any other public spaces, affect people differently—though not necessarily predictably—depending on their gender, nationality, class, race, age, and sexuality. Historians of empire have tended to understand archives as a delineated physical space from which to reconstruct an equally delimited imperial past. Colonial and imperial archives are also museological sites, whispering galleries, land mines, and crime scenes, to name only a few of the metaphors available to signify the kind of work that goes on in these repositories of historical knowledge.[3] As such, they set up boundaries, guard against intruders, recognize only some forms of expertise, and privilege some credentials over others. As sites of transnational labor relations (by which I mean, as places where "locals" and "foreigners" work, one typically in the service of the other), they are implicated in a matrix of global power relations and—in light of corporate research funding—also in international capitalism. Because such archives are important "contact zones" with the imperial past, it is not too much to say that they produce a variety of colonial encounters that are thoroughly, if not exclusively, gendered. Like the historical experience of colonialism itself, research in imperial archives is, then, as much an embodied experience as it is a political project. Understanding how and why this is so is arguably crucial for appreciating the achievements and the limits of women's and gender history in the imperial context and for identifying new archival horizons for future feminist research on the British empire.

Evidence gathered in 2002 through a multipage questionnaire suggests that confronting the logics and the logistics of the imperial archive has posed particular challenges to scholars of women and gender.[4] Although a number of historians can recall positive experiences with archivists, some working in the 1970s faced hostile or indifferent librarians. One historian of Africa remembered

> the sheer effort and energy I (and everyone else) put into finding references to "women" in the files of the medical department, the public works dep[artment], and whatever else made me exceptionally alert to what I was reading. Long before anyone talked of reading against, or with, the grain anybody who spent the late 1970s and early 1980s looking for hints that women were recorded in the documents they were reading learned to read carefully and problematise as they went. You had to think about what was there and what wasn't there at the same time. All the time.

The specter of card catalogues and their categories recurred across generations among the historians who shared their experiences with me. Another respondent remarked on the fact that: "the 'woman' and 'women' entries, say, in the B[ritish] L[ibrary catalogue] proved [an] extraordinarily useful point of entry in my early searches. . . . It always struck me how these classifications and entries were being used in an altogether different way than intended." For those doing their research in the 1990s, the absence of women per se in catalogues or collections necessitated a "conceptual shift" from women to gender in their work, itself a response to a changing secondary literature, but also to the availability of sources. Significantly, scholars who have been working in archives since the 1970s commented on the ways in which many collections had been rationalized over the years, especially through computer technology.[5] Even with technological advances, however, the need to read *against* the classificatory systems that remain in place was a persistent theme. One historian of aboriginal peoples and women's reform culture insisted that "lateral thinking is required":

> Looking under education, health, welfare, motherhood, girls' clubs, women's organizations is useful. Sometimes individual white women held government positions, or were of wealthy families and left personal papers. "Native" women are the subject of government programs or inquiries re health, sexuality, motherhood, etc. Their evidence occasionally appears, but they are usually only glimpsed through the accounts of white women.

Whether such lateral thinking was also required to work out more practical issues remains an open question, as the memory of "being the only woman in the archives of an order of priests . . . [was] a bit of a hoot, once you find out where you can go to the toilet" testifies.

Memories of the solitude and isolation of archival work were intense in some cases but not distinctive for their gender difference. Though a number of scholars recalled frustration, no one admitted to panic in his or her encounter with the archive, as Nicholas Dirks has recently done.[6] The relationship between femaleness, legitimacy, and professional embodiment was a persistent theme among the women surveyed. The men who responded registered no such connection; one even commented that, despite arriving at the House of Lords Record Office with a shaved head, a nose ring, and Doc Martens, he was subjected to no more scrutiny than any other patron. The contrast for women—and especially for women of color—is striking. One respondent spoke frankly of the impact of being an African American woman working on women and slavery:

> The fact that I was looking for enslaved women seemed to reflect directly on my person. When I think back on it, it seems quite obvious that the lack of attention from most archivists was not simply about their ignorance of available source material, but it was also about the fact that somehow my historical work was personalized. You can't be a real historian if you share the characterizations of your historical subjects, now can you?

To a person, the women of color among the respondents commented on the ways in which their "respectability" was an issue in archival spaces. One recounted being required to show her passport on demand in an archive in Britain, just one example of what she called "the insolence of petty functionaries . . . who could so materially interfere, if they took a dislike to [you]." Another recalled being subjected to unwanted overtures from a senior male historian, again in a British archive, leading her to remark that "the archives remain a kind of untamed jungle when it comes to gender harassment."

Being the object of archival predators was not limited to women of color, or even to archives in the West. Nor was nationality irrelevant in the archival experiences of those surveyed. Several recalled anti–American feelings among archive staff in Britain and more general anti–Western sentiment in some South Asian archives, an effect of what one respondent called the asymmetrical "economies of the post-colonial world." A young Australian researcher remembered being made to feel like a "colonial" in London and Oxford in the 1990s, thereby echoing the peculiar reverberations of white settler colonialism in the metropole.[7] By no means all who responded to my inquiry wished to attribute their archival experiences to gender alone, or to gender at all (even the person who made the toilet remark). One commented that "being white, and middle class (at once young . . . and female) means I am acceptable in certain ways that I would have difficulty even quantifying." Youth was a factor for many as graduate students, in whom sufficient "gravitas" was deemed lacking, and status played a role for both junior and untenured faculty, whether men or women. One respondent explained:

> When I was a graduate student researcher, there were certainly occasions when I felt I wasn't taken seriously. I think it had as much to do with my age as my gender. . . . In Britain, I really don't have a sense of how race or national identity shaped my gendered/aged experiences. . . . But when I first began to be a presence in the Ghanaian archives, I am sure that being a white American in many ways mitigated gender and age experiences. I don't think that a young [African] woman would have been given the same respect or attention.

Another senior historian of India concurred. "As my status has risen and I have become [a] full professor, received awards, etc., I am treated very well and in many cases get what I want. And this is far and above what a young Indian male student could get." These observations raise questions for imperial history that are very similar to those that currently beset postcolonial studies—namely, who researches and writes the histories of colonized women so sought after in the Western academy? And how do questions of uneven development and even more uneven resources shape the political claims that undergird the production of these new histories? Equally pressing (and not unrelated) are the uneven power relations at work in archives between patrons and workers, "the legion of 'fetchers'" whose class and status resentment was understood by some and less so by others. The extent to which these "structures and relations of access" are embedded in larger frameworks of transnational capitalism on which historians rely for their livelihoods was not addressed by respondents as frequently as it could, and perhaps should, have been. Nor were the ways in which the "archive hound" model—with its presumptive freedom and mobility—remains a white, male, middle-class ideal in a context of female academics trying to balance professional labor and production with "domestic" labor and reproduction.

Tellingly, perhaps, the basic task of locating women in the archives remained the preoccupying challenge for those who responded to my questions. Most agreed that the ease of turning up evidence by or about women depends on the particular archive. As one historian of Africa observed:

> I've found that in the case of government archives it is particularly difficult to "locate" women . . . unless they are the focus of some sort of an official inquiry. Otherwise, you just have to use your intuition and dig through mounds of files that are likely repositories. . . . Most of the mission societies whose papers I've worked with began to focus on "women" in the 1920s, so it is extremely easy to locate women after the First World War. Before that time, . . . well, it's pretty much like the government archives—hunt and peck. . . . For social history topics, therefore, I end up thumbing through medical records, customary law records, government diaries, sanitation reports, etc.—you name it.

There was general agreement on the comparative accessibility of mission archives, though at least one respondent commented, "When I first started using the microform records of the Society for the Propagation Gospel (Series E, marketed in the 1980s as the 'complete' archives), the records of the Committee on Women's Work were simply not filmed."[8] There was an overwhelming consensus, however, on the relative invisibility of indigenous women compared with white British women. Another Africanist commented:

> It is often hard to find even the mediated voices of African women in the colonial archives, because Colonial and Foreign Office representatives generally did not interview African women and seldom reproduced their translated testimonies in correspondence, let alone reports. British officials privileged the opinions of male representatives of African communities, and, more broadly, they privileged property ownership on a colonialist model.

Whether this was a question of "collection priorities," the "pell-mell" method of archival acquisition, or the insouciance of some archivists about material on natives and women was a matter of some debate across the questionnaires I gathered. Several respondents insisted that the imbalance was as much an effect of class as of race, reasoning that white women of the past were more likely to be literate and to recognize the market value of the written word. In turn, their "imprint" on the historical record was more highly prized. Indeed, the problem of elite voices was, if not a universal concern, then certainly a consistent one among those surveyed. One scholar recalled:

> I spent quite some time at Wellcome / GLRO [Wellcome Institute, London; Greater London Record Office] reading [Florence] Nightingale on Indian women, Aboriginal women in Australia, need for women practitioners, etc. In that archive, there simply was no utterance from indigenous women. The expert and philanthropic women were very loud! The local archive—e.g., Mitchell [Library] in Sydney, Queensland— offered much more by indigenous women—although still fragments. I think the "colonial" public record offices (in the colonies) offer much more in the way of native voices [than metropolitan ones].

The pressures of contemporary political developments could be felt especially by historians interested in indigenous populations in the Antipodes and in Canada. As a feminist historian of Australia remarked, "While I support the protocols governing this sensitive material, the bureaucracy surrounding access to Aboriginal material has become rather obstructive."

All manner of impediments produced originally by the protocols of colonial government continue to structure the research experience. As one male historian observed, "Non–European women are harder to locate in colonial archives because they've been erased from the official records, often not named at all, or only named in partial or anglicized ways that make it difficult to determine their personal identity and social status."[9] A South Asianist put it more bluntly: "Only a few Indian women have been deemed worthy of archivization." Native women's words were elusive in any number of archival sources, as this account testifies:

> I found no women's voices within the colonial files I looked at in Lucknow. There were a few Indian women's voices . . . in the Sarda reports in Delhi. In the private papers of western men and women in London and in the U.S., there were certainly more western women's voices than Indian women's voices. If there were any utterances by

Indian women, these were elite voices for the most part. For instance Pillay, one of the Indian male advocates, mentions using women as models for different contraceptive technologies, but he provides no information about these women models and of course their voices are totally silent in the traditional archives—colonial and national.

The last point is well worth underscoring, since one of the major contributions of recent work on gender and empire has been to draw lines of connection between the operations of patriarchal colonialism and those of patriarchal nationalism and, increasingly, to read the archives of elite colonized women's participation in nationalist struggles, at least, through that doubly critical lens.[10]

Despite the lingering presumption in some circles that historians of women and gender have neglected archival sources in their scholarship, the majority of respondents professed their attachment to archival research, however critical they were of it as a relatively undertheorized example of colonial power still at work. One respondent called herself an "archive junkie," while another remarked that the archive was both her "favourite place to be" *and* a "millstone" around her neck because of the ways in which it was often used in the profession as an arbiter of truth rather than simply as one investigative tool among many. Still another acknowledged that "certainly there is the thrill of the archival 'paydirt' moment." Not surprisingly, however, nearly two-thirds of the respondents either had or developed an elastic view of what counts as an archive, drawing on alternative sources such as private diaries held in personal or family hands (as opposed to being housed in official repositories) and creating new archives through oral histories. One historian cast this as a question of necessity but also of methodological conviction:

Archive used to mean the [Public Records Office in London], the National Archives in Ghana and other such official government repositories. They always have played an important part in my work, but were never the very centerpiece. The further the "official" archive from the seat of colonial power, the more valuable I have found it to be and more central to my work. So, for example, [the] Manhyia Record Office in Kumasi (sort of the private archive of the Asante king) is chock full of customary court cases from about 1908 to after independence. It is a gold mine of material. In my experience, as I move closer to the center of archival power (Britain), the archive becomes less valuable to me.

That said, I am increasingly interested . . . in extending our notions of archive. It started for me when older folks started sharing their personal papers. But then what do you do with the old woman, non-literate, who (after you ask her about early missionaries in the area) . . . sends her granddaughter inside to bring out her women's fellowship card, her bible and several doilies that she crocheted? Is that a personal archive? I think that the term is really up for grabs now—and that is a very good thing.

"Official archives" are often, of course, the fillip for the creation of alternative archives. As Susan Geiger recounts, she was led to Bibi Titi Mohamed (a Tanzanian nationalist) and her oral life history by an offhand comment about her in the papers of a District Officer in Rhodes House, who described her as a "great mountain of a woman, and a reputed bitch."[11]

One respondent to the survey comments on the skepticism with which all archival sources—even and especially oral histories—must be treated, in part because individuals and families were wary of narratives that might be humiliating. Indeed, contrary to what some critics have said about the status of oral testimony as evidence, the majority of those who reported developing alternative archives of whatever kind (textual or material) displayed tremendous sensitivity about the benefits and dangers of such evidence.[12] Such maneuvers often result in creative disciplinary borrowings and methodological mixings. So, for example, in *A Colonial Lexicon*, Nancy Rose Hunt reads missionary narratives as "inscribed forms of oral tradition" and "postcolonial routines as historical evidence" in part to track the ways in which colonialism was negotiated, and in part to understand what she calls "the hygienic modality of colonial power."[13] Lest there be any doubt, what we learn about women and gender resonates well beyond the confines of the domestic and the private, manifestly demonstrating the capacity of feminist history to shed light on the political, the social, the economic, all domains where imperial historians as recently as fifteen years ago did not think women existed, let alone exercised power as historical subjects.

In the search for women and for evidence of gendered experiences under colonialism, analytical and methodological rigor has not, in other words, been sacrificed. To the contrary. Work on women and gender in the British empire has raised challenges to the discipline that continue to be grounds for animated debate.[14] By insisting that the traces of women and other "Others," however ghostly, testify to their capacity to stand as subjects of History, feminist historians of empire have thrown the burden of proof of their presence (back) onto History itself, thereby making women's historicity a question of recognition rather than of certain standards of empirical depth. And yet, as must be clear, the problem of evidence—who has access to it and with what consequences—emerged as the dominant theme among the scholars from whom I heard. Although a number of people commented on the protectiveness of archivists of their collections, three historians of quite different parts of the British empire recounted occasions on which librarians allowed them, or someone they knew, to remove material on women from the archive and photocopy it themselves. Yet another recalled an incident in which a similar flexibility was accorded her inside the space of the archive itself:

> One year when I was . . . [doing research] with my entire family, the kids had to be at school quite early, but the archive didn't open until an hour or two later. I mentioned this to someone one day, and he volunteered to walk over and open the place up at 7:30 A.M., so that I could get a good start each morning after I dropped the kids at school! At this particular archive, there was no archivist on staff for the year I worked there. However, I was allowed into the repository and just set up shop in there. The files were in a complete shambles when I first arrived, and I spent two months of my time just putting things into order and making a class list so that I could actually begin looking at documents in some kind of a systematic way. I also worked with several local scholars to get funding from the Danish Embassy to pay for an air conditioner and pesticides to kill the silverfish and rats.

If this is a long way from the genteel ornamentalism of the India Office Library, it is also evidence of the enduring asymmetries of colonial power and of their persistent reinscription in postcolonial archival spaces. Imperial historians would do well to remain vigilant about the ways in which the official archive "reflects the forms and formations of historical knowledge that have been so markedly shaped by their implication in the history of the state whose past it is meant to enshrine," materially as well as symbolically.[15]

Clearly, all historians, regardless of what they work on, have archive stories. Most if not all of us read against the grain; we all stumble around in unfamiliar surroundings to find the facilities; and we all invent creative strategies so we can excavate the material we need to answer the questions we have and produce new ones in the process. Strategic antagonism toward sources is, or should be, the hallmark of all historians interested in a critical engagement with the past, rather than in its reproduction. I do not wish to suggest that historians of women and gender work harder, longer, or under worse conditions than other historians of empire, not only because they do not, but because such a claim would replicate both the moral-superiority argument that undergirded the Victorian imperial gender system *and* the logic of archive as boot camp that has been invoked as the dominant disciplinary regime in debates about the old versus the new imperial history. More significant perhaps for the future of British imperial history, the archive stories that feminist historians have to tell interrogate the presumptive objectivity of traditional history, surely one of the discipline's more cherished foundations. By laying bare the conditions of production, we can more fully appreciate the logics of archival spaces as well as their irrationalities; the serendipity of "discovery" as well as its careful management by representatives of the national and postcolonial state; the predictability of some absences as well as the often totally unlooked-for presences. Imperial archives are not, and never have been, sites of pure knowledge, bearing as they do the still legible traces of imperial power and colonial rule. Although this is not a uniquely feminist insight, the search for women in imperial archives dramatizes it in irrefutable ways. The more deliberately we acknowledge the impact of our archival experiences on our research and our teaching, the better we are able to historicize the British empire, its strategies of containment, its disciplinary mechanisms, and its visible and invisible forms of rule.

If feminist work of the past quarter-century has taught us anything, it is to be creative about what counts as an archive and to learn to recognize that history resides in any number of locations, some of which resemble the India Office Library, and some of which may be scarcely embodied at all. Indeed, the new frontier of imperial history, whether focused on women and gender or not, is arguably the virtual archive, that breathless corridor of cyberspace where you find your way to evidence not through card catalogues but via search engines, often from the comfort of your own home. Collections such as those in the process of being mounted online by Adam Matthew Publications are vast. They range from India to Africa to Ireland to Australia and New Zealand, and they reproduce everything from travel writing to antislavery archives, personal papers and diaries, and entire runs of missionary print journals.[16] Clearly, such archives have their own aesthetics and architectures. They also are not necessarily any more accessible than repositories in Britain, India, or Africa, given the high cost of technological access and the uneven distribution of technological resources worldwide. In fact, the Internet creates the possibilities for new "virtual empires" available for discovery by browsers tellingly named Navigator and Explorer. These are financed not by the state but by multinational corporations that, in turn, derive revenue from the virtual tourism such sites provide.[17] As feminist historians knew from experience, there is no place outside power when it comes to archives, imperial or otherwise. Rather than representing the end of history, this is the very condition from which future feminist histories of empire can and must proceed.

7

Gender, Colonialism, and Feminist Collaboration

WITH JEAN ALLMAN

The graduate seminar "Gender and Colonialism" that we have offered at the University of Illinois, Urbana-Champaign (UIUC), both jointly and individually, over the course of the past six years is very much the product of a long-term process—a feminist collaborative that is difficult to capture with a single syllabus. The syllabus we present here is a freeze-framed version of that process, the iteration of the course as we first taught it collaboratively in 2003. What follows is an account of how we came to develop a relationship with each other, with our respective fields and intellectual commitments, and with the limits and possibilities of the transnational as a historical concept and a feminist analytical look in the context of thinking through what the combination—via collision and collusion—of gender with colonialism might mean.

Antoinette Burton developed this course in the spring of 2001 in response to curricular imperatives in the graduate field we call "comparative women's and gender history" at UIUC. At the time "Gender and Colonialism" was itself a comparatively new rubric. While the concept of transnationalism had scarcely come into view as an analytical approach, let alone as a methodological procedure, she can see now that she was trying to combine questions of empire and colonialism with a transnational approach. She did this by taking what she had identified as major conceptual questions at the heart of imperial studies and colonial scholarship—domesticity, sexualities, subalternity, citizenship, medicine, commodity capitalism, race, and the nation itself—and routing them through varied physical geographies that might be considered part of the (mostly modern) colonial world.

In part because it was a new course and in part because there was what turned out to be a generation of graduate students at UIUC in a variety of disciplines who were hungry for feminist perspectives on these questions, the course ended up being chock-full of historians, kinesiologists, literary folks, and anthropologists. The diversity reflected students' curiosity about feminist history and colonialism and was the product of humanities and social-science disciplines' struggling to come to terms with gender and postcoloniality. The iteration of the class in 2001 ranged from Cuba to Shanghai, from British Columbia to the black Atlantic.

Looking back, it was probably more diffuse, geographically and methodologically, than it was genuinely *transnational*, partly because there were no mechanisms for comparison built into the syllabus and very little self-conscious reflection on Burton's part about what the grounds of such comparison might be. In this sense, "gender" and "colonialism" served as heuristic devices designed to produce examples of parallel play across a host of diverse and sometimes incommensurate spaces. This is arguably one example of how transnationalism operates as an analytical method, although, of course, this does not exhaust its interpretive potential; historiographically, it is indebted to comparative history, but in the context of colonialism, at any rate, it entails webs or connective tissues that allow us to read gender difference across linked domains (domesticity, labor, citizenship). The result was a series of useful provocations. How does gender act? What are the limits of imperial power? How do women act as agents in the context of colonial regimes? And what does it mean to think transimperially—that is, across differently gendered regimes of colonial power? An equally consequential result was that at the end of the course, Burton was ultimately left with unsatisfying questions: If colonialism is everywhere—one effect of her ham-handed attempts to transnationalize the syllabus—is it nowhere? Or, what are the historical and cultural specificities of its gendered power?

One response to Burton's experience was to produce a more distilled version of the course that sought perhaps to cover less geographical territory while refining the questions we put to the readings and ourselves. After Jean Allman joined the UIUC faculty in January 2001, we began to think about a number of ways to collaborate. Co-teaching this course seemed like a good place to begin. When we began our collaboration in 2003, we used the 2001 syllabus as a template but foregrounded our own areas of expertise and interests both geographically and thematically. This meant, in the first instance, a greater focus on African history in the revised syllabus and more point–counterpoint between area studies work and empire-centered scholarship. We have since realized that by narrowing our territorial coverage, we have not only been able to bring greater thematic coherence to the syllabus but also to provide students—many of whom had no expertise in British, Indian, or African history—with at least some security in terms of locational footing.

As the course unfolded over the weeks, two related meta-narrative debates fueled and focused our discussion. The first pitted the literature on gender and colonialism generated by scholars of empire, who have focused primarily on the power and hegemony of the imperial state, including in realms of the intimate, against that developed by area-based scholars, who have tended to foreground local, subaltern agency and the episodic, uneven nature of imperial rule. The second meta-narrative debate demanded that we bring historiographies of two very different parts of the British colonial world—South Asia and Africa—onto the same page. These are historiographies that, despite their shared concern for understanding the ways in which colonialism affected gendered systems of power, have very little in common. South Asian gender history is focused primarily (though not exclusively) on elite women, questions of the nation, and the domain of the social, while African gender history has largely engaged questions of economy and polity, especially women's marginalization by the colonial state in alliance with male elites. While the question of women's rights is implicit in both bodies of scholarship, it is rarely named as such; more common is a concern about agency, its conditions of production, and its limits and possibilities.

Of course, no one will be surprised to learn, given the dialectics built into the course (dialectics that we only came to fully appreciate as the weeks wore on) that we would each end up occupying one side in these metanarrative debates (sometimes in a staged way, other times not), as we "represented" the literatures we separately brought to the course. It was through that process of enacting and then battling through the historiographical binaries that the course discussions began to move from empire versus area, through South Asia versus Africa, to ultimately translocal and transnational insights about power and difference and the ways in which they are daily constituted, reproduced, challenged, and remembered— from the hearts of empire to their margins. As important, the dissolution of our original binaries generated important and lively discussions about method that were easily portable to the various geographical and temporal fields of interest among our students—the role of audience in historical writing, the power of language and of naming, the ambiguities of translation, the constitution of an archive. The possibility of mediation across a multiplicity of geographical contexts and spaces, in other words, became a standard for measuring the transnational capacity of specific intellectual projects and of a feminist history of gender and colonialism.

In addition to bringing our own expertise to bear more fully on the content of the syllabus, we decided that it would be useful if students wrote their ways through these disparate literatures during the entire semester and not just attempt to pull them all together in one big historiographical essay at the end. We therefore asked students to write and present one book review (a process that brought another source or two to the table each week), as well as compose weekly reflection papers, a midterm essay, and a final essay. In the first essay, we asked students to think about the ways in which the scholarship we had read up to that point challenged the binary of colonizer and colonized. In the final essay, we asked students to imagine that they were assembling an edited volume of ten essays on gender and colonialism and to develop a book prospectus for the collection that set out its main themes and explained its intellectual architecture and coherence. In other words, we asked students to contemplate new or different ways to organize and think through gendered colonialisms across time and space.

The collaborative process that took root in the classroom in 2003 forced us both to reflect very carefully on the politics of location, our different training and academic experiences, and the distinct audiences we hoped to engage with our work. It also encouraged us to contemplate in new ways the challenges of speaking across areas and boundaries without fetishizing the specificities of the local or subsuming everything under an empire, the global, or the transnational—and to begin to fashion more interpretively responsible definitions for all those categories. Those kinds of conversations have continued in a number of guises, including in the special issue of the *Journal of Colonialism and Colonial History* that we co-edited and introduced with the essay "Destination Globalization: Women, Gender, and Comparative Colonial Histories in the New Millennium." These conversations have also sustained and animated our co-editorship of the *Journal of*

Women's History since 2004 and our American Historical Association (AHA) roundtable "Transnationalizing Women's, Gender, and Sexuality History: The View from the Journals" at the 2008 AHA in Washington, D.C.

But little did we realize how precious the opportunity was in 2003 to engage these questions in a pedagogical context. By 2004, we both had been swept into administrative work, editing the journal, and upholding our area teaching duties. Sadly, we have not had the opportunity to co-teach "Gender and Colonialism" again and have had to fly solo. Allman taught the course in 2005 with only a few alterations, the main one being the incorporation of readings that placed gender history of the U.S. in colonial and transnational contexts. While students have come to the course from a range of disciplines and areas, we have increasingly been seeing students with expertise in American history and have wanted to ensure that they could see the ways in which critical debates about gender in the contexts of area / empire and local / global / transnational did not exclude the United States. Burton taught the course the following year, with an emphasis on the body, the archive, and a self-conscious focus on the question of scales of hierarchy and value entailed by what counts as the local and the global in a newly aggressive age of Anglo-American imperialism.

The point–counterpoint, or the dialectical fuel, that brought so much energy to the course in 2003 was very difficult to replicate when teaching alone. In many ways, our scholarly work and our intellectual locations embodied the thematic debates we were trying to move students through. Without both of us in the classroom, discussions never moved quite so provocatively. When we taught together, we were able to generate an open free space in which students could speak. It seemed that our dialogues diffused the tendency (of even very pedagogically savvy students) to say something to please the teacher. As two rather than one, we occupied very different locations in the debate and from those positions were able to recognize and to interrogate the binary quagmire of empire versus area studies and to identify some of the possibilities of the transnational, even as we were determined to remain alive to the ways in which the latter has inherited some of the methodological presumptions and operations of both fields.

As we face the prospect of continuing to teach the course solo (we are now in different institutional locations), we realize that ideally a course such as this should move among a cohort of teachers as an ongoing experiment in what teaching gender and colonialism, whether in comparative or transnational perspective, can look like. In this sense the course will, we hope, continue to be a living archive of the field itself.

History 493a—Problems in Comparative
Women's History: *Gender and Colonialism*

DESCRIPTION: This course provides a thematic overview of the intellectual questions, methodological challenges, and historiographical innovations that arise when gender as a category of historical analysis is brought to bear on colonialism as a world-historical phenomenon. The first half of the semester is devoted to exploring the multiple and conflicting sources through which historians have sought to reconstruct gendered colonial pasts. In the second half of the course, we examine a series of recent historical works that address conceptual problems entailed by attempts to historicize the relationship between gender and colonialism as analytical categories. Among the specific subjects under consideration are the civilizing mission; the subaltern subject; domesticities; sexuality and intimate colonialisms; racialized pathologies; gender, citizenship, and nation.

We will be operating from the assumption that colonial regimes are never self-evidently hegemonic but are always in process, subject to disruption and contest, and therefore never fully or finally accomplished. As we shall see, the gendered and sexualized social orders produced by such regimes are equally precarious, and hence they offer us unique opportunities to see the incompleteness of colonial modernities. In this sense the course is not simply about gender and sexuality as self-evident categories but also about their capacity to interrupt, thwart, and sometimes reconfirm modernizing colonial regimes—in part because they are not simply dimensions of the sociopolitical domain but represent its productive and uneven effects.

FORMAT: This is a participation-intensive seminar that meets once per week. Seminar sessions are devoted to discussions of our readings and the broader issues, theoretical and comparative, raised by those sources. One or two members of the seminar are responsible for leading the discussion each session. In addition to discussing shared readings, we will hear short reviews of books prepared by seminar participants. Book reviews and discussion roles will be assigned during our first meeting.

Required Readings:

Allman, Jean, Susan Geiger, and Nakanyike Musisi, eds., *Women in African Colonial Histories*. Bloomington: Indiana University Press, 2002.

Mani, Lata. *Contentious Traditions: The Debate on Sati in Colonial India*. Berkeley: University of California Press, 1998.

McCord, Margaret. *The Calling of Katie Makanyna: A Memoir of South Africa*. New York: Wiley, 1995.

Stoler, Ann Laura. *Carnal Knowledge and Imperial Power: Race and the Intimate in Colonial Rule*. Berkeley: University of California Press, 2002.

Thompson, Elizabeth. *Colonial Citizens: Republican Rights, Paternal Privilege, and Gender in French Syria and Lebanon*. New York: Columbia University Press, 2000.

Vaughan, Megan. *Curing Their Ills: Colonial Power and African Illness*. Stanford, Calif.: Stanford University Press, 1991.

Wexler, Laura. *Tender Violence: Domestic Visions in an Age of U.S. Imperialism*. Chapel Hill: University of North Carolina Press, 2000.

White, Luise. *Speaking with Vampires: Rumor and History in Colonial Africa*. Berkeley: University of California Press, 2000.

COURSE REQUIREMENTS: Each seminar participant must come to class prepared to discuss the session's required readings. Part of that preparation will include writing a brief (one-half to one page) reaction paper on those readings. Reaction papers will be turned in at the end of each session, but they will not be graded. (They will count toward your attendance and participation, which constitute 20 percent of your final grade.) Additional requirements are as follows:

1. *Lead discussion:* Lead discussion once during the semester. *The week before* you lead discussion, you should bring to class a set of discussion questions to distribute to the seminar. The questions should help us draw out important theoretical, comparative, and historiographical issues as we read and during our discussion the following week (10 percent of final grade).

2. *Book review:* Write one three- to four-page review of a book (or of a collection of four to five articles) and make copies of that review for all the participants in the seminar. (Readings available for review are listed under "Recommended" on the schedule of meetings.) You must provide enough information so that those who have not read the book or

collection will have some basis for participating. Your review should include: a summary of the author's thesis; a synopsis of the book's or articles' content; a consideration of the author's point of view, location, or theoretical groundings; a critique of the book's or articles' weaknesses; and an evaluation of its or their contribution to an understanding of the theme under consideration. In class, you will offer a brief (five minutes) discussion of the work, highlighting its connections with and contributions toward the themes we are discussing at that particular session (10 percent of final grade).

3. *Two questions / topics* will be distributed during the semester well in advance of essay due dates. They will require you (in eight to ten typed pages) to explore one of the themes we have encountered in our readings. The essays each constitute 30 percent of your final grade.

Schedule of Seminar Meetings:

January 22: Introduction to the Course

Required: None

Recommended: Joan Scott, "Gender: A Useful Category of Historical Analysis," *Gender and the Politics of History* (New York: Columbia University Press, 1988), 28–52; Edward Said, "Introduction" and "Knowing the Oriental," *Orientalism* (New York: Vintage, 1978), 1–28, 31–49.

January 29: Points of Departure: Gender and Conquest

Required: Holly Hanson, "Queen Mothers and Good Government in Buganda," in Allman et al., *Women in African Colonial Histories*, 219–37; Julie C. Wells, "Eva's Men: Gender and Power in the Establishment of the Cape of Good Hope, 1652–74," *Journal of African History* 39 (1998): 417–37; Adele Perry, "The State of Empire: Reproducing Colonialism in British Columbia, 1849–1871," *Journal of Colonialism and Colonial History* 2 (2001): 1–39; Mire Koikari, "Rethinking Gender and Power in the U.S. Occupation of Japan, 1945–1952," *Gender and History* 11 (1999): 313–35.

Recommended: Richard C. Trexler, *Sex and Conquest: Gendered Violence, Political Order, and the European Conquest of the Americas* (Ithaca: Cornell University Press, 1995); Kathleen Brown, "Native Americans and Early Modern Concepts of Race," *Empire and Others: British Encounters with Indigenous Peoples, 1600–1850*, ed. Martin Daunton and Rick Halpern (Philadelphia: University of Pennsylvania Press, 1999), 79–100; Stuart Schwartz, ed., *Implicit Understandings* (Cambridge: Cambridge University Press, 1994); Mary Louise Pratt, *Imperial Eyes: Travel Writing and Transculturation* (New York: Routledge, 1992); James Muldoon, *Empire and Order: The Concept of Empire, 800–1800* (New York: St. Martin's Press, 1999); Ramon Gutierrez, *When Jesus Came, the Corn Mothers Went Away: Marriage, Sexuality, and Power in New Mexico, 1500–1846* (Stanford, Calif.: Stanford University Press, 1991); Jennifer Morgan, " 'Some Could Suckle over Their Shoulder': Male Travelers, Female Bodies, and the Gendering of Racial Ideology, 1500–1770," *William and Mary Quarterly*, no. 54, 3rd ser. (1997): 167–92; Rebecca Overmeyer-Velazquez, "Christian Morality in New Spain: The Inimical Nahua Woman in Book Ten of the Florentine Codex," *Journal of Women's History* 10 (1998): 9–37; Martha Abreu, "Slave Mothers and Freed Children: Emancipation and Female Space in Debates on the 'Free Womb' Law, Rio de Janeiro, 1871," *Journal of Latin American Studies* 28 (1996): 567–80; Kelvin A. Santiago-Valles, " 'Higher Womanhood' among the 'Lower Races': Julia McNair Henry in Puerto Rico and the 'Burdens' of 1898," *Radical History Review*, no. 73 (1999): 47–73; Patricia Grimshaw, "Settler Anxieties, Indigenous Peoples, and Women's Suffrage in the Colonies of Australia, New Zealand, and Hawai'i, 1889 to 1902," *Pacific Historical Review* 69 (2000): 553–72; Catherine Hall, ed. *Cultures of Empire: A Reader* (New York: Routledge, 2000).

February 5: Gender and the Colonial Archive:
The Story of Sara Baartman

Film: *The Life and Times of Sara Baartman,* dir. Zola Maseko, 1998

Required: Zine Magubane, "Which Bodies Matter? Feminism, Poststructuralism, Race, and the Curious Theoretical Odyssey of the 'Hottentot Venus,' " *Gender and Society* 15 (2001): 816–34; Sander Gilman, "Black Bodies, White Bodies: Towards an Iconography of Female Sexuality," *Critical Inquiry* 12 (1985): 204–42; Nakanyike Musisi, "The Politics of Perception or Perception as Politics," in Allman et al., *Women in African Colonial Histories*, 95–115.

Recommended: T. Denean Sharpley-Whiting, *The Black Venus* (Durham: Duke University Press, 1999); Anne McClintock, *Imperial Leather* (New York: Routledge, 1995); Ania Loomba, *Colonialism / Postcolonialism* (New York: Routledge, 2005); David Arnold, *Colonizing the Body* (Berkeley: University of California Press, 1993); Jean Comaroff, "The Diseased Heart of Africa: Medicine, Colonialism, and the Black Body," *Knowledge, Power, and Practice*, ed. Maragaret Lock and Shirley Lindenbaum (Berkeley: University of California Press, 1993), 305–29; Annie Coombes, *Reinventing Africa: Museums, Material Culture, and Popular*

Imagination (New Haven: Yale University Press, 1994); Jan Pieterse, *White on Black: Images of Africa and Blacks in Western Popular Culture* (New Haven: Yale University Press, 1995); Gayatri Spivak, "The Rani of Sirmur: An Essay in Reading the Archives," *History and Theory* 24 (1985): 247–72; Tony Ballantyne, "Archive, Discipline, State: Power and Knowledge in South Asian Historiography," *New Zealand Journal of Asian Studies* 3 (2001): 87–105; Natalie Zemon Davis, *Fiction in the Archives: Pardon Tales and Their Tellers in Sixteenth-Century France* (Stanford, Calif.: Stanford University Press, 1990); Alan Sekula, "The Body and the Archive," *October* 39 (1986): 3–64; Antoinette Burton, *Dwelling in the Archive: Women Writing House, Home, and History in Late-Colonial India* (New York: Oxford University Press, 2003).

February 12: Speaking Subjects?

Required: Mani, *Contentious Traditions*

Recommended: Gayatri Spivak, "Can the Subaltern Speak?" *Marxism and the Interpretation of Culture*, ed. Cary Nelson and Lawrence Grossberg (New York: Macmillan, 1988), 271–313; Partha Chatterjee, "The Nationalist Resolution of the Woman Question," *Recasting Women: Essays in Colonial History*, ed. Kumkum Sangari and Sudesh Vaid (Delhi: Kali for Women, 1989), 233–53; Kamala Visweswaran, "Small Speeches, Subaltern Gender: Nationalist Ideology and Its Historiography," *Subaltern Studies XI*, ed. Shahid Amin and Dipesh Chakrabarty (Delhi: Oxford University Press, 1996), 88–125; Carolyn Martin Shaw, "The Production of Women" and "Kikuyu Women and Sexuality," *Colonial Inscriptions: Race, Sex, and Class in Kenya* (Minneapolis: University of Minnesota Press, 1995), 28–59, 60–94; Susan Pederson, "National Bodies, Unspeakable Acts: The Sexual Politics of Colonial Policy-Making," *Journal of Modern History* 63 (1991): 647–80; Antoinette Burton, "Tongues Untied: Lord Salisbury's 'Black Man' and the Boundaries of Imperial Democracy," *Comparative Studies in Society and History* 43 (2000): 632–59.

February 19: "Capturing Voices?"

Required: McCord, *The Calling*

Recommended: Luise White, Stephan Miescher, and David Cohen, eds., *African Words, African Voices* (Bloomington: Indiana University Press, 2001); Sherna Berger Gluck and Daphne Patai, *Women's Words: The Feminist Practice of Oral History* (New York: Routledge, 1991); *I, Rigoberta Menchú: An Indian Woman in Guatemala* (London: Verso, 1984); Robert Carr, "Crossing the First World/

Third World Divides: Testimonial, Transnational Feminisms, and the Post-modern Condition," in *Scattered Hegemonies: Postmodernity and Transnational Feminist Practices*, ed. Inderpal Grewal and Caren Caplan (Minneapolis: University of Minnesota Press, 1994), 153–72; Linda Alcoff and Elizabeth Potter, eds., *Feminist Epistemologies* (New York: Routledge, 1993); Gayatri Spivak, "Can the Subaltern Speak?"; Megan Vaughan, "Reported Speech and Other Kinds of Testimony," *Journal of Historical Sociology* 13 (2000): 237–63; Isabel Hofmeyer, *"We Spend Our Years as a Tale That Is Told": Oral Historical Narrative in a South African Chiefdom* (Portsmouth: Heinemann, 1994); Susan Geiger, *Tanu Women: Gender and Culture in the Making of Tanganyikan Nationalism, 1955–1965* (Portsmouth: Heinemann, 1997); Susan Geiger, "What's So Feminist about Women's Oral History?" *Journal of Women's History* 2 (1990): 169–80; Harold Scheub, *The Tongue Is Fire: South African Storytellers and Apartheid* (Madison: University of Wisconsin Press, 1996); Allman and Tashjian, *"I Will Not Eat Stone": A Women's History of Colonial Asante* (Portsmouth: Heinemann, 2000); Elizabeth Tonkin, *Narrating Our Pasts: The Social Construction of Oral History* (Cambridge: Cambridge University Press, 1992); Belinda Bozzoli, *Women of Phokeng* (Portsmouth: Heinemann, 1991); Charles van Onselen, *The Seed Is Mine* (New York: Hill and Wang, 1996).

February 26: From Source to Narrative to Analysis:
Toward a Practice of Gendered Colonial History

Required: Heidi Gengenbach, " 'What My Heart Wanted,' " 19–47; Teresa Barnes, "Virgin Territory?" 164–90; Lynette Jackson, "When in the White Man's Town," 191–218; Misty Bastian, "Vultures of the Marketplace," 260–81; Tanya Lyons, "Guerrilla Girls and Women," 305–26; Hawkins, " 'The Woman in Question,' " 116–43; and Wendy Urban-Mead, "Dynastic Daughters," 48–70, all in Allman et al., *Women in African Colonial Histories*.

Recommended: Margo Badran, ed., *Harem Years: The Memoirs of an Egyptian Feminist*, by Huda Shaarawi (New York: Feminist Press, 1987); Susan Mann, *Precious Records: Women in China's Long Eighteenth Century* (Stanford: Stanford University Press, 1997); Bonnie Smith, *The Gender of History: Men, Women, and Historical Practice* (Cambridge: Harvard University Press, 2000); Ann Stoler and Karen Strassler, "Castings for the Colonial: Memory Work in 'New Order' Java," *Comparative Studies in Society and History* 42 (2000): 4–48; Nwando Achebe, "Getting to the Source," *Journal of Women's History* 14 (2002): 9–32; Barbara Harlow, "Looked Class, Talked Red," *Meridians* 3 (2002): 226–51.

March 5: Rumors and True Stories

Required: White, *Speaking with Vampires*

Recommended: Jane Hill and Judith Irvine, *Responsibility and Evidence in Oral Discourse* (New York: Cambridge University Press, 1993); Bozzoli, *Women of Phokeng*; David Cohen and A. Odhiambo, *Burying SM: The Politics of Knowledge and the Sociology of Power in Africa* (Portsmouth: Heinemann, 1992); Gyan Prakash, *After Colonialism: Imperial Histories and Postcolonial Displacements* (Princeton: Princeton University Press, 1995); Heidi Gengenbach, "Truth-Telling and the Life Narrative of African Women: A Reply to Kirk Hoppe," *International Journal of African Historical Studies* 26 (1994): 619–27; Kirk Hoppe, "Whose Life Is It Anyway? Issues of Representation in Life Narrative Texts of African Women," *International Journal of African Historical Studies* 26 (1993): 623–36; Ann Laura Stoler, " 'In Cold Blood': Hierarchies of Credibility and the Politics of Colonial Narratives," *Representation*, no. 37 (1992): 151–89; Joyce Appleby, Lynn Hunt, and Margaret Jacob, *Telling the Truth about History* (New York: Norton, 1994).

March 12: Reading, Writing, and Consultation Week

March 19: Seminar Roundtable:
Practicing Gender and Colonial History

This is a week to take stock. Our previous weeks dealt, implicitly and explicitly, with the craft of writing—the troubled nature of sources, the limits of traditional disciplinary conventions, and the problem of silences that face those wishing to take a historical approach to gender and colonialism. In this roundtable, we want you to think about the relevance of the work so far to your interests in history and, ideally, to your dissertations and works in progress.

March 26: Spring Break

April 2: Colonialism, Race, and the Intimate

Required: Stoler, *Carnal Knowledge*

Recommended: McClintock, *Imperial Leather*; Kumari Jayawardena and Malathi de Alwis, *Embodied Violence: Communalising Women's Sexuality in South Asia* (London: Zed Books, 1997); Laura Mulvey, *Visual and Other Pleasures* (Bloomington: Indiana University Press, 1989); Lynn Thomas, "Imperial Concerns and 'Women's Affairs': State Efforts to Regulate Clitoridectomy and Eradicate Abortion in Meru, Kenya, c. 1910–1950," *Journal of African History* 39 (1998): 121–

46; Diana Jeater, *Marriage, Perversion, and Power: The Construction of Moral Discourse in Southern Rhodesia, 1894–1930* (Oxford: Oxford University Press, 1993); Pederson, "National Bodies, Unspeakable Acts"; Lisa Bloom, ed., *With Other Eyes: Looking at Race and Gender in Visual Culture* (Minneapolis: University of Minnesota Press, 1999); Timothy Mitchell, *Colonising Egypt* (Berkeley: University of California Press, 1988); Ruth Bernard Yeazell, *Harems of the Mind* (New Haven: Yale University Press, 2000); Reina Lewis, *Gendering Orientalism: Race, Femininity, and Representation* (New York: Routledge, 1996); Carol Summers, "Intimate Colonialism: The Imperial Production of Reproduction in Uganda, 1907–1925" *Signs* 16 (1991): 787–807; Malek Alloula, *The Colonial Harem* (Minneapolis: University of Minnesota Press, 1986); Vera Kutzinski, *Sugar's Secrets: Race and the Erotics of Cuban Nationalism* (Charlottesville: University of Virginia Press, 1993).

April 9: Pathologizing Colonialism

Required: Vaughan, *Curing Their Ills*

Recommended: David Arnold, *Colonizing the Body* (Berkeley: University of California Press, 1993); David Arnold, *Imperial Medicine and Indigenous Societies* (Manchester: Manchester University Press, 1988); Dagmar Engels and Shula Marks, eds., *Contesting Colonial Hegemony: State and Society in India and Africa* (London: Tauris, 1994); Roy Macleod and M. Lewis, *Disease, Medicine, and Empire* (New York: Routledge, 1988); Diana Jeater, *Marriage, Perversion, and Power;* Marinez Lyons, *The Colonial Disease: A Social History of Sleeping Sickness in Northern Zaire, 1900–1940* (Cambridge: Cambridge University Press, 1988); Sean Hawkins, "To Pray or Not to Pray: Politics, Medicine, and Conversion among the Lo-Dagaa of Northern Ghana, 1929–39," *Canadian Journal of African Studies* 31 (1997): 50–85; Luise White, " 'They Could Make Their Victims Dull': Genders and Genres, Fantasies and Cures in Colonial Southern Uganda," *American Historical Review* 100 (1995): 1379–402; Rajeswari Sunder Rajan, "Beyond the Hysterectomies Scandal: Women, the Institution, the Family, and State in India," *The Preoccupation of Postcolonial Studies*, ed. Fawzia Afzal-Khan and Kalpana Seshadri-Crooks (Durham: Duke University Press, 2000), 200–33; Frantz Fanon, *Black Skin, White Masks*, trans. Charles Lam Markmann (New York: Grove, 1991); Jonathan Sadowsky, *Imperial Bedlam: Institutions of Madness in Colonial Southwest Nigeria* (Berkeley: University of California Press, 1999); James H. Mills, *Madness, Cannabis, and Colonialism: The "Native-Only" Lunatic Asylum of British India, 1857–1900* (New York: Macmillan, 2000); Michael Bourdaghs, "The Disease of Nationalism, the Empire of Hygiene," *Positions* 6 (1998): 637–73;

Nancy Rose Hunt, *A Colonial Lexicon of Birth Ritual, Medicalization, and Mobility in the Congo* (Durham: Duke University Press, 1999); Waltraud Ernst, *Mad Tales from the Raj: The European Insane in British India, 1800–1858* (New York: Routledge, 1991); Warwick Anderson, "Excremental Colonialism: Public Health and the Poetics of Pollution," *Critical Inquiry* 21 (1995): 640–69; Sean Quinlan, "Colonial Bodies, Hygiene, and Abolitionist Politics in Eighteenth-Century France," *History Workshop* 42 (1996): 107–25.

April 16: Domesticating Gender

Required: Wexler, *Tender Violence*

Recommended: J. Hunter, *Gospel of Gentility* (New Haven: Yale University Press, 1984); K. T. Hansen, *African Encounters with Domesticity* (New Brunswick: Rutgers University Press); Jean Allman, "Making Mothers: Missionaries, Medical Officers, and Women's Work in Colonial Asante," *History Workshop Journal* 38 (1994): 23–47; Deborah Gaitskell, "Devout Domesticity? A Century of Women's Christianity in South Africa," *Women and Gender in Southern Africa to 1945*, ed. Cherryl Walker (London: Currey, 1990), 251–72; Deborah Gaitskell, "At Home with Hegemony? Coercion and Consent in the Education of African Girls for Domesticity in South Africa before 1910," in Marks and Engels, *Contesting Colonial Hegemony*, 110–28; Shula Marks, *Not Either an Experimental Doll* (Bloomington: Indiana University Press, 1984); Pam Scully, *Liberating the Family? Gender and British Slave Emancipation in the Rural Western Cape, South Africa, 1823–1853* (Portsmouth: Heinemann, 1997); Maila Stevens, "Modernizing the Malay Mother," *Maternities and Modernities: Colonial and Postcolonial Experiences in Asia and the Pacific*, ed. Kalpana Ram and Margaret Jolly (Cambridge: Cambridge University Press, 1998), 50–80; Elisabeth Locher-Scholten, "Marriage, Morality, and Modernity: The 1837 Debate on Monogamy," *Women and the Colonial State* (Amsterdam: Amsterdam University Press, 2000), 187–218; Vincente Rafael, "Colonial Domesticity: White Women and United States Rule in the Philippines," *American Literature* 67 (1995): 639–66; Elizabeth Schmidt, *Peasants, Traders, and Wives: Shona Women in the History of Zimbabwe, 1870–1939* (Portsmouth: Heinemann, 1997); David Barry Gaspar and Darlene Clark Hine, eds., *More than Chattel: Black Women and Slavery in the Americas* (Bloomington: Indiana University Press, 1996); Susanne Zantop, *Colonial Fantasies: Conquest, Family, and Nation in Precolonial Germany, 1770–1870* (Durham: Duke University Press, 1997); Julia Clancy-Smith and Frances Gouda, eds., *Domesticating the Empire: Race, Gender, and Family Life in French and Dutch Colonialism* (Charlottesville: University of Virginia Press, 1999).

April 23: Gender, Citizenship, and the Nation

Required: Thompson, *Colonial Citizens*

Recommended: Scully, *Liberating the Family*; Mahmood Mamdani, *Citizen and Subject* (Princeton: Princeton University Press, 1998); Aiwha Ong, *Flexible Citizenship: The Cultural Logics of Transnationality* (Durham: Duke University Press, 1999); Tani Barlow, ed., *Formations of Colonial Modernity in East Asia* (Durham: Duke University Press, 1997); Caren Caplan, Norma Alarcón, and Minoo Moallem, eds., *Between Woman and Nation: Nationalisms, Transnational Feminisms, and the State* (Durham: Duke University Press, 1999); Paul Gilroy, *The Black Atlantic: Modernity and Double Consciousness* (Cambridge: Harvard University Press, 1992); Antoinette Burton, "Who Needs the Nation? Interrogating 'British' History," *Journal of Historical Sociology* 10 (1997): 227–48; Elizabeth Povinelli, "Sex Acts and Sovereignty: Race and Sexuality in the Construction of the Australian Nation," *Diacritics* 24 (1994): 122–50; Kenneth M. Wells, "The Price of Legitimacy: Women and the Kûnuhoe Movement, 1927–1931," *Colonial Modernity in Korea*, ed. Gi-Wook Shin and Michael Robinson (Cambridge: Harvard University Press, 1999), 191–220; Geiger, *Tanu Women*; Renata Salecl, "The Fantasy Structure of Nationalist Discourse," *Praxis International* 13 (1993): 213–23; Mrinalini Sinha, ed., *Mother India* (Ann Arbor: University of Michigan Press, 1999); Prasenjit Duara, *Rescuing History from the Nation: Questioning Narratives of Modern China* (Chicago: University of Chicago Press, 1995); Etienne Balibar, "Is European Citizenship Possible?" *Public Culture* 8 (1996): 355–76.

April 30: Reading, Writing, and Consultation Week

May 7: Final Seminar Roundtable on Gender and Colonialism

— *Part II* —

THEORY INTO PRACTICE

Doing Critical Imperial History

8

Fearful Bodies into Disciplined Subjects

Pleasure, Romance, and the Family Drama of Colonial Reform
in Mary Carpenter's Six Months in India

Everywhere the appearance of men, women, and children was sufficiently novel and curious. The deficiency of clothing in the men struck me peculiarly. They seemed to consider that a black skin supersedes the necessity of raiment, and in this respect the lower orders appear perfectly devoid of any sense of decency. I never became reconciled to this, and believe now, as I did then, that living thus in a sort of savage state in the midst of a civilised people increases that want of proper self-respect and that separation from the higher classes which is so painfully characteristic of Hindu society. . . .

Multitudes of both men and women assembled before sunrise to perform their ablutions. . . . Strange was the scene which was here every morning pre-sented to an English eye; for the women appeared wholly devoid of any feeling akin to decency, and in this public place, to avoid wetting their garments, left the greater part of their bodies uncovered. It would seem as if the great seclusion of the women of the higher classes withdraws the refining influence of their sex from society;—those who are not so shielded are thus left in the rude position of barbaric life, where the weaker sex is oppressed by the stronger and being de-graded, is deprived of its special excellence.
—Mary Carpenter, *Six Months in India* (1868)

Social reform was serious business in Victorian Britain, especially where "the woman question" was concerned. Josephine Butler, writing in her introduction to *Woman's Work and Woman's Culture* in 1869, epitomized the public face of Victorian feminism when she insisted that "all who look upon this question of women's interests from a grave and lofty point of view must behold it, as it is indeed, a question which concerns humanity at large, and that very vitally."[1] With social duty the most readily available justification for women's public work—and women's natural frivolity one of the most readily available arguments against the possibility of female emancipation—gravity of purpose was among the prerequisites of respectability and hence of respectable action for middle-class women in the public sphere. If there was any pleasure to be had in the pursuit of reform, convention or shrewdness inhibited its disclosure. To be taken seriously, one had to appear both solemn and cognizant of the solemnity of the reform enterprise; to do otherwise was to endanger the cause "by perpetuating the delusion that women are so many kittens—charming to play with but no more fit than Caligula's horse to be made a Consul."[2] Combating such presumptions was as much of a crusade as the work of social reform itself—so much so that when Barbara Leigh Smith Bodichon argued that the care of the nation's poor was "the serious duty" of single women, her choice of words helped to guarantee the sobriety of her cause rather than functioning, as it does for us, as a quaint redundancy.[3]

Yet pleasure also informed the experiences and hence the discourses of Victorian female social reformers, where it existed in tension with both the call to seriousness and the strategic necessity of self-erasure. While Millicent Garrett Fawcett urged rationality, dispassion, and impartiality, other nineteenth-century feminists argued that female suffrage was necessary because women "desired" the vote, "cherished" their rights, "yearned" for emancipation—and, not least, could be gratified by the success of reform. The utopian visions that underwrote much of women's philanthropic activity in the Victorian period, together with contemporary evangelical enthusiasm for the possibility of secular transformation, shaped a rhetoric of reform in which duty could be suggestive not just of pleasure but also of romantic desire as well. Frances Power Cobbe, who was given to hyperbole but rarely to rapturous prose, spoke, for example, of women's "ardent longing to bring about . . . sorely needed reform."[4] Isabella Todd, writing to a member of Parliament from Ulster about a franchise bill in 1884, described herself as a "pleader" for the cause, argued that "hope deferred . . . maketh the heart sick," and reminded her readers that, "if our demand is a quiet and unexcited demand, it is also a persistent one."[5] Romantic love was among the languages Victorian women used for talking about the pleasure of sociopolitical reform and the intensity of their commitment to it—partly because it was a conventionally Victorian feminine concern, but equally because, as more than a decade of scholarly work on Victorian feminism has shown, what its practitioners wished was for the women's movement to preserve precisely what was "womanly" about British women in the service of the national good.[6]

If the object of Victorian feminists' reform desire was "true femininity" working for the public good, the language in which this quest was figured focused on romantic pursuit, sexual love, and, ultimately, bourgeois family formation. Metaphorically, reform was a process in which women figured as suitors seeking the attention of the body politic so they could become partnered with it. Getting the nation to take notice of, and then fully to appreciate, the women's movement was one of the chief preoccupations of its advocates. Lydia Becker, writing for the *Westminster Review* in 1872, likened the woman question to a secret passion that, "long dormant but never dead, has remained hidden in the hearts of thoughtful women, to be repressed with a sigh over the hopelessness of the attempt to gain a hearing."[7] Elizabeth Wolstenholme Elmy, writing to the *Times* in 1884, used a stanza of Spenserian poetry to represent the strategies female reformers deployed to gain the attention of the legislative body of Westminster. "The pathetic words of Spenser," she wrote, "but too truly portray the experience of all women who have endeavoured to influence legislative action for the benefit of their own sex, since they can only sue, and have no power to demand, remembering the while with an added pang that at every moment some heart is broken or some life undone by reason of the legislative injustice which they are helpless to remedy."[8] Social reform figures here as a love story, with the national body—in this case, Parliament—as the resistant lover and female reformers as scorned (or, perhaps more accurately, ignored) suitors. Disenfranchisement in these scenarios corresponds to exclusion from the lover's company, and the project of emancipation to the realization of what might be called, in Victorian terms, the quest for a "companionate marriage" between women and the state. Pleasure is derived from the seriousness of the cause and from the suffering it exacted—the capacity for suffering being another characteristic of "the womanly woman" in Victorian culture.

This is not necessarily an argument about the masochism of Victorian feminists but, rather, a comment on the ways in which the desire for traditional femininity underwrote the quest for female emancipation. The means by which this was attained could be unconventional and not without its transgressive pleasures. In the allegories that Becker and Wolstenholme Elmy use, pleasure comes from the kind of cross-gendering that the project of feminism in a patriarchal society can involve. Women play the traditionally male suitor's role as they approach the all-male parliamentary body, thus demonstrating both the validity of their claims and their essential femaleness: they must become men—the supreme sacrifice—to secure the attention and hence the equality they seek as women.

The sentiment these stagings create and the sympathy they work to elicit suggest that feminists were no less attached to what Christina Crosby calls the "melodramatic fix" than other Victorians.[9] Indeed, it could be argued that such scenarios were mobilized in self-consciously ironic opposition to the arguments from chivalry that were used to frame arguments against female emancipation and especially against women's suffrage from the 1860s onward. Recurrent images of heterosexual romantic convention and its inversions are also evidence that the reform vocation not only was not devoid of pleasure but was actually fueled by a desire that could be imagined as sexual longing, even when domesticity and motherhood were considered to be its most gratifying ends. Such longing was by no means without its own dangers. For although it was evidently useful for mobilizing women in the public arena, it threatened to undermine the premises of respectability and self-denial on which the edifice of female emancipation was being established in Victorian England. According to Josephine Butler, "earnest work"—defined in part as "a share in grave national interests"—was the solution to this dilemma, for it regulated the "sentimental tendencies" to which women were prone and guaranteed that they would not be undone by their own unrestrained feelings.[10] In the end, it reconciled the female reformer with the body politic by making her the respectable citizen-mother rather than the illicit—and ambiguously gendered—lover of the nation-state. Reform itself could thus gratify women's desire because of its promise to transform women from unattached, potentially disruptive, and unstably gendered bodies into disciplined, potentially political, and gender-certain subjects. If, as Anne McClintock has claimed, nations have been figured as domestic genealogies,[11] feminists in Victorian Britain appropriated the nation-state as a motherland and imagined their desire for reform as a familial drama. In doing so, they did not replace the narrative of heterosexual romance so much as they regulated it in the form of a domestic, familial script. Inside this particular family romance, the mother was the authoritative parent because of her particular concern for women and children and, above all, because of her self-conscious identification with the motherland itself.

Although romance and melodrama have become keywords in analyses of modern Western women's writing, their strategic use in Victorian feminist cultural production has been less carefully scrutinized.[12] Their appropriation by British women for imperial reform has also gone unremarked. Mary Carpenter's interest in Indian social reform, her four visits to India between 1866 and 1877, and her attempt to institutionalize philanthropic commitment to the improvement of Indian women through the National Indian Association can be read as a sociosexual romance in which the English female reformer attempts to reconcile herself to the imperial body politic through the family drama of British imperial reform. Drawn to the cause of India's women initially by Rammohun Roy and other Indian male social reformers who traveled to England in the Victorian period, Carpenter's colonial concerns were fueled by what she herself called "a sort of romance . . . lying dormant or bottled up, as in the Arabian tales, waiting only to come forth in full vigour."[13] Her encounter with India was mediated, if not exclusively then certainly primarily, through Indian men, with whose anxieties about the practices of child marriage she strongly identified and whose concerns for the future of the nuclear family in India she made her own. Indian women's reproductive capacity, and hence their (hetero)sexual activity, was implicitly at issue here, for Carpenter acted unswervingly on the Victorian presumption that early marriage was the source of Indian cultural stagnation and therefore an appropriate site of British imperial intervention.[14] Her determination to improve Indian women's status was bound up with a desire to manage the bodies of Indian girls by diverting them from immediate marriage into professional occupations—a route toward improvement and "uplift" that brought them, from the 1870s onward, under the discipline of professional, Western, female-supervised teacher training and that had as its ultimate goal the preservation of Indian women's procreative capacities inside the ideal of adult companionate marriage. Carpenter herself never married, but she did adopt a white British girl and, rather more informally, two Indian children. These gestures, along with her manifest satisfaction at being called "mother" by a variety of Indians she encountered during her visits to India, suggest that the pleasures of seriousness could be legitimated in part by the maternal role that philanthropic work provided to female reformers—especially in Victorian imperial culture, where the empire was commonly considered "no place for a white woman" and Britain itself embodied the centrifugal motherland.

As the opening quotation indicates, Carpenter was simultaneously drawn to and disturbed by the variety of "uncovered bodies" she witnessed during her tour of India in 1866–67. It was this troubling fascination that shaped Carpenter's romance with India, her passion for the cause of Indian women, and her cultivation of the role of mother to both Indian womanhood and to British women's reform initiatives in India. Because she was one of the few British female reformers who actually traveled to India in the Victorian period, and because she was in large measure responsible for generating interest in the reform of Indian women among Victorian feminists from the late 1860s onward, understanding her approach to the imperial project is consequential to analyses of the colonial encounter in the modern period, particularly when that encounter occurred between Western women and "Oriental womanhood." *Six Months in India* affirms Gayatri Spivak's definition of liberal imperial ideology: as a narrative of colonial reform, it is a specific historical example of a white woman conferring with brown men over the fate of brown women.[15] Equally significant is how it illuminates the ways in which that triangular relationship was familiarized, romanticized, and subsequently translated into reform initiatives—how, in other words, the "representations and routines" of the colonial female body were linked to the institutionalization of imperial social reform ideologies, particularly though not exclusively among Victorian feminists.[16] If *Six Months in India* represents one Victorian female reformer's negotiations with the romance of empire, it also suggests that women's desire, especially in an imperial context, is not now and has never been historically innocent.[17] Scrutinizing how Western women have been seduced by this imperialized romance is crucial to the production of contemporary feminist ideologies that wish not just to confront their own histories but to engage with critiques of colonialism, as well.

From the beginning of her public career, Mary Carpenter grappled with the tensions between the call to seriousness and the pleasures of reform only hinted at by other female activists of her generation. Born in 1807, Carpenter came from a family that, in the words of her biographer, "belonged to the aristocracy of English Puritanism."[18] Her father, Dr. Lant Carpenter, was a Unitarian minister in Bristol, a fervent antislavery activist, and an author of books on the moral principles of education. His personal high-mindedness, as well as his commitment to social justice and moral reform, meant that Mary grew up in an atmosphere in which seriousness was not only expected but required. Inspired by her father's life of public service and, after his death, compelled to kindred pursuits by his memory, Mary Carpenter distinguished herself in the 1840s and 1850s chiefly by promoting the Ragged Schools system, which laid the foundation for primary and industrial education. She was also involved in anti-slavery agitation, prison reform, and, in the 1860s and after, philanthropic activity in India.[19] Throughout her life Carpenter both publicly and privately invoked the Christian mission as the selfless purpose toward which her "blessed work" was directed, though she was not always totally at ease with the mission she believed she was called to. In a phrase quite characteristic of her peculiar bluntness, she described the whole philanthropic enterprise as "naturally repugnant" to her.[20]

Carpenter's correspondence and diaries are full of indications that such "natural repugnance" was in fact the outcome of a tremendous struggle between the imperative for self-denial that commitment to the Christian mission could demand and the sense of gratification that she experienced in her own work. She referred to the "children of the streets" as "those forsaken young immortals whom I love with a heart's desire" and to her various reform projects as "the desire of my heart." Nor was she hesitant about recording her "unspeakable joy" at the success of her Ragged School in Bristol in 1846 (168, 107). From the time she was a teenager, however, she wrestled with a tendency toward pride in her own accomplishments, as the following passage illustrates: "I profess not to think myself deserving of praise, but I have a secret consciousness of having performed (my duty) better than others would have done. I also feel a very unchristian satisfaction in imagining my own feelings of a superior cast to those of others: this I hope I am correcting" (27). Anxiety about the pleasure she experienced in doing good works surfaces again and again in her writing, causing her to question the seriousness of her commitment to the kind of "real sacrifices" that she believed necessary for true Christian piety—and hence for effective social reform (33).

What Peter Stallybrass and Allon White refer to as Carpenter's "self-critical restlessness" was informed by a mid–Victorian religious ethic that emphasized continuous self-sacrifice as the hallmark of the Christian mission to the secular world.[21] The same ethic encouraged female religious enthusiasm that bordered on the ecstatic and that, in Carpenter's meditations, gave her spiritual yearnings a quasi-sexual character (137). This was particularly true when she prayed to her "heavenly Father," with whom she expressed a sense of intense communion and with whom she often conflated her real father after his death in 1840. Yet Carpenter feared that even this "religious emotion," which she did view as permissible, might "take the place of what is to me far more difficult—that active discharge of the duty of the hour" (57). She justified the suppression of such emotions —such pleasures—and the personal suffering caused by such self-denial by reasoning that "God gives us painful discipline" and that "it was intended that we should suffer sympathetic pain to stimulate us to make efforts for our fellow-creatures" (87, 104). The need for self-discipline was a constant refrain for Carpenter; without it, she became "too full of thoughts which keep me in a constant state of excitement" and could not accomplish her duties in the world (57). In fact, so convinced was she of her tendency to "unchristian satisfaction" that she believed that public action was something "to which my woman's nature quite unfits me" (165).

Fitting herself for Christian reform work involved all kinds of physical rigors, including a vegetarian diet and minimal sleep—routines that astonished her erstwhile housemate, Frances Cobbe, and eventually drove her from Carpenter's company.[22] It also meant renewing on a regular basis the pledge she had made in 1836 to devote her life to the poor and destitute, "caring not at all for my own comfort or labour" (30, 49). Experiencing the pleasures of success in reform projects impelled her to regular self-reproach and periodic regimens of self-discipline, not to mention to endless declarations of solemn purpose. Professions of solemnity were chief among Carpenter's cures for the over-excitement that could be brought on by reform endeavors—partly, of course, because there was pleasure to be had in seriousness and its vocations.[23] Even after her father's death, Carpenter viewed him as the standard against which she measured her own enthusiasm and reform achievements. As Vron Ware has shown, she was not alone in this tendency: the antislavery movement, for example, produced several notable women whose fathers served as emotional center and political inspiration.[24] Unlike the parental figures in other historically situated family dramas, however, her father was not someone Carpenter wished to displace; rather, she wished to approximate his self-governing temperament and his self-effacing social reform efforts through such regulatory feats of her own.[25]

Although these "psychological transactions" were a feature of Carpenter's psychic life before the 1860s,[26] it was the prospect of undertaking reform in India that brought about Carpenter's most impassioned declarations of serious reform commitment and eventually resulted in her most public profession of her desire for reform, *Six Months in India*. In the most immediate sense, her intention to go to India was prompted by an Indian Brahmin convert to Christianity who visited England in 1860 and whose preaching in Bristol inspired her.[27] "Never before had I *seen* an instance of the wonderful power of Christianity to surmount all old prejudices of gross idolatry," she wrote in her journal in September 1860. "His simplicity, unaffected manner, and genuine devotion to the cause of his master, inspired us all with very warm interest and desire to help him. . . . How my Father would have rejoiced to see the day when his pulpit should be occupied by one who reminded us of the early followers of the savior. The chapel was more crowded than I ever remember to have seen it, except when my Father preached the funeral sermon for the lamented Rajah" (273).

Carpenter's earliest biographer, her cousin Joseph Estlin Carpenter, suspected that she had romantic feelings toward this Indian man, who is referred to only as "Mr. G—" in the published excerpts from her correspondence. Mary herself alluded to this possibility, for it was his visit that she described to a correspondent as "a sort of romance to me in the midst of the great tension of the stronger and less poetic parts of my nature. . . . I find that all my old feelings and enthusiasms are as fresh as ever, bottled up, as in the Arabian tales, waiting only to come forth in full vigour. And indeed it is well that they are generally imprisoned, for they sadly interrupt me in my work" (277). Here the familiar pattern of excitement and self-restraint is given an expressly romantic object as well as an overtly Orientalist flavor. The cultural taboos working against any kind of union between a Victorian Englishwoman and an Indian man,[28] notwithstanding his conversion to Christianity, may be adduced by the fact that he is the only Indian visitor who goes unnamed in Joseph Estlin Carpenter's account of Mary's life and is never again mentioned after his departure from Britain.

Harihar Das's research indicates that "Mr. G—" was in fact Joguth Chandra Gangooly, an Indian who had had some theological training in the United States before he went to Britain in 1860.[29] Shortly after Gangooly returned to India, Mary Carpenter recorded her first vow to go to

India to undertake work with native girls and women there (277). Although it is tempting to see Gangooly as the great unfulfilled romance of her life—and, indeed, as the source of her longing for India—he was in fact only one of several Indian men whom Carpenter encountered on British soil who prompted her interest in India and nurtured her fantasies about extending her father's reform work to Indian soil. Rammohun Roy was undoubtedly the first. Roy was a prominent Brahmo Samajist who traveled to Britain in the early 1830s. (The Brahmo Samaj was "a monotheistic Hindu reform movement which ultimately became a separate Hindu sect.")[30] Although he was not a convert to Christianity, Roy's attempts to reconcile reform Hinduism with Christian monotheism encouraged some members of the Unitarian community about the possibility of reform in India. His visit to Bristol, his friendliness with local religious communities, and his untimely death there in 1832 made him something of a cult figure—not least for the young Mary, who prepared a rather gushing retrospective titled *The Last Days in England of the Rajah Rammohun Roy* in 1866. Roy's friendship with her father, together with his progressive views on the treatment of women, inscribed him in Carpenter's memory as both a great man and a great reformer.[31] In death Roy's life story acquired a romantic solemnity among those English women whom he had met during his brief sojourn in Britain. Carpenter noted the effect that Roy had on one of her contemporaries, Lucy Aikin, who had spent long hours with Roy discussing the common ground between reform Hinduism and Christianity and, in particular, the condition of Indian women. "He pleaded for pity toward them with such powerful, heartfelt eloquence as no woman, I think can peruse without tears and fervent blessings on his head."[32] Roy was buried under the elms on the property of the Castle family in Stapleton Grove. A commemorative shrine was established there, to which Carpenter herself made devotional visits, especially when Indian travelers came to Bristol.

The powerful religious personality Carpenter attributed both to her dead father and to the deceased Roy was extended to Gangooly and other Indian social reformers who came to Britain seeking, according to Mary, "to become acquainted with English men and women in their public and private work . . . and thus to qualify themselves on their return to India to transplant there what they have found most deserving of imitation among us."[33] In 1864, two Indians, Satyendranath Tagore (brother of the poet Rabindranath Tagore) and Monomohun Ghose (a Bengali barrister), visited Mary in Bristol while on a pilgrimage to Roy's grave and urged on her the need for girls' education in India. "Having them here," she wrote of her visitors, "has carried me back thirty years to Rammohun Roy and my Father. Indeed, my own private life is chiefly in the past, with the beloved departed" (300). After receiving them at the Red Lodge, she confided the following to her diary: "I here record my solemn resolve that henceforth I devote my heart and soul and strength to the elevation of women of India. In doing this I shall not suddenly abandon my work here . . . but I shall obey the remarkable call which has been given me so unexpectedly, which is in accordance with former deep feelings and resolves. Without any present and apparent change of plan I shall watch openings . . . gain information, and prepare in every way for my great object, going to India to promote the Christian work for the women" (298–99). As she prepared for her departure, she confronted her own torturous relationship to pleasure. "This will be the great event of my life," she wrote to her brother Russell. "I feel some female weakness in my pleasure in looking at my things all getting ready and looking nice" (315). Carpenter continued to discipline these emotional responses, anticipating the kinds of gratification that this Indian trip would bring while at the same time "question[ing] myself, suspect[ing] myself of enthusiasm," and finally embracing her "strong and settled conviction" that India was "a new field . . . about to open to me . . . in which my natural powers will have free scope" (299).

Her emphasis on her encounters with Indian men enabled Carpenter to sustain the fantasy—from the 1830s to the 1860s, and well before she went to India—that Indian reform preserved the mystical union between her and her father and between her and Roy.[34] Most important, they helped to organize Mary's reform project around particular notions about Indian women: first, that they were a "problem" that troubled progressive, evangelically minded Indian men; second, that they were "degraded" (a term whose meanings I shall return to) by child marriage and enforced widowhood; and, finally, that their situation required the attention, intervention, and discipline of English women. Such was not necessarily the intention of Indian male reformers. As Lata Mani has written, although Roy shared some of the presumptions of colonialist discourse about *sati*, he had a complex understanding of how patriarchy worked. He was as convinced as other reform-minded Indians that the condition of women was the index of any culture's "civilization," and he was one of many Indian men in the nineteenth century who viewed English women as a sympathetic audience before whom to plead the case of Indian women's reform.[35] Nonetheless, Carpenter read Indian reformers' descriptions as sensational and in turn sensationalized them. This is not because Orientalism was simply an ineluctable feature of modernity (or even of imperialism) but because of the ways in which Victorian cultural presumptions about a lurid and exotic East intersected the history of both her romanticized associations with India and her commitment to public reform. For Carpenter, it was precisely this intersection of romantic attraction and serious social work that prompted her commitment to Indian reform. In the first chapter of *Six Months in India*, Carpenter recalled that it was the "graphic and fearful . . . picture of the condition of Hindoo women" that inspired her "to form the solemn resolve to do something to ameliorate their condition."[36] She told her readers that she apprehended those "graphic and fearful" images from a public lecture in England in the early 1860s given by a Brahmin convert to Christianity whom she does not name in *Six Months*. What the general reading public could not know was that this unnamed Indian was in all probability Gangooly.

Roy, too, had spoken of "extreme cruelties practised towards Indian women"—specifically with reference to sati—in terms that made a long-standing impression on Carpenter's mind, as had Ghose, Tagore, and others.[37] Thus, Indian women were not only constituted as a "problem" for Carpenter by Indian men before she ever got to India, but her "knowledge" about their status and condition was mediated through men to whom she may well have had romanticized attachments and, at the very least, transgressive associations. They were, moreover, mediated publicly —which is to say, in mixed company—at a historical moment when women speaking (or hearing) in public about sex, disease, and even women was considered a breach of the code of sexual propriety on which Victorian society was based. Although we have no record of the impact such transgressions had on Mary Carpenter, we do know that for Annette Akroyd, another Unitarian female social reformer interested in India, the effect of hearing an Indian man speak in public of Indian women's condition was positively "electrifying."[38]

Carpenter's motivations for traveling to India and the history of her attraction to the cause of Indian women were thus variously implicated in the romance of empire. Even more telling, the romance of empire was implicated for Carpenter in the family drama of colonial reform. She privately identified Indian reform with her romantic longings for Indian men and with her feelings for her father; as we shall shortly see, she translated this into a serious public commitment to supervising Indian women's sexual lives so that they more closely resembled Victorian middle-class heterosexual domestic practices. Unlike some of her contemporaries writing about sexual relations in the East, Carpenter did not view Indian men as tyrannical and hence responsible for Indian women's "subjection." Quite the contrary: she read Roy's and other Indian men's concerns for the fate of Indian women as not only enlightened but chivalrous. In fact, she imagined herself as the reform successor to both her father and Roy and took up their protectiveness toward Indian women. It was from this somewhat ambiguously gendered position that Carpenter sought to appropriate the cause that Indian men had made of Indian women, transferring her own privatized family drama, as well as her romance with India, onto the public project of colonial reform and in the process stabilizing herself as the indubitably female, maternal subject of the British empire.

Mary Carpenter's first visit to India (September 1866–March 1867) was in many ways a pilgrimage—not in a sectarian sense, since she repeatedly disavowed any proselytizing purpose and professed to understand how unwelcome missionary work would be among educated Hindus, but in a spiritual and religious sense nonetheless. As the home of her "noble Rajah," the landscape held a peculiar fascination, even if her search for the traces of Roy in Calcutta proved slightly disappointing.[39] And despite the disclaimer of any "proselytizing objects" (314), Carpenter could not but imagine herself as a pilgrim in India. Concerned friends, worried about her undertaking such an arduous trip at her age (she was almost sixty), urged her at least to go by way of Palestine, thereby making her voyage a true *peregrinatio por christo*. She told one correspondent that "all my strength must be for India; that will henceforth be my Holy Land" (315).

Clearly, Carpenter's trip was unusual for someone of her generation. It was certainly considered dangerous in an age when women traveling anywhere, let alone from West to East, were viewed under that persistent Trollopian trope of "unprotected females."[40] Nor would I wish to deny that by traveling without an attendant, staying with and generally socializing among educated Indians, Carpenter transgressed certain racial and gender boundaries in ways that were probably unimaginable for most of her contemporaries. Her many Indian contacts, gained over the years from visitors to Bristol and through her acquaintance with Roy, meant that she experienced a certain sphere of social and domestic life in India highly unusual for an English woman. She was at moments quite uncomfortable with this realization; recalling the scene at the Tagores' dinner table, she remarked, and not in any braggart way, that "I was the only individual there of the Anglo-Saxon race."[41] As Jo Manton puts it, by "sleeping on a string bed, eating vegetable curry and unleavened bread and listening to mantras [she] was committing two of the worst crimes of Victorian England, blasphemy and letting the side down."[42]

And yet it is precisely for these reasons that *Six Months in India*, essentially an account of a secular reform pilgrimage, functioned as a kind of revealed text—because it could be read simultaneously as a white woman's romance with India and as a serious program for colonial reform. This very duality meant that it worked as a cautionary tale: in classic Carpenter style, the serious business of reform was the solution not only to the problem of India, but also to the troubling pleasures that Indian reform gave her. Carpenter's organization of her text is quite literally instructive. The book is divided into two parts: volume one and the first chapter of volume two narrate her journey, from her arrival in Bombay, through her trips to Ahmedabad, Calcutta, and Madras to her journey back again to Bombay, her point of departure. The second volume is devoted almost exclusively to what Carpenter calls "general observations": "Religious Movement," "Social Position of Women," "The Inhabitants of India," "Education," "Female Education," "Reformatory Schools," "Prison Discipline," and, in an appendix, a variety of speeches, memorials, and the like connected with her trip. This structural division—oddly out of sync with the generic travelogue—would seem to replicate Carpenter's habit of movement from pleasure to seriousness, from romance to reform. Even the dedication ("To the honoured memory of the Rajah Mohammun Roy . . . who first excited in the author's mind a desire to benefit his country, these volumes are respectfully dedicated") evokes Carpenter's well-practiced maneuver of channeling desire into respectability.

What becomes immediately apparent in *Six Months* is how India worked to trouble both Carpenter's authority as a reformer and those well-practiced habits by which she had, until then, managed her own responses to the pleasures of philanthropic reform. First of all, once she left the motherland, Carpenter's claim to colonial authority had to be demonstrated, if not repeatedly proven. What had been a kind of family heirloom—knowledge of and concern for India—suddenly became a constraint on the realization of her aspiration to be recognized as an autonomous woman with colonial expertise. Her determination to displace the claims made by others to "know" India, and hence to make her own what had been handed down as "family knowledge" about Indian women, is discernible from the very first chapter of Six Months. On the voyage out, she canvassed her fellow passengers about their views on India. In Six Months, she describes how those interviews enabled her to claim her own authority over India: "The very different, and even contrary statements I received . . . confirmed my belief that the accounts of India and the Hindoos which we hear in England are greatly coloured by the character and views of the narrator; I perceived especially, that what may be true of one part of India is very incorrect of another . . . [and] that though everything I heard from gentlemen or ladies who had lived long in the country was most valuable . . . yet I must not allow my mind to be influenced by the representations of individuals, however intelligent or however long they had resided in India."[43] Although this passage may be read as a critique of British and Anglo-Indian readings of India, it must also be seen as a rejection of claims to knowledge about the Indian female population by Indian men she knew in England. Carpenter contrasts the diversity of opinion about India at this juncture in the narrative with her own lofty and unified perspective—what Mary Louise Pratt calls a "promontory view" and ascribes to male travel writers such as Richard Burton.[44] Her regulation of the images of Indian women throughout the rest of the book may likewise be read as an attempt to sustain that authority and to confirm herself in the eyes of the public not merely as an "unprotected female" traveler in the empire but as the self-disciplined voice of metropolitan reform knowledge, as well.

Despite the confidence with which she made such claims to authority about colonial matters, however, traveling in India and being in contact with Indian men and women in situ seems to have destabilized Carpenter's regime from time to time. Two such occasions are recorded in Six Months, both of which involve her looking at naked or semi-clothed colonial bodies. The first occurs just as she is disembarking from the boat for the first time in Bombay, where "everywhere the appearance of men, women and children was sufficiently novel and curious." According to Carpenter, the "black" men in the crowd do not wear clothes because they think the color of their skin "supersedes the necessity of raiment"—a powerful comment on the capacity of middle-class reform ideology to construct blackness as a willfully perverse assault on white women's sensibilities. For Carpenter, these naked black men are the totality of "the lower orders." As such, they "appear perfectly devoid of any sense of decency"—devoid, that is, of the self-censure that for Carpenter was a sign of civilization as well as the hallmark of her own individual struggles with passion and propriety.

The fact that these black men were not simply devoid of a sense of decency, but "perfectly" so, suggests that Carpenter's discomfort did not prevent her from admiring the ways in which they were apparently "perfectly" comfortable with it. It suggests, in other words, that there is an ambivalence, a kind of "dreadful delight" operating here that may or may not be related to Carpenter's romantic attachments to Gangooly, Roy, and the other Indian men with whom she had been acquainted before coming to India.[45] Meanwhile, Carpenter herself is acutely conscious not simply of the nakedness of the men she observes but also of the effects it produces. In her view, "Living thus in a sort of savage state in the midst of civilised people" (presumably among the Anglo-Indians, or perhaps upper-caste Indians) "increases that want of proper self-respect and that separation from the higher classes which is so painfully characteristic of Hindu society." Determining who suffers more from these effects is crucial to the regulatory work Carpenter is doing here. In the first instance, those who suffer are the naked men "in a savage state": those who have no access to self-consciousness are alienated not only from Western civilization, but also from the potentially civilizing effects of the higher classes or castes in Hindu society. At the same time, those who observe this scene are also in danger of being "un-civilised," in this case of losing their self-respect, by virtue of the fact that they are looking. It is the potential that the gaze has to disintegrate the viewer's integrity, his or her self, in addition to Indian society per se, that makes the sight of those naked bodies a painful pleasure for Carpenter and, ultimately, for her readers, as well.

In the process of recording her discomfort at this sight, Carpenter thus registers her own ambivalences—ambivalences about her desire to look and, more significant, about the necessity of looking itself. For if Carpenter was to be taken seriously by her readers as the colonial reformer she aspired to be—the voice that articulated at once the critique of Indian society and the terms of its reform—she had to look. Moreover, she had to be seen to be disciplining her look—shaping it into acceptable technologies of colonial reform—before their very eyes. To understand how she performs this, it is worth scrutinizing Carpenter's claim that "the deficiency of clothing in the men" struck her "peculiarly."[46] "Peculiar" is a word that she frequently uses in *Six Months* to describe Indian landscapes or "natural" scenes. Two pages before the passage about naked men, however, she observes that people on the boat referred to Indian natives as "*niggers*"—"a term peculiarly improper, as the Asiatic race is perfectly different from the African, and no term of contempt ought to be applied to the negro or any other human being."[47] By professing a knowledge of taxonomy and a commitment to egalitarianism, Carpenter tries to distance herself from the term "nigger" and from its users. She also signals the crisis of looking that India—and Indians—provokes in her, for it compels her to privilege the scientific explanation over a humanitarian one. In the passage on black bodies without "raiment," this crisis again plays itself out as Carpenter's "peculiar" reaction. By taking refuge in the impersonal as the passage continues, so that the "I" disappears from the analysis of what happens among "civilised peoples," Carpenter situates herself as all-seeing observer who yet sees nothing "improper": the objective Western female reformer in India whose vision is telescoped by the spectacle of colonial masculinity that her eye is drawn to and perhaps even seeks out. Carpenter's response is not primarily one of personal sympathy but, rather, that of the disciplined, self-denying authority of quasi-scientific philanthropy.

The second encounter with colonial bodies that Carpenter notes in *Six Months* occurs during her stay at Surat, a city in western India. Carpenter recalls that she was drawn one morning to the window of her "sleeping-room" after "a great confusion of tongues early broke my rest." Looking out the window, she saw "multitudes of both men and women assembled before sunrise to perform their ablutions, and for various household purposes, such as drawing water and washing clothes." Although this is a mixed group—and perhaps because of it—Carpenter's attention focuses on the women in the crowd, who

> appeared wholly devoid of any feeling akin to delicacy, and in this public place, to avoid wetting their garments, left the greater part of their bodies uncovered. It would seem as if the great seclusion of the women of the higher classes withdraws the refining influence of their

sex from society;—those who are not so shielded are thus left in the rude position of barbaric life, where the weaker sex is oppressed by the stronger, and being degraded, is deprived of its special excellence. In India the voices and manner of the lower classes of women appeared to me more harsh and coarse than those of the men. . . . I felt assured, however, that this did not arise from their nature being inferior, but from the condition in which they are placed.[48]

There are a number of parallels between this passage and the one on naked men. In each instance, Carpenter looks down from above, remarks on the natives' lack of self-consciousness about nakedness, and signals that the act of looking is potentially dangerous to the viewer. Such arrival scenes by the 1860s were a fairly conventional aspect of travel writing. For Carpenter, as for other European travelers, they served (in Pratt's terms) as "potent sites for framing relations of context and setting the terms of its representation."[49] There is, however, some initial instability in these frames: in both cases, the mess of bodies "disrupts and intrudes upon the calm order" of Carpenter's normally "plain speech."[50] For when Carpenter writes that "those who are not . . . shielded [from such sights] are thus left in the rude position of barbaric life where the weaker sex is . . . deprived of its special excellence," she is talking not just about the condition of Indian women but about its disintegrating effects on her. She is also speaking her resolve to "shield" herself and to protect her reading public from the ambivalence of her own reaction. After all, she does not turn away from the window but lingers on the spectacle as she tries to manage her response to it. Her move from desire to solemnity, though scarcely successful, circumscribes without erasing pleasure even while it works to reestablish that "special excellence" of self-regulation on which, as we have seen, Carpenter's self-image as a reformer depended. In terms of its capacity to restore propriety to an "unseemly" scene, Carpenter's maneuver not incidentally stabilizes her as the proper Victorian woman and lady philanthropic reformer.

Yet despite its structural similarities with the first passage, Carpenter is unquestionably fixing on Indian women and, more specifically, on the sight of naked female colonial bodies in public in the second passage. She works hard here to explain, and hence to justify, Indian women's nakedness; she gives the impression that she is more "sympathetic" to it. These women are naked, Carpenter suggests, for a purpose: they are performing their "ablutions"—a term that, in addition to its hygienic meanings, also has religious connotations. They thus are not willfully naked, like the black men, but leave their bodies uncovered for purposes understandable in terms of cultural domestic practices. Moreover, the "condition" in which she views them is, as she explains, not of their own making: they have been "degraded" by the fact of purdah—by the fact that the potentially civilizing effects of upper-class women who are in seclusion are denied them. Although degradation may refer to uncleanness—elsewhere in *Six Months* Carpenter emphasizes the "sunless, airless" existence of *zenana* life as an example of the ways in which Hindu women were degraded—in this context it also connotes a fall from rank, a demotion from the cultural height that Carpenter believed women *qua* women should occupy and that Indian male reformers and Victorian Englishwomen of the period believed Indian women had occupied in the ancient Vedic tradition.[51] The fact that Carpenter is looking down from such a height does more than validate her reading of their degradation. It authorizes her readers to justify the intervention of sympathetic female reformers such as herself in the project of uplifting Indian womanhood.

There is undoubtedly an element of ambivalent attraction in this scenario, as well, for Carpenter sees the Indian women as "wholly" devoid of "delicacy" just as Indian men were "perfectly" devoid of "decency." Her use of "delicacy" resonates with notions of proper, privatized, and perhaps also passionless Victorian womanhood, the kind of ideal womanhood that Carpenter desired from Indian women even as she worked to claim it for herself. At the same time, there is less of an attempt on Carpenter's part to render her gaze scientific than in the first passage, partly because women looking at women was considered a more "natural" phenomenon than women looking at men; women serving as caretakers of other women was a central tenet of Victorian philanthropy and, indeed, of feminism itself. Carpenter would not have been alone among white middle-class Victorians in deriving pleasure from ministering to non-white populations, although little has been written about the dynamics of that pleasure when it arose between women in a colonial setting. What this suggests about the pursuit of "true femininity," and the homoeroticism of that pursuit in the context of Victorian women's reform, is well outside the scope of this chapter. It does, however, raise interesting questions about the pleasures that Victorian women may have experienced in their identification with the suffering of "degraded" Other

women and about how underexamined the notion of women's spectator-
ship has been in the recent literature on gender and empire. My point here
is this: if Carpenter was troubled by the sight of these Indian female
bodies, and she undoubtedly was, it moved her to articulate an apparently
sympathetic, woman-to-woman reading, the end of which was nevertheless the same as the quasi-scientific one.[52] That end was the legitimation
of Western women's authority over colonial natives and, hence, over the
reproduction of the civilizing values—decency, delicacy, and "true femininity" for all women—of Western culture itself.

Although Carpenter intimated that the upper classes or high castes of
Hindu society were an important site for the transmission of Western
values to the whole of Indian society, Hindu women remained the central
"problem" of Indian culture from Carpenter's point of view. "From the
first to the last days of residence in India," Carpenter wrote in volume
two, "the point which most painfully strikes the mind is the position of
Hindoo women. This seems to affect every part of society, both native and
English."[53] Whether she was visiting schools or prisons or Indian families'
homes, it was the condition of Hindu women that moved her first to pity
and then to solemn reform purpose. Carpenter was impressed by the
efforts that educated Indian men were making toward what they considered Indian women's uplift, but she found the state of girls' education
basically unsatisfactory, for reasons I shall discuss momentarily. In a declaration very much in keeping with previous leaps to purposeful social
reform, she decided, on her return to Bombay, "I must make this subject
my primary one . . . and all other plans must be superseded by whatever
seem[s] most likely to promote this."[54]

For Carpenter, it was Hinduism that made Indian bodies threatening
to the colonial status quo and dangerous to the British imperial mission.
Her descriptions of her visit to a Hindu temple are thick with Orientalist
referents and with her own ambivalence about observing Hindu rituals.
"A heathen temple, however picturesque, was no great attraction to me,"
but "repugnant as it was to my feelings, this was an experience I ought to
have."[55] By elision, the totality of "women's condition" in India could be
attributed to their heathen religious practices. "Extreme ignorance, and
the vices connected with idolatry, render woman in India very unfit to
perform the duty nature intended for her—the care of children; for even if
she can take proper care of their little bodies (which is doubtful) she
infuses into their opening minds a degree of deception and willfulness

which years may not be able to eradicate."[56] Sympathy for the condition of Indian women clearly did not prevent Carpenter from articulating the Orientalist equation of Hinduism (here, idolatry), vice (child marriage), and unfitness for motherhood. Because sympathy was grounded in the presumption that Indian women's condition should approximate that of middle-class English women and that "Indian" women desired this (or could be trained to do so), it virtually required such a reductio ad absurdum. Women in India were thus reducible to Hindu women; Hindu women, to Hindu mothers; and Hindu mothers, to universal maternal unfitness in India.

Carpenter, moreover, was not particularly scrupulous in her application of the term "caste"—which, depending on the context, could function interchangeably for Victorians with "class"—so that at times, as in the text leading up to this passage, she begins by talking about lower-caste Hindu women and ends up generalizing from them, and from the "heathenness" of their maternal bodies, to all women in India. This occurred despite the personal contact she had with a variety of educated and upper-caste Indian women during her trip. To Carpenter, it was self-evident that among Hindus their "religion and social habits are indissolubly connected" and that the condition of Hindu women could be taken as representative of the condition of Indian womanhood.[57] Particularity evaporated when she was confronted by what she viewed as a sea of idolatrous masses and when she took as her personal responsibility the task of rescuing those "little bodies"—and, hence, the future of India and empire—from the hands of ignorant Hindu mothers. This passage operates quite differently from the one in which Carpenter is watching generic women bathing in which she attributes little or no willfulness to them. Significantly, it is primarily in the context of motherhood that Indian women are pathologized because of the power they have to shape the bodies (and with them, the minds) of the future colonial population, a context in which the fate of the British empire was at stake.

It was therefore the threats that Indian bodies of different kinds posed to the normative, civilizing effects of the nuclear family that were foundational to Carpenter's commitment to reform in India and, more specifically, to her program of women's education. Like other educational-reform initiatives undertaken by the British in India in the nineteenth century, Carpenter's project was motivated by what Gauri Viswanathan calls a belief in "the sustaining structure of error in Hinduism" and inscribed that error and its sociosexual ramifications on the body of Hindu women, meaning Hindu mothers and mothers-to-be.[58] In theory, this Hindu error blighted the whole female population of India, although, significantly, Carpenter concerned herself primarily with the daughters of the Hindu educated classes. The problem with Indian girls' schools was that they were not, for the most part, supervised by women. There were exceptions to this rule, as she noted. The Bethune School in Calcutta was one of the few places where she observed "a female native convert, a widow . . . teaching with evident success," as well as "a young Hindoo widow . . . receiving instruction with a view to train as a teacher."[59] Such exceptions reassured Carpenter about the possibility of Indian women's improvement, for, as Barbara Ramusack has written, she "clearly desired to socialize Indian girls into Victorian domesticity."[60] Attention to Indian women who were fulfilling Carpenter's reform aspirations in *Six Months* was no doubt intended to reassure a curious philanthropic readership that such a project was not only desirable but also possible.

But the fact that Indian girls—even in these exceptional schools—were not under the watchful and regulating eye of *European* women remained distressing to Carpenter. She was anxious about the idle, "listless," and undisciplined Hindu girls who were not being trained in needlework, not getting enough exercise, not being subjected to the kind of "proper instruction" that would begin to discipline them to be trained professionals on the English female model.[61] Creating desire in Indian girls—and managing that desire so that it bolstered the reform purpose both of Western women and of British imperial rule—was therefore integral to Carpenter's colonial education project. It was these same girls who were in the meantime being "withdrawn from school earlier than they otherwise would be" for teenage marriage.[62] Carpenter considered fitting Indian women for useful work through education instrumental in raising their status in Indian society, but especially in the reclamation of the "Hindu race." "All enlightened natives know," wrote Carpenter, "that their race is becoming physically deteriorated by the social customs to which they are bound. Mothers at twelve, grandmothers at five-and-twenty, cannot be the parents of a strong and hardy race; nor can those who are confined to sunless apartments to which we have been introduced . . . inspire their children with the genial influences of God's beautiful world."[63] For Carpenter, the physical evidence of Hindu mothers' degradation—their lack of status and the suffering it caused them—was visible and readable insofar as it was written on their very bodies. "Those who are acquainted with native customs with regard to women, are well aware why these are too often old and shrivelled [*sic*] when they might be in the full beauty of womanhood—why their minds are dwarfed to the measure of childhood, when they should be able to draw out the faculties of their children, and inspire them with thoughts and principles which should guide their minds through life."[64]

This passage reveals, among other things, the authoritative reform project that was at the very heart of Victorian women's "sympathy" for colonial womanhood, as well as the extent to which it depended on controlling Indian women's bodies. Indian, and more specifically Hindu, culture was "made body" by Carpenter for her readers in these passages: the colonial female body became a "surface on which the central rules, hierarchies and even metaphysical commitments" not just of Indianness or even of "heathenness" but of British colonial reform was imprinted. Normalizing such a body through the discipline and regulation of professional training—and through the delay in marriage it would hopefully ensure—was thus constructed as essential to the survival of the Indian and, by extension, to the durability of the "family of nations" that constituted the British empire.[65] Carpenter claimed to have no doubt that "Hindoo girls were capable of the same development as English girls" and would eventually succeed to the position of lady superintendents themselves.[66] But all of the schemes for reform that she enumerated in the text of *Six Months*—including her letters to the viceroy and the secretary of state for India that she later published—recommend the export of English professional women in the strongest terms possible. These recommendations are accompanied by suggestions about the housing arrangements that might be made and at the level at which salaries might be fixed. Early on in *Six Months*, Carpenter confesses that before she went to India, she had imagined that Indian women might profitably come to England for their teacher training but claims that her observations of Indian girls' schools now suggests otherwise. The conclusion she reaches, repeated practically from the beginning of *Six Months*, is that Indian women first needed the civilizing example of English women—they needed, in other words, the object lesson of English women's physical presence in India—to reach their full potential.

Carpenter did not necessarily view her program for reform as an exclusively public project: "There is," she wrote, "work to do for every lady who employs native women in the service in India, and one which need not remove her from her home."[67] Yet the overarching purpose of *Six Months in India* was to persuade her reading public in Britain (or wherever in the empire or dominions they might be) that the proper response to the romance that was India was not sentiment alone but sentiment transformed into sober reform action. Publicizing such reform action could be pleasurable, as Carpenter's enthusiastic prose in *Six Months* manifestly illustrated. In her view, the organized and systematic training of Indian women as teachers was the best possible vehicle for translating imperial desire into civic responsibility because it held the promise of converting fearful bodies of various kinds into disciplined and ultimately (re)productive subjects of the imperial nation-state. *Six Months in India* vitiated readers' fears that alliances between Indian men and female British reformers were dangerous by presenting them as positively salutary to imperial health. Readers of the travelogue were offered Carpenter herself as evidence that empire would not undo women but would restore them to their true—and truly feminine—selves. As I have suggested in another context, *Six Months* offered gratifying proof to the British public that white women's contact with a colonial population would not corrupt them but, rather, would illustrate what constructive and selfless imperial good the female sex of the motherland could do in the production of imperial values and the reproduction of colonial rule.[68]

Six Months in India opens with an impassioned declaration of Carpenter's "desire of many years" for reform in India and ends with a series of memorials from Indian men and women testifying to the virtues of Carpenter's reform scheme and to their own desire to see that scheme carried out by the government in India. Although there is no reason to doubt the sincerity of such testimonials, they complicate rather than resolve the tensions between desire and reform that characterize both *Six Months* and the totality of Carpenter's interest in India. Ever concerned to proclaim her own disinterestedness in the romance of colonial reform, Carpenter insisted that the project of uplifting Indian women had to come from Indians themselves and that her own plans for teacher-training schemes were generated out of "friendly sympathy" rather than official or even personal commitment. Despite the fact that her alarm at the sight of the "graphic and fearful" condition of Indian women was motivated by evangelical antipathy to Hindu practices—an antipathy complicated by her personal history with Indian men and implicated in her attraction to a variety of colonial bodies—she continued to view and to construct her initiatives as the secular and noninterventionist gestures of a private citizen. She was thereby doubtless able to understand her passion for India as an extension of the liberal reformist impulses of her father and of Roy and was also thereby able to manage, without fully containing, that romance with "unchristian satisfaction" that she pursued all her life.

Rather than serving as the final declaration of her love for colonial reform, *Six Months in India* was just the beginning. Carpenter made three more trips to India before her death in 1877. She continued to petition viceroys, to press secretaries of state for intervention, and to publicize what she believed was the "heart-rending" need for a government-sponsored system of women's training schools. While David Kopf's characterization of Carpenter's role in Indian women's education as "intrusively practical" is perhaps not inaccurate, her biographers have generally been cautious about the institutional impact of her reform initiative.[69] Jo Manton suggests that it was her tendency toward confrontation with government officials—together with their unyieldingly economic approaches to the development of colonial reform initiatives—that prevented Carpenter's passion for India from translating itself directly into the kinds of institutional changes she envisioned. The exercise of maternal authority was not, in other words, countenanced by India Office bureaucrats. This is not, I hasten to add, because they did not subscribe to their own version of the family romance of empire—their motto later would be, "O that England would only trust her sons whom she sends forth to do her business"[70]—but because they preferred the traditions of paternalism that viewed Carpenter (and Florence Nightingale before her) as a sentimental busybody. To these explanations for the resistance that her petitions met must be added the effects that her alliances with increasingly well-organized native male Indian efforts for educational reform doubtless had on imperial policymakers. Such officials were determined both to carry out the philosophical commitment to noninterference that had characterized Indian policy since the mutiny and to keep Indians in India at one remove from the programs of colonial power.

Yet despite the fact that no direct connections can be established between her reform commitments to Indian women's education and formal imperial policy, Carpenter's *Six Months in India* was undoubtedly influential in directing the passions for reform of a generation of Victorian women toward empire and, more specifically, toward India and its women. Her trip attracted more public attention than either her antislavery efforts or her Ragged School movement. It was *Six Months* that made her the celebrity among female reformers that she was to become in the 1870s and after her death, even though she remained personally reluctant to support women's suffrage during her lifetime.[71] Carpenter's travelogue was extremely popular, and the feminist periodical press devoted considerable attention to her Indian reform projects throughout the 1870s, touting her as the mother of Indian reform. As Janaki Nair has suggested, its popularity contributed to the creation of India as a site where British women's imperial role could be imagined and their employment goals realized. In conjunction with other texts, social organizations, and Josephine Butler's repeal campaign for India (1886–95), Mary Carpenter's work and the high profile given to *Six Months in India* by feminist advocates were responsible for justifying British women's careerism in the empire as an essential ingredient of Indian women's uplift and, in turn, of the colonial reform mission in Victorian Britain.[72]

Six Months in India worked to institutionalize feminist imperial reform ideology by encouraging women readers to consider taking up imperial responsibilities beyond the indulgences of armchair romance. As the second volume of the travelogue explained, it was only by institutionalizing the professionalization of women that Carpenter believed she could satisfy her particular desire for Indian reform. In 1870, she founded the National Indian Association (NIA)—which for a time was called the Indian National Association for the Promotion of Indian Female Education—to keep the need for teacher training in the British public eye. It ended up becoming a kind of clearinghouse of information about employment for English women in India, especially where educational opportunities were concerned. The NIA, which was patronized by former viceroys and subscribed to by former civil servants, outlived Carpenter by decades, acting as an influential mouthpiece in Indian reform circles and, most significantly, taking up the debate on Indian women's access to medical education with great vigor in the 1880s.[73] This campaign, which was even more explicitly concerned with the health and welfare of Indian bodies, captured the attention of male and female reformers in Britain and India and that of the British and Indian governments—all of whom, as David Arnold has recently illustrated, attempted to regulate their passions for empire and their dread of colonial bodies with suitably sober discourses.[74] Through the

NIA and its affiliations with both the London School of Medicine for Women and the Countess of Dufferin's Fund, many British women were awarded scholarships to train as doctors and hence were able to pursue professional careers in India—as missionaries, as medical doctors, and as a combination of the two.[75] As did *Six Months in India*, the NIA appealed to a broad spectrum of feminist and missionary women in Victorian Britain. It can be read as a space through which Carpenter and her followers enacted their colonial reform convictions and secured a place for themselves in what Victorians believed was the great march of Western civilization.[76]

Mary Carpenter's legacy to Victorian debates about Western women and imperialism is considerable, not least because she was one of the most prominent English women in the nineteenth century to use the family romance idiom to reconcile her passionate desires for self-realization and emancipation with the needs of the imperial body politic. If, as John Stuart Mill claimed, "the whole government of India is carried out in writing," British feminists displayed through their own considerable literary production a distinct, if not distinctive, desire for the power and authority of colonial rule.[77] That they framed their desire in terms of a maternalist ethic is not exclusively attributable to Carpenter's example or even to her influence. Images of the white father and mother teaching "less civilized races" had been the standard stuff of British imperial ideology since the eighteenth century, although the special Victorian cast Carpenter gave to the familiar familial drama of colonial reform should not be discounted, either.[78] What differentiated Carpenter from other women who were attracted to the cause of Indian women—and who justified it in terms of their own ardent love of empire and motherly concern for Indian women—is that she, unlike the majority of them (including Josephine Butler), had been to India. Her claims to "know" the "authentic Indian woman" firsthand and her determination to make that personal knowledge visible to the reforming public gave other British women access to the problem of the colonial female body as well as what they imagined was the authority to speak of, for, and over it in what can be aptly termed a maternal register. Unlike many who followed, Carpenter never indulged in the language of sisterhood, preferring the expressly imperialized hierarchy that "mother" implied. Carpenter's particular romance with India, together with the passionate commitment to empire that she and other British feminists of her generation shared, meant that Indian women became imaginable as one of the chief sites of female reform desire until the First World War. It was the very seriousness of such imperial concerns—their indispensability to the future of the imperial family—that British feminists believed helped to legitimate their desires for white women's emancipation in Britain, whether that was understood as women's suffrage, women's social reform, or both.[79]

As Gayatri Spivak reminds us, in the last analysis, "There is no romance to be found here." Rather than functioning merely as an archive for the pleasurable dangers that empire offered to Victorian white women, or even as more evidence in the historical drama of modern Western maternalist policies, Carpenter's *Six Months in India* is an allegory for the predicaments of a colonizing Western feminism as well as a genealogy of British imperial feminisms themselves.[80] Lest we, in some unselfconsciously nostalgic desire for empire, mistake her story for heroism, let us be vigilant about reading Mary Carpenter's *Six Months in India* as historical evidence of Catherine Hall's astute observation that "there is never any guarantee that the personal voice of a white woman . . . produces a critique of colonialism."[81]

9

Contesting the Zenana

The Mission to Make "Lady Doctors for India," 1874–85

Recent work in British studies suggests that the project of historicizing the institutions and cultural practices of British imperialism is crucial to understanding metropolitan society in the nineteenth century. Monographs by Catherine Hall, Thomas C. Holt, and Jenny Sharpe, together with the impressive series Studies in Imperial Culture, edited by John M. MacKenzie—to name just a few examples of scholarly production in this field—have effectively relocated the operations of imperial culture at the heart of the empire itself.[1] By scrutinizing arenas as diverse as the English novel, government policymaking at the highest levels, and the ephemera of consumer culture, scholars of the Victorian period are in the process of giving historical weight and evidentiary depth to Edward Said's claim that "we are at a point in our work when we can no longer ignore empires and the imperial context in our studies."[2]

The origins of the London School of Medicine for Women (LSMW), its concern for Indian women in the *zenana* (sex-segregated spaces), and the embeddedness of its institutional development in Victorian imperial mentalities is one discrete example of how ostensibly "domestic" institutions were bound up with the empire and its projects in nineteenth-century Britain. As this essay will demonstrate, the conviction that Indian women were trapped in the "sunless, airless," and allegedly unhygienic Oriental zenana motivated the institutionalization of women's medicine and was crucial to the professionalization of female doctors in Victorian Britain.[3] One need only scratch the surface of the archive of British women's entry into the medical profession to find traces of the colonial concerns that motivated some of its leading lights. For women involved in pursuing a medical education, the specter of the zenana was more than a source of personal motivation; the provision of medical care to Indian women was nothing short of national and, indeed, of imperial obligation.[4] According to Sophia Jex-Blake, one of the first "lady doctors," even those who opposed female physicians practicing in Britain could not "dispute the urgent necessity that exists for their services in India and other parts of the East, where native customs make it practically impossible that women should be attended by medical men."[5]

"The Indian woman," imagined as imprisoned and awaiting liberation at the hands of Englishwomen's benevolence, exercised a generally powerful ideological force in this period, even while Rukhmabai, Kadambini Ganguli, and others entered the medical profession and were active in a variety of social-reform efforts in the 1880s and after.[6] Indeed, given Pandita Ramabai's testimony before the Hunter Commission in 1882 about the need for women doctors in India, her own frustrated attempt to pursue a medical education in England, and Englishwomen's attention to her reform efforts, it is arguable that Indian women were both directly and indirectly responsible for the organized interest in supplying medical women for India in the late Victorian period.[7] My focus here is the metropolitan scene, where ideas about British women's mission to the Indian female population divided some British women from others over what the definition of Western women's "mission work" in the colonial field should be during the 1870s and after. In the process, gender came to be rearticulated in relation to race and empire as women's medical training was institutionalized and women doctors were professionalized in Victorian Britain.[8] For in addition to the struggle against the male medical establishment that the first women doctors waged in the United Kingdom, a contest of authority was going on between British female medical missionaries doing de facto medical work among potential native converts and "scientifically qualified lady doctoresses"—that is, those trained from the 1870s onward either at the LSMW or at other degree-granting institutions.[9] Female physicians of the first generation in Britain worried that the lack of proper training on the part of women attached to religious missions threatened to undermine the claims to women's professionalism that they were working so hard, and against all odds, to ratify. Several of the most prominent of them appreciated the fact that India was a "practically unknown territory,"[10] but they realized at the same time that, if its resources were to be of maximum use, British medical women would have to formu-late and then police their own definition of "women's work" in the empire so they could be taken seriously as medical professionals *and* as workers indispensable to the imperial enterprise. Their quest to carve out a profes-sional sphere in the colonies, therefore, not only shaped the direction that medical education for women in Britain would take but also led female medical reformers to construct their goals as different from, and in some ways superior to, traditional missionary reform as carried out by women.

The question of what Western women *could* bring to *empire* was trans-formed by the first generation of British women doctors into the question of what British women doctors *should* bring to *India*. Such a transforma-tion was predicated on the centrality of the zenana and the imagined passivity of Indian women patients. As presumptions about the zenana were circulated and contested, a public debate emerged that advertised the cause of professionally trained "lady doctors" and produced a shift in the terms on which women's public role in the imperial nation-state was imagined. Examining both the discursive and the institutional practices of the LSMW at its founding historical moment contributes to our understand-ing of how gender categories were reconstituted by imperialism even as they helped to determine how the very concept of empire performed the kinds of ideological work it was capable of later in the nineteenth century. The colonial investments of the LSMW enable us, in short, to appreciate more fully how what Laura Tabili calls "the material mechanisms through which colonial racial inequalities" came to be articulated in Victorian imperial culture, not just in the empire, but at home, as well.[11]

In 1878, the annual report of the LSMW recorded its satisfaction at the progress that the movement for the qualification of women in the medical profession in Britain was making in the wake of Russell Gurney's Enabling Act, which had demolished the legal barriers to medical examining boards' granting licenses to women two years earlier. At the school's annual meet-ing, William Cowper-Temple, member of Parliament, moved that the LSMW raise "a special fund of not less than £5000" to guarantee that it would be able to continue to educate women so that they could, through training in "a complete medical school, including clinical instruction in a hospital," be-come eligible for examination for medical diplomas. In support of his resolu-tion, Cowper-Temple observed that a petition circulated in Britain had been signed by 16,000 women expressing "their desire to be attended by persons of their own sex."[12] He ended his motion by emphasizing "the great advantage which it would be to missions in India if female practitioners attended the Zenana."[13]

The imperial rationale that Cowper-Temple articulated for the professionalization of women doctors is one instance of how crucial a symbolic and material site the zenana was for those involved in establishing the provision of medical education for women in Victorian Britain. Traces of the colonial concerns that informed the organized movement to open the medical profession to British women are evident throughout the historical record of that struggle, though they remain unremarked on or underexamined by historians.[14] One foundational text, Jex-Blake's *Medical Women: A Thesis and Its History* (1886), suggests that commitment to the imperial mission in India was part of the earliest schemes for promoting women's medical education in Britain. Jex-Blake made history when, along with seven other women, she sued Edinburgh University over its exclusion of female students pursuing medical degrees in 1872.[15] Recalling the last meeting of the Committee for Securing a Medical Education for Women in Edinburgh (April 1871), she explained in *Medical Women* how an Indian man, the Reverend Narayaa Sheshadri, had stood up and testified to the need for female medical practitioners in India. There were "innumerable females," he said, "whom no male doctor was allowed to see" because of their seclusion in the zenana.[16] In a footnote to her narrative of this event, Jex-Blake added that shortly thereafter, she had questioned an Indian gentleman who had studied medicine in Britain about the conditions under which Indian women received medical treatment—and that he had confirmed her suspicions about the inaccessibility of good care due to the requirements of zenana life.[17] Such suspicions became the grounds for arguments about the imperially minded mission that underwrote the quest for British women's access to medical education. Frances Hoggan publicized the appeals of a variety of colonial reformers for female doctors in the 1880s, arguing that all who encountered zenana women "strongly insist[ed] on the urgency of the need of medical women in India to attend patients of their own sex."[18]

Certainties about the ready-made clientele the zenana provided for Western professional women were common currency in Britain by the mid-1880s, and not just among female doctors and their advocates. Female teacher-training schemes used similar rationales, particularly after Mary Carpenter's first visit to India in 1866–67 established her commitment to providing a corps of British-trained teachers for India.[19] The argument from colonial necessity presumed the passivity of zenanas' inhabitants, as well as their basic incapacity, save in exceptional circumstances, to train as medical doctors themselves. It was motivated by the woman-to-woman care ethic that helped to justify most, if not all, women's work in the public sphere, as well as by the national-imperial commitments through which Victorian women articulated that ethic from the 1870s onward.[20] Finally, it gained additional currency as a response to arguments put forward from within and outside the male medical profession that women doctors quickly would be redundant in Britain, where the local economy could not sustain an influx of new practitioners. The success in India of newly qualified British women doctors such as Mary Scharlieb, combined with their reports of the possibilities of "that large and unexplored field of labour—the women of India," added legitimacy to the claim that the zenana system in India provided the new female professionals with a necessary outlet. It also gave India a high profile as the most obvious extranational site for Western women's medical work.[21]

I have argued elsewhere and in some detail about how essential images of Indian women were to the construction of feminist ideologies in Victorian and Edwardian Britain, chiefly in terms of discourses about women's suffrage and the repeal of the Contagious Diseases Acts.[22] The centrality of colonial women in the rhetoric and practices of the crusade for women's medical education is integrally related to this sociopolitical phenomenon, not least because a number of pioneering women doctors were affiliated with the women's suffrage and repeal movements and because so many prominent Victorian feminists contributed financially and with their political influence to the cause of medical women.[23] In the Victorian period, the women's movement and the institutions it generated—suffrage societies, the repeal campaign, and the feminist periodical press in all its variety—intersected with and helped to support several corporate bodies expressly devoted to the question of women's medical work for India. Chief among these was the Countess of Dufferin's Fund. This fund is generally recognized as the first initiative launched to coordinate the flow of medical women to India. Also referred to as the National Association for Supplying Female Medical Aid to the Women of India, the fund was organized in 1885 by Harriot Dufferin, vicereine of India, who was galvanized, so the story goes, by Queen Victoria's personal request that she interest herself in "measures for the medical relief of the women in

India."[24] The queen's request was revealingly ambiguous about which women, Indian or British, would provide the necessary medical relief, as was her commitment to the education of Indian women more generally.[25] In fact, the question of whose education should be secured first was one that dominated the early years of the fund's existence, even if later accounts insisted that priority be given to Indian women aspiring to the field.[26] From the outset, the fund repeatedly emphasized its nonsectarian character. Its organizers professed to respect the policy of noninterference in indigenous religious customs promulgated by Queen Victoria's post–Mutiny Act of 1858. In this and in other ways, the Countess of Dufferin's scheme worked, as Maneesha Lal has argued, to "replicate the structure of the colonial administrative hierarchy" by grafting onto India "the English model of philanthropy which colonial rulers believed represented a progressive civic ideal."[27] One of the effects of this arrangement was the perpetuation in the Indian medical service of racial and gender hierarchies. Britons were doctors; Indians were lesser-grade "hospital assistants"; and, even after the Dufferin Fund celebrated its first decade, by far the majority of lady doctors in India were Europeans.[28] Two important nineteenth-century exceptions were Ganguli and Rukhmabai; neither of them, significantly, was educated under the auspices of the fund.[29] The Dufferin Fund effectively managed opportunities for systematic medical training and distributed patronage to qualified women doctors in the form of hospital posts and dispensary positions. While it succeeded in creating opportunities for aspiring female physicians through educational scholarships, grants in aid, and other forms of financial assistance, it did not—and, indeed, perhaps could not—challenge the racialized imperial bureaucracy that structured the medical establishment in British India.[30]

The longevity of the Dufferin Fund, together with its aristocratic patronage, its origins in royal-imperial benevolence, and its vast network of branches at home and in the empire, has eclipsed the role played by the London School of Medicine for Women in promoting the work of female medical women for India. The LSMW predated the Dufferin Fund by a decade and established ideological and structural linkages between British women doctors and their Indian female clientele that the fund would use as the basis of its own network of female medical women for India. The foundation of the LSMW was the immediate result of British women's struggle to win the right to a medical education from unwilling British universities. While a variety of sympathetic male faculty members circumvented official policy and risked their own professional reputations to accommodate determined female medical students, the weight of institutional power was decidedly against them, as the Edinburgh Seven's failure to win a legal victory securing their rights to examination in 1872 demonstrates.[31] Rather than take their case to the House of Lords, the seven women decided to seek admission to examinations elsewhere—some on the continent, others in London. Access to examinations was key in getting onto the Medical Register. Candidacy for examination was also the primary site of institutional exclusion: as late as 1874, only Elizabeth Garrett Anderson and Elizabeth Blackwell had been registered in Britain, and both of them had trained outside the United Kingdom.[32] Sophia Jex-Blake and Isabel Thorne took the lead on the London scene, but with little success. So resistant was the medical profession to their claims that the entire Board of Examiners at the College of Surgeons resigned rather than deal with the applications of two women who had applied for candidacy.[33] Jex-Blake and her sympathizers, among whom were a number of prominent physicians, formed a provisional council that soon handed the institutional planning over to a body of governors. It was decided that the most logical procedure was to provide a full course of study with lecturers who were already recognized teachers at metropolitan schools, on the presumption that one among the nineteen examining boards would accept their certificates. On the strength of £1,800 in subscriptions, they bought the lease of "a quaint old house and garden" on Henrietta Street. The London School of Medicine for Women—which Isabel Thorne called the "Mother School of all British Medical Women"—was now in business.[34]

Its prominent patrons and its three-year course of nonclinical study notwithstanding, all of the examining boards refused to accept certificates of attendance and achievement from the school. Even after the passage of the Enabling Bill in 1876, which gave the boards the power to admit women to their examinations but did not require it, no board acted on it until the summer of 1877, when the Royal College of Physicians, Ireland, decided to admit Jex-Blake, Edith Pechey, and several others to their final examinations.[35] The University of London soon followed suit. There remained the question of clinical training, for which Cowper-Temple recommended a fund-raising campaign at the annual meeting in 1877. The £5,000 was eventually raised, and by midsummer, students from the LSMW were admitted to the wards of the Royal Free Hospital. In light of the arguments from colonial necessity that framed the debate over British women's access to medical education, it is worth noting that Scharlieb obtained admittance, along with four other women, to the three-year certificate course at Madras Medical College in 1875, though this was also a bitter struggle. Thus, as S. Muthu Chidambaram reminds us, "While the universities and medical associations in Great Britain were debating whether women should study medicine, this progressive step was taken in India."[36] It is also worth underscoring that Scharlieb and others who had studied medicine in India tended eventually to go to Britain, and especially to the LSMW, for further training pursuant to qualification. This reflects not so much the higher standards or better quality in London as perhaps the reputation for superiority over colonial courses of study that schools in the metropole might be expected to have acquired in Victorian imperial culture.

Of the fourteen women enrolled in the opening of classes at the LSMW in October 1874, twelve had been students at Edinburgh. Fanny Butler, a member of the Church of England Zenana Missionary Society, was one of the two newcomers. While deeply committed to the work of evangelizing India, and particularly its women, Butler was uneasy about the whole notion of "lady doctoring." She shared many of her contemporaries' prejudices about the "unwomanliness" of the profession and for a time was firm in her opposition. "I could not do it," she wrote. "I could not care for the medical women's movement."[37] Yet like so many other British women of her generation, Butler's understanding of the zenana system in India convinced her that evangelization must go hand in hand with medical treatment, both because she cared about the physical well-being of Indian women and because "it was a means of approach to many who were inclined to be hostile to [missionaries'] teaching, but could not resist it when it was expressed in acts of mercy."[38] Butler's decision to attend the LSMW in spite of her reservations stemmed from this conviction. She won the first Ernest Hart scholarship (£50), took her qualifying exams in Dublin, and set sail for India in December 1880. After a relatively short career, she died of dysentery in Srinagar in 1889.[39] She was the first qualified British female doctor to practice in India and the first of those who trained at the LSMW to do so.[40] Her example of martyrdom, together with the scholarship to the LSMW established in her name, inspired many British women after her to take up practice among what one correspondent for the school's magazine called "zenana patients."[41]

Butler's biography, written by E. M. Tonge under the auspices of the

Church of England Zenana Missionary Society, indicates that Butler found the LSMW a fairly secular place. She helped to start a Bible and Prayer Union at the school, in part because her association with students "of many creeds, and no creeds . . . has forced me to examine the foundations of my own belief, so as to be able to give a reason for the faith that is in me."[42] I do not mean to suggest, and neither did Butler, I feel sure, that the LSMW was a godless place. Indeed, although arguments for women's entrance into the medical profession were most often grounded in claims that women were "natural healers" and that their continued disqualification on the basis of sex hampered the progress of British civilization, the fundamentally Christian commitment to healing the sick was an equally constituent element.[43] Yet it was not an entirely hospitable environment for someone in Butler's position. As one student at the LSMW put it, "The medical skill is not a means to gain surreptitious entrance for Christian doctrine under the pretence of doing something else."[44]

From the very beginnings of the school's foundation, criticisms were made of those seeking a medical education for the purposes of proselytizing by newly minted professionals not expressly committed to evangelizing the mission field. At an inaugural address given at the London School in October 1878, for example, Dr. Pechey (who had trained at Berne and qualified for the British Medical Register at Dublin in 1877), expressed the following reservations:

There may be . . . [those] here, who study not from any special taste for medical pursuits, but as a means to an end; in order, namely, that they may be more useful in the future they have planned for themselves. I refer to medical missionaries. . . . Go out with the best credentials possible and as you belong to two professions, see that you serve both faithfully. I confess that I have been somewhat horrified to hear occasionally remarks from the supporters of medical missions to the effect that a diploma is not necessary, that a full curriculum is superfluous—in fact that a mere smattering is sufficient for such students. I cannot believe that such sentiments are held by the students themselves, and if there are any here to-day, I beg of you not for one moment to give way to this idea. Is human life worth less in other lands, amongst people of another faith? or do such persons imagine that disease there is of a simpler nature, and that the heathen, like the wicked, are "not in trouble as other men"?[45]

While Pechey did not discount the possibility that lady doctors could still be handmaidens to the project of Christian conversion, she was clearly worried about the possibility that female medical missionaries might give the movement for women's medical education a bad name. " 'Christian England' is renowned in every land for adulterated goods. Let it not be said," she exhorted her audience, "that under the very guise of Christianity the medical help she sends out is also an inferior article." For her, the salvation of zenana women required the kind of "science and skill" that she believed only the thoroughly trained professional could provide. Her concern that a woman doctor prove herself "a worthy member of the profession, by saving life, . . . lessening pain and smoothing the passage to the grave" signals one of the ways in which the claims of science and professionalism might compete with those of the Christian religious mission narrowly conceived.[46]

Significantly, those medical missionaries who horrified Pechey with their arguments about the sufficiency of basic medical knowledge for women missionaries were not the only ones opposed to the training of women as doctors for India. Male doctors practicing in India dismissed as overrated and inaccurate claims that zenana women needed English lady doctors to provide medical care. According to Charles West, a fellow of the Royal College of Surgeons in London who canvassed the opinions of medical men in India, those men testified that this was a "demand [that] arose in England, not India." One, a Dr. Ewart, argued that "the native women in India are quite shrewd enough to pin their faith to the colours of the male doctors, native or European. Excepting a few strong-minded European ladies in Madras, and perhaps in Bombay, there is not the faintest demand for female doctors. . . . If these good and wise ladies would turn their attention to missionary enterprise, they might prove useful. But in medicine, their efforts can only result, as has been the case here, in the production of an inferior article for which there is literally no necessity or demand in India."[47] Clearly, the opposition to women doctors was as intense and as territorial in the colonies as in Britain. As Catriona Blake has written about the domestic scene, institutionalized resistance on the part of male medical professionals was proportionate to their ideological commitment to preventing women from learning "about their own bodies from doctors of their own sex," whether those women were British or Indian.[48]

Female medical missionaries and women like Pechey were in fact fighting the same battle. It was a battle against the entrenched patriarchalism of institutionalized religion and institutionalized medicine. Apologists for both wished British women's imperial role to be limited to the work of conversion to which Victorian mores believed they were by nature fit. In some ways, then, Pechey was preaching to the converted (so to speak): presumably, the women in the LSMW audience who were attached to missions were enrolled in the school because they, like Butler, believed in the importance of solid medical training. Perhaps because of the newness of the LSMW and her own investment in its uphill battle for legitimacy, Pechey felt compelled to admonish those who might potentially discredit women's quest for medical credentials. Even if Pechey's talk was intended to alert medical mission work women to the sexism of their male missionary counterparts, she nevertheless made clear what she believed the priorities of degreed medical women such as herself should be: the practice of scientific medicine above all other commitments. Those who thought otherwise might always be suspected of using medicine as a means to an end in India and other British possessions and thus of undermining the professional ethics of disinterestedness that, somewhat paradoxically, even a pioneer medical woman such as Pechey was apparently willing to embrace.

That all British women might be understood to be using India's zenana women as a means to their own professional and status ends evidently did not occur to Pechey. As concerned as she was about the quality of medical mission work, however, she at least conceded that its practitioners were pursuing "two professions" and urged them to pursue one as "faithfully" as the other. The publicity given to the career of Elizabeth Beilby in 1881 and after prompted both a recalibration of that position and an institutional realignment on the part of the LSMW so that it could participate more actively in shaping the ways in which medical women became qualified for, and were directed toward, India as a site of medical practice. According to Edith Moberly Bell's classic study of British women doctors, *Storming the Citadel*, Beilby had been a student at the LSMW in its early days. Like Butler before her, "She was a missionary at heart and entered the School to become a medical missionary."[49] She left the school at the end of 1875 (the year before Gurney's Enabling Act), discouraged by the prospects of women ever being able to get onto the Medical Register. The Zenana Mission sent her to Lucknow, where she established a dispensary and eventually a small hospital. In Bell's evaluation, "She was just sufficiently trained to be very conscious of her own deficiencies."[50] Once the battle for registration had been won in England, she resolved to return home to become fully qualified as a doctor.

On the eve of her return, Beilby became celebrated for the conversation she had with the maharani of Punna before leaving for England. Beilby had been called by the maharaja to examine his ailing wife, whom she successfully treated. The maharani urged Beilby to take a message back to the queen telling her that "the women of India suffer when they are sick." Beilby's account of this encounter suggested that the maharani was asking the queen to send English-trained female doctors to alleviate the suffering of Indian women.[51] Lal has remarked that the attention given to Beilby's eventual meeting with the queen "fostered the presumption that a personal bond existed between Queen Victoria and her female subjects, a bond to be mediated through select Englishwomen."[52] Beilby's return to Britain did indeed help to crystallize the woman-to-woman ideological justification for Western lady doctors' access to the zenana, and in part because of the queen's personal interest in the cause, it eventually led to the formation of the Dufferin Fund as well.[53] Images of the queen as empress-mother of India remained crucial to the narratives through which the fund was historicized and through which the whole medical mission project was memorialized. Tracing the origins of the fund in 1929, Ruth Balfour and Margaret Young recalled that "it is pleasant to think that the Countess of Dufferin's Fund owed its origin to Queen Victoria who will long be remembered in India as 'the Great White Queen and Mother of her People.' "[54]

Less attention has been paid by historians to the fact that Beilby's decision to return home for proper medical training was accompanied by a renunciation of mission work. In a letter to the editor of the *Pioneer Mail*, Beilby reported that after six years of working for the Zenana Missionary Society, she was leaving the organization, "and nothing would make me work under it or any other again." She confirmed Pechey's fears about the attitude of medical missionaries toward the practice of medicine in the following terms:

> I do not approve of the "hybrid mixture with a strain of medical knowledge," but on the contrary I think every lady doctor who comes to this country to practice medicine should have gone through the full curriculum of studies and should have obtained a diploma qualifying her to

practice. . . . [O]ne of my greatest objections to the societies who send out zenana medical missionaries is that they think if the said missionaries have enough knowledge to work as sick nurses at home, such knowledge will be sufficient to fit them to undertake the difficult task of a lady doctor out there. This is a most fatal mistake, and one that sooner or later will bring the work of zenana medical missions into disrepute.[55]

Beilby did not see the qualification of Western medical women as the only solution to this problem. She argued that it was "a duty we owe to the native women to train those who are willing to be of use to their own countrywomen." At the same time, she envisioned Indian women being schooled either as nurses or assistants, rather than as doctors, and she excoriated what she considered the unhygienic practices of untrained *dhais* (midwives), "to whose ignorance and superstition hundred of lives have been and are still sacrificed." Her advice to English women who wanted to help the "prisoners" of the zenana was not only to get a sound medical education, but also *not* to come to India under the auspices of a missionary society at all.[56]

Beilby's declaration caused a tremendous stir among supporters of medical education for women in Britain, many of whom had until then carefully avoided impugning the motives of medical missionaries but for whom the practice of medicine was a matter of science and secular reform rather than faith.[57] Beilby's public disassociation from her missionary sponsors provided an opportunity for leaders of the women's medical movement to move in on the zenana and appropriate it as their particular professional cause. Garrett Anderson, lecturer at and later dean of the LSMW, wrote a letter to the *Times* on 31 October 1881 affirming that indeed "there is in India a field almost indefinitely large in which competent medical women would be of the greatest value." Like Pechey, she did not exactly reject the project of evangelism, but she made her own priorities indisputably clear. She warned against using medicine as an instrument of conversion, in part because "one profession firmly grasped is enough for most people," but also because in the end such a project undermined the very Christian principles its proponents wished to instill. "It will not recommend Christianity to Hindoo ladies to send them missionaries in the disguise of indifferent doctors. Already there is suspicion of this having been done, and we have heard in various quarters of native ladies inquiring critically as to the diplomas possessed by the medical missionaries especially for their benefit."[58] She indicated that the LSMW was ready to step into the breach and could, according to her estimation, provide twenty to thirty qualified lady doctors a year should willing students be able to find the necessary funding. Isabel Thorne, writing for the same issue of the *Times*, echoed Garrett Anderson. In her capacity as honorary secretary of the LSMW, she assured the reading public that, because of the school's recent affiliation with the Royal Free Hospital, English women doctors heading to India would have the benefit of both classroom and clinical training. They would thus be fully equipped to work for "the relief of the suffering women of India."[59]

Isabel Thorne was keen to make the maharani of Punna's request of the queen the basis for her appeal for scholarship money to the LSMW. Garrett Anderson, in contrast, politely rejected royal benevolence and emphasized that this was a problem to be negotiated between "the leaders of native society on the one hand, and by the medical women themselves on the other."[60] The LSMW was instrumental in clearing the way for this negotiation, but it did not act alone. Critical to its success was the National Indian Association (NIA), an organization founded by Mary Carpenter in 1870 in the wake of her visit to India and committed from the outset to promoting women's education generally. The NIA, which was run by Elizabeth Adelaide Manning after Carpenter's death in 1877, had been gathering information on the status of medical mission work even before news of Beilby's defection was made known in Britain. Manning had commissioned Hoggan (licentiate, King's and Queen's College of Physicians, Ireland, 1876) to follow up on information given to the association by Sarah Heckford, who had reported to the NIA on the insufficiency of medical aid being provided to zenana women from her own experience in India in December 1881.[61] In November 1882, the NIA announced a meeting in London for its subscribers and other sympathizers to discuss plans to guarantee the supply of female medical aid to the women of India. It was at this meeting that the first public case for lady doctors for India was made, that the first concerted schemes for paying Englishwomen's passage to India were proposed, and that a concrete proposal for creating an agency to mediate between Britain and India was first suggested in Britain.[62] This was December 1882, three years before the Dufferin Fund was established and before the Countess of Dufferin, vicereine of

India, met with Queen Victoria to discuss her role in establishing a medical scheme for Indian women.

Present at this meeting were Hoggan, who read a lengthy paper on the need in India for women's "professional knowledge and skill";[63] Dr. Blackwell, chair of gynecology at the LSMW; James Stansfeld, member of Parliament and member of the governing board of the LSMW; and Garrett Anderson. The LSMW was thus well represented, with several of its founders and two of its most prominent women doctors in attendance. Hoggan's arguments, which drew on information she had collected from English doctors in India, as well as from India Office records and statistics, stressed both the special needs of female zenana patients and the contributions English medical women could make to the imperial enterprise. The latter would be "the most powerful agents for raising the whole tone and worth of women's lives in that vast empire."[64] Hoggan wanted not just individual lady doctors or even a coordinated flow of medical practitioners but a full-fledged women's medical service for India. Robert Harvey, professor of midwifery at the Medical College of Bengal, who was basically supportive of the idea of Western women doctors in India, dismissed that ambitious scheme as premature, and although it remained a cherished and sought-after goal of British feminists and medical women for decades, it did not materialize until just before the First World War.[65]

Blackwell, for her part, was heartened by the professional possibilities created by the needs of zenana women, though she expressed concern that the kinds of hardships lady doctors faced in India would be daunting and their responsibility all the greater for being imperial. The proper clinical training of midwives was also of great concern to her, and she urged the establishment of "a well organized School of Midwifery with Sanitary Science attached . . . for the training of native women."[66] Garrett Anderson agreed, and, foreseeing the very real possibility that qualified medical women might be exploited in India, warned that a trained lady doctor could not be expected to take up an unpaid position in the empire: "if she desired that, she could get plenty of it in England—in the East End of London, for instance." Given the isolation from friends and the "wear and tear" on their constitutions that an Indian stint would surely involve, English female doctors would, according to Garrett Anderson, have to have considerable financial incentive to choose a colonial post over a metropolitan one.[67] Garrett Anderson was a shrewd institution builder who was prepared to make forceful arguments about the socioeconomic realities Victorian women faced. In a turn of phrase that anticipated Virginia Woolf's a-room-of-one's-own thesis by half a century, she had elsewhere warned that female doctors contemplating going to India would have already "spent their patrimony" to get through medical school and therefore had to earn enough to save money to return to Britain after their time in India was up.[68] Debates about the form and nature of medical schemes for Indian women continued over the course of several NIA meetings and in a variety of articles published in the association's journal, up to and including the announcement in March 1883 that George Kittredge, an American businessman from Bombay, was initiating a fund to guarantee the training of female doctors expressly for the medical care of women in India. Stansfeld, for his part, concluded the NIA meeting in December by pledging that the LSMW would do whatever possible to contribute to "the supply of what is so clearly a want in our great Indian possessions."[69]

Paradoxically, in light of Beilby's revelations, Hoggan reported that she had first learned of the inadequate medical provisions for Indian women from missionaries in India. Whether they were Western, native, or female, she did not specify.[70] The origins of concern for zenana women were quickly lost in plans for how the LSMW could accommodate, coordinate, and exercise some influence over both the disbursement of scholarship money and the kinds of training facilities that operated in both England and India. Distinguishing professional medical training from unskilled medical missionary practice remained the guiding principle behind these efforts. Indeed, insisting on that distinction was what had drawn the LSMW into the public debates in the first place; it was also what justified their continued involvement in overseeing the flow of female medical personnel to India. And needless to say, it was what defined and legitimated their claims to medical professionalism at a critical historical moment when those claims were in danger of being doubted, if not challenged head on, by the mainstream medical establishment and its defenders.[71] Institutionalizing this philosophy in the LSMW was crucial to its professional standing and identity. In 1886, Edith A. Huntley, a second-year student at the LSMW, entered an essay competition sponsored by the school. In her essay, "The Study and Practice of Medicine for Women," a discussion of what English medical women could do for India figured prominently. Just as prominent was her emphasis on the need for "legally qualified lady doctors" and her rejection of inferior medical training for female missionaries. "No!" she wrote. "If lady medical missionaries are to be a recognised evangelistic agency, let them at all costs be good doctors."[72] Once again, evangelism was not discounted, but it was also not to be undertaken at the expense of rigorous and professional training. Huntley won the £10 prize that year. Clearly, she and her peers were being schooled in the role of women in Britain's empire, in the conditions of professionalism in the field of clinical medicine, and in the personal rewards of national-imperial service—as well as in pathology, histology, and materia medica—at the LSMW.

If images of zenana women and their medical needs were undoubtedly essential to the successful contest of opposition to the medical profession-alization of women in Victorian Britain, the voices of Indian women did not figure prominently in discussions of their "condition" in the metro-pole. And while they might demonstrate concern, as Blackwell had, about the training of indigenous women as midwives, qualified British women doctors attributed little or no agency to zenana women. "What about the great dependency of our own Empire," wrote Huntley, "where millions of women, our fellow subjects, are immured in zenana beyond the reach of medical skill unless it be carried to them by a woman."[73] Beilby's remark that zenanas' inhabitants did not even realize their great need for Western women's medical care in many ways typified the attitudes of her fellow female doctors.[74] In fact, according to Lal, contemporary statistics showed that, while Indian women routinely sought medical care at government hospitals staffed by Europeans, "Women's attendance was between 15 and 20 percent" of the total—her argument being that Indian women were not absolutely averse to seeking treatment from male physicians.[75] I do not mean to suggest that the first generation of British women doctors was fabricating evidence; nor is it the case that they were not genuinely con-cerned about the health and welfare of Indian women. There is little reason to question their good intentions. What I would argue is that Western women's sympathy was neither transparent nor disinterested; it was additionally bound up in this context with the need to justify Western women's professional activities and to hierarchize the doctor–patient, along with the doctor–nurse and doctor–midwife, relationship. Imperial ideologies, acting in conjunction with changing presumptions about how gender roles should be played out in the course of professionalization, helped to decide who had the upper hand in these relationships and how they were institutionalized. To paraphrase Sharpe, British women doc-tors' bid for gender(ed) power passed through colonial hierarchies of race, making the zenana the foundational justification for British women's imperial intervention even while Indian women remained an undifferentiated and allegedly compliant colonial clientele.[76]

In an echo of the certainties of the imperial civilizing mission, many Victorian Englishwomen were quite convinced that Indian women would train as doctors in time, but at least in these early years, the emphasis was on training English female doctors whose purpose was to supply not just medical aid but that inimitably English commodity: personal example.[77] Spokeswomen for the LSMW moved easily into the authoritative space that had been the special province of medical mission women, largely because they depended on Indian women as a clientele but also because they were not finally critical of the missionary posture, broadly conceived, in which they found themselves as healers of colonial peoples. To say that they secularized what they characterized as a primarily evangelical concern for Indian women would therefore be going too far, because it was not a question of rejecting Christian principles. As Susan Thorne has observed, the missionary movement was one of the principal sites through which imperialist ideologies "infiltrated Victorian feminist consciousness" and Christian principle, one of the ideological bases that sustained a variety of feminist-imperial commitments in this period.[78] Insisting on professional training was, rather, a question of choosing medical skill over religious persuasion as a primary strategy of self-identification and, finally, of gendered cultural power. Empire not only provided a new and "untapped" domain for the exercise of such power; it gave the very category of "women's work" new and permissible scope, national and imperial prestige, and a secular, world-civilizing status.

Such valences were available because of how embedded the LSMW was, both ideologically and in terms of personnel, in the kind of domestic imperial culture that made supplying medical aid to the women of India seem like the highest form of national-imperial service as well as the best guarantee of a bright and prosperous future for British women entering the medical profession beyond the initial "breakthrough" period of the mid-1870s. Although I have striven to demonstrate how the LSMW and, to a lesser extent, the NIA anticipated the concerns for and the linkages to India that were systematized by the Dufferin Fund, it would be a mistake to conclude that there was anything but goodwill among all three of these institutions once the Dufferin scheme was a reality in 1885.[79] Most, if not all, Victorian women and men involved in the female medical movement welcomed the foundation of the fund, cooperated with its organizers, and worked happily to realize its goals. As the system of scholarship funding suggests, the fund depended on the organizing skills of Elizabeth Manning at the NIA and the prestige of the LSMW to attract female candidates as much as the LSMW depended on the fund to place its graduates in hospitals and dispensaries throughout India.[80] These connections were forged because "medical tuition" was "the backbone of the Fund" and because the LSMW was, until 1886, the only place in England where women doctors could train.[81] Such connections were also assured because of how intertwined the very concept of women's professional medical work was from the start with Britain's civilizing mission in India. Ensuring that British women be trained as doctors for work in the empire was not the exclusive province of any group or scheme, and it was not limited to the patronage of vicereines and monarchs, though their images undoubtedly gave cachet to the cause. It was also the product of middle-class women's professional needs and of their broadly based feminist-imperial commitments. Because reliance on the zenana as a site of civilizing effort, whether secular or religious, was crucial to the justification for allowing medical women into the mission field in this period, the contest over zenana women was one constituent of what J. A. Mangan has called the "making [of] imperial mentalities." It was, more broadly, instrumental in the gendering of imperial ideologies in the Victorian metropole, as well.[82]

The popularity of medical-mission work among LSMW graduates tells us a lot about the conditions under which many British women imagined themselves as doctors before 1900. In an 1890 profile of the LSMW, the *Daily Graphic* observed that "the majority of the lady pupils" who graduated from the school proceeded to India or the East after qualifying as medical doctors.[83] Three years later, *The Young Woman* echoed these sentiments, recommending India as the best place for newly qualified lady doctors to practice.[84] The Royal Free Hospital archives indicate that a significant number of women who attended the LSMW during its first decade did in fact adopt India as their cause. In addition to Pechey and Bielby, Drs. Agnes McLaren, Scharlieb, Mary Elizabeth Pailthorpe, Lilian Trewby, and Helen Hanson are among the most well-known doctors who trained at the school and ended up practicing in India.[85] So prominently did India figure in the career choices of the school's graduates that discussion of their achievements occurred regularly in the Reports of the Executive Council of the LSMW from 1884 until the end of the century.[86] Alumnae wrote about their colonial experiences regularly for the LSMW magazine in the 1890s; in fact, the magazine, which is full of news from India, is itself powerful evidence of both the appeal of colonial work to the first generation of lady doctors and of India's centrality in the history of the school. The archives also document the educational careers of several Indian women, among them Rukhmabai, Merbai A. Vakil, Nalini Bonnerjee, Susila Anita Bonnerjee, and Alice Sorabji, all of whom attended the school around the turn of the century.[87] Rukhmabai, who gained celebrity in India and Britain because she had contested her child-marriage in a Bombay court, qualified in midwifery, as did many of the doctors who went from the LSMW to do service in India. Even when English medical women were willing to concede the capabilities of native women, they tended to be critical if not contemptuous of untrained *dhais,* to whom they attributed most of what they viewed as unsanitary conditions in the zenana and among Indian women in general.[88] The LSMW developed quite a faculty in and a reputation for its midwifery branch, not least because of the school's desire to rectify the perceived inadequacy of indigenous women practitioners in Britain's colonial possessions.[89] If, as Nancy Theriot has recently argued, "woman's [sexual] difference . . . was the object of gynecological knowledge" in modern Western medical systems generally, such difference carried racial as well as gender dimensions in the Indian colonial context, where British women doctors relied on Indian women's bodies both as the site for their clinical experience and as their best hope for on-the-ground specialty training.[90]

What had been tensions in the early 1880s between medical missionaries and fully trained doctors were, if not completely resolved, then at the very least largely subsumed in the greater cause of healing the colonial sick as early as the late 1880s. In an 1888 article for the *Queen* entitled "How to Become a Lady Doctor," Scharlieb explained that "in India the demand is great and is increasingly necessary." Of the three best ways to get to India, she recommended the Dufferin Fund, "various missionary bodies," and service in the family of native princes—in that order.[91] Mission work was not first, but it was also neither last nor completely absent from the list of possibilities. There were some, like Jex-Blake, who continued to excoriate mission organizations for their continued use of insufficiently trained women in the mission field. She called the Church of England Zenana Missionary Society a "notorious offender" and warned that such blatant disregard for the necessity of "professional skill" would end up severely limiting the power and the usefulness of such agencies.[92] For her, the commitment to "sending forth" thoroughly qualified women remained of "paramount importance."[93] And yet despite such fulminations from the leadership, medical missionary women—that is, qualified doctors attached to mission stations—were among the most frequent contributors to the LSMW monthly magazine in the 1890s and after, where they unselfconsciously championed their work as the natural and logical result of their metropolitan training. Her prize-winning essay notwithstanding, Huntley became a medical missionary for the Church of England Zenana Mission—thus robbing Jex-Blake's critique of that organization of some of its credibility.[94] Medical training schemes like the one attached to the mission at Ludhiana (which was founded by Edith Brown, a LSMW graduate) got considerable press and may have even drawn LSMW alumnae to work in the colonial field alongside their missionary counterparts.[95]

This apparent reconciliation between mission work, on the one hand, and trained medical work, on the other, is somewhat surprising and raises important questions about the relationship between institution building and rhetorical strategies, especially where gender is at issue. In the case of the LSMW, it seems quite likely that criticism of medical mission work was a strategy to force mission societies in India to hire the "professionally" trained women being produced in London—women who might otherwise be redundant if they limited their employment horizons to the United Kingdom.[96] Insistence on professionalization over religious enthusiasm may also have been a screen for concerns about the class origins of would-be female doctors. At the very least, the quest for secular medical training may be read as evidence of the power Garrett Anderson and others believed the LSMW had to transform aspiring physicians of any class into indubitably respectable women.[97] It may well be, too, that in the fact of cultural opposition to the "unwomanly" effects of practicing medicine, even arguments for imperial service could not compete with the legitimating appeal of evangelical / medical work to Victorian women seeking emancipation through the newly opened secular professions. There will be some for whom this final allegiance to the evangelical imperial mission signals the fundamental conservatism at the heart of an apparently radical cause such as the movement for opening the profession of medicine to women. If analyses of this kind are historically important, then it behooves us to consider as well how committed to the emancipation of zenana women such lady doctors were in the last analysis—whether they were "medical missionaries" or not. By attempting both to distinguish themselves from what had been an evangelically minded tradition of women's national-imperial mission and to refigure medical work among colonial women into a more self-consciously professional, secular project, female physicians in Victorian Britain linked their cause to the progress of science, medicine, and civilization itself.[98] In so doing, they obscured the extent to which both missionary workers and medical reformers were simultaneously supportive of and resistant to the emancipation of Indian women. Although many Indian women may be said to have benefited from the efforts of the Dufferin Fund, as Lal has observed, almost all women physicians of this period accepted and worked within the confines of the zenana rather than challenging that particular separate sphere.[99] They thus perpetuated the conviction, already pervasive in Victorian culture at home, that seclusion alone was the cause of Indian women's degradation and, in this particular case, of the inaccessibility of adequate medical care. Whether because of cultural deference, ideological commitment to official policies of religious noninterference, professional self-interest, doubts about Indian women's capabilities—or a combination thereof—the zenana functioned as one of the pretexts for women's medical professionalism for Western doctors and for some newly professionalized Indian women practitioners, as well.[100] Nor was this merely a phenomenon of the Victorian period. Rukhmabai's career path, as well as the career paths of other early Indian women doctors, anticipated a long tradition of segregation by sex within the Indian medical profession, where "historically Indian women doctors have worked mainly as gynecologists and obstetricians."[101]

By the time she wrote the preface to the definitive book on female doctors and India of the interwar period, Balfour's and Young's *The Work of Medical Women in India* (1929), Scharlieb appears to have all but forgotten the contests over the colonial terrain of the zenana that shaped the Victorian debates about the nature of British women's medical mission to Indian women. Although she mentions the Dufferin Fund and credits Garrett Anderson—of whose "gallant endeavour to secure medical education, training and success for women in England" the movement for colonial medical women was "the early and excellent fruit"—hardly any trace of the competition between religion and science for the hearts and minds of the first generation of British women physicians remains. In fact, Scharlieb waxes eloquent about the historically harmonious relationship between Christian evangelization efforts in the British empire and the medical mission of professional Western women to India. Looking back over the sixty years since "the first medical woman landed in India," Scharlieb happily conflates mission women and doctors not only with each other but with yet another group: British suffragettes. Her characterization of their collective contributions is worth quoting at length:

> Medical mission work indeed constitutes the most attractive exposition of the work and aims of the Good Physician, but it is also the foundation of the truly educative and statesmanlike endeavours which are meant to draw into one state ancient, spiritually-minded India, and the modern, materialistic West. Indeed it is in the humble mission compound, with its narrow means and its want of earthly prestige, that we find the nearest approximation to the spiritual gladness of the early Christian Church, of those days when all things were held in common, when the poverty of the state was the clearest deed to the wealth of heaven . . . as the authors point out, [these] doctors are almost obsessed by their great mission to
>
> > Take up the White Man's Burden
> >   the savage wars of peace
> > Fill full the mouth of Famine
> >   and bid the sickness cease.[102]

In this remarkable passage, Scharlieb merges Christian evangelism, imperial medical practice, and feminist reform impulses into Rudyard Kipling's all-encompassing exhortation of the "white man's burden"—a responsibility that, despite its originally masculine connotations, she implies has been transformed into a white woman's burden of equal national—and, indeed, world—civilizing importance by the unstinting work of British women doctors. Like all histories, that of British women's mission to make "lady doctors for India" is a complex set of representations that can be retrieved only partially through the narratives that its participants constructed about the past.[103] Working to complicate the picture they have left us helps not just to contextualize those narratives but also to appreciate more fully their authors' investment in them.

10

Recapturing *Jane Eyre*

Reflections on Historicizing the Colonial
Encounter in Victorian Britain

Bertha Mason is introduced into the text by a "low, slow ha! ha!" The sound of this
laughter reverberates through feminist literary history.
—Firdous Azim, *The Colonial Rise of the Novel* (1993)

Even a casual observer of the recent feminist literary and critical scene
must be struck by the fact that *Jane Eyre* is enjoying something of a
renaissance. Whether it is the subject of journal articles or the thematic
linchpin of monographs, Charlotte Brontë's novel of 1847 has obtained a
place in the late-twentieth-century feminist canon—a place its critics stake
and then problematize by questioning the very bases of a feminist canon
itself. Celebration of the female subject (whether it be *Jane Eyre* or Brontë
herself) is not the primary object of this scholarly work; quite the contrary. Understanding how the English heroine has been imagined within,
through, and against the framework of Victorian imperialism—and in
particular, understanding the ways in which Jane's subjectivity was constructed in relation to the ambiguously "colonial" figure of Bertha Mason
—is partly what motivates these new approaches to *Jane Eyre*. Urging
readers of the novel to come to terms with how feminist literary criticism
historically has helped to mask, mute, and even misapprehend the nature
and significance of the colonial encounter between Jane and Bertha is,
therefore, the feminist political project that energizes the kinds of "postcolonial" scrutiny currently being directed at the modern British wom-
en's literary tradition.[1]

I witness this phenomenon as a historian of Victorian Britain, of British imperialism, and of the British feminist movement. I do so also in my capacity as a white, North American feminist woman teaching courses in both women's studies and British history—courses that attempt variously to engage the co-implication of race and gender in ideological formations and cultural identities and to re-map traditional British history so that it attends to the impact of imperialism on what heretofore has been considered almost exclusively "domestic" Victorian culture. As both a researcher and a classroom historian, then, I welcome revisionings of *Jane Eyre* that insist on its colonial context, revisionings that began with Gayatri Spivak's "Three Women's Texts and a Critique of Imperialism" (1985), and will certainly not end with Jenny Sharpe's *Allegories of Empire* or Firdous Azim's *The Colonial Rise of the Novel* (both published in 1993). Among other things, their work permits historians to reconsider *Jane Eyre* as a "colonial" novel, to relocate it in the long tradition of imperial feminist production, and to teach it as part of a critical re-mapping of British cultural geography from the mid–Victorian period to the First World War and beyond. At the same time, although the writings of Brontë and of other white British women from the seventeenth century onward are being recaptured in the service of feminist and postcolonial critique, it is important to ask what this trend signifies.[2] Equally significant, I think, is to consider what other questions this preoccupation with the colonial encounter in British literature prompts and, more difficult still, to begin to imagine what kinds of questions it might foreclose or forestall. What is the relationship between literature and history? How did the dialectic between home and empire work in Victorian culture? Why, and under what historical conditions, has *Jane Eyre* emerged as such a critical center in contemporary scholarship? And not least, how do we put these new readings to use in a variety of North American classroom settings?

What I would like to suggest here is that the revival of *Jane Eyre* provides historians with an opportunity to consider the landscape of Victorian Britain as an imperial culture, a terrain on which the confrontation between Jane and Bertha was and is just one of many such colonial encounters requiring our attention and our critical engagement. It also therefore prompts a reconsideration of the boundaries between the literary and the historical, the social and the cultural, the past and the present —a rethinking that is fruitful for those of us interested in the project of remaking history and recasting its "subjects."

Jane's story is a tempting site on which to ratify claims about both the hegemonic violence of modern subject building and its embeddedness in the colonial encounter. The triumphant scene with Aunt Reed, her child-hood tormentor ("I felt a determination to subdue her—to be her mistress in spite of both her nature and her will"), is important evidence of how Jane's self-fashioning is articulated over time, and not without pleasure, through the languages of mastery and domination over others. Joyce Zonana's recent essay in *Signs* bears out this reading. She insists not only on Jane's invocation of the master–slave relationship as one of the conditions of Jane's subjectivity, but also on the ways in which Brontë Oriental-izes that relation—so that Rochester is the tyrannical sultan and Jane, the resistant seraglio girl.[3] Jane's self-formation occurs in the midst of a variety of colonial matrices and is finally, if not fully, contingent on them. Mr. Rochester's fortunes are embedded in colonial intrigues (his marriage to Bertha, his financial investments in the West Indies), and so are Jane's, both by heritage (her uncle in Madeira) and, toward the end of the novel, by moral conviction and emotional attraction (St. John Rivers). *Jane Eyre* thus becomes one of Spivak's "axiomatics of imperialism," and Brontë's story in turn becomes one of the cautionary tales that give rise to Spivak's quotable caveat, "It should not be possible to read nineteenth-century British literature without remembering that imperialism, understood as England's social mission, was a crucial part of the cultural representation of England to the English."[4]

These re-readings make good historical sense. Britain was, after all, an imperial power in the process of consolidation when Brontë wrote at midcentury. In the wake of the abolition of the slave trade and the grow-ing rhetoric about Britain's "civilizing mission" to the world, men and especially women who were already implicated in the socioeconomics of colonialism by virtue of the spices, sugar, and other goods they purchased were being drawn into the heroic discourses and everyday practices of imperial culture at home.[5] Yet this belated recognition of *Jane Eyre*'s colo-nial inscriptions cannot fully account for what apparently is at stake in recent reconsiderations of the novel. Attention to it has much to do with how its role in feminist literary history is being reassessed at this historical juncture. It is in part because *Jane Eyre* is now understood to have become, at least since Virginia Woolf, a "cult text of feminism" that Brontë's novel is being revived as a subject of radical critique at this particular historical moment.[6] That this is also a moment when many of the foundational texts of Western feminism are being reinterpreted in light of the political claims made by women of color in North America, and postcolonial critics more generally, also helps explain the recurrent attention to Brontë's novel. *Jane Eyre* was produced at a historical moment when British imperialism could not but leave its traces on almost all cultural production, "feminist" productions included. Tracking the ways in which the novel's history as a feminist text has been disconnected from its history as a colonial text is crucial to the work of revision to which recent feminist critics are committed. Making Brontë's complicity with the colonial past visible again is also part of the larger project of requiring Euro-American feminism to confront the colonialist traces of its own history.

As a historian, I was frankly amazed at the tracks *Jane Eyre* has left behind in its trajectory as one of the foundational texts of institutionalized feminist literary criticism in the West. One of the reasons these tracks are so clear is that so many critics make their way to *Jane Eyre* through Woolf's first, and for Cora Kaplan her most devastating, "indictment" of it in *A Room of One's Own* (1928).[7] For Sandra Gilbert and Susan Gubar in *The Madwoman in the Attic* (1979), and for Elaine Showalter in *A Room of Their Own* (1978), *Jane Eyre* functions as a kind of revealed text whose placement at the heart of "the feminist past" helps to establish an individualist heroic narrative as the indicator of feminist struggle. This particular mode of recovery is extremely revealing. As Margaret Ezell has observed, it would seem to bear out Woolf's own claim that "women's books continue each other"—a "thesis of continuity" that underwrites and misrepresents the origins and pathways of women's literary history.[8] It also signifies how synonymous *Jane Eyre* became with the very notion of a women's literary tradition, a tradition that could be recuperated through what Woolf herself lauded as the feminist fore-motherhood of women writers.[9] The quest for a womanist heritage (Showalter's "a literature of their own") was predicated on the belief that gender was a stable, if not monolithic, category of identity and that "the female literary subculture" had a distinctive and separate history from that of the "malestream."[10] Such presumptions about the possibility of recovering a pure, purely female, and implicitly white literary past were themselves the product of a historically specific moment in western feminism, and have certainly not been limited to literary critics. Indeed it might be argued that feminist literary and historical practices colluded in the creation of the category of Woman—a subject difficult, both theoretically and politically, to deracinate from its foundational moorings.[11] Scholars revisiting *Jane Eyre* therefore do us no small service. In addition to reminding us that the birth of the novel and the emergence of women's writing in the West coincided historically with the colonial project, they signal that all feminist practices are historically specific and contestable in the critical present.

Because of this insistence on historicity, Firdous Azim can point to the imperial past out of which *Jane Eyre* criticism has come, and announce with conviction that "the task of defining a coherent and unified female subject that feminist literary criticism set for itself" has come not to an end but, more judiciously, "to a pause." That she pronounces her conviction as a teacher of English in Bangladesh is surely suggestive of the purchase of feminism's historically grounded "politics of location."[12] Nor can she leave *Jane Eyre* at centerstage. Azim and Sharpe (and to a lesser degree, Zonana) enact Sara Suleri's suggestion that "the story of the colonial encounter is a radically decentering narrative," one that in this case displaces the novel from its pride of place in the feminist canon and de-heroinizes Jane while re-materializing Bertha's centrality to the story.[13] All three critics argue for interpretations of Jane that problematize her heroic status as English feminist / female protagonist: she now also represents the ways in which English womanhood was imagined in reference to the British colonial project and, by extension, how English women's writing has been implicated in and shaped by its violence. In thus rearranging *Jane Eyre*'s relationship to the past, Azim and Sharpe clarify the contributions of feminist theory to debates on the historical constitution of modern gendered subjectivity. As Jenny Sharpe succinctly puts it, "the sexed subject of Victorian England is also a racial identity."[14] The fact that they perform this maneuver by insisting on a materialist critique of the social subject marks both their linkages to and departures from Woolf, who claimed white English women's exemption from imperialism[15] even as she pressed future historians to ask under what structural conditions women did or did not manifest their creative potential.[16]

The ramifications of historicizing the colonial meanings of *Jane Eyre* go well beyond the immediacy of Brontë's text. Feminist-historical critiques of the novel's subject—in this case, of the heroine—are part of attempts to re-figure the novel itself not just as a genre enmeshed in capitalist relations but, additionally, as a product of the bourgeois colonial encounter. For Azim this endeavor involves interrogating the subject of "English" and the teaching of English literature as they have been institutionalized in

Britain and its colonies since the nineteenth century.[17] Her work, together with Gauri Viswanathan's *Masks of Conquests*, and Suvendrini Perera's *Reaches of Empire*, takes seriously the call to unmask the collusion of the liberal humanist tradition with imperial ideologies and orientalist assumptions that mobilizes much of the most accomplished work in postcolonial studies.[18] For historians of Victorian culture, Azim's interpolations require an ongoing reevaluation of the subject of "British history" as it has been institutionalized and taught in Britain, in India, and in North America for a century and a half. She is by no means alone in wishing to take up this enterprise. Although much work remains to be done to remap imperial culture at home in Victorian Britain, and while it is important not to be naïve about the institutionalized resistance of academic tradition to challenge and to change, it is clear that revisionists are not always at the margins: feminist and post-colonialist interpretations have shaped debates on the directions that British studies should take in the next century.[19]

Having suggested that the burgeoning of the "new imperial history" promises to sustain debates about *Jane Eyre* and other texts as evidence of the geographical centrality of empire at home, I am nonetheless concerned that too much of the weight of critical attention has fallen on the literary dimensions of the colonial encounter. While historians seeking to confront the impact of imperialism on British culture turn to novels like *Jane Eyre* for use in the classroom or their own research, they are in danger of neglecting or altogether ignoring other dimensions of that encounter in Britain. More significant still, the wide varieties of the colonial encounter "at home" may be eclipsed from view as part of the wider historical context in which *Jane Eyre* and especially Bertha Mason were imagined by Brontë and her readers in the nineteenth century. I want be clear that in making this argument I am not faulting Sharpe, Azim, or others for whom *Jane Eyre* has been of recent historical / literary interest. Indeed, the ways both Sharpe and Azim have chosen to historicize Brontë's work and other Englishwomen's novels have yielded rich insights, and not just about the texts themselves. Nor am I suggesting that literary critics either *should* use or in effect do use "figures of the imagination to personify historical types."[20] I would not like to privilege one kind of historical excavation (the recovery of *Jane Eyre*) over another (the recovery of women's lived experience), or even claim that one is more faithful to purposes of history than the other. This reflects not just a commitment to the dismantling or disciplinary hierarchies but an awareness of how recently, historically speaking, the categories of "Literature" and "History" have been institutionalized as separate sites in the western academy.[21] And yet I *would* like to draw our attention to the proliferation of scholarly work on the colonial encounter in literature compared to the relative lack of work available on colonial encounters in Victorian society—on the streets, in the workplace, in the Houses of Parliament. Literature was and is a crucial site for these meetings and their representations, but it is not the only one. If we wish to (re-)write empire into feminist literary criticism, into British history, and into cultural studies, we must excavate not just *Jane Eyre* but the social subjectivities of Bertha Mason and the historical contexts in which she was imagined both by readers in Victorian imperial culture and by subsequent generations.

Historians of "black Britain" have been at pains for decades to demonstrate that there has been both a nonwhite and a mixed-color population living in Britain since the fifteenth century. Whether they were ayahs, manservants, urbane visitors, unwilling wives or mistresses, runaway slaves, or champions of emancipation like Olaudah Equiano and Mary Prince, colonial peoples and communities were a reality in pre-1945 Britain.[22] Although theirs is a presence still largely absent from historical accounts of traditional British history (even after over twenty years of scholarship on blacks in Britain), people of color—both from the colonies and "native-born"—lived, worked, recreated, died, and were buried in the United Kingdom for centuries before the wave of immigration in the post–Second World War period. They also presumably encountered "fellow Britons" everywhere on the cultural landscape of Victorian Britain, though again the encounter has been only rarely alluded to in historiography about (white) Britain.[23] The recovery of the "creole," "colonial" and/or "black" subject in Victorian culture at home is difficult work, in part because defining the very terms is a vexed enterprise itself. As Jenny Sharpe remarks, at least one scholar of *Jane Eyre* has come to the conclusion that Bertha is black—a conclusion that Sharpe rejects, preferring to see Bertha's creole-ness as a literary stand-in for the West Indian planter aristocracy. More recently, Carl Plasa has remarked on Bertha's presence in the text as "intriguingly equivocal," because his reading allows for the possibility that "creole" can refer to descendants of either Europeans or Africans.[24]

It would be interesting to explore the politics of these readings further; having taught the novel in two very different university classrooms, I can testify that most if not all my students have presumed that Bertha is "black."[25] While the debate on Bertha's race / color / otherness has raged, evidence of the colonial female subject (her speech and her silences) has been rendered even more invisible. Ziggi Alexander's narrative of her own frustrated—and, as of 1990, abandoned—attempts to do a dissertation on "Black Women in Nineteenth-Century Britain" testifies to the structural obstacles facing those who wish to historicize women deemed to be culturally "outside whiteness." She also speaks of the continuing impact of the British colonial past on the availability and accessibility of sources. On the one hand, racism and slaveocratic practices kept many people of color illiterate in Victorian Britain; on the other hand, social history has shown that where there is theoretical creativity and institutional will, the absence of conventional historical evidence need not be prohibitive. We cannot afford, in Alexander's defiant words, to let this state of affairs "lie upon the table."[26] Women and men native to India, Africa, and the Caribbean—as well as people of color and of mixed parentage native to Britain —occupied the landscape of mid–Victorian Britain, either as travelers, temporary residents, or as members of permanent "extracolonial" communities. Bertha Mason is thus not an anomalous figure who happens to structure the narratives of *Jane Eyre* by an accident of history. She is imaginative evidence of the real, elusive presence of "colonial" women in Britain and of the complexities of that descriptor historically considered. The project of historicizing the colonial encounter requires that we rematerialize that presence, and at the same time explain what forces have been and still are at work to make Bertha largely unimaginable except as the figurative "mad-woman in the attic."

What I am suggesting is that when we read and when we teach a text like *Jane Eyre*, we situate it in as full a historical context as possible. Recent work on *Jane Eyre*, together with the growing scholarly literature on gender, feminism, and imperialism, gives us a number of useful directives. Peter Fryer's *Staying Power*, Rozina Visram's *Ayahs, Lascars and Princes*, and Douglas Lorimer's *Colour, Class and the Victorians* are all required reading for situating *Jane Eyre* in the context of domestic race relations in Victorian Britain.[27] Clare Midgley's *Women Against Slavery* read in conjunction with *Jane Eyre* helps flesh out the debates on colonial slavery and women's involvement in colonial affairs that structured Brontë's immediate historical present. Midgley's history also makes clear how black and mulatta women, slave and free, shaped those debates and structured the colonial terrain "at home"—how complicated, in other words, Jane's voice was and is by a variety of other voices.[28] Lata Mani's essay on the uses and abuses of suttee in *Recasting Women*, edited by Sangari and Vaid, and Jenny Sharpe's discussion of suttee in *Allegories of Empire*, similarly contextualize Jane's references to that ritual and her comparison of her own situation and Bertha's to that of the Hindu widow.[29] And, finally, rigorously historicized readings of how women writers before Brontë articulated the European woman's agency "against the ground of a woman of color" (such as Susan Z. Andrade's essay on Aphra Behn's *Oroonoko*) give a much needed backdrop to Victorian representations of the heroine at the same time that they provide evidence of the long colonial literary tradition in which to place novels such as *Jane Eyre*.[29]

Considered together with Jane's story, this recent scholarship raises a number of important questions about the impact of Afro-Caribbean slavery, abolition, and missionary Christianity on a wide variety of social-reform enterprises undertaken in this period, both at home and elsewhere in the empire—even and especially when, as Carl Plasa has remarked, evidence of these historical phenomena appears chiefly as metaphor in *Jane Eyre*.[30] Brontë's novel has the potential to prompt new insights about the relationship of literature to history, about the impact of literary traditions on historical actors (like Brontë), and about the agency of gender and race, women, and colonial peoples in the imperial nation-state in the nineteenth century. *Jane Eyre* might profitably be used in the classroom to enable students to take a long view of Victorian history by reconsidering incidents such as the Mutiny of 1857 in India, the Governor Eyre controversy in Jamaica, and the Boer War as "domestic" incidents that affected women's writing lives, their consciousness as gendered imperial subjects, and their commitments to a variety of colonial reform projects. Here Catherine Hall's *White, Male, and Middle Class*, and any one of the monographs in John MacKenzie's series Studies in Imperialism, provide crucial historical context for examining how mutually constitutive race, class, and gender systems were in the construction of "Englishness" and "Britishness" in the Victorian period.[31] Vron Ware's *Beyond the Pale* and my own work on traditions of feminist imperialism in Britain also help to situate Jane's colonial reform interests in a continuum of Victorian women's and feminists' rhetoric about the civilizing mission in India. It was a rhetoric to be found as commonly in fiction and poetry as in formal political tracts and was not limited to the conventionally "private sphere," as Moira Ferguson's *Subject to Others* illustrates.[32] And not least, the strategic use of research on colonial and former colonial peoples in Britain, together with narratives by people of color such as Frederick Douglass, Mary Prince, and Mary Seacole, who traveled to and throughout the Victorian metropole and influenced Britons' notions of what colonial peoples "looked like," works to help historicize the apparently "dark, abiding, signing" presence of Bertha Mason in the Victorian imagination.[33] The "culture of movement" that colonialism set in motion—and that *Jane Eyre* represents for the late 1840s—reveals that traces of empire, its agents, and its institutions are to be found inside as well as outside Britain proper and requires us to re-evaluate what it meant to be an "imperial Briton" in the nineteenth century.[34]

There is, in short, a wealth of material available to those who wish to read Bertha Mason's story as well as Jane's as part of the history of the English(woman's) novel *and* as part of the social, cultural, and political fabric of "domestic" imperial history itself. If we are careful to interpret the voices of historical actors such as Prince and Seacole in such a way that their representations of their own experiences are read not as if they were transparently "true" but, rather, as partial representations of complex historical realities, then we can negotiate the relationship between literary narratives and historical texts even as we question the boundaries that historically have divided them.[35] Such strategies will help to flesh out Victorian imperial culture and, with it, politically engaged critiques of our own practices as we research and teach historical and cultural contexts other than nineteenth-century Britain. These are among the contributions that feminist scholarship can make to the study of national histories, to the historicizing of national literatures, and to the productive dialogues between practitioners of both. They represent, moreover, an invitation to workers in several different and often disparate quarters of the academy to collaborate in the transformation of British history, British literature, and women's studies classrooms at the same time.

11

From Child Bride to "Hindoo Lady"

Rukhmabai and the Debate on Sexual Respectability
in Imperial Britain

In March 1884, Dadaji Bhikaji petitioned the Bombay High Court to direct that his wife, Rukhmabai, move into his house and live with him. Rukhmabai (1864–1955), a Hindu woman who had married Dadaji in 1876 when she was eleven and he nineteen, had resided for more than a decade with her stepfather, the noted Bombay physician Sakharam Arjun; her mother; and several siblings.[1] Although Dadaji was a distant relative of the doctor's and had visited the house on occasion, their marriage had never been consummated. When Dadaji requested that Rukhmabai live with him, she refused. He filed a case for the "restitution of conjugal rights," thereby initiating one of the most publicized court cases in Bombay—and, indeed, in India—during the nineteenth century.[2]

At first, it looked as if Dadaji's suit would be in vain. Justice Robert Hill Pinhey dismissed the case in the fall of 1885 on the grounds that it was not maintainable, first because restitution could not be claimed where no conjugal relations had occurred, and second, because such claims had no foundation in Hindu law.[3] As Sudhir Chandra has noted, Pinhey so doubted the legality of Dadaji's claim that the counsel for the defense was not even called on at this juncture. After trying unsuccessfully to recover costs, Dadaji appealed Pinhey's judgment, and in March 1886 two appellate judges ordered that the suit be remanded for a decision. Rukhmabai's case was heard this time before a Justice Farran. He determined in March 1887 in favor of the plaintiff, persuaded in part by the argument that while Hindu law did not order restitution, neither did it forbid it. Rukhmabai was ordered to go and live with Dadaji within a month or submit to the court's directive: six months' imprisonment.

Farran's judgment created a sensation among "native" newspapers in India and reached the highest echelons of the British government in India, in part because the Matrimonial Causes Act had removed such penal provisions for English spouses as recently as 1884.[4] Even the viceroy followed the proceedings, cabling A. R. Scoble, the Law Member for India, with this admonition: "I hope you are keeping your eye on the Rukhmabai case. It would never do to allow her to be put into prison."[5] An appeal was filed against Farran's judgment, and there was talk of Rukhmabai presenting her case to the Privy Council in England. In one last attempt by Dadaji to recover costs from Rukhmabai and her family, he agreed to relinquish his claims of July 1888 for a payment of 2,000 rupees—even though, as Meera Kosambi has pointed out, the status of the marriage remained unclear. Because it was not legally dissolved according to Hindu law, some still considered it to be valid and binding.[6] Through the influence of Edith Pechey-Phipson, a British medical doctor practicing in India, and with the patronage of some English feminists in London, Rukhmabai traveled to Britain shortly thereafter, where she trained at the London School of Medicine for Women and qualified as a doctor in 1893. She was appointed head of a women's dispensary at Surat and was eventually hailed as one of India's "pioneering medical women." She died in 1955, "still unattached," as Jim Masselos has recently observed.[7]

Historians of nineteenth-century Indian culture and society have read Rukhmabai's trial as one of the precursors to the Age of Consent Act of 1891, legislation that raised the age of consent for girls in India from ten to twelve years of age, making sexual intercourse illegal with a girl below the stipulated age.[8] The act's most vociferous advocate was Behramji Malabari, a Parsi reformer and Bombay journalist whose "Notes on Infant Marriage and Enforced Widowhood" were published in 1884 and who championed Rukhmabai's cause not just in Bombay but also in Britain. Malabari contended that Britain's claims to be a civilizing power were hollow and its government in India a "sleeping giant" if legislation to ameliorate the fate of child brides were not enacted.[9] Opposition to the act was just as vociferous. B. G. Tilak led the agitation against the act in western India on the grounds that it violated Britain's post–Mutiny pledge of noninterference in religious custom, a campaign that coincided with his emergence as a nationalist leader and with the rise of Hindu militancy in that region. Opposition was also fierce in eastern India, where, according to Dagmar Engels, the mobilization against the Age of Consent Act "played an important part in radicalizing the nationalist movement in Bengal."[10]

The trial of Rukhmabai and the social-reform movements that were galvanized in its wake are thus inextricably bound up with the history of Indian nationalism, especially when we understand how debates about sexual respectability "politicized the restructuring of (hetero)sexual family norms in both colonialist and official nationalist rhetoric in India" from the nineteenth century onward.[11] In keeping with presumptions about Hindu conjugality articulated by male reformers who supported the legal prohibition of *sati* (widow immolation) in 1829 and the Hindu Widow Remarriage Act of 1856, those nationalist leaders who endorsed the legislation of 1891 had their own agendas with regard to the bodies of Indian women, rooting the notion of marital "consent" in biological imperatives (age of puberty) rather than in considerations of choice or compatibility.[12] It is in this context that Tanika Sarkar urges us to consider how Rukhmabai's actions "violently foregrounded the sexual double standard" at the heart of Hindu conjugality and "prised open the imagined community [of Hindus] along the lines of caste and gender." In this respect, the trial helped to reveal the illegitimacy of Hindu male reformers' claims to speak in one voice against British rule and on behalf of "the Indian woman."[13]

While the trial became the stuff of Indian nationalist and social-reform debate in India, it also helped to shape arguments in the imperial metropole about the relationship of Indian women's respectability to the readiness of Indian men for self-government. Rukhmabai's defiance of her husband's claims on her person and her willingness to contest those claims in Bombay's High Court—not to mention in the court of public opinion—was turned by the press in Britain into a spectacle of why the Hindu marriage system represented all that was both wrong with and redeemable about Indian society. Whether conservative, progressive, or even radical in Victorian political terms, newspapers across the United Kingdom all used Rukhmabai's plight to debate the benefits and the limits of the official policy of cultural nonintervention in "native" beliefs and marital practices, as well as to produce their own versions of what the respectable Indian woman looked like. If, as Vinay Lal has argued, the trial in the colonial context was itself a form of knowledge where the micropolitics of imperial power might be played out, the publicity given to Rukhmabai's trial in the United Kingdom helped to foreground for imperially minded Britons the ways in which the regulation of Hindu sexual morality was a "vital political topic" considered crucial to the stability of British rule in India.[14]

This essay argues that the late Victorian metropolitan press "made public" the body of an Indian woman as evidence of the necessity of British imperial rule at the same moment that the Indian National Congress emerged as an organized expression of political will, if not of national sovereignty, in the metropolitan public eye.[15] Implicit in this public display of the Hindu child bride was the argument that, by virtue of their incapacity to protect—or manage—a recalcitrant wife, Indian men were as yet unfit for self-government. The fact that Rukhmabai's trial was turned into a story about women's sexual virtue suggests that contests over morality in the Victorian public realm were not limited to metropolitan Britain but were threaded through the complex domains of imperial culture and the middle-class imperial imagination.[16] British newspaper coverage of the trial of Rukhmabai is one discrete example of how available colonial knowledge was to Western metropolitan audiences at home, as well as how constitutive "domestic" matters—in this case, one Hindu wife's sexual respectability—were to the performance and preservation of colonial rule.

Rukhmabai's case became something of an ideological football, with the stories told about it mobilized by a variety of political actors in both Britain and India. These narratives looped across national boundaries and back again, thereby signaling to the Victorian reading public not just how porous such boundaries might be but also how shaped they were by what Mrinalini Sinha calls "imperial social formation," a geopolitical system in which British cultural forms and practices were not antecedent to empire but were in fact always already constituted by it.[17] In this sense, the late Victorian press was one of the "investigative modalities" through which contemporary imperial ideologies were secured and by which the tenets of the civilizing mission, with its reliance on female virtue and, above all, heterosexual respectability, were naturalized in an age of empire.[18]

The conjuncture of public trials with relatively recent "possibilities of publicity"—that is, print culture—was not new to either the British or the Indian scene. Indeed, making court cases into scandal was crucial to the creation of an imperial public sphere, an imagined and contested space where unseen communities were drawn together through a shared public spectacle that transcended boundaries of "home" and "away" precisely because it brought colonial "domestic" matters directly to the sightline of metropolitan readers.[19] As we shall see, Rukhmabai herself was an important contributor to these debates and the political contests they signified, and not just in India. As she did in Bombay, Rukhmabai used the press in Britain to author her own explanations of what her case signified, what was flawed about the Hindu marriage system, and what should be done to secure socioeconomic emancipation for Indian women, in part by transforming herself from pathetic "child bride" into that indubitably respectable colonial hybrid, "the Hindoo lady." The gendered critique of both imperial rule and indigenous patriarchy that Rukhmabai produced for the English reading public from this peculiarly valenced position meant that in this debate about the fate of empires and civilizations, at least, the speech of an Indian woman had to be reckoned with.

John Cameron MacGregor, the Calcutta correspondent to London's *Times*, introduced Rukhmabai to the English public in March 1886, when her case was being brought before the appellate judges.[20] As A. James Hammerton has pointed out, the Victorian period was an age when "the drama of sexual antagonism in marriage" was a crucial constituent of cultural discourse, as well as the object of relentless public scrutiny.[21] The 1880s was a particularly highly charged moment in this respect, when Britons may well have had the divorce proceedings of Sir Charles Dilke's alleged mistress, W. T. Stead's "The Maiden Tribute to Modern Babylon" prostitution scandal, and the resulting passage of the Criminal Law Amendment Act (which raised the age of consent for girls from thirteen to sixteen and broadened police power over streetwalkers and prostitutes) still fresh in their minds.[22] Readers were referred to Rukhmabai's letters to the *Times of India*, which had been written under the byline "A Hindoo Lady" and excerpted in the *Times* of London the previous year under the same pseudonym. MacGregor, a barrister by training, described the letters, which condemned early marriage and the conditions in which child widows often found themselves, as "striking," "forcible," and "remarkable." Even more remarkable in his view was the sight of Rukhmabai herself. She "has come again prominently before the public," he reported, "as herself affording an example of her own pathetic description of the unhappy lot of her sex in India." From the start, Rukhmabai the child bride was imagined as performing not just the whole condition of Indian women but their pathetic destiny, as well. While narrating the basic facts of the case (their ages at marriage, her upbringing), the *Times* correspondent represented the issue as one of marital incompatibility. Rukhmabai was "well educated . . . a lady of high intelligence," while Dadaji was "said to be little better than a coolie, ignorant, uncultivated, and unable to earn more than ten rupees a month." If class and status were at issue here, so were Rukhmabai's "lady-like" sensibilities—a phrase that conjured up decidedly English aristocratic images and models. "The idea of going to live with such a man," according to the correspondent, "was utterly repulsive to her."[23] When he updated the status of the case some three weeks later, he resumed this theme of the "gifted" lady and the unworthy suitor. After recapping the background details of the court case, he wrote that Rukhmabai refused to live with her husband when he demanded it "on the grounds that she had no voice in the marriage, that he was personally repugnant to her, that his character was bad, that his health was indifferent." While to the *Times* Dadaji was a person of questionable character, Judge Pinhey was, conversely, noble and just, with the best interests of Rukhmabai at heart. Pinhey dismissed the suit without calling the defendant because, it was reported, he believed that "it would be a barbarous, cruel and revolting thing to compel her to cohabit under the circumstances. . . . [N]either law nor the practice of the Courts justified him in making such an order."[24] Even though Rukhmabai was at the center of the case, Dadaji and Pinhey were used to frame this narrative, the colonial native and the English judge facing off over the body of the Indian woman.[25]

It is worth emphasizing that the debate about child marriage set in motion by the *Times* did not arise simply out of the opportunity provided by Rukhmabai's case. Discussions of the good Hindu wife and her "unconquered purity" were crucial to a wide variety of revivalist and reformist debates about politics, religion, and the parameters of colonial rule in nineteenth-century India. In Tanika Sarkar's estimation, not only was the Hindu woman's body "molded from her infancy by the Shastric regimen of non-consensual, indissoluble infant marriage," but her "subjectivity and agency . . . [were] exhausted by this embodiment."[26] Many Indian nationalists, for whom conjugality was the centerpiece of nationalist discourse in the nineteenth century, critiqued the Hindu marriage system (early marriage and compulsory widowhood) even as they placed it at the heart of their sociocultural struggle against Western values and influences. It was at the urging of I. C. Vidyasagar that the government had included an age-of-consent provision in the Penal Code of 1860, making sexual intercourse with a girl younger than ten qualify as rape. In 1878, Mahadev Govind Ranade, a prominent theist and reformer, published an article in an issue of the journal of the Poona Sarvajanik Sabha (a local reform organization) suggesting connections between the problem of child marriage and that of overpopulation. He later exhorted the people of Poona to pledge to raise the age of marriage, and it was he who helped Malabari prepare his "Notes" and present them to Lord Ripon in 1884.[27] We know, too, that Hindu women subjected the Hindu home and its institutional idioms to critical scrutiny from the 1860s onward, especially in the context of Bengali *bhadralok* (respectable folk or class) culture. Rather than extolling the pleasures of early marriage, they emphasized its traumas, including separation from the family home and especially the lack of access to knowledge through education. Although she took some solace in her mother's injunction that leaving home was divine will, Rassundari Devi (one of the first Indian female autobiographers) recalled in 1870 that as a child bride she felt "very much like the sacrificial goat being dragged to the altar, the same hopeless situation, the same agonized screams."[28] Kailashbashini Debi, her contemporary, was more frank about what a girl bride might face. "Conjugal love," she wrote in 1863, "has all but disappeared from our country."[29]

In Britain, it was sati (which had been legally prohibited by the governor-general in 1829) that tended to preoccupy those interested in reforming Indian society, functioning as an exemplar of the pathologies of Hindu tradition and backwardness into the 1880s and beyond—even among those who might have claimed to find it "awe-inspiring."[30] Such presumptions were aided equally by missionary, official / government, and feminist discourses, each of which equated women with tradition and identified traditional gender prescriptions as the chief object of the civilizing mission.[31] The practice of purdah (seclusion) and the existence of the zenana (women's quarters) also played their part in locating women and heterosexual relations at the heart of colonial rule—and in structuring challenges to it by orthodox and progressive reformers in India alike.

If by the end of the 1860s child marriage had also become an important issue in domestic social-reform circles, this was due in large measure to the influence of Mary Carpenter, who popularized many of the observations of missionary men and women who had come before her through her sensational and celebrated two-volume account, *Six Months in India* (1868). For Carpenter, as for many Englishwomen who would take up her call in the later Victorian period, child marriage appeared to be basic to what was wrong with Indian society; it therefore became one of the key ideological and material sites for women's intervention in colonial reform. As she saw it:

> All enlightened natives know . . . that their race is becoming physically deteriorated by the social customs to which they are bound. Mothers at twelve, grandmothers at five-and-twenty, cannot be the parents of a strong and hardy race; nor can those who are confined to sunless apartments to which we have been introduced . . . inspire their children with the genial influences of God's beautiful world . . . those who are acquainted with native customs with regard to women, are well aware why these are too often old and shrivelled [*sic*] when they might be in the full beauty of womanhood—why their minds are dwarfed to the measure of childhood, when they should be able to draw out the faculties of their children, and inspire them with thoughts and principles which should guide their minds through life.[32]

While seclusion in the zenana accelerated the rate at which Indian wives and mothers stultified, early marriage fixed their mental and emotional capacities in childhood, preventing them not just from developing their faculties but, more important, from nurturing their children—part of the "citizenry," the workforce, and the future livelihood of the British empire. Investment in Indian female education became Carpenter's call to action between her return from India in 1868 and her death in 1877 precisely because she saw it as one solution to the problem of child marriage and, with it, of premature sexual relations for Indian girls. It was her hope that if educational opportunities were provided for young Indian girls, it might delay the age of marriage and, in the process, train "native" women to become teachers, inspectors, and even medical doctors so that they might eventually perform the work of "uplift" for Indian—and, by extension, for British—civilization.

Carpenter in fact gleaned much of what she knew about the status of Indian women from "progressive" male Indian reformers whom she met in Britain before her trip to India and during her stay there. Thus, knowledge about child marriage, like that about India more generally, did not originate either "at home" or in the empire but was made available by exchanges and transactions occasioned by movement back and forth.[33] In part because of these influences, Carpenter established the National Indian Association (NIA) in Bristol in 1870. It moved to London under the capable direction of E. A. Manning after Carpenter's death, where it functioned as a clearinghouse for practical schemes for Indian reform until the First World War, chiefly through its monthly periodical, the *Indian Magazine and Review*. Child marriage was frequently cited as the biggest barrier to the intellectual and social progress that was thought to flow from Western education, which was a priority for the NIA. Indeed, reform of child-marriage practices functioned as the linchpin in arguments about the need for Indian girls' education—for example, in the essay "The Evils of Early Marriage," from the issue of the NIA journal of February 1879, where the case against early marriage was essential to the argument in favor of Indian women's improvement.[34]

I would not wish to exaggerate the influence of either the NIA or its monthly organ. Although the *Indian Magazine and Review* occasionally published a list of subscribers in Britain and in India, reliable figures are not available after the 1870s, when circulation was recorded at 1,000.[35] Nor was child marriage the association's main concern. Among its organizational purposes in the fifteen years between its establishment and the Rukhmabai trial was to spread information and knowledge about India in Britain; to host and advise Indian travelers to and students in Great Britain; and, last but not least, to promote women's medical education so that Englishwomen could train as doctors and take improved health care to their Indian "sisters." Moreover, the culture of "women's work for women" that emerged during the 1860s, to which the NIA made an active contribution, helped to characterize the problem of Indian women's education as part of "the woman's question" and frankly to contain it as a "social" or "cultural" rather than a "political" issue. This was not because Carpenter, or Manning after her, did not insist that women's work was the work of the political nation and, indeed, of the empire but, rather, because these arguments did not have the kind of resonance they would acquire in the 1880s and 1890s, when Victorian Britain was more fully in the grip of the crisis of imperial confidence that emerged over the scramble for Africa, the rise of the Indian National Congress, and, at century's end, the Boer War.

Thus, although the NIA had established itself as an important metropolitan authority on the condition of Indian women and had helped to fix child marriage as one of the justifications for British reform intervention, it took the Rukhmabai trial and its publicity in Britain to sensationalize the issue—and to turn the Hindu marriage system into a political issue worthy of the attention of a more mainstream, "national" public at home.

MacGregor of the *Times* set the terms of this national debate when he remarked that "the sympathies of the Court were entirely with the lady" but that "the question they had to try was not one of sentiment, but of law."[36] He predicted that the appellate judges would find against Rukhmabai, and when they did, the *Times* picked up the story again. In March 1887, after Farran had rendered his decision, the *Times* reported that the case was "on the point of reaching a crisis." Rukhmabai started out in this report as the same "refined and highly cultivated lady" she had been when the trial started, again modeling what were held to be quintessentially English female virtues. Dadaji was still "a mere coolie." But now, the English public learned, he was not only "utterly ignorant and uneducated" but "consumptive," as well.[37] All kinds of characterizations were shifting in the wake of Farran's order. The correspondent, who had cast Pinhey as the chivalrous English hero a year earlier, now explained that the appeal judges ruled that he was "wrong in law," and hence they had felt "compelled" to remand the case for trial. This in spite of the fact that they were in "entire sympathy with Rukmibai [*sic*]." Significantly, in its reporting of Farran's decision, the *Times* cast all of the judges as helpless cogs in the wheels of British justice. Farran became "the Court," and the Court "had no option save to pass an order that [Rukhmabai] should join her husband within a month." Even her counsel "could only repeat" his earlier arguments that "his client had never consented to the marriage, and never regarded the man as her husband, [and] that the husband was poor, ignorant and unhealthy." Rukhmabai's punishment was also described in mechanistic terms: "should she fail to do so she would be liable to six months' imprisonment."[38]

This claim of reluctance to enact colonial law did more than echo the theme of empire's unwelcome burden. It worked to all but erase both Rukhmabai's agency in contesting Dadaji's claims on her *and* her determination to resist the claims of the colonial state once she was sentenced, for, as her lawyers had made clear, she anticipated that prison might be the consequence, and she went to court anyway. Rukhmabai herself is the absent presence in these accounts. As Lata Mani has argued with respect to Indian women and the sati debates of the early Victorian period, metropolitan discourse about Rukhmabai represented her as emblematic but passive, the ostensible subject of debate but in fact the passive object on which Indians' claims to civilization depended and on behalf of which British justice must therefore proceed.[39] The *Times* ended its account by lamenting the fact that "hardly a single voice . . . has been raised in her favour" except that of Malabari, and thus, as a result, the Bombay court was "reluctantly compelled to enforce" the "cruel law."[40]

What followed was a host of letters to the editor explaining the workings of the law, debating Rukhmabai's sentence, and often articulating, whether implicitly or explicitly, a connection between the body of the Hindu woman and the stability of British rule in India. Someone who signed himself "Judge," writing from the East India Club, St. James's Square, London, had been a magistrate in India, where he claimed to have "had to decide a great number of these cases" and to "have tried all sorts of devices to set the girls free." In most of those, "The difficulty has arisen from a preferred lover, and not from difference of education or position." His experience had shown him that "in Eastern climates girls are precocious, and, unless early settled in her future home, the girl is almost certain to disgrace her family, and the result of such an event is either her murder or such loss of honour to the family that they will never be able to hold their heads up again." Early marriage, in other words, was the right and proper solution to Oriental women's sexual promiscuity—a solution "Judge" approved of the British courts for enforcing. "It is this feeling [of shame over loss of honor]," he went on to say, "which makes the Indian opinion so decided against any change," a fact that required that "we . . . elect to maintain their customs, however much they are opposed to ours." According to "Judge," the "real mistake" in Rukhmabai's case was "educating her so as to make her unfit company for her husband, or rather in so educating her as to make her think only of her own comfort and not recognize her great mission to spread education and information among her humbler sisters." If these two arguments appear to be somewhat at variance, they resonated with a critique of women's education in Britain prominent during this period: that too much learning alienated women from their wifely and domestic duties, making them selfish and self-serving.[41] But "Judge" did not leave it at that. He argued that pity for

Rukhmabai was misplaced because she would not be sent to jail as a criminal "but . . . only confined with the civil prisoners." Moreover, "At the end of six months she is free, except that she cannot marry else-where." He urged the public to keep in mind that this was not too great a price to pay "for not setting aside a custom so dear to Indian opinion."[42]

"Judge's" was not the only legal opinion proffered in letters to the editor, although it may certainly be counted as among the least sympa-thetic to Rukhmabai. In fact, much of the correspondence to the *Times* was concerned with interpreting the relationship between Hindu law and English law as a means of explaining what had happened in the various phases of the trial.[43] F. L. Latham, advocate-general of Bombay and one of Rukhmabai's defense lawyers, insisted that while Hindu law "enjoin[ed] infant marriage, and, like other primitive laws, declare[d] the absolute subjection of the wife to her husband," at the same time it provided "no legal process by which a wife could be compelled to return to her hus-band's society if unwilling." The possibility of conjugal rape is alluded to here but never directly addressed. If anything, it is the law that intrudes where it is not welcome, acting, as Upendra Baxi has argued, not just as the state's representative but as its phallic emissary as well.[44]

It was Latham's contention that, "unfortunately for [Rukhmabai], En-glish law stepped in"—that is, the English judges had relied on the prece-dents set by the "old Ecclesiastical Courts," precedents that enforced "the duties resulting from the marriage ties and made matters of conscience subject to the supervision of the Church." Latham reiterated the claim that the High Court of Bombay "felt that it had no choice" but to follow the precedents, yet he also reminded his readers that recent English legis-lation had ceased to compel a wife or husband to return to "conjugal society" and used suits for restitution of conjugal rights only to deal with issues of marital property. His outrage was thus reserved for administra-tors of the Indian courts, who seemed incapable of modernizing the law quickly enough so that it could protect an Indian woman from her hus-band's unwelcome "society." "It does seem monstrous," he wrote to the *Times*, "that the Indian Courts should be compelled to administer to Hindoos remedies based on English precedents which have been found intolerable in England, and which were actually abolished here before Rukhmabai's case was tried." He called the order of the Bombay court "the re-enactment in India of the English Act" and questioned its applica-bility to Rukhmabai's case.[45]

Friedrich Max Müller, a German professor of Sanskrit at Oxford University who was well known for his Orientalist admiration of India's "golden" (Vedic) age, agreed. For him, too, the law was the offending party, capable of doing the kind of violence to the body of the Hindu woman that could not be named but that circulated nonetheless throughout discussions of Rukhmabai's case. He argued on 25 April 1887 that "the case of Rukhmabai has really very little to do with Indian law," but his was more of a defense of English law than a criticism of its extended purview, as Latham's letter had been:

> Let the Indian Law be what it is, let public opinion in India sanction the sale and so-called marriage of children of three or four years of age, let those who, like Rukhmabai and others revolt against this degrading slavery submit to being boycotted or outcasted, but what has English law to do with such abomination? The Hindoos themselves protest against foreign tribunals interfering with their sacred customs of marriage. Why, then should English law offer to aid in the restitution of conjugal rights, supposing that conjugal rights exist? . . . Whatever the High Court may have decided, the sooner English judges wash their hands of such iniquities the better for the good repute of English law.[46]

Müller, like Latham above, was unwilling to admit that, although marriage was based on contract, the state, via law, was in fact the enforcer of marital relations; nor was either prepared to confront the role of the colonial state in the "abomination" to which Rukhmabai was subjected. To do so would have required both Englishmen to admit not just the failure of the bourgeois colonial project but also its violation of the very notion of contract relations. As their contemporary W. W. Hunter put it, the chief justification of Anglo-Indian law (and hence of British rule) was the creation of "a common system of law applicable to all." At stake, in other words, was the rule of law conceived of as "the use of standardized impartial procedures for the settlement of disputes."[47] Here, as in Latham's letter, the connection between Rukhmabai's reputation and the "good repute of English law" threatened to unmask the disinterestedness of English legal dicta by revealing their corrupting influences on a particular community—Hindu women—that was supposed to be protected under colonial rule.[48]

Müller's letter prompted a letter of support from "R. H. P." (most likely Judge Pinhey), who wrote to the *Times* to correct the misapprehension he feared lingered in the public's mind that his original decision had been taken purely out of sympathy for Rukhmabai (an impression readers might well have gleaned from the *Times* correspondent's coverage) rather than from carefully considered legal opinions. In elaborating on his opinions, Pinhey implied that it was English law that was in danger of being corrupted if its now rejected statutes (specifically those pertaining to the restitution of conjugal rights) were being resurrected for use in India.[49] Müller, for his part, objected to the very concept of "restitution of conjugal rights" on the grounds that it was an idiomatic expression of "English legal language." According to him, it was "a phrase utterly unknown in Hindoo law" and "quite inapplicable" in Rukhmabai's case. In a letter to the *Times* in August 1887, he also contended that Rukhmabai's case had been aggravated by English law. "Formerly, a woman who committed this so-called breach of contract was under the ban of society. She was *patita*, fallen, but she was not exposed to violence, and the idea of sending her to prison, like a common criminal, never entered the minds of native lawgivers." Müller gave the impression that English judges rushed in where Indian men and Hindu pundits feared to tread. "No Indian Lawyer," he went on, "ever thought of forcing a woman to marry against her will by force of imprisonment, and this anomaly and aggravation caused by a mixture of Indian and English law has only to be pointed out to be removed from the English Code."[50]

Müller wrote four letters in all to the *Times* during the period of Rukhmabai's trial, and his opinions in turn generated several replies.[51] But if he defended Hindu law in this instance, he did so only to make way for his conviction that legal recourse was not the ultimate solution to the problems raised by Rukhmabai's case. Education was what was called for, and Rukhmabai was proof of its success, for it was exposure to Western learning that had made her capable, in Müller's view, of becoming "the best judge . . . herself" of her marriage choice.[52] Müller thereby vindicated the bourgeois civilizing mission (which since Thomas Babington Macaulay's service on the Supreme Council of India had aimed at the internalization through education of English values by brown-skinned subjects) and made the person of Rukhmabai into "evidence" in the case against too rapid change by government intervention. Most of the letter writers were staunchly against government interference through legislation, with one J. Scott stating unequivocally that "the Indian people cannot be made moral by an Act of Parliament."[53]

Others saw in the Rukhmabai case an opportunity to move the discussion away from legislation to philanthropy and, in so doing, to advance specific schemes for the improvement of the condition of Indian women. Müller again led the discussion, first by insisting that the trial called on the conscience not of English judges or lawyers but of Englishwomen to protest that "the strong arm of the English law should not be rendered infamous in aiding and abetting unnatural atrocities" such as early marriage.[54] He later warmed to this theme, suggesting that Rukhmabai's case was but one among many and that, even after it was over, "much remain[ed] to be done, not indeed by government, but by private enterprise. It is chiefly due to English education that the lot of the women of India has become intolerable to many of them. It is therefore the duty of English philanthropists to try to mitigate the misery of those who are bearing the brunt of the battle between effete India, or rather, Mahommedan, custom and European enlightenment."[55] Indian men were banished from the picture, leaving the education and training of Indian women to English colonial reformers, who were chiefly women.

In the process of explicating the finer points of Hindu and Indian law, Müller described the "condition" of Indian women for readers of the *Times*, providing census statistics on widows and emphasizing that those younger than fourteen numbered almost 300,000 in 1881. He quoted Pandita Ramabai (the learned high-caste widow well known to the colonial reform public for her commitment to the uplift of Indian women), as well as a Hindu pundit with whom he was in correspondence, on the plight of Hindu widows and suggested that money be raised through charitable organizations in Britain to establish a widows' home in India.[56] Letters came in to support this idea, especially after Ramabai wrote to the *Times* herself on 27 September 1887, explaining in great detail her own scheme for a child widows' home and calling for donations to be directed to E. A. Manning's address, the site of the NIA offices in London.[57] Ramabai emphasized the plight of child widows, thus linking her particular cause with Rukhmabai's in the public mind—a cause she had already publicized in her book, *The High-Caste Hindu Woman*.[58] Ramabai's letter in turn prompted several others, including one from Frances Power Cobbe, a social reformer and "one of the veteran workers in the woman's cause," who pledged her support to Ramabai's project and advertised Ramabai's book to metropolitan sympathizers.[59] In this sense, the so-called plight of the Indian woman, which was such a staple of Victorian feminism, received national attention at this juncture, reaching audiences well beyond those limited to women's emancipationist periodicals in Britain and coinciding with the beginning of campaigns on the part of the Ladies National Association led by Josephine Butler to extend protests against the Contagious Diseases Acts to Britain's colonial possessions and especially to India.[60]

The debate that followed in the wake of Rukhmabai's trial thus took off in a variety of directions, moving public attention beyond the question of child marriage per se to "the problem of Indian women" and its relationship—practical and symbolic—to the projects of empire. Meanwhile, the *Times* continued to update its readers on events in Bombay related to the case. The newspaper covered Dadaji's legal maneuvers (he sued a newspaper in Bombay and the family of Rukhmabai for libel in the summer of 1887, for example); the development and progress of the Rukhmabai Defence Committee (founded in Bombay to help the defendant with court costs); and, increasingly after 1887, the status of several other legal cases involving child brides and the law (including several in which girl wives were apparently murdered by their husbands).[61] The *Times*'s correspondent in Calcutta remarked that it was due to "the absence of more exciting political topics [that] Rukhmabai's case continues to attract much attention" in India.[62] While it was true that one of the biggest trials of the century in Britain was over (Stead's prosecution for procuring a young girl to research "The Maiden Tribute to Modern Babylon"), there was plenty of other "big" news to occupy Britons during the Rukhmabai case, including the Irish Home Rule controversy, continued fighting in Sudan in the wake of General Gordon's death at Khartoum, and, not least, preparations for and celebrations of Queen Victoria's Golden Jubilee. It was nonetheless observed that "the case of Rukhmabai continues to excite the interest of the British public."[63] Coverage in the capital city was not limited to the *Times*. The NIA's *Indian Magazine and Review* reported on the proceedings of both the case and the Rukhmabai Defence Committee, urging supporters to contribute by sending donations for the fund to Manning's London address. It also reprinted a long excerpt from the *Bombay Gazette*, which recorded the final settlement of the case.[64]

The influence of the *Times* was nonetheless considerable in shaping how news of the trial was reported in Britain, since other newspapers and periodicals depended on it almost exclusively for their information about the Rukhmabai case. The *Pall Mall Gazette*, for example, followed the trial in its "Occasional Notes" section until Dadaji had settled the suit in the summer of 1888. But it tended to rely on the *Times*'s correspondent in India, often reprinting in toto his accounts of the marriage law agitation or his details of the trial.[65] In fact, the practice of extracting from metropolitan weeklies and dailies was standard in the Victorian period, thus affirming Marilyn Strathern's recent contention that knowledge production is in part a process of continuous re-contextualization—a phenomenon that in this case occurred not just between India and Britain but also from site to site within the empire's capital.[66] There was little editorializing when this happened, except for the invocation of the rather hackneyed conviction that "the case will deal a deathblow to the pernicious system of infant marriage, and mark an important step in the progress of social reform in India."[67]

Rukhmabai's trial prompted special attention to Indian marriage customs in the *Pall Mall Gazette*, including one two-page essay titled "Marriage Reform in India" by Pandit Sivanath Sastri in August 1888.[68] As it had not with the *Times*, the settlement of the case did not put an end to coverage about related issues—in part because the *Pall Mall Gazette*'s editor was Stead, who had been so instrumental in sensationalizing his child prostitution scandal. Consequently, the *Pall Mall Gazette* followed cases of child brides in distress after the Rukhmabai case had been decided, including one incident in Patna that was telegraphed in by Alfred Dyer, editor of the *Bombay Guardian*. It looked at first as if the whole question of procuring underage girls—the very issue that had fueled the "Maiden Tribute" controversy—was going to be revisited in the Indian context, with sensational headlines ("Alleged Legal Outrage in India") and rhetorical questions to the secretary of state for India ("Will Sir John Gorst justify this proceeding on the ground that we must pay respect to native customs?") appearing in the paper.[69] The *Pall Mall Gazette* tracked the case for a week, until the particulars revealed that it was an incident about prostitution rather than about procurement per se.[70]

Women's magazines also covered Rukhmabai's case, again relying heavily on the accounts of the *Times* correspondent. Sudhir Chandra has analyzed how *Queen* blamed both Dadaji and the orthodox Hindu community for Rukhmabai's troubles, but not without chastising the more progressive "natives" for bowing to the pressure of public meetings and agitations. Although *Queen* admitted that interference could not be countenanced at this time, the magazine assured its readers that change in India could not but occur "with ever-accelerating velocity, and . . . the time may not be far distant when such outrage on human liberty, as evidenced in the case of Rukhmabai, may be forever at an end." The author of *Queen*'s account worked harder than most to eclipse the role of English law in Rukhmabai's case to pathologize indigenous religious statutes, but he or she shared the more general conviction circulating via the metropolitan press that "the colonized were to be regenerated in spite of themselves."[71] The *Englishwoman's Review*, whose coverage of Indian news was quite extensive because of its ties to the *Indian Magazine* and its support of medical education for Englishwomen in India, noted the Bombay trial and recapped almost verbatim what had been written in the *Times* about the suit, the plaintiff, and the appeals.[72] Like Pinhey had done in his letter to the *Times,* the author of "The Hindoo Marriage Law" for the *Englishwoman's Review* expressed concern that "the exact position of affairs is not understood at home." She was virtually alone among the sources cited here in worrying about what would happen to Rukhmabai once the six months' imprisonment order had been given. In this event, the author pointed out, "Her troubles will not necessarily be at an end, for if her husband again requests her to live with him, and she again refuses, a fresh cause of action will arise, and the whole miserable business may be repeated over and over again after the expiration of each term of imprisonment."[73] Should this occur, the *Englishwoman's Review* hoped, "The force of English and Anglo-Indian opinion will compel the Government to alter the law." In the meantime, "The sympathy shown by the British Press and public is fully appreciated here."[74]

If the *Englishwoman's Review* and *Queen* were the only women's periodicals to follow the case, this was because they were among the few of their kind in this period. The *Women's Penny Paper* did not begin until the fall of 1888, and when it did, an advertisement for Rukhmabai's fund-raising efforts for her travel and medical education in Britain appeared in one of its first issues.[75]

The publicity given to the trial of Rukhmabai cannot compare with the sensation caused by her contemporary Mona Caird's critiques of marriage. Although the Bombay court's decision did generate a number of letters to the editor of the *Times*, the correspondence could not begin to approximate the 27,000 letters sent to the *Daily Telegraph* in the 1880s in response to the question, "Is Marriage a Failure?"[76] Rukhmabai's case also competed in the public eye with the trials and tribulations of Georgina Weldon's divorce case and the spectacular revelations of both Lady Colin Campbell's divorce trial and Sir Charles Dilke's troubles.[77] Nonetheless, the *Times*—"that representative of John Bull," as one Indian observer dubbed it—published a variety of letters to the editor related to the trial, editorialized about her plight, and continued to update its readers on relevant events in Bombay.[78] Publicity was not, significantly, limited either to the *Times* or to other newspapers in the capital city of the empire. Papers as diverse as the *Daily Graphic*, the *Echo*, the *Aberdeen Observer*, the *Western Daily Press*, and the *Manchester Examiner* covered the story, and many of these were less restrained than the *Times* in the rhetoric they used to characterize Rukhmabai and Dadaji, who became tragic characters and figures of romance and melodrama across the provincial press. Although the *Bradford Observer* referred to Rukhmabai as "a Hindoo girl," most papers emphasized her ladylike status, refinement, and education. The *Bristol Evening News* called her "a damsel," and the *Scotsman* called her "the heroine of a battle which is . . . fought not only for herself but for her countrywomen."[79] As in representations offered by the *Times*, the more cultivated Rukhmabai became, the farther Dadaji sank into an irredeemably coolie-like status. A contributor to the *Western Daily Press* declared him an "ignorant and degraded peasant"; readers of the *Aberdeen Observer* were told that he was "an ignorant and idle boor"; and to the *Bradford Observer* he was "very vulgar indeed."[80] The language of class, as marked here by work (coolie labor), thus bore the burden of marking the masculine body as a carrier of disease and (sexual) violence, even as the pleasure to be derived from such a sexually charged spectacle was broadcast throughout metropolitan Britain.[81]

Neither Rukhmabai nor Dadaji was unaware of these representations; while the case was being turned into melodrama for British audiences in Britain, they were each publishing explanations of their conduct and defending their good names in newspapers in Bombay and all over India.[82] Dadaji was particularly incensed by "the intellectual degradation with which the fiction-loving journals accredit me," among which he included the *Times*. He insisted that he was a man of property, education, and good health and that Rukhmabai was not his "intellectual superior" and reminded his "co-religionists" that "Hindu marriage is a sacrament and not a civil contract."[83] Rukhmabai, in turn, rejected his "base suggestions," questioned his claims to property and means, and argued that financial gain, not concern for the morality of marriage or Hindu law, was at the heart of his restitution suit.[84] Their testimonies, which were published in the *Bombay Gazette* in June 1887, make clear that many of the details of the case—namely, that Dadaji lived with an uncle who had had a mistress for fourteen years and that this was among the reasons that Rukhmabai judged him unsuitable to reside with—were kept from the British public, even though they were common knowledge in both the Anglo-Indian (British-owned) and English-speaking (Indian-owned) press in India.[85] Indeed, despite the widespread coverage Rukhmabai's trial received in the British press, as much was suppressed about the context of the case as was publicized. Colonial knowledge, then, was not circulated just at the heart of the empire. In this instance, its circulation was carefully managed and in such a way as to suggest that Rukhmabai's case was the justification that progressive Indian reformers needed to present a case against child marriage to the government of India when, in fact, the mechanisms of its publicity and the disinterestedness of its publicizers were being interrogated throughout the subcontinent.[86]

Despite the control exercised in Britain over Rukhmabai's attempts to influence public opinion in Britain via her letters to the *Times of India*, Rukhmabai herself had made use of the public space afforded to her by the *Times* and other metropolitan papers to articulate her own version of events and her own ideas about what kind of action was appropriate to ameliorate the condition of Indian women. Her first appearance in the *Times* came in July and September 1885 when, as was mentioned earlier, she wrote under the pseudonym "A Hindoo Lady." MacGregor, the *Times*'s Calcutta correspondent, extracted only short selections from Rukhmabai's letters, which had been published in greater length in the *Times of India*.[87] Significantly, it was the National Indian Association that reprinted them in their totality in Britain. The first one appeared in the September 1885 issue of the NIA's journal, with this accompanying prefatory note:

> We mentioned in the last *Journal* a remarkable letter by a Hindu lady on Child Marriages which had appeared in the *Times of India*. We now give the [first] letter, as an important contribution to the discussion of the subject. A certain degree of exaggeration must, we are told, be allowed for in regard to the generalisations, which the writer makes from her own experience, and some of her suggestions might not be

practical; but there must be much truth in the facts and arguments put forward, and we hope that this touching appeal will not be without effect in regard to customs which so greatly need reform.[88]

Thus was the "speaking voice" of "the Indian woman" stage-managed—produced out of specific institutional locations for specific colonialist purposes.[89] Rukhmabai herself admitted to the mediation of a "gentleman" friend in the first paragraph of her letter, someone who "kindly looked over and corrected it, where he thought correction was necessary." (This may well have been Malabari.) In the body of her letter, however, she also anticipated the possibility that her plea might be dismissed as hyperbole. "My English readers," she wrote, "can hardly conceive the hard lot entailed upon Hindu women by the custom of early marriage. They might think the picture a little too highly coloured, but I assure them that there is not, at least intentional, exaggeration."[90]

Rukhmabai's argument consisted of three interrelated parts: the differential effect on men and women of early marriage; the linkage between reform of the custom and women's improvement through education; and the need for government intervention in reform. In her view, the disproportionately negative impact of child marriage on women was crucially linked to the question of women's education, for early marriage rarely prevented boys from carrying on their studies, whereas girls married at eight could continue their studies only until age ten (with the onset of puberty). If they wished to go on after that, they would need the permission of their husbands' families. "But even in these advanced times," she pointed out, "and even in Bombay—the chief centre of civilisation—how many mothers-in-law are there who would send their daughters [sic] to school after they are ten years old?" She chastised those indigenous elite reformers who championed women's education and yet resisted changes in marriage customs. "Unless this state of things is changed, all the efforts at higher female education seem like putting the cart before the horse."[91]

Rukhmabai returned several times to the theme that Hindu men failed to take debates about child marriage seriously because they failed to understand its impact on women *as women*. Her claim—since "*men* among Hindus have much more freedom of action than *women*, they are indifferent to the social reforms which prejudicially affect the other sex"—implied not just that male reformers did not see women as gendered beings who were discriminated against on the grounds of sexual difference, but that they did not see themselves as men with gender-specific privileges, either, a rare enough argument against patriarchy in the nineteenth century. Rukhmabai admitted the influence that Malabari's "Notes" had had on her thinking, and she defended him against charges that, as a Parsi, he was a "foreigner" to Hindu customs and communities. Like Malabari, she was persuaded that it was the duty of the British government in India to take action:

> If, Sir, Government shirks its responsibility and gives up this matter, it may be, in deference to the wishes of these gentlemen [male elites resistant to reform], there is not the smallest chance of our people taking it up themselves for years to come, even if then; and in that case, though we are, by God's grace, living under the beneficent rule of her Most Gracious Majesty the Queen-Empress, there can be no one left to protect the women of India from the tyranny of these abominable customs.[92]

This was followed by a five-point outline of what such legislation might look like, including provisions to raise the age of marriage to fifteen for girls and twenty for boys and one to require young men who married below the stipulated age to give up their right to attend a university. Although Rukhmabai's essay had begun as a letter to the editor, by the end she was addressing the leaders of the Hindu community who claimed to have the best interests of Indian women at heart:

> I entreat you, gentlemen . . . to co-operate with Government in emancipating your sons and daughters from the social thraldom under which they groan. If you succeed in bringing about this salutary reform, [the] spread of education, [the] developments of arts and sciences, the production of an able-bodied and strong-minded race of men and women—in fact, the mental and material prosperity of India, will follow as a matter of course, and India will revert to its once proud position in the scale of nations.[93]

Rukhmabai's second letter, which the NIA reprinted in December 1885 under the title "Widow Remarriage," insisted on the linkages between early marriage and the problem of widowhood for Hindu women by focusing on the condition of early widowhood.[94] Again, her critique went to the heart of the matter: men's blindness to the humanity of all women and to the impact of men's privileged practices on themselves and others. "Instances are not rare," Rukhmabai wrote sardonically, of the edifying spectacle of a green old man of sixty, who is visited with the great misfortune of losing his second or third wife, preparing to play the young bridegroom, and sending his creatures out to seek a girl of ten or eleven to bless the remaining days of his natural life. . . . [N]ow, this same worthy gentleman who is so solicitous to gratify his vanity (to term it in the mildest way) or, as he would put it innocently enough, to provide a guardian angel against the infirmities of old age . . . this same gentleman is philosophically rigid in the case of his widowed daughter or granddaughter of 15. . . . [T]he comfort [offered to her] . . . is . . . "My darling . . . fate has ordained this widowhood for you and what human effect can upset the decrees of fate!"

"A noble exhortation, indeed," Rukhmabai continued. "But alas! it comes from the lips of one whose conduct belies its sincerity." As she had appealed to the British government in her first letter, Rukhmabai closed here with an appeal to "Englishmen" to wonder at such "gross hypocrisy" and "wickedness" as the Hindu marriage system.[95]

These are powerful arguments, which demonstrated Rukhmabai's capacity to evaluate critically both indigenous patriarchy and India's "reform" communities. In an era when speaking in public blurred the line between respectable and "public" women (prostitutes) in Britain—and when upper-caste Indian women's sexual respectability was contingent on seclusion—Rukhmabai's letters to the *Times* must be viewed as both courageous and dangerous to her reputation as "a Hindoo lady."[96] Rukhmabai was not the only Indian woman to take a public position on such questions. As Meera Kosambi has documented, Anandibai Joshee, a Maharashtrian woman who became the first female Indian medical doctor, was an outspoken critic of child marriage as early as 1880 and an advocate of interference by the colonial state fully ten years before the passage of the Age of Consent Act in 1891.[97] According to Padma Anagol-McGinn, Indian women were not consulted when the government canvassed the provincial leaders for evaluations of the effects of child marriage in their localities. But in Bombay Presidency, they made a cogent and impassioned case for government intervention in child marriage in their magazines and via their social-reform organizations in the wake of the High Court's decision, with Rukhmabai and her countrywoman Pandita Ramabai among the most prominent participants.[98] Yet Rukhmabai was perhaps unique among them in that her refusal of her husband's conjugal rights constituted a kind of civil death unlike that of widowhood or even conversion, a position that seriously jeopardized her status as a respectable "public woman."[99]

She took advantage of one other occasion during the height of attention to the court case to address the public in Britain. On 9 April 1887, a letter from Rukhmabai appeared in the *Times*. It was printed with a cover letter by the bishop of Carlisle, whose sister had been in correspondence with Rukhmabai. The bishop prefaced the letter by indicating that Rukhmabai did not know that he was going to publish her letter and that he himself (or his sister) had deleted several sections of it; he was, he announced, sending the letter "as received—with the exception of the rectification of a few words in respect of orthography and the omission of one or two sentences which are suitable for a private letter but not for a public utterance." After giving a précis of the practice of child marriage in India, Rukhmabai offered her own version of her life leading up to "my unfortunate trial." In this narrative, Dadaji is characterized not as a "coolie" but as a schoolboy who "fell into bad companies," "was attacked by consumption," and was so sickly that "he was confined to his bed for three continuous years, in such a state that he was not expected to live another season." She, meanwhile, left school at eleven but

> began to learn English at home . . . [D]ay by day my love for education and social reform increased, and I continued to pursue my studies as much as I could. . . . [B]y aid of the little education which I had been able to gain, I began seriously to consider the former and present condition of our Hindoo women, and wished to do something, if in my power, to ameliorate our present sufferings. On the other hand, . . . habits of the man with whom I had been given in marriage added more to my natural distaste for married life.

According to Rukhmabai, it was her stepfather who "resolved not to send me to [Dadaji's] house to live as his wife." As for Dadaji, he "seemed indifferent to the matter . . . but by some former disputes between the leaders of our caste and the constant instigations of wicked people (very common in India), and in the hope of getting my little money, he was induced to file a suit asking me to go and live as his wife."[100]

Whereas the *Times* correspondent had cast her as simply a "refined" lady, Rukhmabai made it clear that she intended to be a reformer with the improvement of Indian women on her agenda. In doing so, she did not so much reject the model of the English lady—as she attempted to demonstrate how bound up the model was for her with commitments to colonial reform—but to supplant it with a persona that evoked Indian mores but could count as equally respectable. This was the "Hindoo Lady" of her pen name, which provided (initially, at least) the cover of anonymity as well as the stamp of reformist legitimacy, in Britain if not also in India.[101] According to one English contemporary in India, she had never even wanted to marry. "I only want to study—that is my wish," Rukhmabai told Nora Scott. "To learn and help the native ladies of all races."[102] Rukhmabai suggested that the trial itself was part of that work, an angle that had never been hinted at by the *Times*. Justice Pinhey's decision was "humane," and, in her view, "If it had been supported, [it] would have altered the fate of millions of daughters of India, and the longed-for freedom would have been easily secured." Rukhmabai reiterated here what she had written in her letters to the *Times of India* before she had been identified to English audiences at home as their author —namely, that it was the "inevitable duty of the present Government" to reform the matrimonial laws. "The only way to face the difficulties," she insisted, "is the law reform," thus plainly declaring herself in alignment with those reformers inside India, and outside it, who wanted government intervention in the custom of child marriage.[103]

In her concluding paragraphs, Rukhmabai appealed as she had in India to "our beloved Queen Victoria's Government, which has its world-wide fame for best administration." In a shrewd rhetorical maneuver, Rukhmabai reminded her correspondent that 1887 was the year of the Jubilee. "At such an unusual occasion," she inquired, "will the mother listen to an earnest appeal from her millions of Indian daughters and grant them a few simple words of change into the books on Hindoo law—that 'marriages performed before the respective ages of 20 in boys and 15 in girls shall not be considered legal in the eyes of the law or brought before the Court.' . . . This Jubilee year must leave some expression on us Hindoo women, and nothing will be more gratefully received than the introduction of this mere sentence into our law books."[104] The bishop of Carlisle told the editor of the *Times* that "no words can plead [Rukhmabai's] cause more eloquently than her own." But he was only partly right, because her speech was not purely her own. It had been both tampered with and re-presented before the public even read it. Carlisle's certainty "that I shall carry you, Sir, and all your readers with me, when I say that the appeal of the poor afflicted Hindoo woman to the Queen, with the reference to the

Jubilee, is infinitely pathetic" meant that Rukhmabai's own words had to compete with his determination to recast her in the role of the pathetic and "defenceless" Indian woman—a particular remake, as it were, of the delicate English lady.[105]

By appealing to the queen-empress and her worldwide imperial government, Rukhmabai demonstrated her determination to make her case and, with it, the question of child marriage an issue of the highest political importance, a determination that had begun with her first act of resistance and of which her letter in the *Times* was a particularly persuasive example. She did so in a metropolitan context where newspapers such as the *Times*, when it deigned to recognize the Indian National Congress (INC) at all, consistently cast aspersions on its legitimacy as a representative political, as opposed to social, body.[106] In the same columns in which the *Times* gave updates on the trial between 1886 and 1888, it also reported a variety of "native" protests against the government's legal interference with the custom of child marriage throughout India. These were abbreviated stories that formed part of the longer daily report on events in India, but they characterized the protests as "agitations" and "outbursts of fanatical hostility" that were "boisterous and . . . absolutely uproarious."[107] Although the INC, which had had its first annual meeting less than a year before, was often not even mentioned by name, its meetings and activities were being covered extensively in the *Times* during the period of the trial in Bombay, and not in a very sympathetic manner. The Indian correspondent referred to it as "the so-called National Congress," and when Indian delegates visited Britain to canvass for members of Parliament supportive of their cause in the general election of 1885, they were referred to as "ambitious agitators" who were unready for self-government.[108] The meetings of the second Congress of 1886 were labeled "demonstrations," with the *Times* praising the Central Mahomedan Association for declining to participate with the skeptical remark, "It is difficult to see what good the promoters can hope to effect."[109] Most significant for our purposes, the *Times* tried to use the outburst of opinion for and against Rukhmabai in India to discredit the claims then being made on the British government and on British opinion by Indian nationalists for self-rule. As the *Times*'s correspondent in Calcutta advised in his editorial comment in the wake of Dadaji's appeal in March 1886, "Native reformers . . . [should]

direct their energies less to vague political aspirations and more to the pressing evils of their social system."[110]

For all that the *Times* tried to relegate debates about conjugality to the sphere of social relations and social reform, the publicity given to Rukhmabai's trial raised important questions about the rule of law in British India—questions that were *political* insofar as they threatened the tenuous balance of power the British had sought to maintain since 1857 by pledging (nominal) noninterference in religious customs such as age of marriage.[111] Rudyard Kipling's poem "In the Case of Rukhmibhaio" offered a view of the trial that was more satirical than that produced by the *Times* or other metropolitan papers but that made the connections between Indian nationalists' calls for self-rule and the debate about the trial in India unmistakably clear:

Gentlemen reformers with an English Education—
Lights of Aryavarta take our heartiest applause,
For the spectacle you offer of an "educated" nation
Working out its freedom under "educated" laws . . .

Gentleman reformers, you have heard the story,
Weighed the woman's evidence—marked the man's reply
Here's a chance for honour, notoriety and glory!
Graduates of culture will you let that chance go by?

[You can lecture government, draught a resolution—
Sign a huge memorial—that Calcutta saw.
Never such an opening for touching elocution—
as the text of Rukhmibai, jailed by Hindu law]

What? No word of protest? Not a sign of pity?
Not a hand to help the girl, but, in black and white
Writes the leading oracle of the leading city:—
"We the Indian Nation, we hold it served her right. . . ["]

It is then the brutal Briton feels an impulse, wild, unruly—
That tingles in the toe nails of a non-official boot—
Lumps in one mean heap of cruelty the graduate and coolie—
And the old race-instinct answer to the clamour:—Hut you brute.[112]

Kipling's animosity toward the "effeminate Bengali" was, and is, well known.[113] For him, as no doubt for many metropolitan readers, the spectacle of Rukhmabai enabled the collapse of "the graduate" (INC men) into "the coolie" (Dadaji) and suggested that at stake in the display of the Hindu woman was the status and masculinity of Indian men, especially where masculinity was defined as a capacity to protect Hindu women from penetration by even an apparently unwilling colonial state.[114] The ladylike qualities attributed time and again to Rukhmabai thus showed up Indian men's failed gentlemanliness, even as fantasies about her helplessness shored up the need for intervention by a chivalrous English state and appeared to confirm the inadequacies of indigenous political protest.

Opinion in Britain during the trial of Rukhmabai as shown in this essay appeared to be both against legislation and "pro" Rukhmabai. This is at first glance a contradictory posture, since Rukhmabai herself called repeatedly on the government for legislative reform. But the disavowal of intervention produced, to borrow from Gyan Prakash, a kind of imperialist double-speak. Those who sided with Rukhmabai did so to show up the apparent barbarity of Indian male reformers who abandoned her to prison, not to criticize the imperial government for failing in its responsibilities.[115] Moreover, they decried legal intervention only as a temporary measure, pending the sufficient education of the indigenous population in the most civilized (read, British) forms of conjugality. Some, such as Max Müller, did so on the grounds that he understood the laws of Manu better than the pundits; others, such as one contributor to *Queen*, were convinced that discretion in such matters was the very proof of British superiority— and, hence, manifest evidence of Britain's right to rule.[116] The coincidence of debates about Rukhmabai's trial with the sardonic and at times outright hostile reception given to the meetings and the leaders of the INC by the British press suggests that the case was being used to help solidify already implicit connections between the ability of Indian men to regulate Indian women's sexuality and their capacity for self-rule. Even, and especially, when they claimed to have the best interests of Rukhmabai at heart, Rukhmabai's supporters in the metropole disparaged Hindu sexual mores by championing as victim the woman whose very resistance made the court case itself an argument simultaneously against the violence of Hindu conjugality *and* colonial rule. Whether Rukhmabai was reclaimed as the pathetic victim of "primitive" Hindu custom or the courageous spokesperson for a new kind of Indian woman, what emerged from the controversy was a particular model of female virtue: "the Hindoo lady." This hybrid persona was clearly appropriated by Rukhmabai to legitimize her resistance to colonial law. But in the hands of the late Victorian press in Britain, it was repeatedly designed to appear as derivative of presumptively English models of "lady-like" sexual respectability, the only kind of "wronged woman," presumably, who could legitimately seek support in the metropolitan public sphere. In this sense, British newspapers' attention to the trial did more than show up the partiality of the colonial judicial system, make visible the circulation of colonial knowledge, or even lay bare some Victorians' contempt for Indian nationalism. Metropolitan discourses about the trial worked continually to obscure the very relationship between empire and "home" that Rukhmabai herself was constantly in danger of revealing, for whether it was the *Times*, the *Pall Mall Gazette*, the *Western Daily Press*, or even *Queen*, journalists of all stripes were deeply invested in the idea that women's respectability was a "full-grown, stable model" that originated in Britain and was transplanted wholesale to colonies, to be appropriated by or imputed to Indian women aspiring to "civilization."[117] To the contrary, Rukhmabai's trial demonstrates that, like Victorian domestic ideology itself, performances of women's virtue were staged neither in Britain nor in India alone but in the transnational communities of colonial culture that imperial social formation generated, of which the press was a crucial discursive technology. Though a relatively "small act" in the long history of colonial rule, Rukhmabai's speech is suggestive of the dialectical and "mutually sustaining process of cultural reconstruction" that empire guaranteed as the structural relationship "between" Britain and India in the nineteenth century.[118]

The debate on child marriage was far from over when Dadaji and Rukhmabai reached their settlement in 1888. In 1890, a child named Phulmonee was "raped to death" by her husband, Hari Mati. Ahe was a girl of eleven or twelve; he was a man of thirty-five. According to Tanika Sarkar, "The event added enormous weight and urgency to Malabari's campaigns for raising the age of consent from 10 to 12" in India. It did not go unnoticed in Britain, either.[119] Encouraged by supporters of Rukhmabai in Britain, Malabari traveled to London in the spring of 1890 specifically to work up support for consent legislation, a campaign that revived the public debate in the *Times* and the *Englishwoman's Review* and carried it into new discursive spaces via a number of mainstream Victorian periodicals. Müller, Cardinal Henry Manning, and Millicent Garrett Fawcett all lent their support to his crusade; fifty-five female doctors practicing in India memorialized the government; and Malabari flooded the British public with his treatise *An Appeal on Behalf of the Daughters of India*.[120] He was hailed in Britain as the spokesman for the marriage-reform movement, and his book received favorable reviews in the press while Tilak raised the cry, "Hinduism in Danger," in Maharashtra, and crowds were organized to protest the possibility of reform in the Indian Penal Code in various regions of India.[121] Geraldine Forbes and Charles Heimsath have suggested that it was the impact of public opinion in Britain that helped pass the act of 1891, because "The Home Government . . . took a decidedly pro-reform stand, under pressure from British societies interested in the welfare of Indians."[122] If they are right, it was not Malabari's campaign in London alone but also the interest generated by the trial of Rukhmabai several years earlier that helped to establish that extra–Parliamentary pressure and ensure its political influence. And although Malabari dominated the debate in Britain in 1890, the impact of Rukhmabai's participation at this juncture must not be discounted. She was studying medicine at the time in London, where she published a lengthy piece in the *New Review* in September 1890 titled, "Indian Child Marriages: An Appeal to the Government." In it, she sounded her earlier themes: that child marriage impeded women's educational progress; that women suffered as a result of it more than men; and that the only remedy could come from the British government. Those in Britain who had followed her trial from the mid-1880s no doubt recognized her ideological positions. They may well have also sympathized with her lament, "Child marriage. Infant marriage. Cradle marriage. . . . [W]hat a repetition of words, and how wearisome the sound of these words has become to some of us!"[123]

12

Tongues Untied

Lord Salisbury's "Black Man" and
the Boundaries of Imperial Democracy

In the general election of 1886, Dadhabai Naoroji (1825–1917), onetime mathematics professor in Bombay and longtime Parsi merchant and entrepreneur, ran on the Liberal Party ticket for the constituency of Holborn and lost, with a total of 1,950 votes against 3,651 cast in favor of the Tory candidate, Colonel Francis Duncan.[1] Naoroji's candidacy received little publicity outside Holborn itself, and, indeed, but for Naoroji's second bid for a parliamentary seat in 1892, the Holborn debacle might have gone unnoticed in the annals of parliamentary history, as did the attempts of two compatriots: David Octerlony Dyce Sombre, who was elected for Sudbury in 1841, and Lal Mohan Ghose, who ran as a Liberal candidate for Deptford just a few years before Naoroji.[2] Even so, Naoroji's accomplishment—that is, election to the House of Commons as the spokesman for a colonial territory that many contemporaries, even those who were sympathetic to the cause of India, scarcely recognized as a legitimate nation, let alone a viable electoral constituency—remains one of the last untold narratives in the high political history of the Victorian period.[3] This omission persists despite the availability of information on Naoroji's career in Britain through the work of Rozina Visram and others, not to mention the attention given to it in the contemporary Victorian press. More remarkable still, Naoroji's bid for parliamentary representation as an Indian for "India" remains obscure despite recent attempts to understand how thoroughly empire helped to constitute "domestic" politics and society across the long nineteenth century.[4]

By the time the votes were counted in the general election of 1892,

Naoroji had managed to capture the seat for Central Finsbury, also a London constituency.[5] He again ran as a Liberal, this time successfully, though his margin of victory was exceedingly slim: he won by just five votes. In the late 1930s, Naoroji's biographer, R. P. Masani, attributed Naoroji's success to his hard work among the electors and to the indefatigable support of those in and outside Parliament who had canvassed on his behalf, both on the eve of the election and during the months and years preceding it. Masani was equally convinced that it was a fortuitous "slip of the tongue" on the part of the Conservative Prime Minister, Lord Salisbury, that helped Naoroji win the election by making his name a household word throughout Britain in the aftermath of his defeat in 1886. In a speech in Edinburgh in November 1888, Salisbury explained, with the following evidently careless remark, why the election in Holborn turned out the way it had. In his view, it was because "Colonel Duncan was opposed by a black man; and however great the progress of mankind has been, and however far we have advanced in overcoming prejudices, I doubt if we have yet to go to that point of view where a British constituency would elect a black man."

"I am speaking roughly," continued Lord Salisbury amid laughter and cries of "Hear, Hear," and "using language in its colloquial sense," according to one contemporary account, "because I imagine the colour is not exactly black, but, at all events, [Naoroji] was a man of another race."[6] The impetus that Masani ascribed to the incident bears scrutiny. "Those two words," he wrote—referring to Salisbury's designation of Naoroji as a "black man"—did nothing less than "kick . . . Dadhabai into fame. The name of the hitherto little-known Indian, difficult of articulation as it had so far been, was within twenty-four hours on the lips of everyone throughout the United Kingdom."[7]

The Edinburgh speech and the storm that followed became highly politicized spectacles that easily could be used in the service of what Naoroji believed was the ultimately righteous cause: Indian self-government. Practically since his arrival in Britain in the 1850s, Naoroji had been thinking, writing, and speaking publicly about the need for Indian representation in Parliament, as well as about the injustices of British rule in India. He did all of this while calling himself a loyal "servant of empire" and claiming to be the representative of both the masses and the various cultural and religious communities of India. Indeed, his insistence that "Hindu, Muslim, Parsi, Sikh and Christian" constituted the disparate but collective basis of "India" was to become a mantra for nationalists seeking a foundation for Indian citizenship in the early twentieth century.[8] The office of president of the Indian National Congress (INC), which was bestowed on Naoroji in 1886 (and again in 1893 and 1906), was undoubtedly a great honor, but it may have fallen temporarily short of his most cherished aspiration. That aspiration was to convince the British public, by means of personal appeal, rational economics, and, above all, his capacity to "speak for" India that Indian self-rule was nothing less than the fulfillment of Britain's great imperial destiny.[9] The "black man" incident should therefore be read as part of Naoroji's decades-long attempt to harness the British public and, no less significantly, the machinery of the Liberal Party to his determination to make the Parliament at Westminster a truly imperial democracy by forcing it to recognize an Indian colonial subject as one of its representatives. Although he would not have used the term, Naoroji clearly recognized that this was a transnational project insofar as it could not be achieved without negotiating power across a variety of national-political boundaries, both imagined and real.

Could Dadhabai Naoroji have been elected to Parliament if Lord Salisbury had not made him into such a national cause célèbre? I wish to be clear that the causal relationship, if any, between Salisbury's passing remark in the fall of 1888 and Naoroji's eventual election in 1892 is not of prime concern here. Of interest instead are the terms through which the public discussion of Salisbury's comment—which was referred to alternately as an epithet, a joke, an attack, an insult, and, most commonly, a "slip of the tongue"—was carried out. Salisbury's comment is significant as much because it was innocent as because it was derisive and racist. It was innocent, that is, not of moral accountability or even, one presumes, political guile. But it was arguably innocent of the reverberations it was to have in local and national political culture, innocent of the path it would open, not just for Naoroji but for the late Victorian press more generally, to articulate the categories of racial hierarchy and the exclusionary premises of political citizenship that circulated throughout the culture at large but were rarely so visible or so publicly on display in national forums. Here, Judith Butler's claims about "excitable speech" are irresistibly germane, and not just because the speech act always says and does more than it intends to, or even because "the risk of appropriation accompanies all performative acts," thereby "marking the limits of their sovereignty."[10] These interpretations are undoubtedly ratified by Salisbury's remark and the veritable Babel of tongues it unleashed in the late Victorian metropole. What Butler's theory enables us to see with particular clarity—especially in a case such as this, where the excitable speech at hand inflicts a culturally agreed-on verbal injury—is why the impulse to fix on the speaker himself as the author of violence (or here, racism) is inadequate for understanding the kind of ideological work that language, in its unavoidably institutional and cultural settings, is always capable of doing. Salisbury's words, together with the torrent of response to them, were "excitable" precisely because they dramatized the ways in which a subject like Naoroji, who was "excluded from enfranchisement by existing conventions," might, through his engagement with such speech, expose the "contradictory character" of the very universal discourse that claimed to represent him and, moreover, worked to naturalize its claim.[11]

That universal discourse was, of course, Victorian democracy, a political arrangement with an implicitly white, male, and middle-class character, which by 1886 had managed successfully to contain, mostly by incorporation, some of those who sought entrance into the body politic. Such was the great constitutional compromise espoused by Conservative and Liberal alike since the Reform Act of 1832 and guaranteed by the subsequent adjustments of the legislation of 1867 and 1884. British women of all classes were a notable, and increasingly organized and politically shrewd, exception to the much touted process of incorporation at the national level. The Irish were an even more menacing threat to this process and were only momentarily crushed by the defeat of their cause at the polls in 1886. Despite Naoroji's considerable sympathy for both English women and the Irish question, he nonetheless sought participation in this compromise through the opportunity created by Salisbury's unwitting invitation into the battleground of extra–Parliamentary democracy in an imperial age. Thereby, one might infer, Naoroji effectively turned the tables on the Tory party and its prime minister, revealing not just the imperial and racist foundations of Victorian democracy but also the vulnerability of its very processes to appropriation and transformation by an outsider and, as was then common parlance, a person of "alien" race and affiliations. In other words, he not only exposed the contradictory character of Victorian imperial democracy but exploited it to win himself a place at the political table. Naoroji's triumphal election to Parliament in 1892 would seem to further bear out this inference, signaling the arrival of an Indian "native" at the very heart of the imperial government's domestic machinery while announcing, as well, the basic fairness and good sportsmanship of modern Western democracy.

If this conclusion seems too neat, it is in part because the Whig narrative cannot fully account for Naoroji's election or the complexities of his relationship to imperial democracy itself. Although Naoroji professed not to take offense at what many of his friends and supporters deemed Salisbury's slander against him, he did not seek any kind of identification with the phantasmagorical "black man" who was the object of the prime minister's scorn. As late as the 1880s, "black man" was an appellation that could in no way enhance—and, indeed, could only endanger—any subject's chances to achieve recognition as a citizen, much less as a civic representative of the people in the Mother of all Parliaments. It carried with it associations of slavery and subjugation that imperiled Naoroji's claims about the special qualification of Indian civilizations and peoples to direct representation, not to mention the august reputation he had cultivated and no doubt deserved as one of India's most respected statesman. To be sure, the metropolitan press, both urban and provincial, helped to excavate and refine this web of associations, updating it in terms readily accessible to its late Victorian readers and, in the process, contributing to a historically specific, though not totally new, disaggregation of "the Indian" from "the African." This disaggregation helped secure certain imperial taxonomies and, possibly, to frustrate what might have been political solidarity between and among colonial peoples.[12] In this sense, Naoroji's rise to parliamentary power may be said to be as much an effect of the new journalism of the 1880s as of his own individual efforts, the consequence of a diffuse yet tentacled visual and textual medium that vied with party-political organizations for the attention and allegiance of an ever more sophisticated, literate middle- and lower-middle-class citizenry and that, not incidentally, helped to make and remake the racial assumptions of the time and place in ways not confined to local or regional culture but affecting politics in the highest places.[13]

Among the contributions that an analysis of the Salisbury–Naoroji "black man" debate can make to our understanding of the history of Victorian democratic culture is to illuminate how some colonial nationalists could be implicated in its populist bargains and how questions of color and citizenship figured in the tradeoffs that were required. I also want to suggest that when we take discourses seriously—as sites of political power and cultural knowledge produced out of concrete conditions—they can be viewed as an archive, a material resource where the "socio-economic and political relations of colonial domination" are both visible and contestable.[14] Finally, rematerializing this Victorian debate demonstrates that although, as Butler notes, injurious speech can be untethered or untied from its original context of utterance and used as a tool for political ends, those ends are rarely as predictable as one might think. The "black man" debate cannot, in the end, be dismissed as merely a case study of a "world in a grain of sand." It represents, rather, an example of how language can be made to matter in the public sphere and of how discourses about color and complexion helped to make and remake Victorian racial assumptions in ways that were not confined to local or regional culture but affected politics at the very heart of the empire, thereby revealing the fundamentally transnational nature of British political culture in the fin de siècle.

The press debate which followed on the heels of Lord Salisbury's remarks revolved around whether or not Naoroji could really be called "black" and whether or not that designation was accurate, appropriate to political discourse, or representative of the opinion of "the great heart of the English nation."[15] While some might contend, as did the *Notts Daily Express*, that "there is nothing criminal in being black," most agreed that "the fact that Mr. Naoroji is not black hardly lessens the sting of the insult."[16] Those who rejected the association with blackness imposed by Lord Salisbury did so primarily through reference to Naoroji's complexion or skin color. So, for example, the *St. James Gazette* argued that because Naoroji was "as fair as a Spaniard . . . it is not only incorrect but impolite to call him a black."[17] The *Yorkshire Post* chided those who "professed to be greatly shocked" by Salisbury's reference to the alleged blackness of Naoroji's skin and reminded readers that "of course Parsis are not black, or any shade of colour approaching it in the majority of instances." According to a contributor to the *Christian World*, Naoroji was "singularly deficient in color even for a Parsee," while the *South Times* opined that "Mr. Naoroji is anything but a black man. He is slightly copper coloured but his complexion is nearer white than black."[18] For all the public discussions of the variations of non-white skin color that followed in the wake of Salisbury's remarks, it was the instability of whiteness, not of blackness, that became the issue, with Naoroji's approximation of it posing as a dangerous challenge to presumptions about who and what could count as

English in an imperial culture such as Britain's. Naoroji's relative "color-lessness" was attributed most often to his Parsi background, a feature that enabled him to pass in India, if not in Britain. As one commentator observed, "To the great mass of the Indian population [he] is almost as much of a foreigner as an Englishman is."[19] For this very reason, as a correspondent for the *Leader* insisted, Naoroji was "not at all black. Many an English man is not so fair. He has lived 30 years in England. In speech, costume, and manners he is indistinguishable from a refined, educated and courteous English gentleman; and it requires a quick eye to tell from his colour that he is not English."[20]

In light of such remarks, it would be easy enough to read such news-paper responses as if they meant to suggest that English gentlemanliness, at least, was a function of "speech, costume and manners" rather than of color or of race. Yet it would be a mistake to imagine that a preoccupation with race and, more specifically, with the alarming fluidity of racial tax-onomies did not motivate these public pronouncements at virtually every turn, or that the racialized debate sustained by the late Victorian press did not also carry political and cultural meanings that far exceeded what appeared in, if not as, black and white. In the first instance, Salisbury's remarks created an opportunity for enemies of the Tory leader to invert the hierarchies of the British class system. The *Somerset Express* remarked that "apart from the low coarseness of such acts, coarseness that would disgrace a working man, could any words be imagined more foolhardy, reckless, mischievous and unstatesmanlike than calling the Honorable Dadhabai Naoroji a black?" It is "only Tory aristocrats," the author con-tinued, "with their dislike of the toiling masses who make their wealth, that can speak so vulgarly of those who differ in complexion or accent."[21] In a letter to the editor of the *Star*, a correspondent who signed himself "B.—A 'Blackman,'" called Salisbury's remark "unworthy of an English gentleman, and more so of an English Prime Minister. The sweet epithet of a black man as a designation for the dark races has hitherto been confined only to 'roughs' and ill-mannered children." The Tory leader, he went on to say, "does them honour by adopting their language and elevat-ing it into a political phraseology, and finally giving it the sanction of his high name and authority. . . . [I]f the colour of a man's skin be any disqualification for high offices or positions, surely Lord Salisbury of all men should not be the Prime Minister."[22] The *Star*, for its part, main-tained that "there is really nothing surprising in it. Gentlemanly ruffians like Lord Salisbury are in the habit of using such language to what they are pleased to call their inferiors."[23] And according to the *Glasgow Mail*, "Lord Salisbury makes no secret of his opinion that, at least within the British Empire, there are no men but Englishmen, and that other races and nationalities are only inferior creatures made for Englishmen to rule." The *Mail*'s emphasis on the "Englishness" of the speaker and his offense was surely not lost on Scottish readers of the day and suggests some of the ways in which class politics and regionalism might converge. "His lordship is the most highly developed type of native English snob—the flower of aristocratic culture," it continued. "If there be the germs of disaffection in India, his words will bring them into active life."[24] The *Accrington Times* saw its opportunity to exploit the images that wordplay might conjure among readers with even the vaguest notions of British history and English convictions of civilization and progress. Its contributor had the temerity to observe:

> While Lord Salisbury's unknown savage ancestor was hunting wild beasts in the "woad paint of Aboriginal Britain" the Indian plains were teaming with fertility and were ruled by "principalities and powers." The finely woven fabrics of India adorned the ladies of Roman patricians and were esteemed more highly and were far more costly than the shawls of Cashmere known to our grandfathers. . . . Moore's "Lalla Rhook" is written about these "black" people. They are no more black than Persians or Egyptians.[25]

Not only are Salisbury's ancestors reduced to savagery here, but the authenticity of their whiteness is called into question by reference to both the woad paint used by ancient Britons and the invocation of "aboriginal," which connoted the native, non-white peoples of Australia and even in some cases the tribal peoples of India in this period. Well might a Victorian reader smile at the implied connection between blue paint and the blue blood that was alleged to run through Salisbury's veins.

For all the subtlety of these jibes, however, no retorts more neatly or more succinctly summed up the ways in which Salisbury's remark undid his claim to be the arbiter of the color of citizenship than the following. The first was attributed to Herbert Gladstone, who is supposed to have said, " 'I know Mr. Nowroji very well, and I know Lord Salisbury by sight, and I am bound to say that of the two, Lord Salisbury is the blackest.' "[26] The second is a remark attributed to an unnamed London politician:

"Well, if [Naoroji] is black, he is not a blackguard like a certain aristocrat we know."[27] Whereas for many the prime minister's comments were thought to be "unspeakable," here Lord Salisbury himself has become the unmentionable object of public satire, ridicule, and fun. It should be noted that despite its wittiness, such speech was hardly less vulnerable than Salisbury's. As a contributor to the *St. Stephen's Review* was quick to remark, "Mr. Gladstone seems to think that it is a disgrace for a man to be black. Perhaps it was in the days when the Right Honorable gentleman's ancestors dealt largely in black ivory."[28] The risks of speech were many, in part because the domains of the discursive and the political were often one and the same. In this case, "excitable" speech was deemed dangerous because it had the power to influence imperial stability and, with it, the very terms of colonial rule. More than one commentator echoed the sentiments of the *Leicester Daily Mercury*, which warned that if "native Indians are to be treated in the spirit that induced the application of the words 'black man' to Mr. Naoroji, we are sowing the seeds of another mutiny."[29]

As should be clear from the variety of speech elucidated here, the counterattacks on Lord Salisbury were never a question of simple inversion. Even if the Tory leader was the real "blackguard" in the affair, the full effect of that term depended on associations between blackness and class status. "Blackguard," in other words, gained its rhetorical force in the context just cited precisely because it was incompatible not only with Salisbury's whiteness but, equally crucially, with his aristocratic standing, as well. In addition to the class valences that helped to shape the public debate around Naoroji and Salisbury, the discourses that emerged depended on the triangular relationship among Englishness as whiteness, Indianness as brownness, and blackness as Africanness. Africa, in other words, was the unspoken Other not just of Englishness but of Indianness, as well. Admittedly, this transnational grid—or, rather, the triple matrix on which it was established—was constantly in danger of being obscured by the polarity of white–black that the debate itself reinscribed with every newspaper column. Yet the triangularity of black–white–brown could not, finally, be suppressed. Take, for instance, the following excerpt from a *Manchester Guardian* article:

> Of course a Parsee is not a "black man" at all, but a man of Aryan race and light olive complexion, often no darker than Lord Salisbury him-

self. A little inquiry into the rudiments of Indian history would show Lord Salisbury that the Aryan races who entered India from the north prided themselves on their fair complexions, and praised their gods for subjecting the black skin to the Aryan man. That, however, is not the main point. Even if our Indian fellow-subjects were all full negros, it should be the first care of a British statesman to avoid any invidious insistence on differences in race and colour. The raw subaltern who goes out to India and calls every native a "nigger" is a mischievous idiot, but then he knows no better. The Prime Minister should know better, and Englishmen cannot impress the lesson on him more effectually than by finding seats in Parliament for one or two of the "black men" in the next election.[30]

References to India's Aryan past were not uncommon and could be used as a cautionary tale about the folly of presuming Western culture to be the apex of civilization.[31] But as Thomas Trautmann has shown, it was the theory of Aryans' racial superiority, by virtue of their putatively light skin color, that elevated nineteenth-century Indians to a special status and required their participation in a colonialized racial hierarchy that placed them above "the negro."[32] At some moments it must have been difficult for Victorian readers to tell who *did* count as "black" (or, alternately, as "full negros"), since the press spilled so much ink explaining who could not reasonably fall under that rubric. Indians certainly did not, in the view of many of the newspapermen writing about the "black man" incident. As the writer in the *Accrington Times* remarked, "Moore's 'Lalla Rhook' [an eighteenth-century verse poem about India] is written about these 'black' people. They are no more black than Persians or Egyptians." He ended by concluding, "It is doubtful whether [Indians] are darker than the inhabitants of Palestine. Professor Max Müller maintains that they are descended from a branch of the great Aryan race to which we ourselves belong."[33]

In addition to being the heyday of the Aryan race theory *and* the "scramble for Africa," this was the period in which ideas about the whiteness and blackness of ancient civilizations such as Greece and Egypt were being consolidated into historical "fact" in both Britain and Germany.[34] Geopolitical events and the ideological projects that both produced and reflected British claims on "black" bodies and all manner of non-white native peoples are clearly crucial, in other words, for understanding the larger historical context in which the "black man" controversy was mobilized for public consumption. The relationship in the debate between gradations of skin color, on the one hand, and geographic location and culture, on the other, may have been imprecise, but it was nonetheless revealing—both about what kinds of scientific and ethnographic knowledge circulated in popular culture during the late Victorian era and about what impact that knowledge might have on apprehensions of domestic politics and political culture. The 1880s in particular witnessed an explosion of colonial exploration literature, a genre made popular by penny dreadfuls (novels) and the variety of metropolitan newspapers, journals, and periodicals that were emerging as shapers of public opinion during this decade. In addition to the images of "savage" and "heathen" blacks that accounts of Livingstone's mission to Africa helped to circulate throughout Britain, minstrelsy was still popular in this period—so much so that a commentator in 1885 believed that most English people formed their views about "Negroes" from stage representations and other caricatures.[35] The year 1885 also saw the publication of John Beddoe's *The Races of Britain*. It was subtitled "A Contribution to the Anthropology of Western Europe," and it devoted considerable space to the variations of hair color, head shape, and physiognomy of Britons because, as Beddoe argued, "The ever-increasing rapidity of local migrations and intermixtures, due to the extension of railways and the altered conditions of society, will in the next generation almost inextricably confuse the limits and proportions of the British races."[36] Given the attachment of the famous Orientalist Friederich Max Müller and his popularizers to the historical and linguistic connections between Britons and Aryan Indians—not to mention the persistent associations of "blacks" with Africa, uncleanness, baseness, unregulated sexuality, and cultural backwardness—it cannot be surprising that defenders of Naoroji were invested in maintaining the distinction between the "Indian" and the "negro."[37] Two degrees of separation was a distance entirely too close for comfort. Indeed, policing the boundaries between brown and black was a critical rhetorical maneuver for those who insisted on refusing the designation "black man" for Naoroji. The term was repeatedly rejected not just as uncivil but as wholly inaccurate because "in the ordinary and colloquial sense of the word [sic] 'black man,' especially in a contemptuous connection, is synonymous with 'negro,' and that hardly improves the matter."[38] That blackness and "negroes" were the irreducible signifiers of Africa—and, by extension, therefore *not* of India—there seemed to be little doubt. The author of a letter to the editor put it quite plainly: "I somewhat agree with the ministerial Marquis in his antipathy to niggers, but

I am bound to confess that I have never regarded our Indian subjects in an African light. Mr. Naoroji is no more a nigger than any of the Cecil family (family of Lord Salisbury) and, as far as talent is concerned, he unquestionably can give good points to the younger generation."[39] But it was the *Hawk* that framed the necessity of disaggregating Indians from "black men" most explicitly when its correspondent wrote, "All the things [Lord Salisbury] should have called him—Baboo, Asiatic—would have been less offensive than 'black,' " which is "an adjective . . . to be avoided, at all costs and hazards, by those orators of talent, whose power over the idioms of their native tongue enables them to imagine and coin equivalent phrases."[40]

The terms "baboo" and "Asiatic" were laden with their own derisive, Orientalist connotations even while, much as blacks themselves used "nigger," these labels could be used by Indians—and were, in the nineteenth century—in the service of political and cultural critique.[41] What is significant here is the concern for the crudeness of the term "black" that the *Hawk* articulated and the paper's attempt to protect Naoroji and Indians in general from it, a concern that was typical of the rhetorical mode of chivalry that characterized the debate over Salisbury's "indiscretion." As the *Daily News* put it, "It is our interest and our duty to cultivate the best and most honourable relationship with the people of India—not to snub their eminent men from the public platform." Most importantly,

> Loyal and educated Indians must not be exposed to unseemly and unwise jeers of the "black man" type. Unity and loyalty of feeling between England and her vast Indian dependencies is a necessity of the present time; but undignified epithets and contemptuous taunts will not strengthen that spirit of unity. . . . [T]he best way to answer my Lord Salisbury . . . would be to elect Mr. Naoroji to the first vacant seat—and have a "black man" in the House of Commons.[42]

Remarks like these enable us to see with particular vividness what was at stake here—and to appreciate the ways in which the discourses of chivalry and protection, with their "feminine" connotations, revealed the inseparability of racial identities from gendered ones in the "black man" debate. Not only was it "unseemly" to expose educated Indians to the term; Lord Salisbury's comments were considered "indiscreet," "indecent," "caddish," and—repeatedly—"wanton." Why should the vocabulary of sexual morality—and more particularly, of heterosexual misconduct—have entered into this discussion? The answer lies partly in traditions of colonial discourse, which effeminized Bengali men especially, but that also effeminized all communities of Indian men who were not from among the "martial" races, Parsis included.[43] If Indian men could be said to occupy the same place as (middle-class) English women in the patriarchal / colonial imagination, then their protection from "unseemly" sneers and jibes would represent the fulfillment of English manhood, even as it showed up the limits and failures of a certain kind of gentlemanliness (Salisbury's aristocratic background) in the process. That this exposure was carried out by a largely urban press corps, fresh from the "Maiden Tribute of Modern Babylon" scandal and well versed, presumably, in the conventions of journalistic chivalry, suggests a kind of extra–Parliamentary attempt to reorient the codes of English masculinity along more democratic, though still thoroughly heterosexist, lines. The body of the African slave was arguably central to the model of colonial English masculinity articulated, however briefly, during the extended debate about Lord Salisbury's remarks, for in contrast to the tremulous, base, and degraded body of the "black" that haunted even the briefest of allusions to slavery, Naoroji was continually constructed as "cultured," "highly intelligent," "well-educated," "distinguished," "refined," "courteous," and "an eminent Indian scholar."[44] His fitness for representing "India" did not go unquestioned; objections had more to do with the impossibility of any one man being able to speak for the various ethnic and religious communities on the subcontinent than with any defect or disqualification on his part.[45]

We might push the analysis further and say that the characteristics invented to describe and, in most cases, to defend Naoroji made him appear self-possessed rather than un-free, in contrast again to the specter of the African black and, more particularly, the slave. While the adjectives supplied by the press to characterize Naoroji could certainly be applied to a Victorian Englishman, with the possible exception of "scholar" they resonate more with the image of the bourgeois Englishwoman than with that of a robust, muscular figure such as John Bull—or, for that matter, than with the body at work of the slave, whose connections to the artisan set him decidedly against the scholarly Naoroji. As with the mockery of Salisbury, class played a constitutive role. It was Naoroji's education and refinement that provided him with upper-class credentials and guaranteed that he could not be mistaken for a slave; if anything, he was a distinguished "servant" of empire, to use Naoroji's own phrase, in his capacity as onetime leader of the INC and self-professed imperial loyalist.

Nor can the "gentle" quality of Naoroji's manliness be gainsaid. If he was "indistinguishable from an English gentleman," he was also "more of a gentleman than Lord Salisbury."[46] He was, in the end, not-black (but brown or olive or "pale" or, simply, "colorless") precisely because of these distinguishing features. It could even be argued that as long as Naoroji was neither fully black nor fully white, determining his color with certainty was unimportant—a possibility that suggests the extent to which blackness was the determinant against which all aesthetic value was measured and from which, in turn, all valuable possessions had to be shielded. The real scandal, the real injustice, therefore, was that Naoroji should be mistaken for a "black man," a mistake that did not simply offend but violated the carefully managed relationships between whiteness and manliness, blackness and savagery, and Indianness and culture on which the late Victorian imperial imagination depended and that a variety of contemporaries—Indians included—were evidently prepared to defend. Such was the equilibrium Salisbury threatened to upset; such were the cultural and political stakes that prompted "the manhood of England" to launch a "chivalrous attack" on Salisbury and to "condemn . . . unequivocally the gibes and flouts and sneers of the Prime Minister."[47]

Clearly the political and cultural significance of the speech act cannot, and should not, be underestimated, especially since the pathos of the whole Salisbury debacle rested on the presumption that the prime minister had merely misspoken—a kind of informal consensus that the unfortunate phrase "black man" was nothing more or less than a "slip of the tongue." Some called it "clumsy"; others, "insulting" or "scandalous"; still others, "pitiful," "uncourteous," "coarse," and even "brutal."[48] The sustained play on "slip of the tongue" is quite remarkable, particularly since it appears across a wide range of newspapers and other public forums. "Lord Salisbury's bitter tongue may cost us dear in India," lamented the *Star*, while the *Dundee Advertiser* called the "black man" comment "a pretty precept to fall from the lips of the leader of a party which makes the integrity of the Empire its peculiar care."[49] The *Pall Mall Gazette* reveled in the damage done: "Few more unfortunate utterances have ever fallen from the lips of a Prime Minister."[50] "If 'Pears' soap' is really what it professes to be, [that is] 'makes foul look fair,' " wrote a correspondent to the same paper, "a copious lather of it may be recommended to the noble lord, to be applied to his eyes and tongue six times a day."[51] Whether contributors were for or against Salisbury, tongues, mouths, and lips predominated in their remarks. The *Dundee Advertiser*, for example, called for the Tories to "show the value they put on the Empire which is so much in their mouths by offering Mr. Naoroji one of their safe seats, . . . [so that they may] thus atone for Lord Salisbury's boorishness."[52] Judgments about the tastefulness of Salisbury's remarks conjured the mouth metonymically, if not literally, as when the *Hereford Times* complained that Salisbury's joke was "a piece of execrable bad taste," an image even a public apology from the prime minister could not banish from the debate.[53]

And apologize—or, at the very least, explain—he did, at Scarborough on 20 December 1888. To those who claimed that the term "black man" was derogatory, he had this to say:

> Such a doctrine seems to me to be a scathing insult to a very large portion of the human race, a portion which contains some of the finest members of the race. The people who have been fighting at Suakin . . . are amongst the finest tribes of the world, and many of them are as black as my hat. But that is a small matter. What I deny is that I said anything about the people of India. I indulged in no contemptuous denunciation of them and in no denunciation of any kind. I did not mention them. . . . All I did was point out that you could not understand the meaning of the Holborn election of 1886 unless you remembered that the Liberal candidate was not only of a distant race—widely separated from us—but that it was marked by his complexion that it was so, so that the whole constituency knew it, and that the existing state of English opinion was a very strong factor in the decision which they gave. Whether it ought to have been a strong factor or not I did not at the time enter on. My own impression is that such candidatures are incongruous and unwise. The British House of Commons, with its traditions and understandings, having grown fitted to the people, and grown out of their daily life, is a machine too peculiar and too delicate to be managed by any but those who have been born within these isles.[54]

Salisbury's contention that when he used the term he intended to distinguish Indians from Africans—such as those "people who have been fighting at Suakin" who are "as black as my hat"—did little to exonerate him, but it does confirm the depth of the division between brown and black in the late Victorian cultural imagination. It also suggests the kinds of pressures that contemporary British military policy might have been exerting on Salisbury's thinking, as well as the larger geopolitical context in which debates about the relative virtues of "brown" versus "black" might have resonated.[55] Finally, Salisbury's defense demonstrates that even when the distinction was maintained, the *sight* of racial difference was believed by some to take precedence over "customs, manners," and whatever other cultural practices might be held in common.[56] One had to be "fit to be seen" not only to be represented, in other words, but also to claim the fitness required to represent others.[57]

It must be noted here, if only briefly, that Lord Salisbury suffered during his entire career from embarrassing and potentially politically costly "slips of the tongue." Peter Marsh has called him a "powerful debater" whose style of oratory was "lean, with little literary or rhetorical embellishment . . . lightened by cynical wit." Though his speeches were largely extemporaneous he was, in Marsh's opinion, one of the "best half a dozen speakers of the day." Significantly, however, "His wit was the one talent he feared."[58] It was a fear that may have been well founded. His comment in 1886 that the Irish were as incapable of governing themselves as Hottentots may have been in line with a visual culture where caricatures of Irish nationalists with "negroid" features were a staple of politics, yet it could not fail to aggravate what was already a tense political mood, at a time when Home Rule for Ireland divided opinion in the country and literally rent the Liberal party.[59] John Morley, Salisbury's contemporary and William Gladstone's biographer, was quoted as saying that Salisbury hardly made a speech that did not contain "at least one blazing indiscretion."[60] Constraints of space do not allow for an extensive discussion of his infamous tendency for gaffes, which included derisive comments about Jews and Scots as well as the Irish.[61] Suffice it to say that Salisbury (who called himself "an illiberal Tory") had little consideration for the niceties of civil discourse—or, for that matter, for the subject peoples of the empire.[62] To be sure, his imperial attitudes were scarcely different from those of many of his contemporaries. As Marc Gilbert observes, Salisbury's Indian policy, "like his overall imperial policy, was unashamedly expressed in racial terms."[63] He was, in W. T. Stead's assessment, "John Bull through and through."[64]

Salisbury, moreover, had nothing but contempt for democracy, and never more so than when it was embraced by his Tory leader, Benjamin Disraeli, whose pandering to the masses he deplored and whose embrace of the necessity of democratic government he could only regard with terror—even as, to quote Marsh, he at times "danced along the banks of the mainstream of British politics toward democracy" himself.[65] The people, in his view, were "a myth," in part because they lacked the capacity to speak either properly or in ways that merited their participation in government and politics:

> Except on rare emergencies, when they are excited by some tempest of passion . . . the "people" do not speak at all. You have put an utterance into their mouths by certain conventional arrangements, under which assumptions are made which, though convenient, are purely fictitious: as for instance . . . that a man's mind is a perfect reflex of the minds of fifty-thousand of his fellow-citizens on all subjects because he was chosen, as the best of two or three candidates, in respect to a particular set of subjects . . . by a bare majority of those who took the trouble to vote on a particular day.[66]

That Salisbury should have referred to democracy as a kind of "speech" put into the people's "mouths" through the ballot box is by no means exceptional. It was one of the chief metaphors for representative government throughout the mid– to late Victorian period. Nonetheless, the question of speech and its symbolic meanings continued to shape the discussion that followed Salisbury's "apology" and, not incidentally, to keep the image of the mouths and lips alive. "He says the word 'black' does not necessarily involve contempt," reported the *Weekly Despatch*. "Perhaps, but in his mouth it did."[67] The *Leader* was even more explicit: If there were a seat available, Naoroji would get it, and "that would be a well-deserved slap in the face from the black man to the still blacker one— in heart and mouth—who traduced him."[68] Liberal reformer Robert Spence Watson echoed this hope, expressing his conviction that "the day would come when [Naoroji] would be the mouthpiece of his people in the British House of Commons."[69] Indeed, it would seem that the principal effect of Lord Salisbury's comments was to secure a place in the public imagination for Naoroji, that "modest and retiring Parse whose name has been on every one's lips for weeks past."[70]

The hazards of orality in general and of particular speech, as well, quickly emerged as a dominant theme in the nationwide debate about the prime minister and the Indian congressman, for when tongues were untied, as in Salisbury's case, the words he uttered might end up being "quoted in every paper and pass[ed] from mouth to mouth in every bazaar in India." It was a kind of verbal intercourse guaranteed in part by the metropolitan press itself, which undoubtedly helped to spread the word from London to Calcutta, to Delhi and beyond.[71] The possibility of miscegenation, not to mention homosexual contact across the color line, that such language had the power to conjure adds another dimension to the sexual politics of the Salisbury episode by demonstrating—to the Victorian middle-class public and to us—just how unstable the heterosexist economy of colonial masculinity was and how crucial to imperial politics its preservation might be. The *Worcestershire Echo* was oblique but on the mark in this regard: "Lord Salisbury possesses, as everyone knows, a tongue which is subject to a most deplorable knack of running away with its owner."[72] Of significance here is the fact that the capacity for careful, controlled speech—versus the excited, excitable kind—was recognized as a mark of civilization, culture, and, of course, Englishness itself in Victorian Britain. Salisbury had become a slave to his own tongue, and for many he had thereby forfeited his claim to represent the English people. The equivalence of controlled speech with Englishness made itself felt through the insinuation that, by letting his tongue run away with him, the prime minister had spoken in a fashion "unworthy of an *English* gentleman."[73] The equation of good speech with perfect English was also sometimes made by reference to that revered master of English linguistic perfection, William Shakespeare. Like the images of tongues and lips and mouths, Othello and Hamlet dotted the discursive landscape of the Salisbury debate, appearing sometimes by name, sometimes by allusion. The most common occurrence was via a quotation from *Othello*, "Mislike me not for my complexion," which Naoroji partisans jokingly suggested should be his retort to Salisbury's "black man" comments.[74] The *Surrey Advocate*, however, unleashed Shakespeare against Naoroji's supporters, borrowing from *Hamlet* to accuse his friends in the press of "tearing a passion to tatters" on his behalf.[75] So did another of Naoroji's opponents, Sir Lepel Griffin, when he wrote to the *Times* that Naoroji should have known that his hosts at a National Liberal Club dinner "cared as little for him as did Hamlet's player for Hecuba."[76]

In the end, Griffin asked what was essentially Salisbury's question, but in a different way: "what qualifications beyond a gift of fluency common to all Orientals, has Mr. Dadhabai Naoroji which should commend him to an English constituency?" His reference to the "fluency" of "Orientals" was an example of the contempt with which many members of the Indian

National Congress were viewed in the English press. Especially in the wake of a visit to London by delegates of the INC in 1885, the press had characterized the group as "gushing, vaporing" politicians whose pretensions to the platform were poor imitations of the Englishman's true oratorical skills.[77] The INC was referred to as "the Indian talking shop" and its delegates were referred to as "persons of considerable imitative powers," as well as in less flattering terms.[78] As the *Globe* wrote of the first INC session, it was "a mere congress of mosquitoes. . . . [T]he delegates buzzed and created a certain degree of momentary irritation . . . but that sums up the entire result of their labors."[79] These idioms were not new in the 1880s.[80] Since Macaulay and perhaps before, Indian men had been seen not as incapable of speech, like Africans or slaves, but as capable only of inexactitudes, of speech that mimicked and approximated English but never actually succeeding in *being* English.[81] Nor was this limited to the empire "over there." As Patrick Joyce has shown, school inspectors gathering information for the parliamentary reports on popular education of 1861 displayed considerable contempt for local dialects. Well into the later part of the century (and beyond), language "stood for decidedly different ideas of what 'culture' was."[82] At the same time, the conviction that Indians only used "jargon," that they "frothed" and "bubbled" at the mouth, speaking about matters of which they had no real knowledge, produced images of failed speech with a particular colonial inflection that continued to animate public discussions of Indian nationalism in the 1880s and 1890s, spurred on in part by the "black man" controversy but by all accounts also antecedent to it.[83] The failure to be anything except an imitation of the Englishman was part of what secured Indians' "Indianness," as well as their status as subjects and not citizens. What could Naoroji possibly have *said*, one wonders, to contest these challenges to his legitimacy when such challenges revolved around the very mastery of language that Indian men were supposed to fall short of, especially since even his friends could not deny "that electors could not feel enthusiastic about a candidate whose name they were unable to pronounce"?[84]

Naoroji's biographer, Masani, reports that electors had no trouble remembering how to pronounce his name after the election in 1892, when he succeeded to office by a margin of merely five votes. They promptly, and memorably, dubbed him "Mr. Narrow-Majoritee."[85] Naoroji's public engagements with the effects of his notoriety in Britain are equally intriguing. His response to the "black man" debate was careful and cautious, befitting the reputation for statesmanship that had helped to shape his image as a gentleman in the Victorian press. At the first of several banquets held in his honor following Salisbury's gaffe, Naoroji was reported as saying little or nothing after being toasted by the assembled group. He "gave us no figures and no rhetoric, and was as cool as the water in his wine glass"—a subtle reference to his sobriety, both literal and figurative, on such a potentially volatile occasion.[86] But Naoroji did not hold his tongue for long. He was back on the stump immediately, hammering away at many of the same arguments he had been propounding, in print and in private, in India and in Britain, for nearly three decades—about the necessity of Indian self-government, the injustice of the economic drain through which Britain exploited the resources of India, the negative impact of an unreformed civil service, the promise the INC offered in its role as "a national body" for India. References to the fact that Indians wished to be viewed as citizens and "not as slaves" peppered his speeches as he canvassed for Central Finsbury in the late 1880s and early 1890s. It is tempting to read these instances as evidence that Naoroji was deliberately refusing the identification with the image of the black man that had been pressed on him. But the invocation of slavery versus citizenship was a rhetorical practice that had a long history in British political culture, dating from at least the seventeenth century, and it cannot therefore be exclusively attributed to the association with blackness Salisbury had tried to attach to him. Nor was the binary opposition of slave and citizen new to Naoroji's speech in the 1880s. As early as 1866, he had mobilized similar terms to argue for Indian self-government. These speeches were given publicly, in London, in the context of the Second Reform Act and in the wake of the controversy over Morant Bay (the rebellion in Jamaica in 1865)—historical circumstances that, as Catherine Hall has persuasively shown, brought the subject of black men and "niggers" before the Victorian public in ways that made the debate about legislative reform as much a matter of imperial as of domestic politics.[87] The rhetoric of slavery was, in other words, a discursive convention so well established in British political culture that it functioned simply as one of a number of well-chosen idioms that could be counted on to resonate with an English public whose Liberal Party sympathizers, at any rate, possessed a strong sense of English history and a familiarity with its tropes and signifiers.[88] In this respect, Naoroji may be said to have neutralized the negative effects of being associated with blackness by proving that he could walk the walk, talk the talk, and speak the speech as it had been pronounced for centuries—"trippingly on the tongue," as it were. As Henry Louis Gates has shown, blacks' supposed incapacity for correct speech and above all, for articulate "English," was believed by many Britons and North Americans to disqualify Africans and others deemed "negroes" not just from access to culture and civilization, but from humanity, as well.[89] Given the severity of this test of personhood, and the conditions it required with respect to literacy and the speech act itself, Naoroji's embrace of the electoral platform, his public orations, and his innumerable performances on the hustings may well have been interpreted by the late Victorian reading and listening public as evidence of his difference from a black man, if not of Indians' essential differences from Africans. Thus, by demonstrating his capacity for speech in the longstanding British oratorical tradition, Naoroji distanced himself—implicitly, at least—from whatever notions of primitiveness Salisbury's epithet might have succeeded in pinning on him. He made it clear, in other words, that *he* could tell "black from brown," and this quite literally, since it was in the "telling"—that is, in the sophistication of the speech itself—that such differences would be audible, if not also visible.

In fact, at the variety of dinners and gatherings at which he appeared in the months and years after the "black man" debate had ceased to be front-page news, Naoroji rarely spoke directly to or about Salisbury's "slip of the tongue." This was so in part because the chairmen who introduced him inevitably made a reference to Salisbury's comments, as at a meeting in Glasgow in February 1889 when Sir William Wedderburn prefaced his remarks by saying that "some men sneered at others because of the colour of their skin. As well might they sneer at men because of the colour of their hair." Applause followed.[90] Whether he wished it to or not, the specter of the "black man" followed him to one of the high points of his public career. When he won Central Finsbury in 1892, Naoroji was greeted by crowds of supporters who raised three cheers to "Lord Salisbury's Black Man." The phrase itself was sometimes printed as "Blackman," suggesting that, attempts to distinguish him notwithstanding, he may have become synonymous in public discourse, if not also in the public mind, with blackness *tout court*. As accounts of his appearances around the country in the late 1880s make clear, no one actually needed to refer to the incident to make it the subject of Naoroji's speeches or public appearances. In this sense, the moniker was not unspeakable, exactly. Rather, Naoroji had become so identified with it that it was scarcely necessary to name "the black man" for "him" to be present.[91] If a retort were needed, Naoroji's return to Parliament in 1892 was, arguably, the ultimate comeback—articulated, no less, through the voice of the people. On those rare occasions when Naoroji did address Salisbury's remark, however, he did so by vowing not to "enter into a discussion of the incident," a maneuver that participated in the unspeakability of the whole affair while allowing him to claim the moral and, one must add, rhetorical high ground. In a speech in Liverpool, he went so far as to say that the comment "meant something deeper than words seemed to indicate," but he left that meaning unspoken and focused instead on the promise for reform and justice held out by the INC. "For what [is] Congress?" he asked the audience. It was "men of different castes, creeds and races, speaking different languages, from north, south, east and west, collecting together, *speaking one language*, and aspiring to [the] political condition" of equality.[92] That "one language" might be Indian nationalism, but it was also equally the *English* language. And if Naoroji was loath to articulate the obvious, his supporters were not as reticent. In the preface to Naoroji's speech at Glasgow, Wedderburn reminded the audience that "the millions of India had long been dumb. We had now for a generation given the people of India education, and . . . they had now found a voice. Not only had they found a voice, but they were now speaking in very articulate tones." Though in this context Wedderburn was referring to the INC, Naoroji's capacity to speak for the "dumb" Indian millions was more than implied. It was, thanks in part to Lord Salisbury's excitable speech, the very presumption on which Naoroji's claims about participation in imperial democracy were based.

Salisbury may have been a racist, but this did not make him exceptional, and it certainly cannot account for the explosion of public debate following his remarks about Naoroji. More significantly, Salisbury flaunted contemporary usages: he got the syntax of racial discourse wrong, and when he did so, he brought the fury of the political press down on his head because his imprecisions threatened the certainties of Victorian racial discourse.[93] The "black man" debate can thus be read as an exercise in the restoration of public order through speech that was equally, if differently, racist, in part because it aimed to stabilize meanings through a recourse to persistently racialist categories. If all speech entails risk, then Lord Salisbury's "black man" remark surely illustrates that not all speakers entertain the same risks, whether of degree or of kind. It was arguably more dangerous for an Indian seeking inclusion in the imperial body politic to be identified with the body of the black man than it was for a prime minister to be identified as a racist, though the fact that Naoroji was in a position to make even ambiguous meaning out of that racism surely signifies his relatively privileged position, as well.[94]

Yet these conclusions beg several larger questions, the first involving the nature of Victorian democracy in an imperial culture. There is little doubt that, despite the system of two-party politics the Liberals and the Tories worked to create and manage—and also no doubt because of it— there were those in the press and in the extra–Parliamentary public sphere more generally who were determined to interrogate the leadership precisely because such a dialectic was considered proper to the democratic process. That this was a conviction with roots in plebeian traditions long preceding the rise of the two-party system has also been well documented.[95] What remains virtually unexplored in the historiography of Victorian politics is how and under what circumstances that democratic process was framed by imperial questions. The debate about Lord Salisbury's remarks, together with national, public events such as the discussions around the Eyre controversy and the Second Reform Act (as described by Catherine Hall), require us to "rethink" Victorian domestic political history as a scene routinely introduced on, if not always fully constituted by, the fact of empire.[96] The attention paid by the metropolitan press to the "slight" against Naoroji may not have been organized enough or sustained enough to be counted as an expression of political will, but it *was* nonetheless an exercise in the display of colonial knowledge that aimed to wield cultural authority to shape political outcomes. Here, cultural authority was clearly not limited to local, regional, or national politics. It encompassed knowledge about the larger imperial context, its history, and its meanings for participation no less than its ramifications for citizenship and subjecthood. The public debate about Naoroji stands as a challenge to the persistently insular historiography of Victorian high politics, which has largely stood aside from recent work on empire, except occasionally to critique it either for not being "historical" enough or for privileging the category of culture over the domain of the political. Salisbury's gaffe and its many reverberations signal how imperial social formation, to use Mrinalini Sinha's phrase, was one of the contexts for whatever collective identities existed in Victorian society, as well as for whatever consensus there may have been about "civic virtue" in the late nineteenth century—a context so naturalized that it remains difficult to see it, let alone to read it, as a complex (and contested) imperial terrain at the "high" political level.[97] If the risks inherent in democracy mean that "one cannot know the meaning the other will assign to one's utterance, what conflict of interpretation may well arise, and how best to adjudicate that difference," then the "black man" case also demonstrates that the effort to "come to terms," as Judith Butler puts it, "is not one that can be resolved in anticipation but only through a concrete struggle of translation, one whose success has no guarantees."[98] In the transnational context produced by British imperialism, where those terms involved not just Englishness but speech acts in the English language itself, what ensued cannot be viewed simply as an incidental debate or an innocent dialogue. It must be understood as Victorians represented it—that is, as an essentially conflictual social and cultural dynamic.[99]

As important as Naoroji's story is to the project of rethinking the Whig national frame of British political history, however, to leave it there would be to reproduce the circularity of imperial logic and obscure the multiplicity of terrains on which racial and cultural identities were being articulated in this period. In the first instance, we cannot ignore the role that organized Indian nationalism played both in promoting Naoroji as a candidate for Parliament and in organizing the "black man" debate for public consumption, both in Britain and in India. In 1889, G. P. Varma Brothers Press of Lucknow assembled excerpts from British metropolitan newspapers that had covered the Salisbury–Naoroji debate. Lucknow was a site of tremendous newspaper activity in the late nineteenth century. Ganga Prasad Varma, of the Varma Press, published two prominent papers in the city and, as Sanjay Joshi notes, "was the real organizing force behind Congress activities in Oudh in the early days of the party"—so much so that he has come to be known as "the maker of modern Lucknow."[100] The anonymous author of the preface to Lord Salisbury's Blackman made it clear that one reason for reprinting the newspaper selections and other ephemera (including verse and some images) was to prove that, the prime minister's insult notwithstanding, the British public had demonstrated that it did not view Indians as inferior peoples "whom, like the proverbial dog, any stick is good enough to beat with"—a concern that suggests how intimately related the protocols of sociability and the promise of political equality might have been.[101] He also noted with satisfaction that as a result of the Salisbury affair, "There is, we believe, hardly a borough in England where 'The Blackman' is not known, and hardly a town of political importance where he is not only known but loved and respected."[102]

While British newspapers had displayed knowledge of and cultural authority over racial hierarchies and imperial taxonomies, nationalist leaders in India broadcast not just their familiarity with the intricacies of the British electoral system (as evidenced by pride that Naoroji was known in towns of "political importance") but also their desire to influence its political outcomes. The fact that, with a few exceptions (such as the *St. James Gazette*), the compilers chose quotes from liberal, radical, or Gladstonian newspapers (such as *Reynolds* and the *Newscastle Daily Chronicle*), signals their canniness about the ins and outs of Victorian political culture and their willingness to use that inside knowledge for their own political purposes, especially since, as they must have known, the liberal press was virtually decimated in the wake of 1886.[103] In fact, the practice of extracting from metropolitan weeklies and dailies was standard in the Victorian period, so that G. P. Varma Brothers was simply using familiar customs for its own nationalist ends.[104] The impact of this selectivity on circulation of the final product in India and in Britain cannot be underestimated. Indeed, the preface to *Lord Salisbury's Blackman* borrows liberally from the idioms used in the British press to characterize the insult, calling Salisbury's remarks "wanton" and invoking the same critiques of Salisbury's alleged gentlemanliness as were common currency in the newspaper coverage. In this sense, Indian public opinion and its makers must be factored into whatever "dialogue" was going on between the British public and its political leaders in this instance, especially since *Lord Salisbury's Blackman* was published after the prime minister made his "explanation" but well before Naoroji's election contest in 1892.

This dialectical relationship—between British government and popular sentiment, on the one hand, and Indian nationalism, on the other—effectively removes "domestic" imperial democracy from the heart of the narrative, a central location that the urban and provincial press in Britain seemed invested in staking out, despite occasional references to and even sympathies for the INC's activities. Nor is the political struggle for Indian self-government and against colonial rule the only one that merits our attention where debates about race and Englishness are concerned. Given the role of Home Rule in the fate of the Liberal Party, not to mention Indian nationalists' attachments to and coalitions with Irish radicals in and outside Parliament, the landscape in which the Naoroji incident took shape was influenced by "imperial" social formations in quite complicated ways.[105] Add to this the fact that Irish nationalists were often caricatured as "Negroes," and the relationships between Naoroji, blackness, and colonialism become yet more complex. The facts that Parsis were often compared to Jews and that Lepel Griffin did not believe Naoroji had any more right to represent Englishmen than "a Polish Jew settled in Whitechapel" makes any simple or dichotomous reading of late Victorian "racial politics" virtually impossible.[106] These convergences serve to remind us that discourses are products of concrete, material social conditions and struggles, even as they also shape the terms through which such conditions are experienced, articulated, and circulated throughout culture.[107] "Black" men themselves were also implicated in contemporary contests over what color colonial subjects were and what color British citizens could or should be, in part because of changing social and political conditions across the colonial landscape. By the 1880s, for example, Africans were beginning to play a role in electoral contests in the Cape Colony, where their votes not only brought about political outcomes but also gave shape to discourses on race, which affected Indian populations in South Africa and, in turn, the direction of the INC and the African National Congress equally, as Gandhi's political trajectory eloquently testifies.[108] Elsewhere, as Belinda Edmondson and Faith Smith have both argued, elite West Indians of African descent were deeply invested in marking themselves off as legitimate, sovereign political subjects against conventions of African "savagery" *and* against stereotypes of Indians as represented in Caribbean discourse and culture in the late Victorian period. The parallels and overlaps between these debates and the issues of color and citizenship raised by the "black man" incident are quite remarkable. J. J. Thomas' *Froudacity* (1889) was a searing indictment of J. A. Froude's *English in the West Indies* (1888), which actively engaged the terms of Englishness and blackness in an effort to prove the vexed connection between literary/linguistic mastery and the political equality that all black men claiming status in modernity were required to demonstrate.[109] The position of the Indian man was crucial to this claim, even while it was often white metropolitan Britons who encouraged the contest between black and brown in the first place. As Froude put it in 1887, "The two races are more absolutely apart than the white and the black. The Asiatic insists the more on his superiority in the fear perhaps that if he did not the white might forget it."[110] Meanwhile, Smith argues, "Pronouncements about 'Indians' were part of the discourses of 'race vindicators' like William Herbert, who took Charles Kingsley to task in the Grenada *Chronicle and Gazette* for suggesting that 'Hindoo peasants' could teach African 'natives' about good husbandry and thrift."[111]

Like Naoroji, Herbert was at worst a collaborator in the ideological work of empire; at best an ambivalent and contradictory reader of imperial ideology and its twisted promises.[112] Taken together, the two men exemplify the predicament of imperial and colonial histories that fail to recognize what Madhavi Kale calls "the mutually constitutive and complicating stories of the British empire in India and the Caribbean, and of Britain."[113] The figure of "the black man" was by no means confined to or contained by the narrow parameters of British "domestic" imperial culture or democracy. It exceeded the boundaries of home and away, crisscrossing as it did to India and the Caribbean and back again in a circuitous and highly politicized trajectory. Such motility highlights what Kale, again, calls "the prolific instability of empire as a discursive resource," precisely because it illuminates how dangerous it is to privilege one contact zone over another or to imagine that the temptation to do so is not part of the seductive legacy of imperialism itself.[114] If neither speech nor democracy is a self-evident subject whose historical meanings we can predict or stabilize, how could it be otherwise for the nation or the empire, which are even more at risk because of the very sovereignty that they—through their historians and other cultural representatives—traditionally have been at pains to claim?

13

India Inc.?

Nostalgia, Memory, and the Empire of Things

Will the British empire ever be over, or are we destined to witness its eternal return in the form of nostalgia masquerading as history, of drama pretending to rehearse its relentless end? The transfer of Hong Kong to China, the devolution of Scotland, and, on the very eve of the new millennium, the precarious shift of power from London to Belfast: if these, taken either separately or together, do not signify the final, halting end of the British empire, it is hard to imagine what would. And yet, as Ackbar Abbas has suggested, we must be suspicious of the "cultures of disappearance" that have emerged in the context of postcolonial history, in part because disappearance rarely means erasure and, indeed, often entails a "pathology of presence" that permits that which is "gone" to be reincarnated in new historical or cultural forms. Our skepticism is also warranted, Abbas argues, because "it is as if the possibility of [certain] social and cultural space[s] disappearing . . . has led to our seeing [them] in all [their] complexity and contradiction for the first time, an instance, as Benjamin would have said, of love at last sight."[1]

In the case of empire, the danger is not that it will disappear as a subject but, rather, that the staging of its end will produce heroes and heroines in new, and newly seductive, romances of empire. In the case of Raj nostalgia, the challenge is to understand the ways in which the loss of India offers an apparently endless opportunity to see empire—the *déjà disparu*—one last time, as well as to experience (if not enjoy) its peculiar forms of commodification in the present.

Tom Stoppard's *Indian Ink*, first performed in London at the Aldwych Theatre in 1995, stages just such a paradoxical disappearing act, for what does "india ink" offer if not the promise of indelibility in the face of erasure, disappearance, history? As with that performance, the earlier BBC Radio 3 version (titled *In the Native State* [1991]) centers on a painting of uncertain provenance that holds the key to the mysteries of the imperial past as set against the background of India in the early 1930s. Although the pun evoked by the original title is lost in the stage version, "Indian Ink" has its own significance. It doubles first as the title of a book of poems being written by Flora Crewe, a poet on London with socialist connections and modern ideas about sex who goes to India in 1930 to give a lecture tour while recuperating from an undiagnosed pulmonary condition; and second, as a symbol of the lingering imprint, the permanent stain, the indelible inscription of India on the British imperial imagination. While on her tour, Flora meets an Indian painter named Nirad Das. What begins as a rather innocent flirtation ends up as a rather more complex, if unelaborated, tryst,[2] the only evidence of which is a watercolor by him of her in the nude. Flora's bohemianism is reflected in the fact that she has been painted in the nude before—by Modigliani, in Paris—and that she is fairly insouciant about being a subject in "her native state." More important, the life of the painting after the death of its subject is a major theme in the play, as the voice of Flora reading her poetry sounds a stirring contrapuntal note.

Simultaneous with these events in India of 1930 is the quest by two men to discover "the truth" about Nirad Das and Flora Crewe in the mid-1980s: Eldon Pike, an American professor of literature whose research speciality is Flora Crewe, half a century on, and Anish Das, Nirad's son. Having traveled across the globe to find the lost canvas, Pike is a veritable torrent of words in footnote form. Because he can only manage to perorate, however, he ends up not just as a caricature of an American academic but also as an emblem of the failure of Americans to understand history *tout court*. Das's son is a stark contrast. Like the protagonist of Hanif Kureishi's novel *The Buddha of Suburbia*, Anish is "a funny kind of Englishman, a new breed, as it were, having emerged from two old histories."[3] The nexus of past and present in both versions of Stoppard's play is Eleanor Swann, also known as Nell, who is Flora's sister and the keeper of her effects, including the Modigliani oil painting. In each of the two acts of the play, the story moves virtually seamlessly between India and Nell's home in Shepperton —that is, suburban London and its environs. Laurie Kaplan has parsed the radio play against the stage play, and I do not want to repeat her work here.[4] What I do want to emphasize is that the staging at the Aldwych by Peter Wood (Stoppard's long-time collaborator and director) effectively dramatized the imaginative coincidence of time and place by juxtaposing India of the 1930s with post-imperial Britain physically, as in side by side.[5] Though not intended as a "blueprint" for all productions, the published version of the text endorses overlapping furniture, shared floor space, and even common characters such as the maharajah of Jummapur, head of the fictitious princely state in which the action in India is set.[6] One effect of this collapse of time and space is that certain objects—Flora's suitcase and a variety of teapots, as well as the controversial canvases themselves—take on a heightened significance: they are the visual reference points that allow the audience to follow the action across time and space and back again. We become invested in their travels, in part because we quickly realize that they will end up telling the story of Flora's and Nirad's encounter. Whether as ethnographic artifacts or works of art, these "things" serve as witnesses to history, and their material presence testifies to the persistence, durability, and commodification of empire in the contemporary present.

To understand the purchase of things in *Indian Ink*, some background on Stoppard is necessary. Born in Czechoslovakia in 1937, Stoppard was living with his family in Singapore when the Japanese invaded in 1942. Women and children were evacuated, and young Tom and his mother went to India, where she eventually became the manager of a Bata (shoe) store in Darjeeling. His father was killed during the Japanese occupation, and his widowed mother later married an English army man, Kenneth Stoppard. Stoppard admitted rather sheepishly to an interviewer in 1974 that her marriage had placed them squarely in the "lower sahib" class.[7] Or, as he told another critic, "We weren't really Raj people"—perhaps in part because, as Stoppard recently announced, they were not only exiles but Jewish exiles, as well.[8] They moved to England in 1946, where he went to school, began working as a journalist, worked as a theater critic, and wrote *Rosencrantz and Guildenstern Are Dead*, his first hit, in 1964. When *In the Native State* aired on Radio 3 in the spring of 1991, theater critics were eager to match Stoppard's latest success with his story of childhood displacement in and experience of India, but he resisted their efforts to overdetermine his work in that way. He made a point of saying that he did not return to India until after he had written the radio script, and only then in connection with the making of *Rosencrantz and Guildenstern Are Dead* into a film.[9] "The visit back actually was in the nature of an experiment with memory," Stoppard told Paul Allen in an interview for the radio program *Third Ear*. "I had quite a few images in my head which really were as nebulous as dreams."[10] He had earlier confided to an American journalist who interviewed him in California (where a production of *Hapgood* was being mounted) that writing the play was something of a struggle for him. This was not necessarily a break with his usual pattern of writing, but apparently the idea of India, and the fact of his childhood relationship to it, was having some effect. "I was eight when I left India for England," he is quoted as saying in 1989. "I felt I should be able to use my own experience of India to write about the ethos of empire. But right now [the idea] isn't really going. I've never really abandoned a play. In the end I've always found something I wanted to do, and I hope that happens with this one, too."[11]

One of the ways that this "ethos of empire" manifests itself in *Indian Ink* is through the subtle but powerful seduction of things that move across the stage throughout the play. Stoppard has long been open to the criticism that he is not as interested in characters as he is in ideas. In this case, the repertoire of household objects familiar to life under the Raj creates an authenticity that Stoppard feared his Indian characters especially did not have.[12] His investment in reproducing the material culture of daily life in colonial India—part of "that re-creation of the English Eden,"[13] as he referred to it—is clear from the first few lines of the play, in which Flora describes her train journey from Bombay to Jummapur:

> Darling Nell, I arrived here on Saturday from Bombay after a day and a night in a Ladies Only, stopping now and again to be revictualled through the window with pots of tea and proper meals on matinee trays, which, remarkably, you hand back through the window at the next station down the line, where they do the washing up, and from the last stop I had the compartment to myself, with the lights coming on for me to make my entrance on the platform at Jummapur.[14]

Here, as throughout *Indian Ink*, we are drawn into the story through images of objects such as teapots and tea trays, which stand in for—and in this case, anticipate—the process of cultural encounter and exchange between Britons and Indians even as they evoke the unequal power relations characteristic of the Raj.[15]

But as Arjun Appadurai has argued, "things" are rarely mere passive objects: they have social, cultural, and political lives of their own.[16] In

Indian Ink, they give the narrative precisely the momentum it needs to negotiate the relationship between past and present, Britain and India, "home" and "away." Flora's suitcase is a particularly compelling visual prop, since we see her arrive with it in Jummapur; we watch it being spirited away by an Indian servant; we look on as Eldon Pike arrives at Nell's house in Shepperton to ask for it because he feels sure it contains the oil painting he has been searching for; and in the last scene, we see her carry it onto the train with her as she heads out of Jummapur.[17] Things like the suitcase do more than simply carry the plot across time and space. They act as souvenirs, evoking and commemorating a past cultural experience and an equally distant historical moment by keeping it alive, and in sight, in the present.[18] Eleanor's tea tray is instructive, as well, for the one she uses in Shepperton came from India, from the days when her husband was a district officer there, and reveals to us that she is no mere disinterested observer of the Raj but is, in fact, an old India hand. It is Anish, Das's son, who recognizes the tray as Nepalese, prompting Eleanor to comment on the movement of people and goods from home to away and back again across the twentieth century. "In India we had pictures of coaching inns and foxhunting, and now I've landed in Shepperton I've got elephants and prayer wheels cluttering up the window ledges, and the tea-tray is Nepalese brass."[19] Eleanor's remark suggests the equivalence of aristocratic foxhunting scenes and Buddhist prayer wheels. It also underscores the portability of imperial commodities and their interchangeability with common metropolitan household items—as well as the visible presence of the old Raj in contemporary domestic space. Eleanor is written as a stiff-upper-lip character with a soft spot for India. Her identification with the objects stranded in her living room leads her momentarily into a recollection of how good the tea was in India and how hard it is to approximate in England. "I expect it's the water. A reservoir in Staines won't have the makings of a good cup of tea compared to the water we got in the Hills."[20] Although brief, her nostalgia for better days—and better cups of tea—erupts into the text and even manages to conjure the Himalayas just beyond the audience's horizon.

If the staging of various objects helps to carry the past into the present, it is the two paintings that dominate the scene in *Indian Ink*. Through these canvases, the past becomes accessible to those who desire it, and through their elusive presence, Flora's and Das's love affair is brought to our sightline.[21] Fear about the fragile state and possible loss of the paintings is shared by all the characters in the play. At the same time, however, and true to Stoppard's inimitable passion for dialogue, it is words that compete with characters and things—and above all, with art—as the enduring legacy of the Raj in *Indian Ink*.[22] Reflecting on the BBC radio script on which *Indian Ink* was based, Stoppard remarked, "I thought I was going to write a play simply about the portrait of a woman writing a poem and her poem is about being painted. Then I found the idea of her poetry so perversely enjoyable I went on writing her poetry for far longer than you'd believe."[23] In this offhand comment to Gillian Reynolds of the *Daily Telegraph* in an interview in 1991, Stoppard captures the dialectic between words and images, between language and things, that structures the play and makes the final disappearance of empire a matter of form rather than a matter of fact. The debate at the heart of the play revolves around the relative merits of words versus image, art versus logos. For Stoppard, it would seem, the fate of colonial empires seems to hang in the balance, as the following scene between Das and Flora suggests.

Das has given Flora a copy of Emily Eden's book *Up the Country* (1866), which describes Eden's tour of India. The gift prompts Flora's to complain that Das is too "English," too enamored of Dickens and Holman Hunt and Chelsea and Bloomsbury, despite the fact that he has never been to Britain. She even has the temerity to suggest that she is more nationalist than he, since she is willing to say, however obliquely, that the English should get out of India. Her criticism provokes him, and he cries out ("passionately," according to the stage directions), "The bloody Empire finished off Indian painting!"[24] What ensues is a lively discussion in which they debate the merits of the British empire (it brought roads and schools, but all the saris are still made in Lancashire), with Das ending the riff by prophesying the end of empire. "The Empire will one day be gone like the Mughal Empire before it, and only their monuments remain—the visions of Shah Jahan!—or Sir Edwin Lutyens!" Flora responds with a line from Shelley, "Look on my works, ye mighty, and despair!" The script continues:

> *Das:* (Delighted) Oh yes! Finally like the Empire of Ozymandias! Entirely forgotten except in a poem by an English poet. You see how privileged we are, Miss Crewe. Only in art can empires cheat oblivion, because only the artist can say, "Look on my works, ye mighty, and despair!" There are Mughal paintings in London, in the Victoria and Albert Museum.[25]

The watercolor he is working on while they converse turns out to be Das's attempt to imitate a Mughal miniature, and it survives both of their deaths to keep the debate about art alive into the present, as Anish and Nell engage in a similarly spirited discussion when he brings it to her in Shepperton fifty years on. The nude itself ends up being a kind of hybrid aesthetic form: the mosquito netting in Flora's bungalow serves as the house within the house (read, mock harem), and Flora herself serves as a modern-day Radha in Das's own re-creation of the Krishna story from the *Gita Govinda*.

The contest over what forms of art can survive the fall of empires is a major arc in the play, and debates about the relationship of politics to aesthetics under colonial rule are clearly implicated in the sexual encounter between Das and Flora. Their dialogue—the *Hobson–Jobson* words they play on,[26] the jibes and clever retorts—is artistry itself and frankly competes for our attention with both image and poetry as the drama unfolds. Poetry, painting, love, and empires past and present intertwine, in other words, as Das's canvas and Flora's book of poems take shape. The contest between word and image is ever present, as when Das tells Flora that he is Rajasthani, and "all our art is narrative art, stories from the legends and the romances."[27] Among these stories, the favorite of Rajput painters was from the *Chaurapanchasika*, which, Das tells her, is a collection of "poems of love written by the poet of the court on his way to execution for falling in love with the king's daughter, and the king liked the poems so very much he pardoned the poet and allowed the lovers to marry."[28]

Das's own arrest and imprisonment for participating in an antigovernment riot is foreshadowed in this account, an experience that also leads to his untimely death. The survival of his nude of Flora, not to mention the preservation of Mughal art in museums in London and elsewhere, may well signify that in the competition for immortality, painting and literature are equally enduring. Flora herself suggests a similar interpretation when she hopes that "perhaps my soul will stay behind as a smudge of paint on paper, as if I'd always been here, like Radha who was the most beautiful of herdswomen, undressed for love in an empty house."[29]

Yet there is much in Stoppard's play to suggest that, as Das remarked, empires are entirely forgotten "except in the poetry of English poets" like Flora and, by extension, in the English language itself, of which Stoppard is so famously enamored and which he called his "first tongue," despite his birth in Czechoslovakia.[30] For one thing, we scarcely see the famous canvases around which the whole play revolves; they are rolled up, shrouded from view or turned away from the audience, as they often are from Flora, as well. Pike's stentorian footnote readings take up more space than they do on stage.[31] In typical Stoppard mode, words predominate in general, so much so that he has confessed to feeling that all of his plays, for radio and the stage equally, are overwritten and that *Indian Ink* is no exception.[32] More specifically, it is Flora's poetry that is a major presence in the play. She is constantly writing drafts, reading portions aloud, and working it out word by word. As we know from Pike's research, Flora's volume of poems called *Indian Ink* not only endures; it makes a comeback in the 1980s through the efforts of Pike and the market for "exotic" writing by white women of the empire created by Western feminism *and* the craze for Raj nostalgia of that decade, twin phenomena to which Stoppard gives a nod in the stage script. In fact, the role of Western feminism in excavating, re-presenting, and thereby helping to guarantee the "eternal return" of empire in the West has been crucial to the Raj's survival in the fin de siècle, in part because Western feminists have been slow to recognize the costs of recovering the memsahib as a long-lost heroine, and in part because white liberal feminism is no less subject to the seductive fantasies that lie at the heart of the historically imperial romance between English women and India.[33]

Stoppard had never even heard of Emily Eden until he came across her book in a bookshop in London. One cannot help but wonder whether the copy he found was the Virago reprint, made directly possible by the feminist publishing that was one very visible outgrowth of the women's movement in Britain in the 1980s.[34] That feminist publishing houses like Virago —which reissued Eden's *Up the Country* in 1983 as part of its effort to rescue women from the invisibility of traditional history—should have participated in Raj nostalgia in such a direct and unselfconscious way is telling evidence of the ways in which traditions of imperial feminism in Britain (from the antislavery campaigns to the campaign for women's suffrage) have made their way into twentieth-century popular culture through the logic of late capitalism.[35] Stoppard's romance with India may thus be said to be derivative of (if not reliant on) a certain version of postcolonial feminist imperialism, especially where the character of Flora is concerned. Eden, significantly, is not merely Flora's foil. Stoppard makes Eden an unmistakably Victorian antecedent to Flora's modern version of "English womanhood," offering a progressive, evolutionary model of that identity. Equally powerful, it is Emily Eden and her text that have the last word. The play ends with Flora boarding the train to Jaipur with her copy of *Up the Country* in hand. As the train "clatters loudly" and the light fades on-stage, Flora is heard reading aloud from a passage of the book, dated 1839, which gives an account of the Queen's Ball in Simla:

> It was a most beautiful evening; such a moon, and the mountains looked so soft and *grave*, after all the fireworks and glare. Twenty years ago no European had ever been here, and there we were with a band playing, and observing that St. Cloup's Potage à la Julienne was perhaps better than his other soups, and that some of the ladies' sleeves were too tight according to overland fashions for March, and so on, and all this in the face of those high hills, and we are one hundred and five Europeans being surrounded by at least three thousand mountaineers, who, wrapped up in their hill blankets, looked on at what we call our polite amusements, and bowed to the ground if a European came near them. I sometimes wonder they do not cut all our heads off and say nothing about it.[36]

Things can, and do, get lost. Suitcases, teapots, paintings are all perishable, as is, of course, the empire itself. But words—especially English words—live on, as the survival of Flora's poems and the text of her historical double testify.

In an important sense, then, gender is more than incidental to the script. This is not just because women are the heart of the play, or even because the encounter between Flora and Nirad Das is a source of mystery and intrigue. White women are, rather, the keepers of imperial memory, and in the end, like many memsahibs before 1947, they remain guarantors of empire's reproduction for future generations. And yet if Flora and Eden are intended as evidence of the liberalism of empire, they succeed in revealing the limitations of political critique in the heroic mode, even and especially when women get to be the heroes.[37] To imagine that Eden wished the end of British rule is nothing short of fantasy. Not only was her brother then the governor-general of India, but *Up the Country* is in many ways a classically Orientalist text, not least because of its "sympathetic" view of "the natives." That someone like Flora, even with her Bloomsbury and socialist connections as alluded to in the play, would have welcomed the end of British India is less dubious but still unlikely. It is a possibility that is not, in any case, borne out by the rest of the narrative, where we see her demonstrating a number of fairly conventional Orientalist behaviors, including voicing her suspicion that it is Das who has gossiped about her health problems and spread misinformation about the purposes of her visit. Orientalism is not, of course, equivalent to anti-nationalism. But in the end, Flora is a basically apolitical person, as careless about politics as she is about posing nude. To read her as a "mutinous free-spirit," as one critic in London did (and as Stoppard surely intended her), is to overestimate her commitment to the end of the empire in Britain, though it does suggest the enduring purchase of the modern liberal imperialist fantasy that white women were typically predisposed to anti-imperial sympathies.[38] Indian women, meanwhile, make no appearance at all, a vacuum characteristic of most, if not all, imperialist narratives about decolonization in India and one that perpetuates the myth that British India and its fate rested solely in the hands of Anglo-Indians, colonial officers, native servants, and a few Indian men.[39]

Indeed, despite the play's representations of the anticolonial resistance that helped to determine the last days of the Raj, *Indian Ink* is not subversive of imperial histories or ideologies; it is, rather, one of empire's contemporary residual effects. Nowhere is this clearer than in the character of Nirad Das. Stoppard writes Das's public protest against colonial rule as a sad, pathetic, and finally futile attempt to attack the British government in India. As Peter Kemp put it in his review of the production at the Aldwych Theatre in 1995, under the title "Flinging Mangos at the Resident's Daimler":

> That the missile is nothing more than a menacing fruit typifies this play's softening of political antagonisms. In other ways, too, Stoppard seems insouciantly content not to probe too deeply into the situation he re-stages; he remains, for instance, apparently heedless of his play's curious suggestion that, in order to liberate himself from colonial promptings, an Indian needs an erotic nudge from an Englishwoman.[40]

Stoppard is not interested either in staging a full-scale critique of empire or in moving beyond a kind of friendly caricature of its foibles. As he remarked to Mel Gussow in 1995, he thought the play was "worryingly cosy," but he "really enjoy[ed] its lack of radical fierceness. It has its checks and balances. There's no ranting or storming around; there are no long monologues."[41] Nor is he careless where the sexual politics of the play are concerned. The relationship between Flora and Das is quite carefully and deliberately crafted so that it replaces—or, at least, distracts from—the political action of nationalists and nationalism on the ground, against which the lovers are made to seem far more sophisticated and Flora, quite "radical." The fact that all the turmoil of 1930 happens off-stage, and that news of unrest and riots and violence is carried onto the set by various Indians who have encountered it, further distances the audience from it and makes it easier and, indeed, more pleasurable to read decolonization as a highly individual, personal process. By moving political questions into the bedroom, *Indian Ink* effectively domesticates the end of empire and arguably de-politicizes the whole "affair." More accurately, the play re-politicizes the last days of the Raj as a comfortable, consumable tale that does little to disrupt dominant narratives of empire's end in India as the "granting" of autonomy rather than as the concession of independence in the face of a popular anti-imperialist movement that, by 1947, was several decades old.

How audiences would have responded to the play in the spring and summer of 1995 is, of course, notoriously difficult to evaluate. But it is possible to speculate about what the total theater experience would have been like for them by looking at the playbill—which, it must be said, is a monument to a bygone imperial era. The program was oversize compared with the usual *Playbill* variety, and that alone may have caused ticket holders to take a closer look than they otherwise might have. It featured a map of India, sketches of various "native scenes," and quotes from Charles Allen's *Plain Tales from the Raj*, a coffee-table book that originated as a BBC production. A reprint of an image of Emily Eden, complete with a short biography, also appears, just underneath two photos—one, a vintage photograph taken in the 1930s of "native" crowds in India being beaten back with *lathis*; the other, a Modigliani nude. Theatergoers were obviously being encouraged to admire the facticity of the play, to embrace not just its historical accuracy but its aesthetic verisimilitude as well. The program also contains excerpts from *Hobson–Jobson* with definitions of various words used in the play, including *"punkah," "dawk,"* and *"verandah."*[42] In addition to being an Orientalist production, the Aldwych Theatre's version of *Indian Ink* was clearly an exercise in feeding what was left of the Raj nostalgia machine in the 1990s. For the price of a pound sterling, theatergoers could come away with a souvenir program as well as the memory of the play itself. The commodification of *Indian Ink* in this form suggests the ways in which Stoppard's play participated in a larger economy of "India, Inc." in the 1980s and 1990s, a phenomenon manifest in this case as a species of "tourist art" that continued the ideological work of the play beyond the confines of the Aldwych by moving public history into private hands.[43]

Critics writing about the play rushed to pigeonhole it as a Stoppardesque equivalent of *The Jewel in the Crown* and so to reiterate what were, by the time the BBC aired *In the Native State* in 1991, the familiar lineaments of the Raj nostalgia syndrome. Stoppard was as aware of the appetite the British public displayed for rehearsals of the Raj's glory days as he was of the fact that the subject was in danger of exhausting its appeal. "I mean the whole Anglo-Indian world has been so raked over and presented and re-presented by quite a small company of actors who appear in all of them," he told Paul Allen almost apologetically when interviewed in 1991 about the radio play. By 1995, the genre presumably had become even more hackneyed, although this did not prevent the producers of the stage version from continuing to capitalize on what was left of Raj nostalgia. Art Malik, who had played Hari Kumar to such critical acclaim in the British television production of *The Jewel in the Crown,* was cast as Nirad Das. Even if viewers did not know his name, they may well have recognized the face. And if they read reviews of the show, they could not help but notice Malik—"That old Raj drama hand," as Peter Kemp dubbed him—to whom critics invariably drew attention. Stoppard professed not to have known that Malik was in *The Jewel in the Crown*. He claimed in 1995, in fact, that he had never seen the television production or read *The Raj Quartet*, but he did admit to knowing that Malik had appeared as the Arab terrorist in Arnold Schwarzenegger's blockbuster film *True Lies*.[44] Given the fact that many London theatergoers, especially in summer, are white, middle-class Americans, the role of *Indian Ink* in sustaining Raj nostalgia is even more interesting, stoking what seems like an inexhaustible market for the exotic allure of British imperialism—all of this in the wake of a historical moment in which the "special" Anglo-American relationship had undergone a highly publicized revival, with Margaret Thatcher and Ronald Reagan cavorting about the international stage like transatlantic cousins. Unlike *Arcadia* (1993), however, which was a huge hit in London and New York, *Indian Ink* did not make it to Broadway, though it did debut in Washington, D.C., in the fall of 1999 to rave reviews ("The jewel in the Crown of the season").[45] Nor has it yet been made into a film, despite Stoppard's position as "a leading playwright on either side of the Atlantic" and despite his express desire for a movie version.[46]

Stoppard's images of India in the 1930s are wistfully inaccurate, at best, and regrettably unrepresentative, at worst. His representations of Britain in the 1980s are perhaps more unsettling, not so much for the ideological work they actively do as for the absences they enshrine at the heart of the narrative. It bears emphasizing that the "contemporary" portion of the play is meant to be the mid-1980s, and *not* the early 1990s, as some reviewers of the radio play seemed to assume. The difference of five years is not to be dismissed as negligible, for the 1980s were a decade of tremendous racial contention, when Britain's post-imperial status was vigorously debated, and images of black–white–brown violence in London and elsewhere in the British Isles circulated widely on television and in film.[47] This is crucial for understanding the politics of *Indian Ink* and its critical reception, if only because one could come away from the play with no knowledge of such volatile events, despite their prominence in the headlines during the very years the contemporary action is supposed to be occurring—that is, during the later part of Thatcher's prime ministership, for which race and the legacy of empire were such defining questions.[48] Nor did these debates express themselves only through violence. They occurred in City Council and County Council elections, in television drama, and in the pages of national newspapers virtually daily, as Thatcher's quest for "enterprise culture" alternatively scorned black Britons and wooed Asians for capitalist ventures.[49] Britain was, in other words, a veritable racial battleground in which contests over national identity as racial identity were continually played out. In Stoppard's play, in contrast, Britain in the mid-1980s "takes place" in suburban London, in the living room of the former memsahib Nell, whose world is intruded on by a brash American scholar and a more softly spoken England-resident "Indian" man, but never by even a hint of the tumult that was going on in the streets of cities in the United Kingdom over the racial makeup of fin-de-siècle Britain. This occlusion, and the blind eye it turns toward the impact of empire at home in economic and political terms, is in many respects far more revealing than the imperial sexual politics of the play. The complete lack of reference to the kind of racial strife evident in Hanif Kureishi's *My Beautiful Laundrette* (1985) and *Sammy and Rosie Get Laid* (1987), on the one hand, and the enclosure of Nell in her house in Shepperton, on the other, are, of course, intimately related. They are the effects of the same de-politicizing strategy, one that re-politicizes the end of empire as a kind of domestic quarrel that is easily consumable from the comfort of one's arm-chair—or theater seat.

In a plot evidently determined to merge home and empire—or, at the very least, to suggest the ways in which they overlapped imaginatively and in terms of the traffic of goods and people—the omission of any allusion to the racial violence and contestation of the 1980s is surely a remarkable one. Not a single critic has asked Stoppard about this in print. Not surprisingly, given the stranglehold that the culture of celebrity has exercised on public intellectual life and political debate in both Britain and America in the postwar period, the British press at the time was more interested in the fact that Stoppard and the actress who played Flora Crewe in the Aldwych production, Felicity Kendal, were lovers. Although Kendal had been the leading woman in several of his other plays, news of their relationship broke just before the Radio 3 broadcast, prompting the *Radio Times* to speculate on Kendal's "love affair . . . with India."[50] Once again, and in ways that echo the work of the play itself, *Indian Ink* was touted as a love affair, with its sins of commission and omission cast to the side in favor of "sexual scandal" of the most prurient—and hence, market-able—kind.

The re-domestication of the end of the British Raj in and around the production of *Indian Ink* has, moreover, an intimately familiar history. As Stoppard explained to Mel Gussow as the Aldwych production was about to open, the stage play is dedicated to Laura Kendal, Felicity's mother.[51] She and her husband, Geoffrey, had a company of actors who toured South Asia and Southeast Asia, a story that was made into the film *Shake-speare Wallah* (1965) by Ismail Merchant and James Ivory.[52] *Shakespeare Wallah* was also Felicity Kendal's movie debut, and, as many theatergoers might have known, Felicity's sister Jennifer also appeared in that film and was married into the Hindi film family of Shashi Kapoor, who in turn had a role in *Shakespeare Wallah*.[53] Thus, the transnational film and celebrity culture of the late twentieth century gave Stoppard an insider's view that his own, somewhat marginalized, childhood relationship to British India could not begin to approximate. In an echo of the historical experience of many lower-class Britons who emigrated to India, Stoppard's return to Britain and his rise in the British theater gave him the kind of cultural capital, as well as the class status, that his family could not achieve during the final days of the Raj.

As Yasmin Ali has observed, the British empire had many echoes at century's end.[54] The productions of *Indian Ink* and the brief traces they left on the fin-de-siècle cultural scene prompt one to ponder, among other things, the relationship of BBC radio plays to films such as Kureishi's; of the Strand to Brixton and South Shields; of television to Hollywood and "Bollywood"; of tea trays and Mughal painting and the Victoria and Albert Museum to Pakistani groceries and Indian takeouts and other targets of violence and racial hatred in contemporary Britain. Surely the stories that each of these "opposites" tells compete in the contemporary imagination not just for the ground of memory and history, but also for commodification in a global capitalist marketplace. Perhaps the story about British citizens and subjects of color who "have borne the brunt of elite and popular anger that the Britain of 1995 is not the Britain of 1945" simply will not sell in a West End patronized mostly by middle- and upper-class white Britons and Americans.[55] This may be especially true of the white American clientele, who prefer their Britain PBS-style, where they can avoid the images of racial tension and violence that crowd network television in the U.S. and can escape into Georgian, Victorian, and Edwardian worlds where bourgeois existence is uninterrupted by such things. When race does intrude, it is packaged, as in *The Jewel in the Crown*, as nostalgia with just the appropriate tinge of regret and self-censure about "what we did over there."

Like the past and the present, however, the "Orient" and the West End are not merely opposites; they work dialectically in culture *and* through the cultural imagination, sometimes to unmask hegemonies, but more often to reconsolidate them in new historical forms. Is *Indian Ink* simply another form of colonial knowledge, to be ranged against a long history of other such knowledges?[56] How different it is in this respect from its Irish contemporary, Brian Friel's *Dancing at Lughnasa,* which was published in 1990 and is also set in both the 1930s and the 1980s. As Declan Kiberd observed, "By exploring the parallels between African and Celtic harvest festivals," Friel's play "brought to the fore the post-colonial elements of Irish culture after a decade of chronic emigration and unemployment had led many to ask whether Ireland might not itself be a third world country."[57] Irish cultural workers have long been willing to admit to "universal boundaries" compared with the resolute embrace of "splendid isolation" that is England's trademark. And Friel was willing to see his stagescapes—his Irelands—in colonial terms long before arguments about postcolonialism were fashionable, no doubt because of his critical appreciation for Ireland's historically colonial relationship to England. This is a comparison worth dwelling on, if only because of the appeal of Celtic nostalgia in the transatlantic public sphere, among middle-class white Americans rapturous about the Raj but unwilling or perhaps unable to embrace Ireland and India as part of a similar, if historically distinctive, world-historical colonial phenomenon. Such a disjuncture is, arguably, merely characteristic of the persistent disaggregation of India from the rest of Britain's colonial possessions and experiences, a disaggregation that means that India returns as the "jewel" in the postcolonial crown.

As with all nostalgia, Stoppard's text longs for a "future past" made possible by the intrusion of the 1930s into the 1980s. As if the rhetorics of nostalgia and mourning, memory and loss, that the play stages are not enough, the death of Flora allows us to experience "elegiac processes of leave-taking" from the past that makes the imperialist nostalgia of both the script and the 1995 production impossible to escape.[58] As a narrative of desire for an empire destined to be history, *Indian Ink* represents a return to and, ultimately, a disavowal of the end of empire, rehearsing for us the role that imperialist nostalgia continued to play in the late-twentieth-century British cultural imagination.[59] Meanwhile, the popularity of Raj productions such as *Indian Ink* in the context of a multiracial, post-imperial culture leads one to wonder at the relentless restaging of empire's end and, more productively, to inquire about what aesthetic forms postcolonial memory takes when empire is apparently gone but continues to "vanish" again and again before our very eyes.

14

New Narratives of Imperial Politics in the Nineteenth Century

Parliament cares about India little more than the Cabinet. The English people, too, are very slow and very careless about everything that does not immediately affect them. They cannot be excited to any effort of India except under the pressure of some great calamity, and when that calamity is removed they fall back into their usual state of apathy.
—John Bright (1860)

The sentiment of empire is innate in every Briton.
—William Gladstone (1878)

The trouble with the English is that their history happened overseas, so they don't know what it means.
—Salman Rushdie (1989)

For historians of the nineteenth century, the question is, arguably, not whether empire had an impact on domestic life and experience, but how. The realm of high politics is a domain where those influences are most evident, though the role of imperialism in shaping it has received comparatively little attention. If historians have been slow to see and to recognize the impact of empire on "domestic" history, Britons who followed high politics from the 1830s until just after Queen Victoria's death in 1901 could not have ignored the ways in which imperial questions impinged on and helped to shape Victorian democracy across the nineteenth century. The Captain Swing rioters and other "criminals" were exiled to Australia; opium debates made their way to the floor of the House; and Irishmen and women, together with former Caribbean slaves, were involved in

Chartist agitations—whose spokesmen drew in turn on metaphors of slavery to inform their political demands.[1] White, English, middle-class women entered debates about citizenship through their interest in the plight of slaves and colonial peoples, an interest that laid the groundwork for Victorian feminism.[2] Whether the issue was abolition or the extension of democracy to the new middle classes, parliamentary statesmen and social reformers understood the linkages between domestic concerns and imperial problems, in part because they viewed empire as a constitutive part of national character, national life, and national political culture.

Political reform at the highest level was carried out in the context of tremendous public debate about imperial questions. As Catherine Hall has shown, the years leading up to the passage of the Great Reform Act, which did away with "rotten" boroughs and expanded the electorate by approximately 60 percent across the United Kingdom in 1832, were preceded by elaborate discussions of citizenship in a variety of "colonial" contexts.[3] Ireland was one. Although Britons did not typically use the word "colony" for Ireland at the time, in Hall's view it was a colony "in that Irish Catholics in Ireland were treated as a conquered people and English Protestants in Ireland acted as colonial settlers."[4] Religious difference carried with it overtones of racial difference, and Irish Catholics were politically disenfranchised as well as culturally subordinated. Daniel O'Connell's work with the Catholic Association, and especially his speeches to Parliament, placed civil rights for the Catholic Irish at the heart of political debate and made it clear that the peace and stability of the whole of the United Kingdom was in peril if political emancipation at the periphery closest in was not forthcoming. Unrest in Upper and Lower Canada in this period added to the sense that the empire was in crisis.[5] Jamaica was another very visible colonial context in which debates about political reform occurred in the 1830s. Parliament was preoccupied with events in Jamaica in the two years leading up to the passage of the Reform Act of 1832, especially in the wake of the Christmas rebellion in December 1831, in which free black men and women sought to overthrow slavery and were brutally repressed.[6] As in Ireland, the language of civil rights and the threat to private property in Jamaica set the stage for a quite conservative Reform Bill in 1832, one that enfranchised about 400,000 men in the United Kingdom but that left the majority of British men and all British women without the parliamentary vote.

The 1830s were a decade characterized by "liberal" reforms shaped by imperial pressures, including the act that abolished slavery in 1833. Indeed, for all of the allusions to their connections across the whole of the nineteenth century in scholarship from the 1940s onward, the direct and indirect connections between imperialism and the slave trade have yet to be fully documented.[7] In any case, some of the men involved at the highest levels of domestic reform were also involved in promoting legislation that would have a huge impact on colonizers and colonized alike. One such man was Thomas Babington Macaulay, who famously supported the 1832 act by arguing that Britain must "reform to preserve."[8] Just three years later, he took quite a different tack when he suggested that Government of India funds for Instruction in Arabic and Sanskrit should not be preserved—and offered the equally famous opinion, "We must at present do our best to form . . . a class of persons, Indian in blood and colour, but English in taste, in opinions, in morals, and in intellect."[9] Debates about citizenship and belonging in the nation-empire persisted into the 1840s, once again with Ireland and Jamaica at the fore. O'Connell continued to press for Irish freedoms, while two of the century's most famous men of letters, Thomas Carlyle and John Stuart Mill, engaged in heated public debate about the impact of the West Indian "Negro question" on issues such as labor, virtue, and civilization. Nor was empire merely debated at the rhetorical level. British imperial ambitions extended to China and Afghanistan in the 1840s. Contests with Russia over the limits of British imperial interests led to a war in the Crimea (1853–55), which in turn led some commentators such as Richard Cobden to reflect on the extent to which imperial ambition could, or should, define national greatness.[10] Others, such as William Greg in 1851, posed an equally provocative question about the financial viability of empire: "Shall We Retain Our Colonies?"[11] Although it was not the only uprising to threaten British imperial stability before mid-century or after, the Indian Mutiny (sometimes called the Rebellion) of 1857 has become the most famous. Karl Marx, writing from New York, declared it a "catastrophe" and chastised the colonial state for its "abominations" against the rebels.[12] Nonetheless, the Indian Mutiny brought images of empire home to Britons like no other event of the century, thereby revealing the fragility of British imperial rule to a generation of Victorians for whom the power of the Raj had appeared untouchable.[13]

The generation of British politicians that oversaw the passage of the Second Reform Act (1867) was equally preoccupied with imperial questions—again in Jamaica, where the Morant Bay rebellion of 1865 exerted enormous pressure on discussions both in and outside Parliament about who could count as a Briton and how race shaped the definition of a citizen.[14] And once again, Ireland played an important role at this political juncture. In 1867 the Fenians sought justice through violent means, and an Irish Republic was briefly declared.[15] That year also witnessed the British North America Act, which provided for the federation of Upper and Lower Canada, New Brunswick, and Nova Scotia, thus rearranging Britain's longstanding relationship with one of its chief white settler colonies.[16] More so than in 1832, imperial power was visible in the legislation that enfranchised 400,000 more British men, some of them laborers, in 1867. The polity to which they gained entrance was decidedly white, male, and middle class, despite attempts by English women to gain access to the vote through voluntary associations, parliamentary petitions, and direct confrontation at the hustings.[17] Perhaps surprisingly, Victorian feminists were no less wedded to empire than their male counterparts. As they made their case for the right to participate in the political nation, they invoked colonial women and other Orientalist images almost casually as part of their case for emancipation.[18] In this sense, they were little different from the leaders of both of Britain's political parties in the Victorian era. William Gladstone and Benjamin Disraeli (prime ministers and political adversaries) each used British imperialism, its limits and possibilities, as a platform for party unity and ideological sparring.[19] Although the Tory party became known as the party of empire, many Liberals embraced imperialism as the inevitable, if not wholly desirable, burden of geopolitical power, especially after the siege of Khartoum and the death of General Gordon (1884–85).[20]

The third and final Reform Act of the century (1884) did little to alter the basically conservative character of Victorian democracy except by enfranchising agricultural laborers. But parliamentary debates in its wake —especially those about Ireland and India—kept empire visible at home. Although it had been a consistent feature of political life since at least the 1870s, the question of Irish self-determination came to a head at this same moment, with the defeat of a Home Rule bill in 1886 ensuring an almost permanent end to Liberal Party power until the twentieth century.[21] The Indian National Congress, founded in 1885, also made a variety of political claims on the idea of English democracy.[22] Despite its links with Irish nationalists, it fell short of demanding Home Rule at this stage. One of its first presidents, Dadhabai Naoroji, was elected member of Parliament for

Central Finsbury in 1892, bringing the question of Indian self-representation directly into the "Mother of all Parliaments."[23]

As Bernard Semmel documented in astonishing detail nearly forty years ago, the discourses and policies of social imperialism provided the major ideological backdrop for British politics from the fin de siècle until the Great War.[24] The so-called Khaki election of 1900 provided an opportunity for many political constituencies to comment on the nature and direction of imperial policy. George Bernard Shaw's confidence in the invincibility of the British empire was to be sorely tested by the Boer War (1899–1902), which many Britons supported as a "holy war" intended to protect the "native races" of its South African empire from the depredations of lesser civilizations such as the Afrikaans-speaking Dutch settlers who posed a threat to Britain's ambitions on the African continent at large.[25] This kind of competitive whiteness signaled an intensified awareness of racial identities at the turn of the century. Indeed, racial exclusion was the precondition of nation formation as well as of empire building, as is evident in the creation of an all-white citizenship policy alongside the foundation of Australia in 1901.[26] By the time J. A. Hobson wrote in his famous treatise *Imperialism* (1902) that "colonialism, in its best sense, is a natural overflow of nationality; its test is the power of colonists to transplant the civilization they represent to the new natural and social environment in which they find themselves," empire was so natural a fact of life in Britain that it has taken historians until very recently to rediscover its many influences and effects at home.[27]

What I have sketched should not, of course, be taken as any kind of definitive new narrative. It represents one of many possibilities enabled by students of imperial political culture, many of whom are now refocusing our attention on the role of Britain's white settler colonies (South Africa, Canada, Australia, New Zealand) in the metropole in ways that recontextualize and may in the end mitigate our emphasis on the role of India and Africa, long considered the dominant colonial influences at home and in the empire.[28] This work, together with the explosion of visual-culture projects in a variety of British metropolitan and provincial museums in recent years, provides the basis for a number of different, and perhaps even competing, paradigms for the study of imperial Britain in the nineteenth century and twentieth century.[29] The challenges of periodization nonetheless remain, beginning with the very term "Victorian," which technically binds us to the years 1837–1901. Few surveys, whether in the form of textbooks or course syllabi, cleave to either that beginning or end date. In my primary-source reader, *Politics and Empire in Victorian Britain*, I suggest as one alternative 1829–1905 on the grounds that bookending the period with Catholic emancipation on one side and the Alien Act on the other restores questions of religion and race to the dominant narratives of both national *and* imperial histories, offering a flexible alternative to both the Whig interpretation and that of the *Oxford History of the British Empire*.[30] Yet there are still "political" events and formations that have left little trace on even alternative narratives of the Victorian period. Fully fledged wars in Afghanistan, China, and the Transvaal before the 1890s, and lesser but equally significant eruptions or rebellions in Canada, South Asia, and Africa across the century, impinged on national consciousness and high politics in ways that have yet to be fully explored by historians of the period, even though Victorians themselves left evidence of the politicizing influence of faraway battles in distant imperial lands.[31] Incidents such as the Don Pacifico affair (in which a Portuguese Jew born in Gibraltar tried to claim British citizenship and sparked an international incident) and events such as the Crimean War (in which Britain sought to contain Russia's territorial ambitions to protect its Indian empire) also brought imperial questions before the popular and the official mind in ways that have yet to be fully historicized, let alone reconciled with accounts of Britain's "imperial century." Whether military in the strictest sense or not, such high-profile imperial episodes helped to gender citizenship as masculine and to underscore it as presumptively white, the very public work of Florence Nightingale (the famous "Lady with the Lamp") and Mary Seacole (a mixed-race nurse who was also in the Crimea) notwithstanding.[32] Taking seriously the intersections between military ideology and "domestic" policy will likely further erode the distinctions between "home" and "empire" and may also give rise to a chronology that interrupts the canonical recourse to the Crystal Palace and the Mutiny of 1857 as the twin embodiments of "mid–Victorian" political culture.[33] Nor has the articulation of political economy and political culture in national, regional, or local landscapes been as fully attended to as it might be. The story of the unequal competition between the Lancashire and Indian cotton mills at the height of the industrial revolution, for example, is among the most celebrated and yet perhaps least well-integrated instances of Mrinalini Sinha's "combined but uneven development," one arguably with ramifications in world history if Mahatma Gandhi's embrace and mobilization of *swadeshi* (a boycott of British products in favor of ones made in India) in the next century is taken as one indirect, *longue durée* effect of India's comparative eclipse with respect to industrial "progress."[34]

Colonial Circuitry and the Politics of Social Imperialism

Despite the purchase of Bernard Semmel's argument that imperialism was a constituent feature of reform politics in the two decades before the First World War, histories of nineteenth-century British labor, British socialism, and British progressivism have not fully countenanced the impact of empire on those movements. The great exception to this is, of course, Anna Davin's germinal article "Imperialism and Motherhood" (1978), which made a persuasive case for the influence of the post–Boer War political climate on the creation of a eugenicist program of social reform and state intervention that targeted Britain's poor and, arguably, laid the groundwork for the twentieth-century welfare state.[35] While Davin's article was remarkable as much for connecting the dots between an imperial war and state-sponsored social programs as it was for emphasizing the role of women and gender in shaping those connections, it has not proved unusual in identifying the Anglo–Boer conflict as the takeoff point for reformers' engagements with imperialism in the post–"scramble-for-Africa" period. Indeed, Britain's Pyrrhic victory in South Africa tends to be the point of departure for past and present work on the history of the left and empire, as if progressives' interest in imperial questions was limited to the duration of that struggle or even its aftermath or could be reduced to an anatomy of who supported and who rejected the government's aims and military campaigns in the Transvaal.[36] There is, in other words, a back story about empire and progressive politics before the onset of the Boer War that remains to be told. Meanwhile, the insularity of late-nineteenth-century liberal-left political culture from imperial influences in British historiography remains one of the most remarkable features of British studies after the imperial turn.[37]

To be sure, social-reform histories, and especially those interested in the late Victorian and Edwardian origins of the welfare state, have long taken a transnational approach with respect to European influences, in part because of the internationalist character of fin-de-siècle socialism and in part because of the attraction of continental models (such as Bismarck's Germany) for social insurance and other reform schemes.[38] But given the tremendous mobility of reformers and politicians—a mobility of people matched by the cross-pollination of ideas and policymaking, as Ian Tyrell and Daniel T. Rodgers have shown in the Atlantic context—the geographical ambit of that internationalism must be extended to include the colonies, which many contemporaries frankly admired as a social laboratory for progressive political and social-reform projects.[39] The white settler colonies, especially Australia and New Zealand, were singled out for scrutiny in the 1890s when a series of socioeconomic crises and liberal government responses there produced a variety of progressive outcomes, including the passage of a women's suffrage act in New Zealand in 1893.[40] If feminists the world over could not resist shaming modern Euro-American democracies for being upstaged by such an Antipodean success story, they were by no means alone in pointing to Australia and, especially, New Zealand as the place where the true future of democracy might be glimpsed.[41]

Although space does not permit me to rehearse this in detail, I would not like to reproduce the historiographical emphasis on the 1890s where metropolitan attention to the Antipodes is concerned. Quite apart from the sustained interest in New Zealand in the 1860s and 1870s in the wake of the Maori Wars, the periodical press in Britain was attentive to political dynamics and developments in the Antipodes, Canada, South Africa, and, of course, the United States in a concentrated way at least from the 1880s, using all these places as sites for evaluating the successes and failures of Anglo-Saxon values and "colonial" projects. The Antipodes were an especially attractive destination for political ethnographers, not least because the vexed histories of their settlement offered myriad comparisons with "English" form and practices, whether political, social, economic, or cultural. The familiarity of Australia and New Zealand—their presumptive whiteness and their apparently recognizable Englishness, especially in the context of decimated aboriginal populations, whose virtual extinction was alternately bemoaned and ignored, and Chinese laborers, whose access to the nation was being restricted—was also an attraction, though one that could reveal the vexed nature of "identification" with fellow Anglo-Saxons. To take only the most famous example, Charles Dilke's *Greater Britain* (1868) surveyed the white settler colonies past and present, combining travelogue with political commentary in ways that put "Australasia" on the map in enduring ways. *Greater Britain* (and its successor, *The Problem of Greater Britain* [1890]) was undoubtedly a species of imperial apologia, but in it the young Dilke professed his admiration for the fact that what he saw in Australia was very much like what Britain was destined to become in the wake of manhood suffrage. He described the colony of Victoria as

> the most interesting place I have been in, since it probably presents an accurate view "in little" of the state of society which will exist in England after manhood suffrage is carried, but before the nation as a whole has become completely democratic. Democracy—like Mormonism—would be nothing if found among Frenchmen, or niggers, but is at first sight very terrible when it wears an English broad-cloth suit, and smiles on you, from between a pair of Yorkshire cheeks.[42]

Dilke's ambivalence about the image of the future he caught sight of in Australia was echoed by many of the well-known or well-heeled Victorians who traveled to Australia and New Zealand in the last three decades of the nineteenth century to engage in the hard work of that uniquely Victorian genre: reform-minded tourism. Of particular interest here are those radicals and progressives who sought out the Antipodes in the 1890s and after for what political events and legislative experiments there could tell them about democracy and progress in action, especially of the socialist variety. The Irish member of Parliament Michael Davitt; the Social Democratic Federation leader H. M. Hyndman; the Labour Party organizer and future prime minister Ramsay MacDonald (with his wife, Margaret); and the Fabians Sidney and Beatrice Webb are just a few among the many fin-de-siècle reformers who traveled to "the Democratic communities of the South Seas" in search of "socialism without doctrines."[43]

What impact did such travels have on metropolitan politics in the making? First and foremost, they brought knowledge about colonial conditions into the discursive space of reform circles and advertised specific legislative innovations that were of great interest especially to radical reformers in the age of Chamberlain and Rosebery. So, for example, Davitt's travelogue *Life and Progress in Australasia* (1898) trumpeted the passage of the Industrial Conciliation and Arbitration Act of 1894 in New Zealand as part of a series of government interventions covering "almost every risk to life, limb, health and interest of the industrial classes." In his view, New Zealand was "the most progressive country in the world today," surpassing even Australia in its emphasis on state responsibility for the problems engendered by a modernizing industrial democracy.[44] The case of the Webbs is equally instructive. Although their diaries are notorious for the general snobbery and contempt they showed over what they viewed as the "vulgar" Australians and New Zealanders (not to mention Americans) they encountered on their tour in 1898, Sidney Webb's public pronouncements were much more positive. In an interview in the *Echo* in 1898, he was quoted as saying:

> We have got to wake up to the fact that Australia must be taken seriously, and studied, not as an infant community just out of the gold-diggings stage, but as an adult Anglo-Saxon Democracy, full of interest and instruction to the political world. We have a vast amount to learn from Australia, especially in the sphere of government. Our statesmen are always running over to the United States, which is essentially a foreign country, as unlike England as Germany itself. But, with the notable exception of Sir Charles Dilke, they seem to know nothing of, and learn nothing from, the Democratic communities of the South Seas, whose experience of Cabinet administration is extensive and peculiar . . . Australia sadly needs studying, as Mr Bryce studied the American Commonwealth, and such a work would be of enormous value.[45]

Sidney admired Australia in direct proportion to the fact that it was so unlike America; in that sense, Australia for him was an attractive Fabian alternative to the dominant liberal tendency to look to the United States for refractions of Anglo-Saxon ideals. Australia was to be admired, in short, because it was not about abstractions or "arbitrary psychology." It was here, in its English-inspired disposition toward practicalities, that "the extraordinary interest of Australian political experience to the English student" lay.[46] Even more remarkable was Beatrice Webb's take on New Zealand. Not known to wax enthusiastic about many subjects, Beatrice declared that if she had to raise a family outside Great Britain, she would choose New Zealand. While not totally uncritical, as Sidney had been on Australia, she took America as her main point of comparison. In contrast to both Britain and the United States, she found in New Zealand "no millionaires and hardly any slums. . . . [A] people characterized by homely refinement, and by a large measure of vigorous public spirit."[47]

The Webbs' experience in Australasia may have been a wake-up call for them about the pedagogical value of colonial experiments, but, as I have suggested, they somewhat belatedly joined a growing group of metropolitan politicians and reformers for whom the view from the Antipodes was less a mirror than a kind of visionary political possibility. In any event, the story of the Webbs' Antipodean experience has several ramifications for the provocation about reverse flow that animates this volume. In the first instance, it is quite likely that the Webbs' determination to visit Australia and New Zealand was the result of their encounter with two New Zealanders in London: William Pember Reeves and his wife, Maud Pember Reeves. Reeves had been a member of the Liberal Party government in New Zealand that oversaw much of the progressive legislation Britons admired in the early 1890s (especially, in his capacity as minister for labour, the Arbitration Act), and from 1896 he became the New Zealand agent-general in London. Maud had political credentials in her own right, having participated in the agitation for women's suffrage in New Zealand that resulted in the franchise in 1893. William Pember Reeves had been an admirer of Fabian socialism since he had read *Essays in Fabian Socialism,* published in 1889; he had corresponded with Sydney Webb from New Zealand, and when he came to London, the two met, and he and Maud were quickly taken into the Fabians' circle.[48] Reeves's biographer intimates that the Webbs' visit to New Zealand in order to get firsthand impressions of a socialist state in action was one consequence of their friendship.[49]

In addition to whetting the Webbs' appetite for what he would later call "experiments in state socialism," Reeves was an active contributor to the dissemination of information about New Zealand, its political accomplishments, and its imperial allegiances in metropolitan opinion forums such as the *National Review* and several Fabian tracts.[50] So confident were the Webbs in Reeves's bona fides that they entrusted him with the directorship of their most enduring Fabian product of all, the London School of Economics.[51] In terms of direct influence on Fabian socialism, however, Maud's role was even more significant, though it perhaps is still largely underappreciated. Not only did she become a member of the Fabian executive committee, taking H. G. Wells's side in his failed bid to take control of the society in 1906–7; she was instrumental in getting and keeping "the woman question" on the Fabian agenda into the early years of the twentieth century, as seen in her contributions to the eventual formation of the Fabian Women's Group in 1908.[52] Nor was her role limited to the suffrage question per se. Maud Pember Reeves was the author of a celebrated Fabian pamphlet, later expanded into a book, that documented the struggles of English working-class mothers and became a bestseller and a classic in both liberal-leftist and feminist circles until the end of the twentieth century: *Round about a Pound a Week.*[53] As late as the 1990s, the historian David Vincent was still citing it as an authority on the Victorian social-welfare mind, its aspirations, and its strategies for reform.[54]

Maud Pember Reeves was not, of course, alone in her efforts to propel women's issues to the centre of the Fabian platform. But her experiences in the New Zealand suffrage struggle undoubtedly helped her to strategize the necessary ways and means to fight the confident but ultimately sexist sexual-liberation program at the heart of Wells's version of socialism. Nor was she the only Fabian woman to draw on colonial experiences to make her case for the necessity of state support for working women and mothers. In 1907, B. L. Hutchins wrote Fabian Tract No. 130, *Home Work and Sweating: The Causes and Remedies*, in which she referred extensively to legislation in Australia and especially New Zealand and in which the Arbitration Act figured prominently in her case for the regulation of sweating. As John Rickard has shown, this was part of a larger cross-relay between Australia, New Zealand, and Britain over the question of labor policy and social reform in the first decade of the twentieth century.[55] Once again, although the heightened attention brought to these questions by, for example, the Exhibition of Sweated Labour at Queen's Hall in 1906 has given them prominence in twentieth-century narratives, this should not occlude the late Victorian roots of these imperial networks. In 1890, Lady Emilia Dilke, in her capacity as president of the Women's Trade Union, had used the example of striking women in Melbourne in 1882 to make her point to English women about the importance of tenacity in their labor struggles, as well as the object lesson their colonial "sisters" could teach them about the path to unionization.[56]

What we see, then, is a pattern not just of reference but of example from colonial to metropole, a discursive universe of cross-relay with pedagogical effects on the political culture of Britain—persuasive evidence of what Alan Lester calls "diverse and dynamic but interconnected imperial terrain[s]" across considerable geographical space and, most significantly, perhaps, equally powerful evidence of the movement of ideas and policies not from home to empire but the reverse. For some, the evocation of this discursive terrain may not be sufficient "proof" that empire was constitutive of "domestic" politics. For skeptics, the accomplishments of Maud Pember Reeves may well seem marginal, despite the impact of a book such as *Round about a Pound a Week* on shaping the culture of care at the heart of the emergent late Victorian / Edwardian welfare state.[57] In this respect, the political work of William Pember Reeves in London is a useful counterpoint. Although he was best known then, and remains so now, chiefly for his promotion in Britain of information about New Zealand's Arbitration Act, he also played a role in the creation of a crucial piece of social-welfare legislation: the Old Age Pensions Act. New Zealand's Pensions Bill—first proposed in 1896 and passed after several failed starts in 1898—was lauded as the first such provision in the British empire.[58] This was virtually simultaneous with the publication of the Report of the Committee on Old-Age Pensions in Britain, chaired by Lord Rothschild.[59] Although it was not mentioned in that report, New Zealand's bill was much talked about in the metropolitan press in the years leading up to the British Act of 1908, with particular emphasis placed on the means tests that the government of New Zealand had applied.[60] Reeves contributed actively to this public discussion, providing valuable evidence about the workings of the New Zealand scheme and thereby contributing to the debate about what kind of pension model should be enacted in Britain.[61] Clearly, Reeves was not directly or even indirectly responsible for the provision of old-age pensions, which grew out of a discussion that had been going on in Britain at least since the 1880s; it had deep roots in Victorian poor law and Elizabethan pauper-relief systems, as well.[62] At the same time, the Pension Act that eventually passed in Britain in 1908 borrowed from the Antipodean model rather than the German one (by relying on a redistribution of income rather than taxes to pay for the outlays).[63] Nor is this the full extent of colonial influence on the making of the social-welfare state in Britain. Although the "native" English roots and the European context of that debate have been scrutinized, the ways in which public discussion in Britain was imprinted with imperial reference points, as writings by Canon Samuel Barnett and others in the press at the time testify, have not been fully considered.[64] Reeves is not, in the end, the proverbial smoking gun, proof positive that imperial experience "made" the proto-welfare state in Britain, as Peter Coleman has claimed for New Zealand's role in American Progressivism.[65] And his role in imperial social-reform politics is in many ways "fitful," if not tenuous, with respect to the larger story of political imperial culture writ large, especially given the unrepresentativeness of the Fabians in the socialist and larger political landscape.[66] But Pember Reeves's post-1896 career in London does offer persuasive evidence that politics and even some policy outcomes in modern Britain were influenced by colonial encounters "at home," if not by the total experience of imperial power abroad, as well.[67]

Such evidence does not mean that the "domestic" and European contexts of incipient welfare statism are to be eclipsed by new imperialized narratives, though this seems often to be one fear effect of the new imperial studies. Yet the imperial context of continental references and borrowings should not be discounted, either. Recourse to German examples can easily be seen as a reflection of larger imperial competitive anxieties in the aftermath of the partition of Africa. In any case, Reeves himself was a political polyglot, gleaning what he knew and valued about progressive politics and reform from contemporary English, German, French, American, and Australian writers and practices, so it would be a mistake to see his contributions to metropolitan debates as purely "colonial"—or to view the vectors of imperial political culture as linear (rather than multidirectional or "web-like," to invoke Tony Ballantyne's metaphor).[68] It is also worth remarking, as did his late Victorian and Edwardian contemporaries, that Reeves articulated colonial whiteness as a "component of imperial governmentality" (at least in his metropolitan self-representations) in ways that underscore the racialist agendas of fin-de-siècle liberal and reformist thinking.[69] Indeed, much remains to be said about how the suppression of evidence about "aliens" and treaty work with aboriginal peoples both erased evidence of racial practices in Australasia *and* encoded the social-experiment discourses in the metropole with a certain fictive, if powerful, claim to Anglo-Saxon purity and white-supremacist triumphalism.

Given the fact that, together with democracy, the provision of services of the kind that the incipient welfare state sought to institutionalize is thought to be one of the legacies of the Victorian state to the present (and, by implication, to the world), it is worth lingering on the significance of colonial contributions to social-insurance schemes of the kind Reeves championed during his residence in Britain. This is especially warranted in light of recent work on India and Egypt that points to traditions of both colonial / state-sponsored philanthropy and indigenous forms of provision that belie the highly naturalized and historically ungrounded assumption that Britain or the West is the original home of "welfare" broadly conceived. Although he does not pursue this line of questioning, Sanjay Sharma's work on northern India, for example, opens the door to future scholars interested in tracing the connections between famine relief on the subcontinent and in Ireland in the 1830s and 1840s.[70] He and the late Mine Ener both excavate examples of poor relief provision by local elites in northern India and Cairo / Alexandria, respectively, thereby implicitly challenging the chronology of first-the-West-then-the-rest when it comes to concerted efforts to manage the indigent in self-conscious and systematic ways.[71] Relocating Pember Reeves, his wife, and their contemporaries in the long story of imperial state formation—in the combined, uneven, geographically dispersed but ideologically and practically linked imperial developments that Sharma's and Ener's work points to—is admittedly an enormous project, but it is essential to the counter-narratives of political history that we must develop if we are to challenge the persistent insularity of Whig history in toto. It is equally crucial in combating the archaic but still powerful idea that Britain's empire was acquired and sustained in a "fit of absence of mind."[72] By understanding the workings of imperial political culture (which I intend as an analogue of Sinha's "imperial social formation"), we can, I think, appreciate the ways in which imperial ideologies and practices were not orchestrated or coordinated in any necessarily deliberate way, even as we understand how a variety of local, unlooked-for, and ultimately quixotic events and players helped to suture it together —with authority as well as with the kind of porousness and flexibility that allowed contest and resistance—across space and place.

In the end, the concept of "reverse flow" that the Antipodean example illustrates may not prove the most useful metaphor for understanding how imperial political culture was made, insofar as it proceeds from a home–empire imaginary rather than evoking a multiplicity of influences (English, colonial, continental) that could account for what modern Britain looked like at the turn of the twentieth century. Indeed, the very question of "flow" has come in for some criticism for the way it allegedly reproduces "durable liberal conceptions" of movement, though it need not—and, I would say, does not—perforce do so in the new scholarship.[73] Whatever model we adopt, the history of imperial political culture—its uneven development and the convergences and divergences of people, ideas, and power it produced—is surely in the details. Of course, there will always be connections that cannot be cemented, outcomes whose genealogies we can but imperfectly trace, and evidence that the archive, however nimbly we negotiate it, and even exceed it, cannot yield. To admit as much is to acknowledge that, in Jed Esty's evocative words, "We must chart imperial presence not only as visible and narrative data but as unexpected formal encryptments and thematic outcroppings" in presumptively "domestic" contexts.[74] It is these unanticipated codes and recurrent, if fugitive, instances that require our attention. This is the terrain on which anti-imperial histories of the British empire—political or otherwise—can, should, and doubtless will be written.

— *Coda* —

EMPIRE OF/AND THE WORLD?

The Limits of British Imperialism

Getting Outside of the Global

Repositioning British Imperialism in World History

This is an interesting, if not defining, moment in British empire historiography. Students of imperialism in a global age—that is, those interested in global empires of the past and those aware of the ramifications of
global imperialism in the contemporary moment—are seeking comprehensive syntheses and authoritative overviews of the British empire, and
historians of empire are obliging.[1] Publishers have flocked to meet market
demand through series and short titles, through primers and blockbus-
ters, many of which rehearse the rise and fall of Victorian imperialism
from its early triumphs through its mid-twentieth-century dissolution
from a variety of perspectives. It is hard to imagine a historical moment
when the British empire has been more popular in the international
marketplace; British imperial history is big business. Niall Ferguson's *Empire* is a case in point. Three years after its initial publication in 2004, its
sales rank was in the top 1,700 titles on Amazon.com.uk—only marginally
behind, in proportional terms, the latest Harry Potter book—and it had
no fewer than sixty-nine reviews on the American Amazon.com website.
Aided in part by the urge for comparison that the American-led war in
Iraq has produced, accounts of British imperial supremacy are flying off
the shelves, virtual and otherwise.[2] Imperial knowledge is not just in
demand, it would seem; it is on its way to becoming the basis of a global
publishing phenomenon.

Historians of the British empire such as Niall Ferguson and Linda
Colley, the author of *Captives: Britain, Empire, and the World* and *Elizabeth
Marsh: A Woman of the World*, are well placed to capitalize on these condi-
tions insofar as they have cast their narratives as evidence of the British

empire's distinctively global character.[3] Moving simultaneously beyond the old-fashioned core–periphery model of traditional imperial history and the reverse-flow paradigm of the new imperial studies, historians of British imperial power over and above Ferguson and Colley readily acknowledge not only its global reach and impact, but also its capacity for forging and sustaining interdependent networks, multiple forms of authority and legitimacy, and connective circuitries that cast "a girdle round the earth," to recall an early-twentieth-century imperial suffrage metaphor.[4] In addition to a set of convictions about the need to think differently than has been done about Britain's empire, what this recent body of work shares is the enthusiasm of arrival: arrival at a place past not just the first post—that of, say, the multivolume *Oxford History of the British Empire*—but past the most controversial one, that of postcolonialism, as well. Thus, we are beyond postcoloniality, beyond sovereignty, beyond the nation, beyond the metropole, beyond even the colonies, though very much still in the empire, especially in its "British worlds."[5] In addition to offering a new paradigm for empire studies, the global would also appear to represent a new horizon of possibility, the last frontier, perhaps even the highest stage of imperial history—one that makes doing British empire studies feel respectable, politically relevant, and even redemptive, especially in an age of aggressive American imperialism.[6]

But what, exactly, is the global as it is being professionally developed by academics, popularly consumed in the marketplace, and appropriated and applied by university administrators and department curriculum committees in North America and Britain, at the very least? For some, it is similar to (if not exactly coterminous with) the transnational, an analytical framework that has enjoyed great favor among historians of empire of late. As Kevin Grant, Philippa Levine, and Frank Trentmann, editors of *Beyond Sovereignty: Britain, Empire, and Transnationalism, c. 1880–1950* put it, "The seeds of transnationalism are imperial, rather than post-colonial" and "empires . . . were critical sites where transnational social and cultural movements took place."[7] Durba Ghosh and Dane Kennedy aspire to track the same phenomena when they aim for "an ecumenical approach" that "exposes the cross-colonial, multivalent nature of the relationship between ruler and ruled" in their edited collection *Decentring Empire: Britain, India, and the Transcolonial World*.[8] David Lambert and Alan Lester thrill to a similar rhetoric of multidimensionality in the introduction to their edited volume, *Colonial Lives across the British Empire*, where they map what they call "imperial careering" onto the various spaces of the British empire to demonstrate how such experiences "constituted meaningful connection" and outline "the trans-imperial life path[s] by the traveling and dwelling of . . . colonial subjects."[9] To be sure, students of British imperialism have been taking a transnational view and employing transnational methods for some time, as Lester's own work and that of Tony Ballantyne, to name just two such practitioners, testifies, although research that works on and from multiple imperial sites rather than just between metropole and colony is still rare enough.[10] Meanwhile, it is not such a great leap from the transnational to the global—a bigger stage, perhaps, with a scope whose difference can be measured in degree, if not kind.[11] What concerns me here is the question of how the "imperial transnational" or the "global imperial" functions in recent British empire work. I would argue that, despite their internal variations—for I would not deny that Grant and colleagues or Ghosh and Kennedy share little enough intellectual ground with, say, Ferguson—current work in British imperial history circling around these questions treats the transnational and the global much as earlier historians treated the national—that is, as de facto exceptional for being rooted in English / British contexts and (tautologically, if not Whiggishly) Victorian English histories, as well.

In fact, the national exceptionalism accorded to (and derived from) English democracy, English abolitionism, the English civilizing mission has by and large eclipsed the extensively, extranationally global imperial contexts in which English / British imperialism came of age in the modern period and has prevented us from factoring those global imperial pressures into narratives of Britain's claims to globality *tout court*. Much as the national did—and, in fact, much as English iterations of whiteness continue to do not just in imperial studies but in Atlantic history and "British world historiography," too—the globality of British imperialism operates as the site of an unacknowledged, naturalized rule of imperial difference.[12] In a paraphrase of Ferguson's admittedly hyberbolic bestselling prose, the British empire dominated the globe and thereby changed the world unlike any other power before or since (though as is also famously known, in his view the U.S. is next in line for that distinction). Even in their use of violence, Britain's imperial officials and policies were (he argues) exceptionally benign, at least compared with those of the Dutch empire, which helps account for the former's success and the latter's demise.[13] Inside this argument—and it is an inside view that I would submit even critical historians and theorists of empire often inhabit—the global impulse was a presumptively English / British impulse and the empire, a major delivery system for that ambition in world history. Feminist historians, for all their critique of the metropole–colony binary and for all their insistence on the need to think globally about empire as a gendered project, have not moved much beyond the boundaries of their respective imperial remits, myself included. Even work that addresses the centrality of the exceptional political economy of Victorian gender to British imperial hegemony falls short of asking an antecedent question: to what extent has gender itself, as a historical field of power and as a contemporary methodological tool, been an effect of (in this case mainly Western Anglocentric) imperium rather than simply (if strenuously) a dimension of its ideological and material power?[14]

There is little point, of course, in denying the particularities and peculiarities of British imperialism. In terms of territorial expansion alone, Britain extended its spatial reach significantly, if not exponentially, in the nineteenth century, bringing a variety of social, cultural, linguistic, and religious communities into equally various spheres of influence and formal and informal control. In terms of sheer numbers (whether the calculus is subject bodies or square miles), Britain outpaced its European rivals significantly, with the result that the British imperial experience has—especially in recent blockbuster accounts—become emblematic in historiographical terms of "the imperial encounter" *tout court*. If the litmus test for imperial global-imperial power is economic hegemony, Britain's pre-eminence at the close of the nineteenth century has not been challenged, though if work exploring the limits of "the great divergence" between Europe and Asia (Britain and its European rivals) were undertaken for a period later than the eighteenth century, this truism might be under duress, as well.[15] As the heart of the "developing capitalist core" both in the West and in the world, Britain—and England and London within it—was undoubtedly the center of the imperial globe, not least because it served as the fulcrum for both industrial production and commercial consumption *and* as the centrifugal capital of a vast empire of financial services.[16] As significant, the structural conditions it had long established for realizing profits across its Eastern imperial territories, where both full colonial and semi-colonial power was operative, meant that aspiring empires such as Japan were compelled to grapple with British imperial foundations as they sought to enhance their own economic and territorial power.

Let me be absolutely clear, then: there is no denying that in terms of technological development, economic prowess (in almost every register in which that might be assessed), and superstructural reality, the British empire was—and remains—critical to the definition, in practical and symbolic terms, of modern imperialism as such. In this sense, the appellation "Anglo-globalization" is not without merit as a characterization of the processes through which the contemporary moment came into being.[17] Yet recognition of the British empire's centrality to the establishment of a certain species of globality need not mean conceding the floor, as it were, to British imperialism as a static, fully accomplished, or (worse yet) teleologically hegemonic phenomenon untouched by the threat of competitors or the specter of native resistance from within. Indeed, as Duncan Bell has recently argued, the planetary imagination that undergirded schemes for imperial federation—and discourses of British imperialism more generally—from the 1870s onward grew out of anxieties about the spread of democracy and developed in the context of an equally keen awareness of the threat of imperial rivals (not least the United States.): hence, the future conditional tense of an observer such as Charles Oman, who wrote in 1899 that "a firm and well-compacted union of all the British lands would form a state that *might* control the whole world."[18] Like the nation's imperiality, empire's global dimensions were always in the process of becoming, hegemonic by design but the effect, ultimately, of many different historical forces, of stop-and-start political maneuverings, of the ebb and flow, the crisis and rupture of economic pressures and the uneven ground of social relations to such a degree that, again, like the nation's imperial dimensions, empire's global character was ever in flux, rarely fully articulated, perpetually in need of reiteration. Without putting too fine a point on it, and despite Victorian rhetoric about its worldliness, British imperialism was never only about itself and was scarcely realized merely or even chiefly through its own motor purpose. As Ania Loomba has written in another context, to provincialize Europe (or, in this case, the British empire), we do not need to establish Europeans' provincialism. Rather, we need to "reveal their intersections with the rest of the world"—the world of empires included.[19]

The case of the South African war of 1899–1902 is apposite here. The product of Anglo-German rivalries on the continent (which were moti-

vated in turn by both the prospect of gold and of transcontinental supremacy) cross-hatched by intra-ethnic rivalries (Afrikaner–English and
Afrikaner–African), this fin-de-siècle contest materialized a complex set of
contact zones and colonial encounters that made it a global war whose
center was not self-evidently the British empire, especially when we consider the significant role it played not only in the metropolitan English and
European national scenes but also on the stage of a burgeoning Chinese
national and international politics. Indeed, the Chinese monitored events
in South Africa in the late 1890s alongside those in the Philippines, not
only as a function of a larger concern about "Anglo–American" imperialism but also because they understand their own global possibilities to
be at stake in these conflicts.[20] As Rebecca Karl explores in *Staging the
World: Chinese Nationalism at the Turn of the Century*, these surveillance
tactics and the geopolitical canniness they exemplify suggest how important anticolonial resistance was in principle and in practice to the mobilization of aggressive military force on the part of imperial powers, to the
character and contour of European regimes, and, not least, to the cosmopolitan national identity of would-be non–Western power brokers—
which is to say, aspiring imperialists—such as the Chinese. That the end
result of the South African war was a pyrrhic victory for the British—
"success" on the ground but at enormous cost, both in terms of dead and
wounded and with respect to imperial confidence as the new century
dawned—suggests how unstable "British imperialism" actually was even
at one of its most self-consciously jingoistic moments.

"Upending the telescope" on the British empire in the way that seeing
the Boer War from the vantage point of Peking allows does not so much
reverse our gaze as it reorients our understanding of what the global arena
looked like from outside the precincts of both the British imperial experience and a British empire–centered world history.[21] If nothing else, it
reminds us that in the last quarter of the long nineteenth century, a host of
players on the global stage were jockeying for elbow room (and *Lebensraum*, of course). In doing so, they not only articulated many of the same
justifications for territorial expansion and cultural contact as their Western
counterparts; they had their eye as much on other global imperial powers
as they did on the indigenous people they aimed to colonize, a phenomenon across empires both full-bodied and embryonic that suggests the profound historical inaccuracy of casting the imperial encounter as a binary or
dichotomous experience. This is true even if we recognize, as we must,

that colonizer-to-colonizer encounters were also unevenly constituted by the realities of global power and that mutually constitutive hierarchies of scale and value, often expressed in raced and gendered terms, exercised reciprocal effects on those encounters. The Russian experiment in Tashkent is a case in point: the quest to become recognized as equivalent to the Western powers was a huge motivating factor in the imposition of administrative rule in Central Asia. Officials such as Governor-General K. P. fon Kaufman had one eye on Moscow and Paris and the other on the Muslim communities subject to their authority as they sought to redraw the map of cities such as Tashkent so that they showcased Russia's capacity to civilize native populations through all the canonical means, including sanitation, education, and, of course, the imperially designed ceremonial occasion. The boundaries Kaufman and his successors tried to establish and the reform projects they strove to carry out met with both local collaboration and outright resistance, evidence that "the predicaments of progress" were, if not universal features of the imperial encounter in this period, then very much locally specific ones. Meanwhile, the complexity of the hierarchies and the cross-referentiality both inside the colony and beyond it that they entailed is evident in the common comparison of Sart traders (Turkicized inhabitants of Central Asian regional urban centers) with European Jews, both of whom were viewed as preternaturally unhygienic.[22] While it might be too much to suggest that pogroms and Muslim persecution emanated from the same national/imperial cauldron, subcolonial connections like these must give us pause when we think about cordoning off "non–Western" empires from histories and theories of European nation building and colonialism—or about writing narratives of empire that render the Raj as the outer edge of globality.[23]

This is especially the case if we recognize not simply the territorial reach of the Russian empire but the ways in which Russian historians have taken the imperial turn and engaged in the creation of a new imperial history at the exact historiographical moment British historians have engaged these questions.[24] Whether "family resemblances" is the appropriate lens through which to appreciate the relationship between British and Russian/Soviet empires, as Mark Beissinger has suggested, is indeed a provocative question.[25] What might be called the "extreme relationality" of Russia's imperial ambition—its sense of itself as only ever a quasi-imperial power always looking to the West as an imperial model and example—as well as of Japan's stands in stark contrast to the splendid isolationism of both Britain's dominant imperial identity and its imperial historiography.[26] Equally fruitfully, Dina Khouri and Dane Kennedy have argued for the urgency of examining the commensurability of the British and Ottoman empires, breaking with a kind of parallel historiographical tradition that has failed to appreciate or historicize them in the same analytical space.[27] Khouri and Kennedy are, instructively, less concerned with the question of British imperial supremacy that has preoccupied several generations of British imperial historians than in exploring the degree of "structural resemblance" between the two empires.[28] Their work makes us usefully conscious, I think, of the degree to which presumptions, never mind convictions, about the supremacy of British power and the exceptionality of its ambition have driven accounts of imperial territorial aggrandizement in this period, convictions typically attributed to Whitehall's fixation on both the long-term security of the Indian empire and (relatedly) the establishment of a corridor of power from the Cape of Good Hope to the Mediterranean.

This fixation in turn was, of course, globally apparent throughout the 1880s and especially after the Berlin conference of 1884–85, proposed by Bismarck, whose own *Weltpolitik* bespoke a pan–Germanism that aimed to rival British imperial aspirations with fateful consequences for the future history of total war—let alone total empires—in the twentieth century. As one prewar German writer put it, "We must have lands, new lands!"[29] But the most historically accurate way to view these contests for imperial hegemony is surely not through a competitively nationalist frame. For one thing, such an approach casts the history of imperial encounters in a purely international framework, thereby reproducing the Europe-centered, state-to-state presumptions of the Congress of Vienna model and extending its interpretive reach well beyond its temporal limits in the process. Not only does this prevent us from understanding how deeply enmeshed the scramble for Africa was in an emerging global field of imperial power, one in which an "Eastern question" like the one that animated the late 1870s can and should be seen as an uneasy relationship between empires (British and Ottoman) with ramifications for aspirant ones (like Russia and Japan), it also potentially obscures our ability to look beyond the arenas of diplomacy and the military for sites of consequential imperial encounters, and the conceit of global empire more generally.[30] What we need are histories that acknowledge the double, even triple and quadruple, helix of imperial and global power—the unevenness of that intertwining on the ground—*and* narrative procedures that enable us to capture the fiction of English / Anglo global imperial exceptionalism that has such tremendous consequences for imagining contemporary geopolitical power. We also need comparative frameworks that look beyond the paramountcy of the British model and enable us to see parallels between some European empires—such as Germany's, for example—and other continental and multiethnic ones, such as the Russian, the Ottoman, and the Austrian.[31]

One need not read deeply into the history of imperialism—Japanese, Russian—to realize how crucial the conceit of exceptionalism itself was to modern global empires, whether Western or not.[32] As important, the call to reposition British imperialism in world history resonates with one of the objectives of self-styled transnational imperial history—namely, the aim identified by David Lambert and Alan Lester to trace transimperial networks of the kind that can go "beyond comparison" and seek "actual historical connections and disconnections between different sites of empire" between and across empires, as well as inside the dominant one.[33] On the whole, however, the multi-axial approach that I believe such a project requires is not one that recent work on the transnational or the global British empire has come to terms with, despite calls by A. G. Hopkins to (re)situate the history of British imperial ambition and design on a broader geopolitical landscape.[34] Typically, scholars have focused inward, back toward the intra-colonial, exploring comparisons between colonized sires (India and Ireland), the exchange of ideas between lateral sites (Egypt and India), or the movement of troops between one imperial outpost and another (Punjab to Peking) in an attempt to re-plot histories of empire (mainly of the Raj) on a more complex, "trans-colonial" grid.[35] There is no gainsaying the importance of this work, especially, in my view, if it succeeds in de-centering India from the heart of imperial history, where it continues to reside—resulting in an "empire of the Raj" not just historically but also historiographically.[36] Such a de-centering project involves both provincializing India and revealing its nodal relationships with so many "sub" regions of the empire, from the post–Mutiny of 1857 period through independence. The "jewel in the crown" approach to India is one instance of the many lingering Victorian preoccupations of that body of scholarship, whether "old" or "new," and dethroning India is certainly one salutary effect of collections such as Ghosh's and Kennedy's *Decentring Empire*.[37] But even such trans-colonial work is arguably a very particular kind of "globalizing" maneuver, one that remains largely within the perspectival confines of the Victorian and post–Victorian imperial nation-state, even when it takes culture and social relations (as opposed to policy and diplomacy) as its analytical focus. As telling, if not more so, might be to explore cross-imperial connections and referents, as with the persistent arguments in Japan that colonial Korea was to Tokyo what Egypt was to London and that the Japanese therefore should not merely aim to colonize Korea but to "Egyptianize" it, as well.[38]

As Joe Cleary has recently made clear in his wide-ranging essay on Ireland in empire studies in international context, the "spatial fix" characteristic of imperial hegemonies seeking sovereign authority in the face of both "national" competitors and a variety of colonized others is both here to stay and the right and proper object of anti-imperial critique, postcolonial or otherwise, even as it also positions nationalist histories and their historiographies in unique ways.[39] At this juncture, I would like to draw attention to recent work that represents exciting and provocative challenges to what I have been describing as a variant of that fix: an implicit, unremarked insiderism in the newest imperial/transnational history focused on the British empire. Both Manu Goswami and Mrinalini Sinha have given us rigorous and detailed accounts of how deeply implicated both metropolitan imperial politics and colonial nationalist movements were in what Sinha calls a "globally articulated imperial structure," and what the ramifications of those structural entanglements were, not just for the histories of those phenomena, but for their interpretive fates, as well.[40] Significantly, though their research is rooted in a British imperial story, these two scholars work in fact at the intersection of imperial history and U.S.–based "area studies," the latter offering a space potentially further outside the universalizing grasp of the imperial global, even as—at least, in the U.S.—it is also bound up historically with Cold War imperial structures and institutional exigencies.

From a different quarter, the work of Lydia Liu, James Hevia, Rebecca Karl, and Ruth Rogaski has demonstrated the cosmopolitan, universalizing, and global imperial perspectives of Qing political culture and its legators, putting paid to the conviction that the British idiom for those aspirations was the only one during either the run-up to or at the high noon of Western imperialism.[41] Whether in the realm of high politics or in what Rogaski calls "hygienic modernity," Qing rule was historically coincident with British imperial power rather than derivative of it, even while it was in extended crisis. As important, they shared ground with other empires—the Japanese and the American—and operated on a geopolitical landscape where a variety of competing imperial interests, including Russian and Ottoman, shaped the discursive and material conditions in which they worked. Nor is the late Qing empire the only one to suffer being branded as comparatively backward imperially in historiography of the nineteenth century as written in the U.S. and Europe. This, too, has been the fate of Spain, raising questions about the relationships between decline, deterioration, and crisis among empires.[42] The scholarship on China also dispels the notion that the British imperial idiom erupted sui generis, generated in isolation from, rather than in dynamic tensions with, Asian empires.[43] The "return of the repressed" to which Hevia refers in the last chapter of *English Lessons: The Pedagogy of Imperialism in Nineteenth Century China* might just as easily be the global framework of the clash between the British and Qing empires as the fact of Chinese territorial ambition itself.[44] Even if we concede that the Qing and the British empires are not coeval or even analogous, we should at least countenance the fact that each operated inside a China-centered and Britain-centered world—and that each sought to challenge that spatially centered notion of empire at overlapping and divergent moments in the nineteenth century.[45]

Last, but certainly not least, though in a somewhat different vein, I want to note Barbara Bush's *Imperialism and Postcolonialism* (2006). This book, part of a series emphasizing history's "concepts, theories, and practices," shares more ground with historians working "inside" British imperial history than those just cited; it comes more intelligibly out of imperial history than area studies and is more concerned with addressing an imperial history audience, both traditional and less so, as a consequence. But what makes Bush's contribution unique among the recent gaggle of British empire books is her conviction that "new approaches to imperial history need to build upon existing conventional studies within a critical framework that incorporates fresh insights informed by postcolonial theory."[46] This objective produces a fairly predictable congeries of counternarratives, many of which grow out of her expertise in African and Caribbean history. More ambitious, and more apposite to my own argument, is Bush's attempt to reposition the British empire in a more expansively global context—that is, to see the global as a genuine reorientation device (to borrow from Sarah Ahmed's *Queer Phenomenology*) rather than merely as a residue of British imperialists' self-referential view of the empire's reach, power, and historical distinctiveness.[47] Although she does not cite the work of Liu or Karl or Hevia, Bush emphasizes the simultaneity of British imperial ambition and Chinese and Japanese imperial aspiration, positioning the latter both literally and figuratively alongside the former, thereby disrupting a longstanding, if unacknowledged, presumption that these "other" empires were insignificant to the grand narrative of British imperialism in all its geopolitical complexity. In the end, her treatment of China and Japan ends up being fairly self-contained; as imperial players (rather than as objects of British global design), they inhabit very discrete spaces in the text rather than being integrated more purposefully into the larger analytical framework of the book. In this respect, the Asian empires are not fully constitutive of the big picture Bush wants to draw. Some might argue that the story of British imperialism still drives that narrative, that it remains the standard against which those others are measured. There is some truth to this. As an enduring, if implicit, ground of comparison, the British empire remains at the heart of the book, in part perhaps because the postcolonial theory Bush is so determined to engage is itself so derivative of the career of the British empire and its worldly ambition.[48] This is a shame, not least because recent work on Asian imperialism especially has emphasized the effects of "multiple imperialist presences" on geographical spaces such as those under Japanese imperial rule, as well as the "uneven colonial relations" between and among imperial powers—an approach that simultaneously provincializes Britain and accords Chinese and Japanese imperialism agency while acknowledging the asymmetries of power and influence that this confluence produced.[49] If, as Shu-Mei Shih has suggested, the "semi" in semi-colonialism is taken not as half but, rather, as "the fractured, informal, and indirect character of colonialism, as well as its multi-layeredness," then this term might reasonably apply to the British empire in all its imperial globality rather than just to British imperial power—*especially* as a competitor with Japanese imperial ambition—in China per se.[50]

While Bush is not able to capture this kind of multidirectionality, hers are flaws of execution that I believe are symptomatic of the gargantuan challenges she has set for herself, and that we must continue to set for ourselves if we aim to break from the inheritance of Victorian imperial presumptions about the global that undergird contemporary apprehensions of transnational imperial history and global imperial studies. Readers may well have already rebelled against the alternative imperial history syllabus I have effectively embedded in this chapter. But we must continually, and purposefully, cast our eye well beyond the precincts of British imperial historiography, as Bush has done, to appreciate empires contemporary to the British empire more fully, as well as how historians of other empires past and present are figuring the imperial and the global and the spaces in between. De-centering the British empire *in* global history so that British imperial history is no longer understood as self-evidently synonymous *with* global history requires a leap of imagination and a methodological reorientation of the kind that few historians of empire have begun to imagine, let alone think through or practice. Like the project of thinking with and through the nation, this does not mean abandoning the analytic of empire per se; rather, it means recognizing the burdens of British imperial history it carries with it—and the impact of those burdens on the subjects we choose and the methods we use, not to mention on audiences we aim to address and the bodies of literature through which we seek to (re)educate ourselves. Of course, to lead with empire as a kind of territorialized given is potentially to obscure from the outset other ways to imagine imperialized space, whether oceanic or arctic, littoral or inland, contiguous and hybrid in both form and function. This I take to be the critique embodied especially by recent work on the Indian Ocean world, projects that work mightily to imagine a more expansive spatial economy in and for South Asia.[51] It is also a problem that comparison and an awareness of intra-imperial contiguities—as in the nineteenth-century circumpolar region, the fin-de-siècle Spanish Caribbean centered in Cuba, or the domains of Europe's three interlocked modern empires (Ottoman, Russian and Hapsburg)—allow us to see with particular vividness. It is also, of course, a vantage point on offer via women's, gender, and feminist histories of empire that, however various in their methods and scales, have aimed to trouble the presumptively self-evident spatial grounds (territorial, discursive, reproductive) that empires have purported to put and hold in place. Yet only comparatively rarely have feminist historians of empire recognized that imperial space was scarcely sovereign, not only because native peoples constantly contested it, but because it was always a borderland often several times over, potentially abutting and thereby foxing the dream of integrity cherished by neighboring empires.[52] Despite these limitations, it is certainly an extension of two decades of feminist imperial history to observe that, for all their competing logics, modern empires enjoyed an intimacy—and an *interdependent* flexibility—that scholars are only beginning to fully countenance, but that can and should be one of the grounds for a resolutely rather than a simply presumptively global history.[53] This is to say nothing of the overlaps of densely colonial spaces with local, internally cosmopolitan, and insouciantly contiguous spaces at the heart of empire—as in wartime Calcutta, for example, a conurbation where a communist in the making such as Muzaffar Ahmad might both wander and take root, aware of the shifts in global and imperial power at Versailles, if vaguely so, but caught up in deeply tentacled communities of writers, thinkers, booksellers, and mess dwellers in ways that only graze the sightline of "global" histories even now.[54] How does imperial history even in its most flexibly comparative mode register these kinds of histories, gendered or not? Or are such pasts to be considered outside the technical purview of "imperial history" per se?

In light of the reality of multiple and mobile imperial, anti-imperial, and non-imperial spatialities "on the ground" as well as in the colonial / modern imagination,[55] I am convinced that historicizing empires in a worldly way means understanding the global, along with the national, the local, the regional, and the transnational, not only as spatial frameworks but also precisely as positioning techniques, or "instituted perspectives," to quote Sanjay Krishnan—perspectives whose ideological work has become extremely powerful in Western social science even as its Anglo-imperial origins are pretty consistently naturalized or obscured. Indeed, for all the claims that they have been remade, undermined, and destroyed by postmodernism and postcolonialism, the academic disciplines continue to participate in "the conceit of objective description" that underpins most, if not all, of those descriptions of the world that are considered "proper," authoritative, and legitimate today.[56] While interdisciplinarity is no guarantee of anti-objectivism, the fact remains that History as a discipline, especially in the context of British empire and commonwealth studies—and especially, it would seem, in Britain—continues to exert an astonishingly tenacious hold on the arbitration of what counts as fact, as archive, and articulates a correlative suspicion of practice of theorizing, by which I mean, among other things, rigorously historicizing the conceptual terms through which we produce imperial histories in favor of History per se. Again, the history of Japanese imperialism is apposite, for as Stefan Tanaka has suggested, insisting on the objectivity of history is, in the end, a project bound up not just with imperial self-reckoning but also with the history of competition between empires as well.[57] The critical position I am reaching for is not merely a *cri de coeur* either for post-colonialism or against Orientalism. Again, as Krishnan (in the critical tradition of Edward Said and of much of postcolonial criticism) suggests, Orientalism (and Eurocentrism with it) "is less an ideologically motivated misrepresentation than the condition of knowledge production" in a pre-ternaturally imperialized world.[58] Indeed, I would argue that the real challenge is to think about how to resist, in part by simply recognizing and then by trying to exceed, the extraordinarily seductive grasp of British imperial globality on all of our work in this field. In short, if convictions about the discrete and hegemonic territoriality—its exclusive spatial reach—have been an exceptional feature of British imperial globality, re-materializing the histories of other contemporary empires makes that globality look like a co-production rather than a distinctively English/British phenomenon.[59]

Historians of global empires (and students of imperial globality, as well) might look to postcolonial studies for models of the kind of methodological approach I have been reaching for here—not simply out of a political reflex but because historical actors and agents of empire, like many propo-nents of nationalism and anti-imperialism, thought and operated in—and, indeed across—the world that way. Elleke Boehmer and others have sug-gested we take seriously the "multi-axial alliances" and "polyphonic dis-course" at the heart of twentiety-century anticolonial movements, and historians interested in exceeding Anglo-imperial concepts of the global might look to their work for examples of how this might be done.[60] In-deed, anticolonial movements typically operated across a number of impe-rial terrains simultaneously, and it is partly by studying their agents, their successes, and their failures that we can more fully appreciate the relation-ship between empires and globalization. This "vast, rhizomal network," as Benedict Anderson recently called late-nineteenth-century Filipino re-sistance, offers both pattern and method for genuinely global histories of modern imperialisms.[61] Critics of this approach have called it out for a number of reasons, its loose sense of politics and the political prime among them.[62] But even if we were to concede the point (and that is the subject of another paper!), such a critique is much less relevant for the history of imperial globality because modern empires continuously colluded and conspired to protect each other even as they did so out of a sense of strate-gic anxiety—collusions and conspiracies with very real political effects and, of course, consequences in world history, political and otherwise, even and especially when they failed.[63] The idea that the British empire operated above or beyond this matrix of global power is a fiction that is only possible if one reads only British imperial history—and if, in doing so, one ignores or turns a blind eye to the empire's embeddedness in a world of interdependent trans-colonial footholds, economic concessions, territorialized encounters, and "international frontiers."[64] It is precisely these "coordinates of simultaneity" that warrant our attention if we want a truly multidimensional historical view of modern power.[65]

In the meantime, getting outside the global means recognizing, as Neil Smith (following Lenin) has so cogently argued, that "the loss of an outside"—of a political, intellectual, and, of course, territorial imaginary beyond empire—"is actually a hallmark of twentieth century imperialism" itself.[66] Such a project clearly also requires acknowledging the impact of another Anglophone empire on the shape of the global that nurtures a cult of exceptionality even as it disavows the imperializing force of its own universalism: that of the post–Cold War, postcolonial U.S. empire, in the making at accelerating rates as we speak. Its influence on both globality and postcoloniality (as historical conditions and methodological practices) is both obvious and yet to be fully historicized. It is American soil that has served as the dominant locative position whence postcolonial theory and discourses of the global have been imagined, articulated, and deployed, most often in ways that have directly addressed the relationship between American nationalist discourses and geopolitical ambition of the U.S. only rarely, at least until very recently, in historical terms.[67]

As significant, on those rare occasions when historians of empire interrogate the exceptionality of the British empire, they do so not in the service of a truly global vision of modern imperialism—one that would map it as a co-authored enterprise in all its unevenness across space and time—but to call out the specificities of a "new" American empire, one that, of course, had deep roots across the world before 1945. The U.S. was in the global imperial mix from the moment of independence from Britain, positioning itself alongside and in contrast to the mother empire. It was invested in its own exceptionality and enmeshed in and shaped by a complex set of racial hierarchies that themselves were crosshatched by events and policies in China, in India, in Africa, and in the Pacific. Despite how tempting—or politically satisfying—it is, comparing the British and American empires to predict the next colossus (Ferguson) or to critique American-style imperial history (Colley) does little more than corral us inside the same limited parameters through which the contemporary paradigm of imperial globality routinely repackages itself, not least through the shared Anglo–American "grid of racial intelligibility" that continues to rationalize "global" power as presumptively, if anxiously, white as well as northern in hemispheric terms.[68] Rejecting this bind or striving to work in a critical relationship with it means, among other things, recognizing what historians of other non–Western empires can clearly see—that is, that what is at stake is the production of genealogies of what Peter Duus calls "the synergy of . . . parallel efforts" among imperial powers (British, Japanese, Russian, Ottoman, Chinese) rather than simply competition between them.[69] It also means asking who the audience is for British empire history and who it is not—and, of course, remembering that if the "global" marketplace for the work with which I opened this essay is simply Britain and the U.S., or even Anglo–America and Europe, then it is scarcely global at all. Otherwise, what we have is a "parochial fantasy of global relations" rather than a self-critically expansive vision for and practice of globality as geopolitics.[70]

Last, but not least, thinking beyond the imperial global or the transnational imperial means recognizing that the global career of the English language itself—and the relative linguistic provincialism of most practicing historians, imperial or not—is a huge impediment to getting at any place "outside" an ineffably Anglo-centric worldliness. As must be clear, even and especially my own apprehensions of comparative scholarship in this essay are bounded by my inability to read work about Japanese, Chinese, Russian, or Ottoman imperialism except if it is in English—and if it is in English, it likely speaks to an orientation already imprinted by a geographically delimited (if naturalized) articulation of "the global" and is embedded, arguably, in a historiographical tradition of discourse of greater and lesser imperialisms in which Britain is the center and against which I am trying to think, if not get fully outside.[71] This is to say nothing of the opaqueness of most indigenous languages, in all their post-encounter imperial hybridities, to most historians of empire, whether in the U.S. and Britain or elsewhere—not to mention the embeddedness of non–Western historiographies in many languages in Western (and, after 1945, Euro- and America-centric) concerns and presumptions.[72] In the end, the agenda entailed by this diagnosis of the provincialism of even transnationally informed British imperial history requires more than new reading lists and more expansive bibliographical tools. It would necessitate a total transformation of how we train graduate students, let alone how we retrain ourselves—an agenda that is scarcely achievable in the context of nationally bounded structures of research funding across the global and, as significant, in light of the profoundly uneven access to transnational travel resources and mobility in "First" versus "Third" worlds.[73] My own modest hope is that if we are vigilant about understanding the global as an optic—a continuously and at times aggressively *spatializing* device, as well as the articulation of a spatial *claim*—we can perhaps begin to write the British empire into world history in terms of its proportionality rather than its exceptionalism, in terms of its role in the co-production of imperial globality rather than its originary character, in terms of its limits rather than its inflated and ultimately self-serving image. Only then, if then, can we admit the possibility that the fundamentally imperial logics of the modern international order and their histories might someday be exceeded.[74]

Afterword   C. A. BAYLY

Even a generation ago, British domestic history still seemed like a celebration of G. M. Trevelyan's vision of English exceptionalism. This was a history only occasionally, if rudely, interrupted by neo–Marxist historians' stories of class struggle. As for imperial history, the Whig picture of the progressive development of colonial freedoms had, it is true, been eroded by the rise of a nationalist hagiography and a related Marxian historiography of colonial exploitation. Yet much of what was taught about empire in Britain and the U.S. still concerned constitutions and the "man on the spot," while colonized people were either "collaborators" or politicians on the make, often both at the same time. The changes that have occurred since about 1970 have encompassed a conceptual revolution that has further destabilized the Whig model and focused attention on race, gender, and the formative influence of empire on British life and thought. Antoinette Burton, as these essays show, has been a leader and exemplar in this revolution in historical writing.

Many of the most fully researched and powerfully argued pieces in this collection concern women, gender, and empire. Burton began, as it were, with the "woman on the spot," appalled by the absence of women in the archive and in imperial historiography. She was spurred on by Gayatri Spivak's classic article "Can the Subaltern Speak?" But she moved forward, through studies of Mary Carpenter and the Zenana Mission in India, not only to analyze what has been called "maternal imperialism," but also to show how women's activism in the empire contributed powerfully, if ambivalently, to gender politics in Britain itself and to the rising demand for women's suffrage. Empire, then, was a field of forces within which Britain itself emerged as a modern nation.

One of the great strengths of Burton's methodology is that it can also be extended to colonial territories outside India, and even beyond. Scholarship on campaigns against female child slavery (*mu tsai*) in China, Hong Kong, and Malaya, or against female genital mutilation in East Africa, can be set alongside Burton's studies to create a connected picture of female British imperial social activism. Yet we can perhaps extend and complicate the range of analysis further by considering the role of colonized men and women in civil-society "networks of empire," to use Tony Ballantyne's phrase. These indigenous activists and intellectuals emerged not as free agents or as collaborators but often as moral insurgents within their own societies. Rammohan Roy, for instance, whom Burton mentions in her essay on Mary Carpenter, embodied within his own family a growing reaction against the Kulin Brahmin system of multiple child marriage. This social form began to buckle after 1750 as the Indo-Mughal extended household came under pressure from numerous ideological and economic pressures during the onset of colonial rule. As Burton implies, Christian, and especially Unitarian, missionary onslaughts on Indian domestic patters were important here. Yet Rammohan was not simply the subject of imperial "epistemological violence." He also inherited and recast several emerging South Asian ideological programs, including late Mughal Muslim rationalism, the inheritance of Bengal's own anti-caste Chaitanya tradition, and recessive elements in more orthodox Hindu vedantism, which could be interpreted to stress this-worldly piety and companionate marriage. For Rammohan, the degradation of women, especially in Bengal, mirrored a wider degradation of a godly and balanced "ancient Indian constitution."[1] Through Rammohan, a certain type of subaltern spoke loudly and articulately, drawing on a range of arguments mined from the Upanishads, through Chishti rationalists, to Tom Paine and de Sismondi, the Swiss political economist who opposed European colonization.

One of Burton's strongest arguments in favor of the idea that imperial sensibilities permeated and, in many ways, "constructed" nineteenth-century Britain itself concerns the issue of race. Here her essay "Lord Salisbury's 'Black Man' and the Boundaries of Imperial Democracy" is again exemplary. Burton argues that reactions in Britain and India to the prime minister's famous gibe at the expense of the liberal nationalist Dadabhai Naoroji during the general election campaign of 1886 reveals the taxonomies of contemporary racial attitudes. The ensuing controversy contributed to the disagreggation of "the Indian" from "the African," so helping to frustrate conceptually what might have become political solidarity among subject peoples. Africans were reinstated at the bottom of the hierarchy in the widespread rush to disavow the idea that Naoroji was "a black." The British were repositioned at the apex of the racial ranking as protectors of even "gentle" and implicitly feminized Indian intellectuals. Yet this position was unstable. It was undermined, as liberals and radicals argued, by the "blackguard" Salisbury's own coarseness. Between these two poles, the Irish, the Jews, and West Indians were represented in a shifting kaleidoscope of fluid racial signs, ranked according to the reporting of political events across the empire. Thus, in India, Max Müller and Aryan race theory were invoked to refute the slur. In short, Burton interprets the whole controversy as an example of the manner in which imperial issues framed the emergence of a democratic electorate in Britain, comparable with the case of Governor Eyre's atrocities in Jamaica or Catherine Hall's analysis of the racial politics surrounding the Second Reform Act.

Burton's analysis could be both broadened and particularized in productive ways by future scholars. European comparisons are highly relevant. In France as in Britain, the public appearance of non-white subjects raised similar problems of categorization but, here, often complicated by matters of religion. Were French-educated West African évolués more civilized than Arab Muslims? As an "ancient Mediterranean people" with kinship to the Romans, were the Kabils of North Africa more civilized than their Arab neighbors? If the vibrant French race had itself been created by an admixture of Celtic and Roman types, what were the boundaries of race and racial mixing? In Germany, by contrast, which had few colonial ambitions before the 1880s, and where Aryan race theory had its home, it was Jews who became the most potent signifier. In Nietzsche's thought, for instance, Indians had created a perfect hierarchy of virtue in the caste system. Africans were outside the pale, but Jews had instituted a religion of servitude that had corrupted and debased the European races. Burton's model could here be used to interrogate racial ideology and practice across the whole later-nineteenth-century Western world. But so far, we have few comparative studies to match it.

Just as important is the question of how these racial signifiers were appropriated or rejected by subject non–European peoples. Dadabhai Naoroji himself was no stranger to argument and controversy about race.

Indeed, well before 1886, the educated public would have associated him with views of Aryanism, religion, and even the Jews. This was one reason the Salisbury controversy became so animated. In a lecture to the Liverpool Philomathic Society in 1861, he argued that the Parsi religion, and hence the Parsi "race," was not debased by idolatry, as evangelical Christians claimed. Fire, in the monotheistic belief of Zoroastrian Aryans, was merely a symbol, equivalent to the symbols used in rationalistic Christian practice, he asserted. Naoroji's most interesting point of comparative anthropology, however, related to his analogy between the Jews and the Parsis. Both these "national types" had preserved their integrity over thousands of years, surrounded by "idolatry" and "fanaticism."[2] They had emerged from this long period of trial still monotheistic and monogamous. There had, of course, been some "contamination" by Hindu practices, but Naoroji used Leviticus to show that Parsi marriage and death customs, on the whole, were similar to those of the Jews rather than to those of the Hindus. A few years later, Naoroji set out to denounce the view of the former Southeast Asian colonial administrator, John Crawfurd, on the "mental inferiority of the Asiatic races." Naoroji argued that Europeans were as racially divided as Asians; that they were, if anything, more dishonest than Asians; and that the "rise of the West" was the result of a confluence of chance rather than innate character. All in all, races needed careful study before "innate difference" was posited.[3] The use of this phrase by an Indian intellectual in 1866 is striking.

Naoroji's passages of arms concerning race took place on British soil. But the debate had raged in India itself from the earliest days of Indian-owned print media. The cartoons from *Hindi Punch* noted by Burton had many antecedents. Before colonial rule, Indians classified people in terms of color in matters of marriage, for instance. They were also aware of ethnicity as an embodiment of cultural difference with strong political connotations. But color and "race" were not closely linked in their worldview, while ethnicities were not generally forced into a hierarchy by Indian writers of the Mughal period, as they were in the European tradition that culminated with Count Gobineau. By the 1830s and '40s, as Shruti Kapila has shown, emerging Indian elites in Calcutta had certainly begun to adapt and use Western sciences such as phrenology, which had strong racial overtones. But a sense of racial hierarchy was difficult to instill in the broader world of popular physiognomy and color grading.

So while there was much slippage and contact between Indian popular understandings of embodied difference and emerging Euro-American race science, the two categories remained largely incommensurable. It was only within the context of debates about representation in the late nineteenth century (as with Salisbury's gibe) that Indians began to use racial arguments to pursue claims for autonomy and dignity within the imperial system. Indian authors referred to the "color line" and the "color bar" in arguments about the status of Indian subjects in South Africa. Indians generally wished to disassociate themselves from rural Africans, though not necessarily from urban ones. Indian intellectuals' ideas of race remained, in general terms, softer and less politicized than those of most of their European contemporaries. They reflected ideas of proper deport-ment and of correct ritual and domestic practice and culture (*sanskriti*) rather than intellectual and moral inferiority. So the proponent of rural uplift, Radhakamal Mukerjee, could state in the 1930s that "colour" was an outward and visible indication of mankind's "fitness for life under certain geographical conditions."[4] International legislation would be needed "to ratify the judgement of nature" to help "non-adult" races of the world such as Africans, Kalmuks, or Asian and Australasian aboriginal peoples. An international agreement on trusteeship (which included a free India) would decide whether economic regions should be open to trade and settlement or closed and segregated. What we see here, then, is the convergence of Indian conceptions of embodied virtue with European ideas of race within a transnational sphere of debate about colonialism, decolonization, and diaspora. Burton's work has helped to open up that transnational sphere for study.

It is no longer possible to work on empire or British identity without taking account of race. Gender studies have become almost canonical as elements in history teaching at universities in the U.S., Britain, and India. Burton's third and broadest claim—namely, that Victorian Britain and the political and social form of the country's modern identity was fundamen-tally shaped by the experience of empire—has encountered much stiffer resistance not only in Britain, but also tacitly from some British historians in North America. Again, it is not only domestic British (or, rather, "En-glish") historians who have reacted with skepticism but also significant historians of empire itself (e.g., Peter Marshall and Bernard Porter).

It is worth considering why this should be because the reasons are rather different in the United Kingdom and North America. In Britain, the "laager mentality" of domestic British historians is certainly one good reason. Even in a well-regarded history faculty, one hears the cry, "British history should be taught in a British university," when there is any suggestion of diminishing the number of compulsory courses in this field. It could also be that methodological conservatism ("empiricism," as Burton puts it) is a factor. The U.S. has perhaps been more adept at picking up new ideas from the intellectual world of France and Germany, which, at least up to the 1990s, were the real innovators in historical studies. Yet modern empire has been on the margins of continental European historiography, and actively discouraged in France. Instead, I suggest a number of other reasons that empire remained hived-off from domestic British political and social history.

First, many British historians remained concentrated on the issue of class even after the Marxist wave of the 1960s and '70s had spent its force. Whatever role empire played in the progress of parliamentary reform, for instance, British historians still argue, *pace* Catherine Hall, that class conflict in Britain remained the essential context. To take Burton's key case: it could be argued that the attack on Salisbury for his "black man" jibe had less to do with empire than with being part of a growing assault on the political role of the landed aristocracy that reached its height when Lloyd George emasculated the House of Lords in 1911. Similarly, race was assimilated to class as non-white immigration increased in the late twentieth century. Stephen Lawrence was black, but he was also the victim of a lower-class white "sink council estate." A large part of the British Indian population continues to vote Tory for reasons of class and capitalism. Second, British historians argue that the state—a much more obtrusive force in British than American history—was formed in its outlines well before imperial territorial expansion, or even the slave trade, became significant. The ghost of Geoffrey Elton's "Tudor revolution in government" hangs over British historiography. The only "imperial" issue here was the Irish one, and Ireland had an ambivalent status as part colony and part metropolis, with a big stake in the empire. Finally, British economic historians remain suspicious of arguments that the "drain of wealth from India," the slave trade, or colonial exploitation more broadly were critical features, either in the industrial revolution or in the economic stability of nineteenth-century Britain. Europe, the U.S., and, most important, rising domestic demand were vital here. British economic historians have lined up to critique Kenneth Pomeranz's argument that the economic "great divergence" between Britain and China came late and was a consequence of features external to the Western European economy itself.

All of these claims, of course, can be, and have been, vigorously contested. I repeat them only to indicate that the resistance to giving empire the critical role in British domestic history among British historians, correctly noted by Burton, arises not only from empiricism or parochialism but from longstanding historiographical traditions, which are themselves ideologically informed. They reflect, in fact, a sensibility of *l'angleterre profonde* that is both a powerful myth in history and a set of historical theories in its own right. It perhaps bears comparison with the contestation between the cosmopolitan America of the East and West coasts and the "small-town America" of the Midwest and the South that played such an important part in the election of Barack Obama.

Historians of the British empire and its regions have struggled hard to gain recognition from domestic historians as their subjects passed from a Whiggish constitutional phase, through the anti–Marxism of Robinson and Gallagher, to their present state of decentralization and theoretical pluralism. In Britain, the apartheid of language-based "Oriental studies" from history has hardly begun to break down. The trope of globalization quite often seemed to re-empower the dichotomy of "center" and "periphery." Relatively few Anglophone historians have grappled with the Iberian, French, or Dutch experience of empire. To this extent, the work of Antoinette Burton and her peers in thrusting race, "maternal imperialism," gender, and empire onto the agenda of British historians has been liberating. I end this afterword by suggesting some areas that should, perhaps, bulk larger in scholarship in the next decade. Many of these themes are suggested in Burton's essays.

First, the role of the "white dominions" in imperial Britain needs to be reasserted. Recent work by John Mackenzie, Andrew Porter, Tony Ballantyne, Peter Cain, Anthony Hopkins, Elizabeth Hofmeyer, and, most recently, Saul Dubow have in different ways reasserted the importance of "Britishness" in the colonial world. They have also traced connections between different dominions and colonies. The presence of the "white empire" in British history remains greatly underestimated, however. This is true across the board, from economic history to the history of social mores. It was, after all, Naoroji himself who pointed out that, per head of population, British exports to Australia dwarfed exports to India. Burton has puzzled at the failure of personal reflexivity among British historians. But if I look at my own middle- and lower-middle-class family history, it is unquestionably Australia, Canada, and, above all, New Zealand that play the dominant role as points of emigration, points of comparison, and "homes from home." Even the food we ate, from beef to the iconic Marmite, came from parts of the "informal empire" such as Argentina. If anything, the U.S. was more important than India or Africa, too. Racial ideas were omnipresent, of course, in family debate within my grand-parents' and parents' generation. Irritating colonial nationalists, such as Gandhi, were occasionally denounced. The "dying races"—Maori, ab-origines, American Indians, even South African blacks, at one stage—made brief appearances on the debating platforms of family and school. But the most vigorous racial stereotypes were always applied to Euro-peans, particularly Catholic Europeans and the Irish. As Burton argues, postcolonial studies have been "Indo-centric," but British understandings and constructions of the world were centered at least as much on domin-ions, on the U.S., and on Europe. It was perhaps only among the upper-middle-class service families who had their careers in Asia and, later, Africa, or families of soldiers who served in Asia during the Second World War or the Mau Mau insurgency, that these regions assumed the over-whelming importance that they have now achieved in postcolonial stud-ies and the historiography of empire in the domestic context.

Second, it would be well for historians to consider the interaction and mutually reinforcing features of the European, American, and imperial ex-perience in the creation of modern Britain within one frame, rather than vainly trying to assert that one or other of these—or what I have called l'angleterre profonde—was ever dominant. All of these different influ-ences were transformed in the domestic context. They "fed off," supple-mented, and reinforced one another at different times and in different places. At the level of transnational diaspora, for instance, twentieth-century waves of South Asian, Caribbean, and Polish migrants followed a path and lived in the same places earlier created by Huguenots and Irish in London's East End and elsewhere. These migrants encountered similar waves of religious and racial prejudice. At the economic level, it is impossi-ble to say that the empire was more or less important than Europe, the U.S., or domestic demand, *tout court*. During the Napoleonic Wars, when Britain was barred from Europe, or again in the late nineteenth century, when Britain faced severe competition from the U.S. and newly unified

Germany, the empire was undoubtedly a critical redoubt for British world trade. By the 1920s and '30s, however, the domestic economy was massively more important than the empire. That, of course, was one reason decolonization could be contemplated after 1945. Even in the realm of ideas, these varied influences intersected. Aryan theory might well be traced to William Jones and India, but Aryanism in the nineteenth century was preeminently a German concept made hospitable in Britain by powerful German philological and philosophical influences. Theosophy was a globalized ideological mongrel. Gandhi, in turn, found a hospitable moral space because John Wesley, John Ruskin, and Tolstoy had already contributed to a tradition of moralized anti-industrialism and "atonement politics."

The value of this type of analysis is that it can be developed for the dominions and colonized world, too. In Canada, for instance, Scottish educational projects, Irish American anticolonialism, and French cultural separatism all interacted within "the webs of empire." A Canadian prime minister stated at the beginning of the twentieth century, "To be better imperialists, we must first be better Canadians." Similarly, British India, far from being defined solely by the metropole–colony tension, was open very early to influences from Iberian liberals, French Comtians, "Germanism," and, later, Japanese ideas of "Asia for the Asians." All of these were transformed and recast by Indian intellectuals. Antoinette Burton's essays have been critical markers for the development of this project, which simultaneously analyzes the local and the global while it avoids essentializing either.

Notes

Foreword

1. See Gail Hershatter, *Women in China's Long Twentieth Century* (Berkeley: University of California Press, 2002), 107.

Introduction

Epigraphs: Adrienne Rich, *Atlas of the Difficult World* (New York: W. W. Norton, 1991), 6; William Ewart Gladstone, "England's Mission" (1878), in *Politics and Empire in Victorian Britain: A Reader*, ed. Antoinette Burton (New York: Palgrave, 2001), 135; Salman Rushdie, *The Satanic Verses* (London: Viking, 1988), 353.

1. See Antoinette M. Burton, "Introduction: On the Inadequacy and Indispensability of the Nation," in *After the Imperial Turn: Thinking with and through the Nation*, ed. Antoinette M. Burton (Durham: Duke University Press, 2003), 2.

2. Heather Streets, "Empire and 'the Nation': Institutional Practice, Pedagogy, and Nation in the Classroom," in *After the Imperial Turn*, 57–69.

3. Gayatri Chakravarty Spivak, "Can the Subaltern Speak?" in *Marxism and the Interpretation of Culture*, ed. Cary Nelson and Lawrence Grossberg (Urbana: University of Illinois Press, 1988), 271–313.

4. Gayatri Chakravarty Spivak, "The Rani of Sirmur: An Essay in Reading the Archives," *History and Theory* 24, no. 3 (1985), 247–72.

5. bell hooks, *Teaching to Transgress: Education as the Practice of Freedom* (New York: Routledge, 1994), 48–50.

6. Kumkum Sangari, "The Politics of the Possible," in *Interrogating Modernity: Culture and Colonialism in India*, ed. Tejaswini Niranjana, Pillarisetti Sudhir, and Vivek Dhareshwar (Calcutta: Seagull, 1991), 32.

7. Spivak, "The Rani of Sirmur," 248.

8. Ibid., 267.

9. See Paul Gilroy, Lawrence Grossberg, and Angela McRobbie, eds., *Without Guarantees: In Honour of Stuart Hall* (London: Verso, 2000), 283. The term "problem-

space" is developed most elaborately in David Scott, *Conscripts of Modernity: The Tragedy of Colonial Enlightenment* (Durham: Duke University Press, 2004).

10. I am thinking here of Peter Fryer, *Staying Power: The History of Black People in Britain* (London: Pluto Press, 1984); Rozina Visram, *Ayahs, Lascars, and Princes: Indians in Britain, 1700–1947* (London: Pluto Press, 1986); Ron Ramdin, *The Making of the Black Working Class in Britain* (Aldershot: Gower, 1987); and Raphael Samuel, ed., *Patriotism: The Making and Unmaking of British National Identity*, 3 vols. (New York: Routledge and Kegan Paul, 1989).

11. See Valerie Amos and Pratibha Parmar, "Challenging Imperial Feminism," *Feminist Review* 17 (1984), 3–19.

12. Hazel Carby, "White Women Listen! Black Feminism and the Boundaries of Sisterhood," in *The Empire Strikes Back: Race and Racism in 70s Britain*, ed. Centre for Contemporary Cultural Studies (London: Routledge, 1982), 212–35.

13. Audre Lorde, *Sister/Outsider: Essays and Speeches* (Trumansburg, N.Y.: Crossing Press, 1984); Cherríe L. Moraga and Gloria E. Anzaldúa, eds., *This Bridge Called My Back: Writings by Radical Women of Color* (New York: Kitchen Table–Women of Color Press, 1981).

14. Ellen Carol Dubois, *Feminism and Suffrage: The Emergence of an Independent Women's Movement in America, 1848–1869* (Ithaca: Cornell University Press, 1978); Angela Y. Davis, *Women, Race and Class* (New York: Vintage Books, 1983).

15. For a particularly instructive example of the tenacity of empiricism in imperial history, see Bernard Porter, *The Absent-Minded Imperialists: Empire, Society, and Culture in Britain* (Oxford: Oxford University Press, 2004); Jonathan Rose, *The Intellectual Life of the British Working Classes* (New Haven: Yale University Press, 2001). For the two autobiographical essays, see Catherine Hall, "Introduction," in *Civilising Subjects: Colony and Metropole in the English Imagination, 1830–1867* (Chicago: University of Chicago Press, 2002), 1–22; David Cannadine, "Appendix: An Imperial Childhood?," in *Ornamentalism: How the British Saw Their Empire* (Oxford: Oxford University Press, 2002), 181–200.

16. Laura Lee Downs and Stephanie Gerson, eds., *Why France? American Historians Reflect on an Enduring Fascination* (Ithaca: Cornell University Press, 2007).

17. Geoff Eley, *A Crooked Line: From Cultural History to the History of Society* (Ann Arbor: University of Michigan Press, 2005).

18. Jeremy D. Popkin, *History, Historians and Autobiography* (Chicago: University of Chicago Press, 2005).

19. For an account of his war experience up to, but not including, his hospitalization in Britain, see in David H. Burton, "Unit," *Animating History: The Biographical Pulse* (Philadelphia: St. Joseph's University Press, 2007), 283–313. He returned to active duty at Lichfield and was later assigned to a Military Police detachment in Ogborn St. George (a military training area for the British army). I thank Laura Mayhall for showing me how to address this.

20. Margaret Barrow, *Women, 1870–1928: A Select Guide to Printed and Archival Sources in the United Kingdom* (London: Mansell, 1981), contained a short reference to the Josephine Butler collection, then held at the Fawcett Library (London), and empire.

21. P. J. Marshall, "No Fatal Impact? The Elusive History of Imperial Britain," *Times Literary Supplement*, 12 March 1993, 8–10. Peter Marshall has always been a trenchant and generous interlocutor.

22. Joan Scott, "The Evidence of Experience," *Critical Inquiry* 17, no. 4 (1991), 773–97.

23. For an especially germane example of this, see Durba Ghosh, "National Narratives and the Politics of Miscegenation: Britain and India," in *Archive Stories: Facts, Fictions and the Writing of History*, ed. Antoinette M. Burton (Durham: Duke University Press, 2005), 27–44.

24. Mrinalini Sinha, *Colonial Masculinity: The "Manly Englishman" and the "Effeminate Bengali" in the Late Nineteenth Century* (Manchester: Manchester University Press, 1995); idem, "Teaching Imperialism as a Social Formation," *Radical History Review* 67 (1997), 175–86.

25. Ann Laura Stoler, *Race and the Education of Desire: Foucault's History of Sexuality and the Colonial Order of Things* (Durham: Duke University Press, 1995); Frederick Cooper and Ann Laura Stoler, eds., *Tensions of Empire: Colonial Cultures in a Bourgeois World* (Berkeley: University of California Press, 1997).

26. Henry Mayhew, *London Labour and the London Poor* (New York: Dover Publications, 1968 [1861]).

27. John Darwin, "Imperialism and the Victorians," *English Historical Review* 112, no. 447 (1997), 614–42; Stoler, *Race and the Education of Desire*.

28. Catherine Hall, "The Rule of Difference: Gender, Class and Empire in the Making of the 1832 Reform Act," in *Gendered Nations: Nationalisms and Gender Order in the Long Nineteenth Century*, ed. Ida Blom, Karen Hagemann, and Catherine Hall (New York: Oxford / Berg 2000), 107–35; Catherine Hall, Keith McClelland, and Jane Rendall, *Defining the Victorian Nation: Class, Race, Gender and the Reform Act of 1867* (Cambridge: Cambridge University Press, 2000). For the first comprehensive attempt to track the domestic impact of modern British imperialism, see Catherine Hall and Sonya O. Rose, eds., *At Home with the Empire: Metropolitan Culture and the Imperial World* (Cambridge: Cambridge University Press, 2006).

29. Hall, *Civilising Subjects*.

30. Catherine Hall, *White, Male, and Middle Class: Explorations in Feminism and History* (New York: Routledge, 1992); Paul Gilroy, *The Black Atlantic: Modernity and Double Consciousness* (Cambridge: Harvard University Press, 1993).

31. Porter, *The Absent-Minded Imperialists*; see also Richard Price, "One Big Thing: Britain and Its Empire," *Journal of British Studies* 45, no. 3 (2006), 602–27.

32. See the "NACBS Report on the State and Future of British Studies in North America," available on the North American Conference on British Studies (NACBS) website, http://www.nacbs.org/.

33. Bernard S. Cohn, "Representing Authority in Colonial India," in *The Invention of Tradition*, ed. Eric Hobsbawm and Terence Ranger (Cambridge: Cambridge University Press, 1993), 161–210.

34. Alan Lester, *Imperial Networks: Creating Identities in Nineteenth-Century South Africa and Britain* (London: Routledge, 2001); Felix Driver, *Geography Militant: Cultures of Exploration and Empire* (Oxford: Blackwell, 2001); Tony Ballantyne, *Orien-*

talism and Race: Aryanism in the British Empire (Houndmills: Palgrave, 2002); David Lambert and Alan Lester, eds., *Colonial Lives across the British Empire: Imperial Careering in the Long Nineteenth Century* (Cambridge: Cambridge University Press, 2006); Michael Hardt and Antonio Negri, *Empire* (Cambridge: Harvard University Press, 2000).

35. Iniva (Institute of International Visual Arts), and *Making Britain: South Asian Visions of Home and Abroad, 1870–1950*, a inter-disciplinary research project led by the Open University and sponsored by an Arts and Humanities Council Grant, are just two examples. See http://www.iniva.org/ and http://www.open.ac .uk/Arts/south-asians-making-britain/.

36. Jeffrey A. Auerbach, *The Great Exhibition of 1851: A Nation on Display* (New Haven: Yale University Press 1999); Peter H. Hoffenberg, *An Empire on Display: English, Indian, and Australian Exhibitions from the Crystal Palace to the Great War* (Berkeley: University of California Press, 2001); Annie E. Coombes, *Reinventing Africa: Museums, Material Culture and Popular Imagination in Late Victorian and Edwardian England* (New Haven: Yale University Pres, 1997); Louise Purbrick. ed., *The Great Exhibition of 1851: New Interdisciplinary Essays* (Manchester: Manchester University Press, 2001).

37. For a comprehensive review, see Douglas M. Peers, "Is Humpty Dumpty Back Together Again?: The Revival of Imperial History and the Oxford History of the British Empire," *Journal of World History* 13, no. 2 (2002), 451–67.

38. For one account of this relationship, see Antoinette M. Burton, *The Postcolonial Careers of Santha Rama Rau* (Durham: Duke University Press, 2007).

39. See, e.g., Simon During, "Postcolonialism," in *Beyond the Disciplines: The New Humanities*, ed. K. K. Ruthven (Canberra: Australian Academy of the Humanities 1992), 88–100; idem, "Postmodernism and Postcolonialism Today," *Textual Practice* 1, no. 1 (Spring 1987), 58–86. See also Ania Loomba, Suvir Kaul, Matti Bunzl, Antoinette M. Burton, and Jed Esty, eds., *Postcolonial Studies and Beyond* (Durham: Duke University Press, 2005).

40. Ann Curthoys, "We've Just Started Making National Histories and You Want Us to Stop Already?," in *After the Imperial Turn*, 70–89.

41. Ann Curthoys and Marilyn Lake, eds., *Connected Worlds: History in Transnational Perspective* (Canberra: Australian National University Press, 2005); Marilyn Lake and Henry Reynolds, *Drawing the Global Colour Line: White Men's Countries and the International Challenge of Racial Equality* (Cambridge: Cambridge University Press, 2008).

42. I am grateful to Tony Ballantyne for urging me to make this point and for personifying it in his work.

43. Sugata Bose, *A Hundred Horizons: The Indian Ocean in the Age of Global Empire* (Cambridge: Harvard University Press, 2006), 40.

44. The reference is to Dipesh Chakrabarty, *Provincializing Europe: Postcolonial Thought and Historical Difference* (Princeton: Princeton University Press, 2000).

45. See Ballantyne, *Orientalism and Race*; Robert A. Bickers, *Empire Made Me: An Englishman Adrift in Shanghai* (New York: Columbia University Press, 2003); James

L. Hevia, *English Lessons: The Pedagogy of Imperialism in Nineteenth-Century China* (Durham: Duke University Press, 2003). For a short survey of work that has taken a broadly imperial view, see Clare Midgley, ed., *Gender and Imperialism* (Manchester: Manchester University Press, 1998); idem, *Feminism and Empire: Women Activists in Imperial Britain, 1790–1865* (London: Routledge, 2007); Philippa Levine, *Prostitution, Race and Politics: Policing Venereal Disease in the British Empire* (New York: Routledge 2003); idem, ed., *Gender and Empire* (Oxford: Oxford University Press, 2004); idem, *The British Empire: Sunrise to Sunset* (Harlow, U.K.: Pearson Longman, 2007); Kathleen Wilson, *The Sense of the People: Politics, Culture and Imperialism in England, 1715–1785* (Cambridge: Cambridge University Press, 1995); idem, *Island Race: Englishness, Empire and Gender in the Eighteenth Century* (London: Routledge, 2002); idem, ed., *A New Imperial History: Culture, Identity and Modernity in Britain and the Empire, 1660–1840* (Cambridge: Cambridge University Press, 2004).

46. Radhika Mohanram, *Imperial White: Race, Diaspora, and the British Empire* (Minneapolis: University of Minnesota Press, 2007).

47. See "Anglo-Saxon Attitudes," *The Economist* March 29, 2008, pp. 71–73.

48. Thanks again to Tony Ballantyne for this point.

49. For this view, I am indebted to Sarah Ahmed, *Queer Phenomenology: Orientations, Objects, Others* (Durham: Duke University Press, 2006). I am also grateful to Emily Skidmore for putting it into my hands.

50. I thank Mrinalini Sinha for enabling me to grasp this point.

51. Audra Simpson, "On Ethnographic Refusal: Indigeneity, 'Voice' and Colonial Citizenship," *Junctures* 9 (2007), 78.

52. Adrienne Rich, "North American Time," *Your Native Land, Your Life: Poems* (New Yoir: W. W. Norton 1993), 33–36.

53. Charles S. Maier, *Among Empires: American Ascendancy and Its Predecessors* (Cambridge: Harvard University Press, 2006).

54. As Janice Peck says of Stuart Hall eulogizing Allon White, he "embarked on his career committed to the metaphors he now came to interrogate": Janice Peck, "Itinerary of a Thought: Stuart Hall, Cultural Studies, and the Unresolved Problem of the Relation of Culture to 'Not Culture,' " *Cultural Critique* 48 (2001), 200.

55. See Maya Jasanoff, *Edge of Empire: Lives, Culture, and Conquest in the East, 1750–1850* (New York: Knopf, 2005); Anthony Pagden, "Review of *C Is for Colonies*," *London Review of Books*, 11 May 2008, 30–31; Antoinette M. Burton and Tony Ballantyne, "The Politics of Intimacy in an Age of Empire," in *Moving Subjects: Gender, Mobility, and Intimacy in an Age of Global Empire*, ed. Tony Ballantyne and Antoinette M. Burton (Urbana: University of Illinois Press, 2008), 1–28. For an extended discussion of possible futures for postcolonial inquiry, see Loomba et al., *Postcolonial Studies and Beyond*.

56. Manela Erez, *The Wilsonian Moment: Self-Determination and the International Origins of Anticolonial Nationalism* (Oxford: Oxford University Press, 2007).

57. This posture is echoed in Saidiya Hartman, *Lose Your Mother: A Journey along the Atlantic Slave Route* (New York: Farrar, Strauss and Giroux, 2007); in idem, "Venus

in Two Acts," keynote address delivered at the Ninth Annual Graduate Student Symposium in Women's and Gender History, University of Illinois, Urbana-Champaign, March 2008; and, I think, in Antoinette M. Burton, *Dwelling in the Archive: Women Writing House, Home and History in Late Colonial India* (New York: Oxford University Press, 2003).

1. Rules of Thumb

This paper has benefited from the support and criticism of Paul Arroyo, Catherine Candy, Gary Daily, Chandra de Silva, Darlene Hantzis, Mike Kugler, Philippa Levine, Arvid Perez, Barbara Ramusack, Deborah Rossum, Sudipta Sen, Nyan Shah, Susan Thorne, and Jocelyn Zivin. Special thanks to Barbara Ramusack and Kali Israel for their commitment to organizing the Feminism, Imperialism, and Race: India and Britain Conference in Cincinnati, which provided the critical spaces within which this paper developed.

1. For a useful discussion of the problems inherent in the historiography of the "United Kingdom," see Keith Robbins, "Core and Periphery in Modern British History," *Proceedings of the British Academy* 52 (1984), 275–97.

2. Seeler quoted in David K. Fieldhouse, "Can Humpty-Dumpty Be Put Together Again?: Imperial History in the 1980s," *Journal of Imperial and Commonwealth History* 13, no. 2 (1984), 9–10.

3. For a set of discussions on doing Irish history as colonial history, see Terry Eagleton, Frederic Jameson, and Edward Said, *Nationalism, Colonialism, and Literature* (Minneapolis: University of Minnesota Press, 1990).

4. A. P. Thornton, *The Imperial Idea and Its Enemies: A Study in British Power* (New York: St. Martin's Press, 1985 [1959]), x. Thornton, a Scot, headed departments at the University of Toronto and at the University of the West Indies, thus plotting his own particular imperial / colonial trajectories. See Nicholas Mansergh, "A. P. Thornton: Realism Tempered by Wit," in *Studies in British Imperial History: Essays in Honour of A. P. Thornton*, ed. Gordon Martel (New York: St. Martin's Press, 1986), 1–7.

5. Michael Hechter, *Internal Colonialism: The Celtic Fringe in British National Development* (Berkeley: University of California Press, 1975); Robert Colls and Philip Dodd, eds., *Englishness: Politics and Culture* (London: Croom Helm, 1986).

6. John M. MacKenzie, *Propaganda and Empire: The Manipulation of British Public Opinion, 1880–1960* (Manchester: Manchester University Press, 1984), 254.

7. History was by no means the only stage for such apprehensions of imperial power. See Jacqueline S. Bratton, *Acts of Supremacy: The British Empire and the Stage, 1790–1930* (Manchester: Manchester University Press, 1991); Bernard S. Cohn, "Representing Authority in Victorian India," in *The Invention of Tradition*, ed. Eric J. Hobsbawm and Terence Ranger (Cambridge: Cambridge University Press, 1983), 165–210.

8. Shula Marks, "History, the Nation, and Empire: Sniping from the Periphery," *History Workshop Journal* 29 (1990), 117. See also Catherine Hall, *White, Male, and*

Middle Class: Explorations in Feminism and History (New York: Routledge, 1992), 20. Even some who have recognized the importance of domestic discourses on race, such as Douglas Lorimer, have downplayed its imperial significances: see Douglas A. Lorimer, *Colour, Class, and the Victorians: English Attitudes toward the Negro in Mid-Nineteenth Century Britain* (Leicester: Leicester University Press, 1987).

9. Hugh A. McDougall, *Racial Myth in English History: Trojans, Teutons, and Anglo-Saxons* (Montreal: Harvest House, 1982), 89–116.

10. J. G. A. Pocock, "The Limits and Divisions of British History: In Search of the Unknown Subject," *American Historical Review* 87 (1982), 314.

11. John Darwin, *The End of the British Empire: The Historical Debate* (Oxford: Basil Blackwell, 1991).

12. Arnold P. Kaminsky, *The India Office, 1880–1910* (New York: Greenwood Press, 1986), chap. 1.

13. For an overview of Robinson's and Gallagher's contributions to imperial historiography, see William R. Louis Jr., ed., *Imperialism: The Robinson and Gallagher Controversy* (New York: Franklin Watts, 1976).

14. Partha Chatterjee, *Nationalist Thought and the Colonial World: A Derivative Discourse?* (London: Zed Books, 1986); Gyan Prakash, "Writing Post–Orientalist Histories of the Third World: Perspectives from Indian Historiography," *Comparative Studies in Society and History* 32 (1990), 383–408.

15. P. J. Marshall, "Empire and Authority in the Later Eighteenth Century," *Journal of Imperial and Commonwealth History* 15 (1987), 105.

16. Quoted in Homi K. Bhabha, "Dissemination: Time, Narrative, and the Margins of the Modern State," in *Nation and Narration*, ed. Homi K. Bhabha (New York: Routledge, 1990), 317.

17. Joanna Liddle and Rama Joshi, "Gender and Colonialism: Women's Organizations under the Raj," *Women's Studies International Forum* 8 (1985), 521–29; Nupur Chaudhuri and Margaret Strobel, eds., *Western Women and Imperialism: Complicity and Resistance* (Bloomington: Indiana University Press, 1992), 1–2.

18. Prakash, "Writing Post–Orientalist Histories of the Third World," 384. Jane Haggis calls it "a dialectic complexity of 'meetings' between two social formations": Jane Haggis, "The Feminist Research Process—Defining a Topic," in *Feminist Praxis: Research, Theory, and Epistemology in Feminist Sociology*, ed. Liz Stanley (London: Routledge, 1990), 73.

19. Helen Callaway, *Gender, Culture, and Empire: European Women in Colonial Nigeria* (London: Macmillan, 1987), 5.

20. Marks, "History, the Nation, and Empire," 113. See also Liz Stanley, "British Feminist Histories: An Editorial Introduction," *Women's Studies International Forum* 13 (1990), 3–7.

21. Bernard Semmel, *Imperialism and Social Reform: English Social-Imperial Thought, 1895–1914* (New York: Anchor Books, 1960).

22. MacKenzie, *Propaganda and Empire*, 1–10; idem, *Imperialism and Popular Culture* (Manchester: Manchester University Press, 1986).

23. Arthur Godley, undersecretary of state for India, 1883–1910, quoted in Kaminsky, *The India Office*, 174.

24. James Walvin and J. A. Mangan, eds., *Manliness and Morality: Middle-Class Masculinity in Britain and America, 1800–1940* (New York: St. Martin's Press, 1987); J. A. Mangan, *The Games Ethic and Imperialism* (London: Viking, 1986); Brian Stoddart, "Sport, Cultural Imperialism, and Colonial Response in the British Empire," *Comparative Studies in Society and History* 30 (1988), 649–73.

25. Jane Haggis, "Gendering Colonialism or Colonizing Gender? Recent Women's Studies Approaches to White Women and the History of British Colonialism," *Women's Studies International Forum* 13 (1990), 105–15.

26. Anita Levy, *Other Women: The Writing of Class, Race, and Gender, 1832–1898* (Princeton: Princeton University Press, 1991), 5; Chandra Talpade Mohanty, "Feminist Encounters: Locating the Politics of Experience," *Copyright* 1 (1987), 32. See also Kumari Jayawardena, *Feminism and Nationalism in the Third World* (London: Zed Books, 1986); Margaret Strobel, *European Women and the Second British Empire* (Bloomington: Indiana University Press, 1991).

27. Suvendrini Perera, *Reaches of Empire: The English Novel from Edgeworth to Dickens* (New York: Columbia University Press, 1991); Jenny Sharpe, *Allegories of Empire: The Figure of Woman in the Colonial Text* (Minneapolis: University of Minnesota Press, 1993).

28. Leonore Davidoff and Catherine Hall, *Family Fortunes: Men and Women of the English Middle Class, 1780–1850* (Chicago: University of Chicago Press, 1987); Catherine Hall, "The Economy of Intellectual Prestige: Thomas Carlyle, John Stuart Mill and the Case of Governor Eyre," *Cultural Critique* 12 (1989), 167–96.

29. Mary Poovey, *Uneven Developments: The Ideological Work of Gender in Mid–Victorian Britain* (Chicago: University of Chicago Press, 1988). See also Judith Rowbotham, *Good Girls Make Good Wives: Guidance for Girls in Victorian Fiction* (Oxford: Basil Blackwell, 1989). Rowbotham devotes an entire chapter to the imperial dimension of girls' fiction because "by the middle of the nineteenth century the British empire was already a part of the consciousness of middle-class society, featuring in its cultural artifacts from art to literature and considered by that class to involve all levels of society": Rowbotham, *Good Girls Make Good Wives*, 180.

30. Clare Midgley, *Women against Slavery: The British Campaigns, 1780–1870* (London: Routledge, 1992).

31. Susan Pedersen, "National Bodies, Unspeakable Acts: The Sexual Politics of Colonial Policy-making," *Journal of Modern History* 63 (1991), 647–80; Michael Roper and John Tosh, eds., *Manful Assertions: Masculinities in Britain since 1800* (New York: Routledge, 1991). On the use of the term "amnesia" as it relates to these issues, see Hall, *White, Male, and Middle Class*, esp. chap. 1.

32. Gayatri Spivak, "Three Women's Texts and a Critique of Imperialism," in *The Feminist Reader: Essays in the Politics of Literary Criticism*, ed. Catherine Belsey and Jane Moore (New York: Basil Blackwell, 1989), 175.

33. Nigel Leask, *British Romantic Writers and the East* (Cambridge: Cambridge University Press, 1992), 86, 103.

34. Gauri Viswanathan, "Raymond Williams and British Colonialism," *Yale Journal of Criticism* 4, no. 2 (1991), 47–66. I am grateful to Mrinalini Sinha for pressing me to recognize the ways in which the relationships between "national" and "imperial" culture are themselves contested in postcolonial studies.

35. It had become a commonplace observation in 1866 that Britain's center of gravity had moved to Calcutta. What Benjamin Disraeli wished to do was to reflect back into Europe the strength that Britain drew from India, and the policy that he pressed Lord Derby to adopt in 1866 was designed for this purpose: Freda Harcourt, "Disraeli's Imperialism, 1866–1868: A Question of Timing," *Historical Journal* 23 (1980), 97. I thank Susan Thorne for bringing this essay to my attention.

36. In a similar vein, Paul Rich points out how the Martian invasion of the English countryside in H. G. Wells's *The War of the Worlds* brought the colonial experience home: Paul Rich, "The Quest for Englishness," in *Victorian Values: Personalities and Perspectives in Nineteenth-Century Society*, ed. Gordon Marsden (London: Longman, 1990).

37. Although empire, and especially "imperial anxieties," tend to function more as an unelaborated backdrop than as cultural agents in her book, and the ramifications of London as an "Imperial City" are underdeveloped from my point of view, *City of Dreadful Delight* raises important questions about how the map of empire was inscribed onto London itself: Judith R. Walkowitz, *City of Dreadful Delight: Narratives of Sexual Danger in Late–Victorian London* (Chicago: University of Chicago Press, 1992), 17–19, 25–26, 42–48. See also Tracy C. Davis, *Actresses as Working Women: Their Social Identity in Victorian Culture* (New York: Routledge, 1991), esp. chap. 5.

38. Peter Fryer, *Staying Power: The History of Black People in Britain* (London: Pluto Press, 1984); Rozina Visram, *Ayahs, Lascars, and Princes: Indians in Britain, 1700–1947* (London: Pluto Press, 1986); Bhikhu Parekh, ed., *Colour, Culture, and Consciousness: Immigrant Intellectuals in Britain* (London: George Allen and Unwin, 1974).

39. Seamus Deane, "Introduction," in *Nationalism, Colonialism and Literature*, ed. Eagleton et al., 10.

40. Quoted in Deborah J. Rossum, " 'A Vision of Black Englishness': The Black Press in England and the Construction of Black Identity," paper presented at the joint meeting of the North American and Pacific Coast Conference on British Studies, Santa Clara University, 1991, provided by the author.

41. Laura Tabili, " 'A Place of Refuge': Black Workers and Black Settlements in Interwar Britain," paper presented at the joint meeting of the North American and Pacific Coast Conference on British Studies, Santa Clara University, 1991, provided by the author.

42. I am grateful to Catherine Candy for sharing this insight with me in correspondence. See also Thomas C. Holt, *The Problem of Freedom: Race, Labor, and Politics in Jamaica and Britain, 1832–1938* (Baltimore: Johns Hopkins University Press, 1992); Michel-Rolph Trouillot, "Discourses of Rule and the Acknowledgment of the Peasantry in Dominica, West Indies, 1838–1928," *American Ethnologist* 16 (1989), 704–18.

43. Anna Davin, "Standing on Virginia Woolf's Doorstep," *History Workshop Journal* 31 (1991), 73.

44. Christopher A. Bayly, *Imperial Meridian: The British Empire and the World* (London: Longman, 1989), 11. The term "field" is itself imperially marked, and when invoking it we might remember, with Vivian Twostar, that the terms we use are part of the vocabulary of the colonizer: Vivian Twostar, "Discovery. Possession. How Different Was I from the Construct I Fabricated?," in *The Crown of Columbus*, ed. Louise Erdrich and Michael Dorris (New York: Harper Paperbacks, 1991), 269.

45. Antoinette Burton, "The Feminist Quest for Identity: British Imperial Suffragism and 'Global Sisterhood,' 1900–1915," *Journal of Women's History* 3, no. 2 (1991), 46–81; Vron Ware, *Beyond the Pale: White Women, Racism and History* (London: Verso, 1992); Brian Harrison, *Separate Spheres: The Opposition to Women's Suffrage in Britain* (New York: Holmes and Meier, 1978).

46. Kumari Jayawardena, *Feminism and Nationalism in the Third World*; Adelaide M. Cromwell, *An African Victorian Feminist: The Life and Times of Adelaide Smith Casely Hayford* (London: Frank Cass, 1986); Huda Shaarawi, *Harem Years: The Memoirs of an Egyptian Feminist*, trans. Margot Badran (New York: Feminist Press, 1986); Rokeya S. Hossain, *Sultana's Dreams and Selections from the Secluded Ones,* ed. and trans. Roushan Jahan (New York: Feminist Press, 1988); Margot Badran and Miriam Cooke, eds., *Opening the Gates: A Century of Arab Feminist Writing* (Bloomington: Indiana University Press, 1990); Geraldine H. Forbes, "Votes for Women: The Demand for Women's Franchise in India, 1918–1937," in *Symbols of Power: Studies on the Political Status of Women in India*, ed. Vina Mazumdar (Bombay: Allied, 1979), 11–23; Margot Badran, "Dual Liberation: Feminism and Nationalism in Egypt, 1870s–1925," *Feminist Issues* 8 (1988), 15–34.

47. Edward W. Said, "Identity, Authority and Freedom: The Potentate and the Traveler," *Transition* 54 (1991), 12. I am grateful to Sherifa Zuhur for sharing this essay with me.

48. Stephen Hay, "The Making of a Late–Victorian Hindu: M. K. Gandhi in London, 1888–1891," *Victorian Studies* 33 (1989), 74–98; Mohandas K. Gandhi, *An Autobiography: or, The Story of My Experiments with Truth* (Boston: Beacon Press, 1957), 113–17.

49. Madhu Kishwar, "Gandhi on Women," *Race and Class* 28 (1986), 43–61; Geraldine H. Forbes, "The Politics of Respectability: Indian Women and the Indian National Congress," in *The Indian National Congress: Centenary Hindsights*, ed. D. A. Low (Delhi: Oxford University Press, 1988), 54–97; James D. Hunt, "Suffragettes and Satyagraha: Gandhi and the British Women's Suffrage Movement," paper presented at the Annual Meeting of the American Academy of Religion, St. Louis, Mo., 1976, on file at the Fawcett Library, London.

50. Burton, "The Feminist Quest for Identity," 46–81; Barbara N. Ramusack, "Cultural Missionaries, Maternal Imperialists, Feminist Allies: British Women Activists in India, 1865–1945," in *Western Women and Imperialism*, ed. Chaudhuri and Strobel, 118–36.

51. For a debate on the fate of national histories in the era of internationalism, see Ian

Tyrrell and Michael McGerr, "American Historical Review Forum," American Historical Review 96 (1991), 1031–72. Ian Tyrrell, Woman's World, Woman's Empire: The Women's Christian Temperance Union in International Perspective, 1880–1930 (Chapel Hill: University of North Carolina Press, 1991), is an interesting example of international history in practice.

52. Stanley, Feminist Praxis, 64.

53. Kumkum Sangari and Sudesh Vaid, eds., Recasting Women: Essays in Colonial History (New Delhi: Kali for Women, 1989); R. Radhakrishnan, "Nationalism, Gender, and the Narrative of Identity," Nationalisms and Sexualities, ed. Andrew Parker, Mary Russo, Doris Sommer, and Patricia Yaeger (New York: Routledge, 1992), 77–95.

54. Mrinalini Sinha, " 'Chathams, Pitts and Gladstones in Petticoats': The Politics of Gender and Race in the Ilbert Bill Controversy, 1883–1884," and Ramusack, "Cultural Missionaries, Maternal Imperialists, Feminist Allies," both in Western Women and Imperialism, ed. Chaudhuri and Strobel, 98–118, 119–36. See also Barbara N. Ramusack, "Embattled Advocates: The Debate over Birth Control in India, 1920–40," Journal of Women's History 1 (1990), 34–64; Janaki Nair, "Uncovering the Zenana: Visions of Indian Womanhood in Englishwomen's Writings, 1813–1940," Journal of Women's History 2:1 (Spring 1990), 8–36; Catherine Candy, " 'Mother India' and the Ideal 'Femaculine': An Irish Orientalist Feminist in India," paper presented at the Annual Meeting of the American Historical Association, Chicago, 1991, provided by the author.

55. This is an extrapolation of Sara Suleri's claim that "the story of the colonial encounter is itself a radically decentering narrative": Sara Suleri, The Rhetoric of English India (Chicago: University of Chicago Press, 1992), 2.

56. This literature is rich in both theoretical innovation and evidentiary sources. In thinking about new ways to conceptualize imperial culture, I have been particularly influenced by the concept of diaspora, used primarily, though not exclusively, by African American historians: see, e.g., Rosalyn Terborg-Penn, Sharon Harley and Andrea Benton Rushing, eds., Women in Africa and the African Diaspora (Washington: Howard University Press, 1987).

57. Judith Butler, "Contingent Foundations: Feminism and the Question of Postmodernism," in Feminists Theorize the Political, ed. Judith Butler and Joan Scott (New York: Routledge, 1992), 7.

58. Chandra Talpade Mohanty, "Cartographies of Struggle: Third World Women and the Politics of Feminism," in Third World Women and the Politics of Feminism, ed. Chandra Talpade Mohanty, Ann Russo, and Lourdes Torres (Bloomington: Indiana University Press, 1991), 3.

59. Ibid., 2: Eric J. Hobsbawm, Nations and Nationalism since 1780: Programme, Myth, Reality (Cambridge: Cambridge University Press, 1990), 177.

60. Dipesh Chakrabarty, "Postcoloniality and the Artifice of History: Who Speaks for 'Indian' Pasts?," Representations 37 (1992), 1.

61. For an excellent discussion of the problem of constituting "home," see Biddy Martin and Chandra Talpade Mohanty, "Feminist Politics: What's Home Got to

Do with It?," in *Feminist Studies / Critical Studies*, ed. Teresa de Lauretis (Madison: University of Wisconsin Press, 1986), 191–212. B. J. Reagon offers another powerful reflection on home in "Foreword: Nurturing Resistance," in *Reimagining America: The Arts of Social Change*, ed. Mark O'Brien and Craig Little (Philadelphia: New Society Publishers, 1990), 1–8. I thank Darlene Hantzis and the students in "Feminist Theories" at Indiana State University in the fall of 1992 for sharing their insights on this essay with me.

62. Haggis, "The Feminist Research Process," 77.

63. Ann Laura Stoler, "Rethinking Colonial Categories: European Communities and the Boundaries of Rule," *Comparative Studies in History and Society* 31 (1989), 134–61.

64. Mohanty, "Feminist Encounters," 30; Aiwha Ong, "Colonialism and Modernity: Feminist Re-presentations of Women in Non-Western Societies," *Inscriptions* 3, no. 4 (1988), 79.

65. Johannes Fabian, *Time and the Other: How Anthropology Makes Its Objects* (New York: Columbia University Press, 1983), x.

2. Who Needs the Nation?

This essay owes much to Bernard S. Cohn, for whose generosity of mind and spirit I have long been grateful. A number of friendly critics, including Nadja Durbach, Ian Fletcher, David Goodman, Rob Gregg, Madhavi Kale, Dane Kennedy, Philippa Levine, Laura Mayhall, Maura O'Connor, Fiona Paisley, Doug Peers, Minnie Sinha, Susan Thorne, and Angela Woollacott, have helped to strengthen my arguments, for which I, of course, bear the final responsibility. Herman Bennett's long-term investment in this essay has made all the difference. I am equally indebted to Peter Marshall's energetic engagements. Finally, I greatly appreciate the feedback I received at presentations for the Australian Historical Association in Melbourne in 1996 and the Workshop on State Formation in Comparative Historical and Cultural Perspectives in Oxford in 1997, especially from Ann Curthoys, Philip Corrigan, Marilyn Lake, Vinay Lal, Derek Sayer, and Sudipta Sen.

1. Perry Anderson, "Origins of the Present Crisis" (1964), *English Questions* (London: Verso, 1992), 25.

2. Ibid., 25–26.

3. Irfan Habib, "Capitalism in History," *Social Scientist* 23, nos. 7–9 (July–September 1995): 15–31.

4. Eric Williams, *Capitalism and Slavery*, repr. edn. (Chapel Hill: University of North Carolina Press, 1994 [1944]). See especially the introduction to this edition, in which Colin Palmer unearths the critical response to the manuscript before it was accepted for publication, followed by its review history: ibid., xi–xxii. Perry Anderson does not cite Williams, though his argument in "Origins of the Present Crisis" echoes much of what Williams had meticulously advanced in *Capitalism and Slavery*: Anderson, "Origins of the Present Crisis." Thomas C. Holt, *The Problem of Freedom: Race, Labor and Politics in Jamaica and Britain, 1832–1938* (Baltimore: Johns Hopkins University Press, 1992), is also relevant here.

5. Gauri Viswanathan, "Raymond Williams and British Colonialism," *Yale Journal of Criticism* 4, no. 2 (1991), 47–67; E. P. Thompson, *Alien Homage: Edward Thompson and Rabindranath Tagore* (Delhi: Oxford University Press, 1993); Catherine Hall, *White, Male, and Middle Class: Explorations in Feminist History* (London: Routledge, 1992); Harish Trivedi, *Colonial Transactions: English Literature and India* (New York: St. Martin's Press, 1995). See also Robert Gregg and Madhavi Kale, "The Empire and Mr. Thompson: The Making of Indian Princes and the English Working Class," *Economic and Political Weekly* 32, no. 36 (1997), 2273–88.

6. In this sense, it was petit bourgeois, as well, although Anderson does not take this up explicitly: see Anderson, "Components of the National Culture," 52, 103. For an instructive colonial take on the question of "national" culture, which was contemporaneous with Anderson's (but to which he does not allude, even in the reprint edition), see Frantz Fanon, "On National Culture," in *The Wretched of the Earth* (Penguin: Harmondsworth, 1967). This chapter is reprinted in Patrick Williams and Laura Chrisman, eds., *Colonial Discourse and Post-Colonial Theory: A Reader* (New York: Columbia University Press, 1994), 36–52. For evidence of the continued search for explanations about why Britain failed to produce a "native" sociology, see José Harris, "Platonism, Positivism and Progressivism: Aspects of British Sociological Thought in the Early Twentieth Century," in *Citizenship and Community: Liberals, Radicals and Collective Identities in the British Isles, 1865–1931*, ed. Eugenio F. Biagini (Cambridge: Cambridge University Press, 1996), 343–60.

7. For a recent response to the literary turn that engages this phenomenon, see Dane Kennedy, "Imperial History and Postcolonial Theory," *Journal of Imperial and Commonwealth History* 24, no. 3 (September 1996), 345–63. The fact that the linguistic turn and the ethnographic turn are related is often overlooked. For a recent discussion of their historical connections, see Sara Maza, "Stories in History: Cultural Narratives in Recent Works in European History," *American Historical Review* 101, no. 5 (December 1996), 1497.

8. Edward Said, *Culture and Imperialism* (New York: Vintage Books, 1993), 6.

9. Peter Hulme, "Subversive Archipelagos: Colonial Discourse and the Break-up of Continental Theory," *Dispositio* 14, nos. 36–38 (1989), 1–23.

10. John M. MacKenzie's editorship of the multivolume Studies in Imperialism series is responsible for much of the wealth of historical material now available on the impact of empire on domestic British culture. See, e.g., John M. MacKenzie, ed., *Imperialism and Popular Culture* (Manchester: Manchester University Press, 1986); idem, *Propaganda and Empire: The Manipulation of British Public Opinion, 1880–1960* (Manchester: Manchester University Press, 1984). Other relevant monographs include Jenny Sharpe, *Allegories of Empire: The Figure of Woman in the Colonial Text* (Minneapolis: University of Minnesota Press, 1993); Firdous Azim, *The Colonial Rise of the Novel* (New York: Routledge, 1993); Hall, *White, Male, and Middle Class*; Vron Ware, *Beyond the Pale: White Women, Racism, and History* (London: Verso, 1992); Antoinette Burton, *Burdens of History: British Feminists, Indian Women, and Imperial Culture, 1865–1915* (Chapel Hill: University of North Carolina Press 1994); Annie E. Coombes, *Reinventing Africa: Museums, Imperial Culture, and Popular*

Imagination (New Haven: Yale University Press, 1994); Mrinalini Sinha, *Colonial Masculinity: The "Manly Englishman" and the "Effeminate Bengali" in the Late Nineteenth Century* (Manchester: Manchester University Press, 1995); Anne McClintock, *Imperial Leather: Race, Gender, and Sexuality in the Colonial Contest* (New York: Routledge, 1995).

11. Gretchen Gerzina, *Black London: Life before Emancipation* (New Brunswick: Rutgers University Press, 1995), 204. See also Antoinette Burton, *At the Heart of the Empire: Indians and the Colonial Encounter in Late-Victorian Britain* (Berkeley: University of California Press, 1998); Peter Fryer, *Staying Power: Black People in Britain* (London: Pluto Press, 1987); Barnor Hesse, "Black to Front and Black Again," in *Place and the Politics of Identity*, ed. Michael Keith and Steve Pile (London: Routledge, 1993), 162–82; Colin Holmes, *John Bull's Island: Immigration and British Society 1871–1971* (London: Macmillan, 1988); Rozina Visram, *Ayahs, Lascars, and Princes: Indians in Britain, 1700–1947* (London: Pluto Press, 1986).

12. John M. MacKenzie, *Orientalism: History, Theory, and the Arts* (Manchester: Manchester University Press, 1995); Marshall, 1993.

13. Benita Parry, "Overlapping Territories and Intertwined Histories: Edward Said's Postcolonial Cosmopolitanism," in *Edward Said: A Critical Reader*, ed. Michael Sprinker (Oxford: Blackwell, 1993), 19–47.

14. Paul Gilroy, *The Black Atlantic: Modernity and Double Consciousness* (Cambridge: Harvard University Press, 1993), 7.

15. Olaudah Equiano was a slave from Benin who purchased his freedom in 1766 and wrote his life story, *The Interesting Narrative of the Life of Olaudah Equiano*, in 1789; Mary Seacole was a Jamaican nurse who served in the Crimean War and wrote the account *Wonderful Adventures of Mrs. Seacole in Many Lands*; see Paul Edwards and David Dabydeen, eds., *Black Writers in Britain, 1760–1890* (Edinburgh: Edinburgh University Press, 1991). For newspaper coverage of the response of Prime Minister John Major's government to the inclusion of these works in British history texts, see "The 'Betrayal' of Britain's History," *Daily Telegraph* (London), 19 September 1995; "Heroic Virtues," *Sunday Telegraph* (London), 24 September 1995; "History Fit for (Politically Correct) Heroes," *Sunday Telegraph* (London), 24 September 1995. I am grateful to Audrey Matkins for these references.

16. See Bill Schwarz, ed., *The Expansion of England: Race, Ethnicity, and Cultural History* (New York: Routledge, 1996); Catherine Hall, "Histories, Empires, and the Post-Colonial Moment," in *The Post-Colonial Question: Common Skies, Divided Horizons*, ed. Iain Chambers and Lidia Curti (New York: Routledge, 1996), 65–77; and P. J. Marshall, *The Cambridge Illustrated History of the British Empire* (Cambridge: Cambridge University Press, 1996). Marshall agrees with two of the definitions of "constitutive" in the Oxford English Dictionary: (1) "having the power of constituting; constructive"; and (2) "that which goes to make up; constituent, component." But he cannot agree with the third: "that which makes a thing what it is": P. J. Marshall, private correspondence, 15 September 1996.

17. MacKenzie, *Propaganda and Empire*, 3.

18. I am grateful to Catherine Hall for pressing this point in conversation. See also

Hall, *White, Male, and Middle Class*, 1; idem, "Rethinking Imperial Histories: The Reform Act of 1867," *New Left Review* 208 (1994), 3–29.

19. Ruth H. Lindeborg, "The 'Asiatic' and the Boundaries of Victorian Englishness," *Victorian Studies* (Spring 1994), 5–40.

20. See Sinha, *Colonial Masculinity*. For one example of how this false homogenization works to obscure the role of the Celtic fringe in empire, see the discussion of how crucial Dundee was in the history of the jute mills in Calcutta in Dipesh Chakrabarty, *Rethinking Working-Class History* (Princeton: Princeton University Press, 1989), chap. 2.

21. Kathleen Wilson, "Citizenship, Empire, and Modernity in the English Provinces, c. 1720–1790," *Eighteenth Century Studies* 29, no. 1 (1995), 70; emphasis added.

22. McClintock, *Imperial Leather*, 36.

23. I am aided in these observations by Prasenjit Duara, *Rescuing History from the Nation: Questioning Narratives of Modern China* (Chicago: University of Chicago Press, 1995).

24. See Elizabeth D. Ermarth, *Sequel to History: Postmodernism and the Crisis of Representational Time* (Princeton: Princeton University Press, 1992), 18, 21. She is not concerned with the imperial contexts of modern Western discourse, but her characterizations of historical convention are extremely useful nonetheless.

25. I am aided in this observation by the reading of Richard Hakluyt in Kim F. Hall, *Things of Darkness: Economies of Race and Gender in Early Modern England* (Ithaca: Cornell University Press, 1995), 48.

26. Anna Marie Smith, *New Right Discourse on Race and Sexuality* (Cambridge: Cambridge University Press, 1995). See also Judith Butler, "Contingent Foundations," in *Feminists Theorize the Political*, ed. Judith Butler and Joan Scott (New York: Routledge, 1992).

27. Ann Laura Stoler, *Race and the Education of Desire* (Durham: Duke University Press, 1995); Ann Laura Stoler and Frederick Cooper, "Introduction: Tensions of Empire: Colonial Control and Visions of Rule," *American Ethnologist* 16 (1989), 609–21.

28. Renata Salecl, "The Fantasy Structure of Nationalist Discourse," *Praxis International* 13, no. 3 (October 1993), 213–23.

29. MacKenzie, *Orientalism*.

30. See, e.g., Harold Perkins, "Review of José Harris, *Private Lives, Public Spirit: A Social History of Britain, 1870–1914*," *American Historical Review* 100, no. 1 (February 1995), 164; Bruce Kinzer, "Review of James Vernon, *Politics and the People: A Study in English Political Culture, c. 1815–1867*," *American Historical Review* 100, no. 3 (June 1995), 900.

31. Most recently, Gilroy, *The Black Atlantic*, was upheld in a review essay by Frederick Cooper as an example of a "transcontinental" study that requires proper historical work to fill in its "gaps": see Frederick Cooper, "Race, Ideology, and the Perils of Comparative History," *American Historical Review* 101, no. 4 (October 1996), 1129.

32. Judith A. Allen, "Feminist Critiques of Western Knowledges: Spatial Anxieties in

a Provisional Phase?," in *Beyond the Disciplines: The New Humanities*, ed. K. K. Ruthven (Canberra: Papers from the Australian Academy of the Humanities Symposium, 1992), 57–77.

33. Ermarth, *Sequel to History*.

34. Arjun Appadurai, "Diversity and Disciplinarity as Cultural Artifacts," *Disciplinarity and Dissent in Cultural Studies*, ed. Cary Nelson and Dilip Parameshwar Gaonkar (New York: Routledge, 1996), 23–36.

35. Kate Brown, "The Eclipse of History: Japanese America and a Treasure Chest of Forgetting," *Public Culture* 9 (1996), 69–91.

36. Kobena Mercer, *Welcome to the Jungle: New Positions in Black Cultural Studies* (New York: Routledge, 1994), 5, 31.

37. Joyce Appleby, Lynn Hunt and Margaret Jacobs, *Telling the Truth about History* (New York: W. W. Norton, 1994).

38. Joanne Meyerowitz, ed., *Not June Cleaver: Women and Gender in Post-war America* (Philadelphia: Temple University Press, 1994).

39. Although the exiles I have in mind in this particular formulation (and in this essay in general) are people of color and formerly colonial migrants in Britain, it must also be said that working-class men and women have a differently ambiguous, though equally painful, relationship to the nation and its ideological apparatus, the state. As Carolyn Steadman writes so poignantly in her autobiography, "I think I would be a very different person now if orange juice and milk and dinners at school hadn't told me, in a covert way, that I had a right to exist, was worth something": Carolyn Steadman, *Landscape for a Good Woman: A Story of Two Lives* (New Brunswick: Rutgers University Press, 1987), 122. I am grateful to Nadja Durbach for this citation and for how it compelled me to refigure the question, "Who needs the nation?"

40. Homi K. Bhabha, "Life at the Border: Hybrid Identities of the Present," *New Perspectives Quarterly* 14, no. 1 (Winter 1997). See also Bernard S. Cohn, *Colonialism and Its Forms of Knowledge: The British in India* (Princeton: Princeton University Press, 1996).

41. Dorothy Ross, "Grand Narrative in American Historical Writing," *American Historical Review* 110, no. 3 (June 1995), 651–77.

42. Anita Chakravarty, "Writing History," *Economic and Political Weekly* (23 December 1995), 3320; Ramachandra Guha, "Subaltern and Bhadralok Studies," *Economic and Political Weekly* (19 August 1995), 2057–58; idem, "Beyond Bhadralok and Bankim Studies," *Economic and Political Weekly* (24 February 1996), 495–96.

43. I am aided in this conceptualization by Greg Dening's "P 905 .A512 × 100: An Ethnographic Essay," *American Historical Review* 100, no. 3 (June 1995), 864.

44. Patrick Joyce, *Democratic Subjects: The Self and the Social in the Nineteenth Century* (Cambridge: Cambridge University Press, 1994); Laura Mayhall, "Creating the 'Suffragette Spirit': British Feminism and the Historical Imagination," *Women's History Review* 4, no. 3 (1995): 319–44; Raphael Samuel, *Theatres of Memory* (London: Verso, 1994); James Vernon, *Politics and the People: A Study in English Political Culture, c. 1815–1867* (Cambridge: Cambridge University Press, 1993); Judith Wal-

kowitz, *City of Dreadful Delight: Narratives of Sexual Danger in Late–Victorian London* (Chicago: University of Chicago Press, 1992).

45. Geoff Eley and Keith Nield, "Starting Over: The Present, the Post-modern, and the Moment of Social History," *Social History* 20 (1995), 355–64.

46. Ermarth, *Sequel to History*, 18, 21.

47. David Lowenthal, "Identity, Heritage, and History," in *Commemorations: The Politics of National Identity*, ed. John R. Gillis (Princeton: Princeton University Press, 1994), 41–59.

48. I am grateful to Maura O'Connor for urging me to appreciate this point and for sharing "Imagining National Boundaries in the Nineteenth Century: English Travelers, Diplomats and the Making of Italy," paper presented at the North American Conference of British Studies, Chicago, 1996.

49. David Goodman, *Gold Seeking: Victoria and California in the 1850s* (Sydney: Allen and Unwin, 1994).

50. Ann Curthoys and John Docker, "Is History Fiction?," *The UTS Review* 2, no. 2 (May 1996), 12–37.

51. Herman Bennett, *Africans in Colonial Mexico: Absolutism, Christianity, and Afro-Creole Consciousness, 1570–1640* (Bloomington: Indiana University Press, 2003), which posits the performative model, is a particularly promising exception.

52. Carlo Ginzburg, *The Cheese and the Worms* (Baltimore: Johns Hopkins University Press, 1980); Emmanuel LeRoy Ladurie, *Montaillou: Cathars and Catholics in a French village, 1294–1324* (London: Scolar, 1978).

53. Eugen Weber, *Peasants into Frenchmen: The Modernization of Rural France, 1870–1914* (Stanford: Stanford University Press, 1976).

54. Philip Corrigan and Derek Sayer, *The Great Arch: English State Formation as Cultural Revolution* (Oxford: Blackwell, 1985).

55. Judith Butler, *Gender Trouble: Feminism and the Subversion of Identity* (Routledge, 1990); Bernard S. Cohn, "Representing Authority in Victorian India," in *The Invention of Tradition*, ed. Eric J. Hobsbawm and Terence Ranger (Cambridge: Cambridge University Press, 1983), 165–209; Greg Dening, "The Theatricality of History Making and the Paradoxes of Acting," *Performances* (Chicago: University of Chicago Press, 1996).

56. Christopher A. Bayly, *Imperial Meridian: The British Empire and the World, 1780–1830* (London: Longman, 1989); Linda Colley, *Britons: Forging the Nation, 1707–1837* (New Haven: Yale University Press, 1992). This is especially challenging, I think, in light of how powerful late Victorian rhetoric about the long history of the English nation-state was in the wake of more recent Italian and German unification, not to mention the challenges posed by Irish Home Rule and the Indian National Congress.

57. George Chauncey, *Gay New York: Gender, Urban Culture, and the Making of the Gay Male World, 1880–1940* (New York: Basic Books, 1994).

58. Hall, "Histories, Empires, and the Post-Colonial Moment," 65–71. See also M. Jacqui Alexander and Chandra Talpade Mohanty, *Feminist Genealogies, Colonial Legacies, Democratic Futures* (New York: Routledge, 1997).

59. Partha Chatterjee, "Beyond the Nation? Or Within?," *Economic and Political Weekly* (4–11 January 1997), 30–34.

60. W. E. B. Dubois, *The Souls of Black Folk* (New York: Penguin Books, 1989), 20.

61. Ruth Behar and Deborah Gordon, eds., *Women Writing Culture* (Berkeley: University of California Press, 1995), 8.

62. I thank Darlene Hantzis for suggesting this possibility to me.

63. Madhavi Kale, "Projecting Identities: Empire and Indentured Labor Migration from India to Trinidad and British Guiana, 1836–1885," in *Nation and Migration: The Politics of Space in the South Asian Diaspora*, ed. Peter van der Veer (Philadelphia: University of Pennsylvania Press, 1994); Liisa H. Malki, *Purity and Exile: Violence, Memory, and National Cosmology among the Hutu Refugees in Tanzania* (Chicago: University of Chicago Press, 1995); Smadar Lavie and Ted Swedenburg, eds., *Displacement, Diaspora, and Geographies of Identity* (Durham: Duke University Press, 1996).

64. Ien Ang, " 'I'm a Feminist, but . . .': Other Women and Postnational Feminism," in *Transitions: New Austrailian Feminisms*, ed. Barbara Caine and Rosemary Pringle (New York: St. Martin's Press, 1995), 57–73. See also Adele Murdolo, "Warmth and Unity? Historicizing Racism in the Australian Women's Movement," *Feminist Review* 52 (Spring 1996), 69–86.

65. Rosemary Marangoly George, *The Politics of Home: Postcolonial Relocations and Twentieth-Century Fiction* (Cambridge: Cambridge University Press, 1996); Aiwha Ong, "On the Edges of Empires: Flexible Citizenship among Chinese in Diaspora," *Positions* 1, no. 3 (1993), 745–78; Vincente Rafael, "Overseas Filipinos and Other Ghostly Presences in the Nation-State," paper presented at the Seminar for Global Studies in Culture, Power, and History, Johns Hopkins University, Baltimore, October 1996.

66. Earl Lewis, "Turning on a Pivot: Writing African Americans into a History of Overlapping Diasporas," *American Historical Review* 100, no. 3 (June 1995), 765–87.

67. Sherry Ortner, "Theory in Anthropology since the 1960s," in *Culture/Power/History: A Reader in Contemporary Social Theory*, ed. Nicholas B. Dirks, Geoff Eley, and Sherry B. Ortner (Princeton: Princeton University Press, 1984), 372–411.

68. Mrinalini Sinha, "*Historia Nervosa*, or, Who's Afraid of Colonial-Discourse Analysis?," *Journal of Victorian Culture* 2, no. 1 (Spring 1997), 113–22.

69. Stuart Hall, "Cultural Studies: Two Paradigms," in *Culture/Power/History*, 520–38.

70. Nicholas B. Dirks, *Colonialism and Culture* (Ann Arbor: University of Michigan Press, 1992).

71. Keith Jeffery, ed. *An Irish Empire? Aspects of Ireland and the British Empire* (Manchester: Manchester University Press, 1996); Hugh Kearney, *The British Isles: A History of Four Nations* (Cambridge: Cambridge University Press, 1989).

72. Sudipta Kaviraj, "The Imaginary Institution of India," in *Subaltern Studies VII: Writings on South Asian History and Society*, ed. Partha Chatterjee and Gyanendra Pandey (Delhi: Oxford University Press, 1993), 1–39.

73. David Harvey, *The Condition of Postmodernity* (Oxford: Blackwell, 1990).

74. Robert Carr, "Crossing the First World/Third World Divides: Testimonial,

Transnational Feminisms, and the Postmodern Condition," in *Scattered Hegemonies: Postmodernity and Transnational Feminist Practices*, ed. Inderpal Grewal and Caren Caplan (Minneapolis: University of Minnesota Press, 1994), 153–72.

75. Carol Breckenridge, "The Aesthetics and Politics of Colonial Collecting: India at World Fairs," *Comparative Studies in Society and History* 31 (Spring 1989), 195–216.

76. Arjun Appadurai, "The Heart of Whiteness," *Callaloo* 16, no. 4 (1993), 796–807; Carole Boyce Davies, *Black Women, Writing, and Identity: Migratory Subjects*. (London: Routledge, 1994).

3. Thinking beyond the Boundaries

This paper originated as a contribution to a roundtable at the Berkshire Conference of Women Historians in Rochester, New York, in 1999. I thank my fellow panelists, Philippa Levine, Laura Mayhall, Sudipta Sen, and Mrinalini Sinha, as well as various members of the audience who offered spirited feedback. The essay that resulted has also been influenced by a number of critical interlocutors, especially Herman Bennett, Rob Gregg, Madhavi Kale, and Susan Thorne, to whom I owe a great debt. Participants in my graduate seminars at Johns Hopkins University and the University of Illinois have also, perhaps unwittingly, left their mark on this essay, and I acknowledge them here. I am equally grateful to Craig Koslofsky and Clare Crowston for indulging me in discussions about the status of the archive. Finally, Geoff Eley's suggestions and interventions have made the essay much more lively and, I hope, persuasive. Any errors of omission or interpretation are indubitably mine.

1. For a digest of some of these events, see Mrinalini Sinha, "*Historia Nervosa*, or, Who's Afraid of Colonial-Discourse Analysis?," *Journal of Victorian Culture* 2, no. 1 (Spring 1997), 113–22. See also John M. MacKenzie, "Edward Said and the Historians," *Nineteenth-Century Contexts* 18 (1994), 9–26; Peter Stansky et al., "NACBS Report on the State and Future of British Studies in North America," North American Conference of British Studies, November 1999.

2. For an instructive counter to this preoccupation, see Sumit Sarkar, *Writing Social History* (Delhi: Oxford University Press, 1997). I am grateful to Mrinalini Sinha, whose "Re-materializing Culture: The National Formation in Late-Colonial India" (paper presented at the Berkshire Conference of Women Historians, Rochester, N.Y., 1999), underscored the importance of Sarkar's work for specifying the geographical limitations of claims about history writing at the end of the millennium.

3. Victoria E. Bonnell and Lynn Hunt, eds., *Beyond the Cultural Turn: New Directions in the Study of Society and Culture* (Berkeley: University of California Press, 1999), 9–10.

4. Edward Said's elaboration of the concept of culture in *Culture and Imperialism* is instructive in this regard, because he sees it, on the one hand, as a set of practices "that have relative autonomy from the economic, social and political realms and that often exist in aesthetic forms," and on the other as "a sort of theater where various political and ideological causes engage each other": Edward Said, *Culture and Imperialism* (New York: Vintage Books, 1994), xii–xiii.

5. Benita Parry, *Delusions and Discoveries: India in the British Imagination*, 2nd edn. (London: Verso, 1998).

6. The quote is from Caren Kaplan, Norma Alarçon, and Minoo Moallem, eds., *Between Woman and Nation: Nationalisms, Transnational Feminisms, and the State* (Durham: Duke University Press, 1999), 4. On the genealogical quest, see Stuart Hall, "Cultural Studies: Two Paradigms," in *Culture / Power / History: A Reader in Contemporary Social Theory*, ed. Nicholas B. Dirks, Geoff Eley, and Sherry B. Ortner (Princeton: Princeton University Press, 1980), 520–38; Benita Parry, "Overlapping Territories and Intertwined Histories: Edward Said's Postcolonial Cosmopolitanism," in *Edward Said: A Critical Reader*, ed. Michael Sprinker (Oxford: Blackwell, 1992), 19–47; Peter Hulme, "Subversive Archipelagos: Colonial Discourse and the Break-up of Continental Theory," *Dispositio* 14, nos. 36–38 (1989), 1–23; Arif Dirlik, "The Post-colonial Aura: Third World Criticism in the Age of Global Capitalism," *Critical Enquiry* 20, no. 2 (1994), 328–56; Patrick Williams and Laura Chrisman, eds., *Colonial Discourse and Post-Colonial Theory: A Reader* (New York: Columbia University Press, 1994); John M. MacKenzie, *Orientalism: History, Theory and the Arts* (Manchester: Manchester University Press, 1995); Dane Kennedy, "Imperial History and Postcolonial Theory," *Journal of Imperial and Commonwealth History* 24, no. 3 (September 1996), 345–63; Iain Chambers and Lidia Curti, eds., *The Post-Colonial Question: Common Skies, Divided Horizons* (London: Routledge, 1996); Cary Nelson and Dilip Parameshwar Gaonkar, eds., *Disciplinarity and Dissent in Cultural Studies* (New York: Routledge, 1996); Lisa Lowe and David Lloyd, eds., *The Politics of Culture in the Shadow of Capital* (Durham: Duke University Press, 1997); Pheng Cheah and Bruce Robbins, eds., *Cosmopolitics: Thinking and Feeling beyond the Nation* (Minneapolis: University of Minnesota Press, 1998); Saskia Sassen, *Globalization and Its Discontents: Essays on the New Mobility of People and Money* (New York: New Press, 1998); Ania Loomba, *Colonialism / Postcolonialism: The New Critical Idiom* (New York: Routledge, 1998); John Tomlinson, *Globalization and Culture* (Chicago: University of Chicago Press, 1999).

7. See, e.g., Vron Ware, *Beyond the Pale: White Women, Racism and History* (London: Verso, 1992); Clare Midgley, *Women against Slavery: The British Campaign, 1780–1870* (London: Routledge, 1992); Antoinette Burton, *Burdens of History: British Feminists, Indian Women, and Imperial Culture, 1865–1915* (Chapel Hill: University of North Carolina Press, 1994); Mrinalini Sinha, *Colonial Masculinity: The "Manly Englishman" and the "Effeminate Bengali" in the Late Nineteenth Century* (Manchester: Manchester University Press, 1995); Anne McClintock, *Imperial Leather: Race, Gender, and Sexuality in the Colonial Contest* (New York: Routledge, 1995); Susan Thorne, *Congregational Missions and the Making of an Imperial Culture in Nineteenth-Century England* (Stanford: Stanford University Press, 1999).

8. See David Scott, *Refashioning Futures: Criticism after Postcoloniality* (Princeton: Princeton University Press, 1999), 3–20.

9. Bill Readings, *The University in Ruins* (Cambridge: Harvard University Press, 1996), 64.

10. See Antoinette Burton, *At the Heart of the Empire: Indians and the Colonial Encounter in Late–Victorian Britain* (Berkeley: University of California Press, 1998), 15.

11. Ibid.

12. Geoff Eley and Keith Nield, "Farewell to the Working Class?," *International Labour and Working-Class History* 57 (Spring 2000), 11.

13. See Sylvia Yanagisako and Carol Delaney, "Naturalizing Power," in *Naturalizing Power: Essays in Feminist Cultural Analysis*, ed. Sylvia Yanagisako and Carol Delaney (New York: Routledge, 1995), 19.

14. Nicholas B. Dirks, ed., *Colonialism and Culture* (Ann Arbor: University of Michigan Press, 1992).

15. I am grateful to Herman Bennett for flagging this formulation. See also Michel-Rolph Trouillot, *Silencing the Past: Power and the Production of History* (Boston: Beacon Press, 1995).

16. Catherine Hall, "Competing Masculinities: Thomas Carlyle, John Stuart Mill, and the case of Governor Eyre," in idem, *White, Male, and Middle Class: Explorations in History and Feminism* (London: Routledge, 1992), 255–95; Gail Bederman, *Manliness and Civilization: A Cultural History of Gender and Race in the United States, 1870–1917* (Chicago: University of Chicago Press, 1995); Maura O'Connor, *The Romance of Italy and the English Political Imagination* (New York: St. Martin's Press, 1998).

17. Laura E. Nym Mayhall, "Reclaiming the Political: Women, the Social and Suffrage in Modern Britain" paper presented at the Berkshire Conference of Women Historians, Rochester, N.Y., 1999. See also idem, "Reclaiming the Political: Women and the Social History of Suffrage in Great Britain, France, and the United States," *Journal of Woman's History* 12, no. 1 (Spring 2000), 172–81.

18. Frederick Cooper, "Race, Ideology, and the Perils of Comparative History," *American Historical Review* 101, no. 4 (October 1996), 1129. Cooper suggests that James T. Campbell's *Songs of Zion: The African Methodist Episcopal Church in the United States and South Africa* (New York: Oxford University Press, 1995), is "helping to turn the study of the Black Atlantic into a historical question": Cooper, "Race, Ideology, and the Perils of Comparative History, 1129.

19. I thank Herman Bennett for this insight. For an interesting example of the persistence of this legacy (even) in feminist thought, see Dorothy E. Smith, *Writing the Social: Critique, Theory, and Investigations* (Toronto: University of Toronto Press, 1999).

20. I am grateful to Clare Crowston for urging me to consider this point. For an instructive attempt to grapple with the social-science model of social history in its encounter with culture, see Miles Fairburn, *Social History: Problems, Strategies and Methods* (New York: St. Martin's Press, 1999). I thank Philippa Levine for this reference.

21. For the ramifications of this in British history proper, see Antoinette Burton, "Who Needs the Nation? Interrogating 'British' History," *Journal of Historical Sociology* 10, no. 3 (1997), 227–48.

22. Bonnell and Hunt, *Beyond the Cultural Turn*. For an alternative reading of the same period that insists on reinscribing European colonialism on the story of Western academic production, see Ann Laura Stoler, *Race and the Education of Desire* (Durham: Duke University Press, 1995).

23. Thorne, *Congregational Missions and the Making of an Imperial Culture in Nineteenth-Century England*. For the debate in *Social History*, see David Mayfield and Susan Thorne, "Social History and Its Discontents: Gareth Stedman Jones and the Politics of Language," *Social History* 17 (May 1992), 165–88; idem, "Reply to 'The Poverty of Protest' and 'Imaginary Discontents,'" *Social History* 18, no. 2 (May 1993), 219–33; Patrick Joyce, "The Imaginary Discontents of Social History: A Note of Response," *Social History* 18, no. 1 (January 1993), 81–86; idem, "The End of Social History?," *Social History* 20, no. 1 (January 1995), 73–91.

24. Eley and Nield, "Farewell to the Working Class?," 18; idem, "Reply: Class and the Politics of History," *International Labour and Working-Class History* 57 (Spring 2000), 76–87.

25. See, e.g., Peter Mandler et al., "Cultural Histories Old and New: Rereading the Work of Janet Oppenheim," *Victorian Studies* 41, no. 1 (Fall 1997), 69–106. For two essays that assess the linguistic turn in different ways, see Sara Maza, "Stories in History: Cultural Narratives in Recent Works in European History," *American Historical Review* 101, no. 5 (December 1996), 1493–515; Kennedy, "Imperial History and Postcolonial Theory."

26. Florencia Mallon, "The Promise and Dilemma of Subaltern Studies: Perspectives from Latin American History," *American Historical Review* 99, no. 5 (December 1994), 1514; emphasis added.

27. See Kennedy, "Imperial History and Postcolonial Theory."

28. For one among many examples, see Akhil Gupta and James Ferguson, eds., *Anthropological Locations: Boundaries and Grounds of a Field Science* (Berkeley: University of California Press, 1997).

29. The phrase is David Greetham's. See his "'Who's In, Who's Out': The Cultural Poetics of Archival Exclusion," *Studies in the Literary Imagination* 32, no. 1 (Spring 1999), 1.

30. Madhavi Kale, *Fragments of Empire: Capital, Slavery, and Indian Indentured Labor in the British Caribbean* (Philadelphia: University of Pennsylvania Press, 1998), 9.

31. Michel Foucault, *The Order of Things: An Archaeology of the Human Sciences* (New York: Vintage, 1994), 15.

32. This is Martha Nussbaum's rather glib critique of Judith Butler: see Martha C. Nussbaum, "The Professor of Parody," *New Republic*, 22 February 1999, 37–45. For the ludic, see Teresa L. Ebert, *Ludic Feminism and After: Postmodernism, Desire, and Labor in Late Capitalism* (Ann Arbor: University of Michigan Press, 1996).

33. On the debate in *Social History*, see n. 23.

34. Robert Gregg, "Class, Culture, and Empire: E. P. Thompson and the Making of Social History," *Journal of Historical Sociology* 11, no. 4 (December 1998), 419–60; Robert Gregg and Madhavi Kale, "The Empire and Mr. Thompson: The Making

of Indian Princes and the English Working Class," *Economic and Political Weekly* 32, no. 36 (1997), 2273–88. See also Robert Gregg, *Inside Out, Outside In: Essays in Comparative History* (London: Palgrave Macmillan, 1999).

35. Gregg and Kale, "The Empire and Mr. Thompson," 2273–88.

36. See, e.g., the special issue "Islands in History," *Radical History Review* 73 (Winter 1999).

37. Eugene D. Genovese, "The Origins and Progress of the Historical Society," president's address presented at the inaugural meeting of the Historical Society, Boston University, 27 May 1999. I thank Patricia Romero for sharing a copy of the text with me.

38. For a detailed exposition of this history, see Bonnie G. Smith, *The Gender of History: Men, Women, and Historical Practice* (Cambridge: Harvard University Press, 1998), esp. chap. 4.

39. See Jacques Derrida, *Archive Fever: A Freudian Impression* (Chicago: University of Chicago Press, 1996); "The Archive, Part 1," special issue, *History of the Human Sciences* 11, no. 4 (November 1998); "The Archive, Part 2," special issue, *History of the Human Sciences* 12, no. 2 (May 1999); "The Poetics of the Archive," special issue, *Studies in the Literary Imagination* 32, no. 1 (Spring 1999).

40. George E. Marcus, "The Once and Future Ethnographic Archive," *History of the Human Sciences* 11, no. 4 (1998), 49–63. The work of Bernard S. Cohn and Nicholas B. Dirks, each of whom bridges the divide between anthropologists and historians, is an exception to this claim. See Bernard S. Cohn, *Colonialism and Its Forms of Knowledge: The British in India*, ed. Nicholas B. Dirks (Princeton: Princeton University Press, 1996); Nicholas B. Dirks, "Colonial Histories and Native Informants: Biography of an Archive," in *Orientalism and the Postcolonial Predicament: Perspectives on South Asia*, ed. Carol A. Breckenridge and Peter van der Veer (Philadelphia: University of Pennsylvania Press, 1993), 279–313.

41. Sanjay Seth, "Rewriting Histories of Nationalism: The Politics of 'Moderate Nationalism' in India, 1870–1905," *American Historical Review* 104, no. 1 (February 1999), 95. For him, the social and the material are ranged against the discursive, although he does little more than set these up as prefabricated categories.

42. "The Postcolonial Critic: Homi Bhabha Interviewed by Daniel Bennett and Terry Collits," in *Literary India: Comparative Studies in Aesthetics, Colonialism and Culture*, ed. Patrick Colm Hogan and Lalita Pandit (Albany: State University of New York Press, 1995), 240.

43. Mary Poovey, *Making a Social Body: British Cultural Formation, 1830–1864* (Chicago: University of Chicago Press, 1995); Tony Bennett, *Culture: A Reformer's Science* (London: Sage Publications, 1998). Rosemary Hennessey and Chrys Ingraham echo this when they claim that culture is "the domain of knowledge production," which they take to have material and symbolic dimensions: Rosemary Hennessey and Chrys Ingraham, "Introduction: Reclaiming Anti-capitalist Feminism," in *Materialist Feminism: A Reader in Class, Difference, and Women's Lives*, ed. Rosemary Hennessey and Chrys Ingraham (New York: Routledge, 1997), 9. Among

their aims is to connect shifts in representation to shifts in the production of goods and lives under late capitalism, a gesture toward contingency with which historians might find fellowship.

44. Quoted in David Lloyd and Paul Thomas, *Culture and the State* (New York: Routledge, 1998), 1.

45. See Judith Butler, "Merely Cultural," *New Left Review* 207 (1998), 33–44.

46. I am grateful to fellow participants in a recent workshop, "The New Imperial Social History," held in Berkeley on 1 May 1999, for helping me to realize this point. Special thanks to Durba Ghosh, Doug Haynes, Madhavi Kale, Dane Kennedy, Tom Metcalf, Philippa Levine, and Mrinalini Sinha.

47. Some of this research resulted in Antoinette Burton, "Tongues Untied: Lord Salisbury's 'Black Man' and the Boundaries of Imperial Democracy," *Comparative Studies in Society and History* 43, no. 2 (2000), 632–59.

48. This was, of course, an echo and refiguration of the way women (white and brown) were regulated by men (colonial and nationalist) in British India: see Kumkum Sangari and Sudesh Vaid, eds., *Recasting Women: Essays in Colonial History* (New Delhi: Kali for Women, 1989); Lata Mani, *Contentious Traditions: The Debate on Sati in Colonial India* (Berkeley: University of California Press, 1998).

49. Mayhall, "Reclaiming the Political."

50. See Adrienne Rich, *Blood, Bread and Poetry: Selected Prose, 1979–1985* (New York: W. W. Norton, 1986); M. Jacqui Alexander and Chandra Talpade Mohanty, eds., *Feminist Genealogies, Colonial Legacies, Democratic Futures* (New York: Routledge, 1997); Kaplan et al., *Between Woman and Nation*. For evidence that this view can be invoked as a "universal" historical value, see Carl Schorske, *Thinking with History* (Princeton: Princeton University Press, 1998), chap. 1.

51. See Kaplan et al., "Introduction," in *Between Woman and Nation*, 6.

52. I borrow here from the description of the archive in the introductory essay in Paul J. Voss and Marta L. Werner, "Toward a Politics of the Archive," *Studies in the Literary Imagination* 32, no. 1 (Spring 1999), ii.

53. For development of the discussion of the unfinished business of hegemonies in a variety of colonial contexts, see Antoinette Burton, ed., *Gender, Sexuality and Colonial Modernities* (London: Routledge, 1999), chap. 1 and passim.

4. Déjà Vu All over Again

1. David Cannadine, *Ornamentalism: How the British Saw Their Empire* (New York: Oxford University Press, 2001), xvii.

2. See, e.g., A. P. Thornton, *The Imperial Idea and Its Enemies: A Study in British Power* (New York: St. Martin's Press, 1989 [1959]); Robin Winks, ed., *The Oxford History of the British Empire, Volume 5: Historiography* (Oxford: Oxford University Press, 1999).

3. P. J. Marshall, ed., *The Cambridge Illustrated History of the British Isles* (Cambridge: Cambridge University Press, 1996).

4. Mrinalini Sinha, *Colonial Masculinity: The "Manly Englishman" and the "Effeminate Bengali" in the Late Nineteenth* Century (Manchester: Manchester University

Press, 1995); Catherine Hall, "Rethinking Imperial Histories: The Reform Act of 1867," *New Left Review* 208 (1994): 3–29.

5. Gyan Prakash, *Another Reason: Science and the Imagination of Modern India* (Princeton: Princeton University Press, 1999), 5. Here Prakash suggests the simultaneous emergence of "Indian" and "English" modernities, in contrast to the serial relationship usually mobilized to describe how such formations emerged in the context of colonialism.

6. See Andrew Porter, ed., *The Oxford History of the British Empire, Volume 3: The Nineteenth Century* (Oxford: Oxford University Press, 1999); Winks, *The Oxford History of the British Empire, Volume 5*.

7. John M. MacKenzie, ed., *The Victorian Vision: Inventing New Britain* (London: Victoria and Albert Museum Publications, 2001).

8. This is in contrast to Philip Morgan's use of the concept of interconnectedness, which Cannadine uses, though in diluted form: see Philip D. Morgan, *Slave Counterpoint: Black Culture in the Eighteenth-Century Chesapeake and Lowcountry* (Chapel Hill: University of North Carolina Press, 1998).

9. Onyekachi Wambu, ed., *Empire Windrush: Fifty Years of Writing about Black Britain* (London: Victor Gollancz, 1998); Yasmin Alibhai-Brown, *Imagining New Britain* (New York: Routledge, 2001); "Black Teenager Dies after Knife Attack by White Youths: Police Fear Racist Backlash," *Times* (London), 24 April 1993; "Race Case Police Fail to Provide Crucial Answers," *Times* (London), 18 July 1998; "Race in the Classroom: The Right Way to Advance Tolerance after Lawrence," *Times* (London), 26 February 1999; Kamlesh Bahl, "Lessons of Lawrence: An Open Letter to the Prime Minister," *Times* (London), 2 March 1999; Brian Cathcart, *The Case of Stephen Lawrence* (London: Viking, 1999); Sir William Macpherson, "The Stephen Lawrence Inquiry Report," available online at http://www.archive. official-documents.co.uk/document/cm42/4262/4262.htm.

10. Bhikhu Parekh, ed., *The Future of Multi-Ethnic Britain: Report of the Commission on the Future of Multi-Ethnic Britain* (London: Profile Books, 2000).

11. Alan Travis, " 'British' a Term of Coded Racism, Says Report," *Guardian Weekly*, 19–25 October 2000, 11.

12. Sarah Lyall, "Provocative Book Says Class System, Not Racial Pride, Ruled Britannia," *New York Times*, 25 August 2001; Fouad Ajami, "Ornamentalism: Married to the Raj," *New York Times Book Review*, 26 August 2001.

13. John M. MacKenzie, "Prejudice behind the Pomp and Baubles," *Times Higher Education Supplement*, 27 July 2001, 25; P. J. Marshall, "Review of *Ornamentalism: How the British Saw their Empire*," *Reviews in History*, no. 202, http://www.history .ac.uk/reviews/.

14. MacKenzie, "Prejudice behind the Pomp and Baubles," 25.

5. When Was Britain?

I take as my ironic point of departure the question posed by Gwyn Williams in the title of *When Was Wales?* (1985). This essay went to press six months before the war with

Iraq, led by President George W. Bush's and Prime Minister Tony Blair's "coalition." It was first given as the Modern European Luncheon Talk at the American Historical Association meeting in San Francisco in January 2002. An earlier version was presented at the Pairing Empires Conference at Johns Hopkins University, organized by Paul Kramer and John Plotz, in November 2000. It has benefited from comments, criticism, and all manner of useful references from Paul Arroyo, Jim Barrett, Catherine Candy, Clare Crowston, Jed Esty, Doug Haynes, Madhavi Kale, Craig Koslofsky, Robert Gregg, Philippa Levine, Ania Loomba, Laura Mayhall, Raka Nandi, Doug Peers, George Robb, Mrinalini Sinha, and Adam Sutcliffe. I especially appreciate Dana Rabin's enthusiastic support for this project. Without the interest and insight of Tony Ballantyne, it would have been a very different thing, indeed. David H. Burton, Catherine Hall, P. J. Marshall, and Peter Stansky have also helped to shape it, however variously and unwittingly, and I am indebted to each of them.

1. I am hardly the first to observe this. See Tom Nairn, *After Britain: New Labour and the Return of Scotland* (London: Granta Books, 2000); Peter Hitchens, *The Abolition of Britain from Winston Churchill to Princess Diana* (San Francisco: Encounter Books, 2000). As George Will observed with some regret, "Bland Tony Blair may have the most radical agenda in British history: the end of Britain": see George F. Will, "Cheshire Cat, Cheddar Man," *Newsweek* (10 July 2000), 72.

2. See Devoney Looser, "Feminist Implications of the Silver Screen Austen," in *Jane Austen in Hollywood*, ed. Linda Troost and Sayre Greenfield (Lexington: University Press of Kentucky, 1998), 159–76.

3. Douglas Haynes, "White Lies: The British Past in Postwar America," *History Teacher* 31, no. 1 (November 1997): 96–100; idem, "The Whiteness of Civilization: The Transatlantic Crisis of White Supremacy and British Television Programming in the United States in the 1970s," in *After the Imperial Turn: Thinking with and through the Nation*, ed. Antoinette Burton (Durham: Duke University Press, 2003). Allison Graham takes up many of these questions in *Framing the South: Hollywood, Television, and Race during the Civil Rights Struggle* (Baltimore: Johns Hopkins University Press, 2001).

4. The literature on this is vast. Most recently, see H. Mark Glancy, *When Britain Loved Hollywood: The Hollywood "British" Film, 1939–1945* (Manchester: Manchester University Press, 1999); Fred Leventhal, "Essential Democracy: The 1939 Visit to the United States," in *Singular Continuities: Tradition, Nostalgia, and Identity in Modern British Culture*, ed. George K. Behlmer and Fred M. Leventhal (Stanford: Stanford University Press, 2000), 163–77.

5. See Adrian Kear and Deborah Lynn Steinberg, eds., *Mourning Diana: Nation, Culture and the Performance of Grief* (London: Routledge, 1999).

6. Warren Hodge, "For the Queen Mother, Solemn Drums (and Offstage Disputes)," *New York Times* (6 April 2002), A4. Despite its critical coverage, the *New York Times* continued to feature the Queen Mother's death, lying in state, and funeral as front-page news (with color photos) on and off in the first two weeks of April 2002.

7. If Peter Mandler is right, and the very elite class that American public television stages as equivalent to "Britain" was in fact "uninterested in its own national past," this is not simply ironic—it speaks to the real use value Britain provides for legitimating Americans' view of themselves as the future, especially given the corporate sponsorship of PBS: see Peter Mandler, "Against 'Englishness': English Culture and the Limits to Rural Nostalgia, 1850–1940," *Transactions of the Royal Historical Society* 7, series 6 (1997): 155–75.

8. See Raphael Samuel, *Patriotism: The Making and Unmaking of British National Identity*, 3 vols. (London: Routledge, 1989); idem, *Theatres of Memory* (London: Verso, 1994); idem, *Island Stories: Unravelling Britain* (London: Verso, 1995); Bill Readings, *The University in Ruins* (Cambridge: Harvard University Press, 1996); Patrick Wright, *On Living in an Old Country: The National Past in Contemporary Britain* (London: Verso, 1985).

9. See Claudia L. Johnson, "Run Mad, but Do Not Faint" (review of Patricia Rozema's film *Mansfield Park*), *Times Literary Supplement*, 31 December 1999.

10. Although no one has written a comprehensive account of these programs of the 1990s in the United States, Jeffrey Miller's history of earlier programming is instructive: Jeffrey S. Miller, *Something Completely Different: British Television and American Culture* (Minneapolis: University of Minnesota Press, 2000).

11. Haynes, "The Whiteness of Civilization."

12. I am grateful to Jim Barrett for this observation.

13. Onyekachi Wambu, ed., *Empire Windrush: Fifty Years of Writing about Black Britain* (London: Victor Victor Gollancz, 1998); Yasmin Alibhai-Brown, *Imagining New Britain* (New York: Routledge, 2001); "Black Teenager Dies after Knife Attack by White Youths: Police Fear Racist Backlash," *Times* (London), 24 April 1993; "Race Case Police Fail to Provide Crucial Answers," *Times* (London), 18 July 1998; "Race in the Classroom: The Right Way to Advance Tolerance after Lawrence," *Times* (London), 26 February 1999; Kamlesh Bahl, "Lessons of Lawrence: An Open Letter to the Prime Minister," *Times* (London), 2 March 1999; Brian Cathcart, *The Case of Stephen Lawrence* (London: Viking, 1999); Sir William Macpherson, "The Stephen Lawrence Inquiry," available online at http://www.archive.official-documents .co.uk/.

14. Russell Baker introducing *Masterpiece Theatre*'s *The Murder of Stephen Lawrence*, 21 January 2002, WILL-TV (Champaign-Urbana, Ill.). The program also aired that night on PBS stations in New York, Philadelphia, and California.

15. The U.S. media coverage of Cathy Freeman in the 1998 Olympics paralleled this in fascinating ways. Freeman, an aboriginal athlete representing Australia at the games, was routinely compared to Jackie Robinson in the 1940s and 1950s in terms of her achievement and its significance. Commentators thereby produced a regressive, racialized timeline similar to Baker's Lawrence and civil-rights narrative and, of course, cast Freeman's "blackness" as unproblematically equivalent to Robinson's African Americanness ("Negro-ness," in the parlance of his times). I thank Tony Ballantyne for making this connection.

16. Available online at http://www.pbs.org/wgbh/masterpiece/lawrence/index

.html. Among other things, the site offers bibliographical links to sources related to the murder of Stephen Lawrence.

17. In fact, *Upstairs Downstairs* was the focus of much early criticism of PBS among those who believed that reliance on such "foreign" programming was "un–American": see David Stewart, *The PBS Companion: A History of Public Television* (New York: TV Books, 1999), 71–82; Timothy Brennan, "Masterpiece Theatre and the Uses of Tradition," *Social Text* 12 (1985), 102–12.

18. Caryn James, "Crime and Race in England, both Factual and Fictitious," *New York Times*, 21 January 2002.

19. See Talal Asad, *Genealogies of Religion: Discipline and Reasons of Power in Christianity and Islam* (Baltimore: Johns Hopkins University Press, 1993).

20. I am grateful to Tony Ballantyne for pressing this point.

21. *New Yorker*, 15 September 1997.

22. Because of its connection to television watching (the small screen), this American love of British history may be connected to what Lauren Berlant calls the "downsizing" and "privatization" of American citizenship, together with the desire for an American citizen (like the fetus and the child) "not yet bruised by history": Lauren Berlant, *The Queen of America Goes to Washington City: Essays on Sex and Citizenship* (Durham: Duke University Press, 1997), 3, 6. That such nostalgia for empire can exist side by side with nostalgia for a "British" nation shorn of its domestic imperial legacies should be no surprise, given (1) the historically concentric relationship between nation and empire; (2) the generally accepted view that empire represented the best Britain had to offer to the world; and (3) the disaggregation of empire from racial questions in popular American culture described above.

23. Peter Stansky et al., "NACBS Report on the State and Future of British Studies in North America," North American Conference of British Studies, November 1999, available online at http://www.nacbs.org/. I thank Peter Hansen for this website reference.

24. Ibid., 15.

25. Ibid.

26. Ibid.

27. Ibid., 15–19.

28. Max Beloff, "Empire Reconsidered," *Journal of Imperial and Commonwealth History* 27, no. 2 (May 1999), 15.

29. Stansky et al., "NACBS Report on the State and Future of British Studies in North America," 10.

30. See David Held and Anthony McGrew, "The Great Globalization Debate," *The Global Transformations Reader*, ed. David Held and Anthony McGrew (Cambridge: Polity Press, 2000), 1–45.

31. E. P. Thompson, *Alien Homage: Edward Thompson and Rabindranath Tagore* (Delhi: Oxford University Press, 1993). See also Robert Gregg and Madhavi Kale, "The Empire and Mr. Thompson: The Making of Indian Princes and the English Working Class," *Economic and Political Weekly* 32, no. 36 (1997), 2273–88; Robert

Gregg, "Class Culture and Empire: E. P. Thompson and the Making of Social History," *Journal of Historical Sociology* 11, no. 4 (1998), 419–60; Samuel, *Island Stories*.

32. This language of inside–outside replicates a long history of dichotomous thinking linked by Rushdie and others to imperialism: see Robert Gregg, *Inside Out, Outside In: Essays in Comparative History* (New York: St. Martin's Press, 1999).

33. Stansky et al., "NACBS Report on the State and Future of British Studies in North America," 17.

34. Ibid., 31; emphasis added.

35. Readings, *The University in Ruins*, 30.

36. Paul Gilroy, *The Black Atlantic: Modernity and Double Consciousness* (Cambridge: Harvard University Press, 1993), esp. chap. 3. Although Gilroy himself underplays it, that music is itself a hybrid of Caribbean and South Asian forms (such as "the bangramuffin" of Bally Sagoo in the early 1990s).

37. J. G. A. Pocock, "The Limits and Divisions of British History: In Search of the Unknown Subject," *American Historical Review* 87, no. 2 (1982), 319.

38. The seed essay of the article in *American Historical Review* was published as "British History: A Plea for a New Subject," *New Zealand Journal of History* 8 (1974), 3–21, and reprinted in the *Journal of Modern History* 4 (1975), 601–24. It was also first given in the United States as the address for the Modern European History section of the American Historical Association in 1978, an itinerary of which I was unaware until recently.

39. Jed Esty, *A Shrinking Island: Modernism and National Culture in England* (Princeton: Princeton University Press, 2003), provided by the author. See esp. part 3, "Insular Times: T. S. Eliot and Modernism's English End," and part 4, "Becoming Minor."

40. Mrinalini Sinha, *Colonial Masculinity: The "Manly Englishman" and the "Effeminate Bengali" in the Late Nineteenth Century* (Manchester: Manchester University Press, 1995).

41. See, most recently, Michael Adas, "From Settler Colony to Global Hegemon: Integrating the Exceptionalist Narrative of the American Experience into World History," *American Historical Review* 106, no. 5 (2001), 1692–720; Robert Tignor et al., *Worlds Together, Worlds Apart: A History of the Modern World from the Mongol Empire to the Present* (New York: W. W. Norton, 2002).

42. See Anthony Hopkins, "The History of Globalization—and the Globalization of History?," in *Globalization in World History*, ed. Anthony Hopkins (New York: W. W. Norton, 2002), 11–46; idem, "Back to the Future: From National History to Imperial History," *Past and Present*, no. 164 (August 1999): 198–243.

43. David Cannadine, *Ornamentalism: How the British Saw Their Empire* (New York: Oxford University Press, 2001).

44. Quoted in Claire E. Alexander, *The Art of Being Black: The Creation of Black British Youth Identities* (Oxford: Clarendon Press, 1996), 5.

45. Bhikhu Parekh, ed., *The Future of Multi-Ethnic Britain: Report of the Commission on the Future of Multi-Ethnic Britain* (London: Profile Books, 2000). For the response of one Labour Party government minister, see the extracts from Robin Cook's

speech to the Social Market Foundation in London, "Robin Cook's Chicken Tikka Masala Speech," *Guardian*, 19 April 2001. http://www.guardian.co.uk/.

46. Robert Cooper, "Why We Still Need Empires," *Observer* (London), 7 April 2002; Emily Eakin, "It Takes an Empire," *New York Times*, 1 April 2002. I thank Tony Ballantyne for these references.

6. Archive Stories

1. Mary Louise Pratt, *Imperial Eyes: Travel Writing and Transculturation* (London: Routledge, 1992).

2. These portraits are the coat of arms of the East India Company from the directors' meeting room; Lord Clive receiving the grant for the pension fund, commissioned by the East India Company, by Edward Penny, 1772; Naqd Ali Beg, commissioned by the East India Company, by Richard Greenbury; Hasan Reza Khan, minister to the nawab of Oudh, by Zoffany; General Sir Jang Bahadur Rana, 1817–77, commander of Nepal, by Bhajuman Citrakar, gift in 1850 (after Nepal had been "pacified"); Asaf-ud-daula, nawab of Oudh, by Zoffany; Fath Ali, Shah of Persia, 1797–1834, by Mirza Babu, presented by Wellesley, 1826; Nadir Shah, shah of Persia who sacked Delhi in 1739, unknown painter, presented by N. Vansittart, 1822; Mirza Abu'l Hasan Khan, ambassador from Persia to George III, commissioned by the East India Company, 1810, by William Beechey. I thank Douglas Peers and Durba Ghosh for confirming these details.

3. See Barbara Harlow, "Sappers in the Stacks: Colonial Archives, Land Mines, and Truth Commissions," in *Edward Said and the Work of the Critic: Speaking Truth to Power*, ed. Paul Bové (Durham: Duke University Press, 2000), 165–86.

4. I circulated a questionnaire to about sixty scholars of gender and empire via e-mail, under the heading "Archive Stories: Gender in the Making of Imperial and Colonial Histories." Thirty-seven responded. Eight were men; twenty-nine were women; twenty-six were white; eleven were non-white; four had earned Ph.D.s before 1980; five had earned Ph.D.s between 1980 and 1989; and twenty-seven had earned Ph.D.s in the 1990s. One did not have a Ph.D. All but four were historians by training. Twelve of thirty-seven live outside North America. Each responded on the condition of anonymity.

5. For longer histories of archive rationalization, see Philippa Levine, "History in the Archives: The Public Record Office and its Staff, 1838–1886," *English Historical Review* 101 (1986), 20–41; Alan Sekula, "The Body and the Archive," *October* 39, no. 3 (1986), 3–64.

6. Nicholas B. Dirks, "Annals of the Archive," in *From the Margins: Historical Anthropology and its Futures*, ed. Brian Keith Axel (Durham: Duke University Press, 2002), 48.

7. Angela Woollacott, *To Try Her Fortune in London: Australian Women, Colonialism, and Modernity* (Oxford: Oxford University Press, 2001).

8. He later discovered them at Rhodes House, Oxford.

9. He went on to say, "All is not hopeless, as Durba Ghosh has shown in her brilliant

dissertation ['Colonial Companions: Bibis, Begums, and Concubines of the British in North India, 1760–1830,' University of California, Berkeley, 2000]."

10. See, e.g., Susan Geiger, *Tanu Women: Gender and Culture in the Making of Tanganyikan Nationalism, 1955–1965* (Portsmouth: Heinemann, 1997); Mrinalini Sinha, "Refashioning Mother India: Feminism and Nationalism in Late–Colonial India," *Feminist Studies* 28, no. 3 (2000), 623–44.

11. Susan Geiger, *Life Histories of Women in Nationalist Struggle in Tanzania: Lessons Learned* (Dar es Salaam: Tanzania Gender Networking Program, 1996), 8.

12. For a discussion of these critiques, see Antoinette Burton, *Dwelling in the Archive: Women Writing House, Home and History in Late–Colonial India* (New York: Oxford University Press, 2003).

13. Nancy Rose Hunt, *A Colonial Lexicon of Birth: Ritual, Medicalization, and Mobility in the Congo* (Durham: Duke University Press, 1999).

14. See, e.g., Robin Winks, ed., *The Oxford History of the British Empire, Volume 5: Historiography* (Oxford: Oxford University Press, 1999).

15. Dirks, "Annals of the Archive," 58.

16. See "Empire On-Line," available online at http://www.adam-matthew-publications.co.uk.

17. Debbie Lee and Tom Fulford, "Virtual Empires," *Cultural Critique* 44 (2000), 3–28. This is a manifestation of the phenomenon Michael Hardt and Antonio Negri describe in *Empire* (Cambridge: Harvard University Press, 2000).

8. Fearful Bodies

This article was prompted by Marjorie Lightman's thoughtful "A Comment: The Pleasure of Social Reform," *Journal of Women's History* 4, no. 1 (1992): 114–18. It has profited from conversations with Paul Arroyo, Chandra de Silva, Laura Mayhall, Jennifer Morgan, George Robb, Hannah Rosen, and Susan Thorne, as well as from the comments of several anonymous reviewers. The careful reading, critical questions, and continued interest of Philippa Levine, Mary Poovey, and Barbara Ramusack have strengthened this project immeasurably. I am equally grateful to Darlene Hantzis for urging me to think through some of the implications and complexities of the "family romance."

Epigraph: Mary Carpenter, *Six Months in India*, 2 vols. (London: Longman, Green, 1868), vol. 2, 19, 85.

1. Josephine Butler, *Woman's Work and Woman's Culture* (London: Macmillan, 1869), xiii.

2. Frances Power Cobbe, "Our Policy: An Address to Women Concerning the Suffrage" (n.d.), in *Before the Vote Was Won: Arguments for and against Women's Suffrage, 1864–1896*, ed. Jane Lewis (London: Routledge, 1987), 94.

3. Barbara Leigh Smith Bodichon, "Reasons for and against the Enfranchisement of Women" (1869), in *Before the Vote Was Won*, 41.

4. Cobbe, quoted in Gwenllian E. F. Morgan, "The Duties of Citizenship: The Proper Understanding and Use of the Municipal and Other Franchises for Women" (1896), in *Before the Vote Was Won*, 471.

5. Isabella M. S. Todd, "Women and the New Franchise Bill: A Letter to an Ulster Member of Parliament" (1884), in *Before the Vote Was Won*, 403.

6. Olive Banks, *Faces of Feminism: A Study of Feminism as a Social Movement* (New York: St. Martin's Press, 1981); Philippa Levine, *Victorian Feminism, 1850–1900* (Gainesville: University Press of Florida, 1994); Jane Rendall, *The Origins of Modern Feminism: Women in Britain, France, and the United States, 1780–1860* (New York: Macmillan, 1985); Martha Vicinus, *Independent Women: Work and Community for Single Women, 1850–1920* (Chicago: University of Chicago Press, 1985).

7. Lydia Becker, "The Political Disabilities of Women" (1872), in *Before the Vote Was Won*, 118.

8. Elizabeth C. Wolstenholme Elmy, "The Parliamentary Franchise for Women: To the Editor of *The Times*" (1884), in *Before the Vote Was Won*, 405.

9. Christina Crosby, *The Ends of History: Victorians and "The Woman Question"* (New York: Routledge, 1991), 69–109.

10. Butler, *Woman's Work and Woman's Culture*, xxxiii; Kate Flint, *The Woman Reader, 1837–1914* (Oxford: Clarendon, 1993), 25.

11. Anne McClintock, "Family Feuds: Gender, Nationalism and the Family," *Feminist Review* 44 (Summer 1993), 61–80.

12. I am grateful to one of my reviewers for urging me to engage with this point.

13. Mary Carpenter, *Letters to the Right Honourable the Marquis of Salisbury, Secretary of State for India* (Bristol: Arrowsmith, 1877, 277).

14. Padma Anagol-McGinn, "The Age of Consent Act (1891) Reconsidered: Women's Perspectives and Participation in the Child-Marriage Controversy in India," *South Asia Research* 12, no. 2 (1992), 100–18; Dagmar Engels, "The Age of Consent Act of 1891: Colonial Ideology in Bengal," *South Asia Research* 3 (1983), 107–34; Geraldine Forbes, "Women and Modernity: The Issue of Child-Marriage in India," *Women's Studies International Quarterly* 2 (1979), 407–19; Barbara Ramusack, "Women's Organisations and Social Change: The Age of Marriage Issue in India," in *Women and World Change: Equity Issues in Development*, ed. Naomi Black and Ann Baker Cottrell (Beverly Hills: Sage Publications, 1981), 198–216.

15. Gayatri Chakravorty Spivak, "Can the Subaltern Speak?," in *Marxism and the Interpretation of Culture*, ed. Cary Nelson and Lawrence Grossberg (Urbana: University of Illinois Press, 1988), 296–97.

16. Thomas Laqueur and Catherine Gallagher, *The Making of the Modern Body: Sexuality and Society in the Nineteenth Century* (Berkeley: University of California Press, 1987), vii.

17. Ann Curthoys, "Identity Crisis: Colonialism, Nationalism, and Gender in Australian History," *Gender and History* 5, no, 2 (1993), 174.

18. Jo Manton, *Mary Carpenter and the Children of the Streets* (London: Heinemann, 1976), 18.

19. Ibid.; Barbara Ramusack, "Cultural Missionaries, Maternal Imperialists, Feminist Allies: British Women Activists in India, 1865–1945," in *Western Women and Imperialism: Complicity and Resistance*, ed. Nupur Chaudhuri and Margaret Strobel (Bloomington: Indiana University Press, 1992), 119–36.

20. Carpenter, *Letters to the Right Honourable the Marquis of Salisbury*, 244. Further references to this page numbers in this work are in parentheses in the text.

21. Peter Stallybrass and Allon White, *The Politics and Poetics of Transgression* (Ithaca: Cornell University Press, 1986), 199.

22. Barbara Caine, *Victorian Feminists* (Oxford: Oxford University Press, 1992), 122–23; Manton, *Mary Carpenter and the Children of the Streets*, 148–52; Ruby J. Saywell, *Mary Carpenter of Bristol* (Bristol: Bristol Branch of the Historical Association, 1964), 14; Harriet Warm Schupf, "Single Women and Social Reform in Mid–Nineteenth Century England: The Case of Mary Carpenter," *Victorian Studies* 17, no. 2 (1974), 311.

23. Philippa Levine reminds us of what odd forms such serious pleasure could take when she recalls Emilia Dilke's girlhood practice of atoning for her sins by lying "for hours on the bare floor or on the stones, with her arms in the attitude of a cross": Philippa Levine, *Feminist Lives in Victorian England: Private Roles and Public Commitment* (Oxford: Basil Blackwell, 1990), 36.

24. Vron Ware, *Beyond the Pale: White Women, Racism and History* (London: Verso, 1992), 91.

25. Stallybrass and White, *The Politics and Poetics of Transgression*; see also Lynn Hunt, *The Family Romance of the French Revolution* (Berkeley: University of California Press, 1992).

26. This is the term that Norman MacKenzie uses to describe Beatrice Webb's negotiations between the "ego that affirms" and the "ego that denies": Norman MacKenzie, "Introduction," in Beatrice Webb, *My Apprenticeship*, ed. Norman MacKenzie (Bath: Pitman 1979), xix. I am grateful to Laura Mayhall for suggesting the application of MacKenzie's term to Carpenter.

27. This, in any event, is how Carpenter referred to him. For some Unitarians, and perhaps even for Carpenter, joining the Brahmo Samaj represented a kind of conversion to Christianity. Whether or not he actually converted is unclear.

28. Mrinalini Sinha, " 'Chathams, Pitts, and Gladstones in Petticoats': The Politics of Gender and Race in the Ilbert Bill Controversy, 1883–1884," in Chaudhuri and Strobel, *Western Women and Imperialism* (Bloomington: Indiana University Press, 1992), 98–116.

29. Harihar Das, "The Early Indian Visitors to England," *Calcutta Review* 13 (1924), 106–7.

30. Judith Brown, *Modern India: The Origins of an Asian Democracy* (Oxford: Oxford University Press, 1994), 77.

31. Manton, *Mary Carpenter and the Children of the Streets*; Ramusack, "Cultural Missionaries, Maternal Imperialists, Feminist Allies"; Niharranjan Ray, ed., *Rammohun Roy: A Bi-centenary Tribute* (New Delhi: National Book Trust, 1984).

32. Mary Carpenter, *The Last Days in England of the Rajah Rammohun Roy* (Calcutta: Riddhi, 1976 [1866]), 77.

33. Ibid., n.p.

34. Schupf, "Single Women and Social Reform in Mid–Nineteenth Century England," 306–7.

35. Anagol-McGinn, "The Age of Consent Act (1891) Reconsidered," 103–5; Uma Chakravarti, "Whatever Happened to the Vedic *Dasi*?: Orientalism, Nationalism, and a Script for the Past," in *Recasting Women: Essays in Colonial History*, ed. Kumkum Sangari and Sudesh Vaid (Delhi: Kali for Women, 1989), 29–35; Lata Mani, "Contentious Traditions: The Debate on Sati in Colonial India," in *Recasting Women*, 89, 102–5; Rozina Visram, *Ayahs, Lascars, and Princes: Indians in Britain, 1700–1947* (London: Pluto Press, 1986).

36. Carpenter, *Six Months in India*, vol. 1, 4.

37. Idem, *The Last Days in England of the Rajah Rammohun Roy*, 65.

38. David Kopf, *The Brahmo Samaj and the Shaping of the Modern Indian Mind* (Princeton: Princeton University Press, 1979), 35.

39. Manton, *Mary Carpenter and the Children of the Streets*, 201.

40. Billie Melman, *Women's Orients: English Women and the Middle East, 1718–1918: Sexuality, Religion and Work* (Ann Arbor: University of Michigan Press, 1992), 1.

41. Carpenter, *Six Months in India*, vol. 1, 34.

42. Manton, *Mary Carpenter and the Children of the Streets*, 202.

43. Carpenter, *Six Months in India*, vol. 1, 14.

44. Mary Louise Pratt, *Imperial Eyes: Travel Writing and Transculturation* (London: Routledge, 1992), 205.

45. Judith R. Walkowitz, *City of Dreadful Delight: Narratives of Sexual Danger in Late-Victorian London* (Chicago: University of Chicago Press, 1992).

46. Carpenter, *Six Months in India*, vol. 1, 19.

47. Ibid., 15–16.

48. Ibid., 85.

49. Pratt, *Imperial Eyes*, 78.

50. Francis Barker, *The Tremulous Private Body: Essays on Subjection* (New York: Methuen, 1984), 7.

51. Chakravarti, "Whatever Happened to the Vedic *Dasi*?"

52. Pratt, *Imperial Eyes*, 68.

53. Carpenter, *Six Months in India*, vol. 2, 74.

54. Ibid., 102.

55. Ibid., 117, 194.

56. Ibid., 80.

57. Ibid., 68.

58. Gauri Viswanathan, *Masks of Conquest: Literary Study and British Rule in India* (New York: Columbia University Press, 1989), 37.

59. Carpenter, *Six Months in India*, vol. 1, 184.

60. Ramusack "Cultural Missionaries, Maternal Imperialists, Feminist Allies," 121.

61. Carpenter, *Six Months in India*, vol. 2, 143.

62. Ibid., 143.

63. Ibid., vol. 1, 77.

64. Ibid., 78.

65. Susan R. Bordo, "The Body and the Reproduction of Femininity: A Feminist Appropriation of Foucault," in *Gender / Body / Knowledge: Feminist Reconstructions*

of *Being and Knowing,* ed. Alison M. Jaggar and Susan R. Bordo (New Brunswick: Rutgers University Press, 1989), 13–15.

66. Carpenter, *Six Months in India,* vol. 2, 143.

67. Ibid., vol. 1, 83.

68. Antoinette Burton, *Burdens of History: British Feminists, Indian Women, and Imperial Culture, 1865–1915* (Chapel Hill: University of North Carolina Press, 1994).

69. Kopf, *The Brahmo Samaj and the Shaping of the Modern Indian Mind,* 41; Y. B. Mathur, *Women's Education in India, 1813–1966* (Delhi: Asia Publishing House, 1973), 30; Ramusack, "Cultural Missionaries, Maternal Imperialists, Feminist Allies," 122.

70. Arnold P. Kaminsky, *The India Office, 1880–1910,* (New York: Greenwood Press, 1986), 110.

71. Manton, *Mary Carpenter and the Children of the Streets,* 205, 217–18.

72. Antoinette Burton, "The White Woman's Burden: British Feminists and 'The Indian Woman,' 1865–1915," in Chaudhuri and Strobel, *Western Women and Imperialism* (Bloomington: Indiana University Press, 1992), 137–57; Janaki Nair, "Uncovering the Zenana: Visions of Indian Womanhood in Englishwomen's Writings, 1813–1940," *Journal of Women's History* 2 (Spring 1990), 8–34.

73. The *Indian Magazine and Review* (called the *Journal of the Indian National Association* until 1886) was the NIA's organ from the 1870s into the 1910s. For the turn toward interest in women's medical education in India see, e.g., C. R. Francis, "Medical Education of Native Women in India," *Indian Magazine and Review,* November 1883, 621–32; Frances Hoggan, "Medical Women for India," *Indian Magazine and Review,* 15 May 1883, 265–69.

74. David Arnold, *Colonizing the Body: State Medicine and Epidemic Disease in Nineteenth-Century India* (Berkeley: University of California Press, 1993).

75. Maneesha Lal, "The Politics of Gender and Medicine in Colonial India: The Countess of Dufferin's Fund, 1885–1888," *Bulletin of the History of Medicine* 68, no. 1 (1994), 29–66.

76. I am indebted to Laura Mayhall for pressing this point.

77. Homi K. Bhabha, "Sly Civility," *October* 34 (Spring 1985), 72.

78. Catherine Hall, *White, Male and Middle Class: Explorations in Feminism and History* (London: Routledge, 1992), 216–18.

79. Burton, *Burdens of History.*

80. Gayatri Chakravorty Spivak, "The Rani of Sirmur: An Essay in Reading the Archives," *History and Theory* 24, no. 3 (1985): 269.

81. Catherine Hall, "Review of *Women's Orients,* by Billie Melman, and *Imperial Eyes,* by Mary Louise Pratt," *Feminist Review* 45 (Spring 1993), 133.

9. Contesting the Zenana

I received a grant from the American Council of Learned Societies in support of this project. I thank Lynn Amidon for assistance at the Royal Free Hospital, London. Versions of this chapter were presented at the North American Conference of British

Studies, Vancouver, in October 1994, and at the twenty-third annual South Asia Conference at the University of Wisconsin, Madison, in November 1994. The essay has benefited from comments by Jeff Cox, Mary Fissell, Maneesha Lal, Philippa Levine, Laura Mayhall, Chandrika Paul, Barbara Ramusack, George Robb, and Angela Woollacott. I am especially grateful to Susan Thorne and Geraldine Forbes for their intellectual engagement with the issues raised here. Without their collegiality, this essay would have been unimaginable.

1. Catherine Hall, *White, Male, and Middle Class: Explorations in Feminism and History* (New York: Routledge, 1992); Thomas C. Holt, *The Problem of Freedom: Race, Labor and Politics in Jamaica and Britain, 1832–1938* (Baltimore: Johns Hopkins University Press, 1992); Jenny Sharpe, *Allegories of Empire: The Figure of Woman in the Colonial Text* (Minneapolis: University of Minnesota Press, 1993). Examples from John MacKenzie's series Studies in Imperialism are John M. MacKenzie, ed., *Imperialism and Popular Culture* (Manchester: Manchester University Press, 1986); David Arnold, ed., *Imperial Medicine and Indigenous Societies* (Manchester: Manchester University Press, 1988); and J. A. Mangan, ed., *Making Imperial Mentalities: Socialisation and British Imperialism* (Manchester: Manchester University Press, 1990).

2. Edward Said, *Culture and Imperialism* (New York: Vintage Books, 1994), 6.

3. The expression "sunless, airless" existence is Mary Carpenter's. For an example of Victorian women's interest in and attitudes toward the zenana, see Mary Carpenter, *Six Months in India*, 2 vols. (London: Longmans, Green, 1868). Janaki Nair, "Uncovering the Zenana: Visions of Indian Womanhood in Englishwomen's Writings, 1813–1940," *Journal of Women's History* 2 (Spring 1990), 8–34, suggests how the zenana was constructed by a variety of female English writers from the early nineteenth century onward as a resourceful ideological and vocational space.

4. Edith A. Huntley, *The Study and Practice of Medicine by Women* (Lewes: Farncome, 1886), 34.

5. Sophia Jex-Blake, *Medical Women: A Thesis and Its History* (London: Hamilton and Adams, 1886), 234.

6. For an extended discussion of this phenomenon, see Antoinette Burton, *Burdens of History: British Feminists, Indian Women and Imperial Culture, 1865–1915* (Chapel Hill: University of North Carolina Press, 1994). Rukhmabai trained at the LSMW; Ganguli trained at Bengal Medical College and, later, at the University of Edinburgh. For details of Rukhmabai's medical career, see S. Bhatia, president, Association for Medical Women in India, to Dr. Lowrie, Medical Women's Federation, letter, 17 April 1967, Wellcome Institute for the History of Medicine, London, SA/MWF/c. 144; "Report of the Cama Hospital's Jubilee Fund," Wellcome Institute for the History of Medicine, SA/MWF/c. 146, 1936, 14–17 (she had been a house surgeon there in 1895); Edith Lutzker, *Edith Pechey-Phipson, M.D.: The Story of England's Foremost Pioneering Woman Doctor* (New York: Exposition Press, 1973), 199–208. On Ganguli, see Malavika Karlekar, *Voices from Within: Early Personal Narratives of Bengali Women* (Delhi: Oxford University Press, 1993), 173–78.

7. See A. B. Shah, ed., *The Letters and Correspondence of Pandita Ramabai* (Bombay: Maharashtra State Board for Literature and Culture, 1977); Meera Kosambi, *At the Intersection of Gender Reform and Religious Belief* (Bombay: Shreemati Nathibai Damodar Thackersey Women's University, 1993), esp. chap. 2; Frances Hoggan, "Medical Work for Women in India," *Englishwomen's Review*, 15 April 1885, 150–51.

8. This formulation is applied to Indian social reform in the context of nineteenth-century nationalism in Susie Tharu and K. Lalita, *Women Writing in India, Volume 1: 600 B.C. to the Early Twentieth Century* (New York: Feminist Press, 1991), 154.

9. *Mayfair*, 27 August 1878, 615; Newspaper Cuttings Collection, Royal Free Hospital Archives, London.

10. Edith Moberly Bell, *Storming the Citadel: The Rise of the Woman Doctor* (London: Constable, 1953), 125.

11. Laura Tabili, "The Construction of Racial Difference in Twentieth-Century Britain: The Special Restriction (Coloured Alien Seamen) Order, 1925," *Journal of British Studies* 33 (January 1994), 62. Tabili's essay is a skillful and long-overdue analysis of this process in twentieth-century Britain.

12. Frances Power Cobbe ratified the claims of these petitioners when she narrated the following anecdote. A London woman was advised by her doctor to consult another male physician at Bath. He sent her along with a sealed note, but her curiosity got the best of her. "The seal was broken, and the lady read: 'Keep the old fool for six weeks, and be sure to send her back to me at the end.'" Cobbe wrote, "I rejoice to believe that thanks to men like . . . Mr. Cowper-Temple, there will soon be . . . women's hospitals attended by women-doctors, in every town and kingdom": Frances Power Cobbe, "The Little Health of Ladies," *Contemporary Review* 31 (1877), 294, 296.

13. "Report of the London School of Medicine for Women," 1878, 12, Cuttings Collection, Royal Free Hospital Archives, London. Cowper-Temple had also been the author of several bills in the mid-1870s that called for the opening of medical courses at British universities to women. See Catriona Blake, *The Charge of the Parasols: Women's Entry into the Medical Profession* (London: Women's Press, 1990), 178, 183–84; Thomas Neville Bonner, *To the Ends of the Earth: Women's Search for Education in Medicine* (Cambridge: Harvard University Press, 1992), chap. 6. For a comprehensive analysis of the Victorian medical profession, see M. Jeanne Peterson, *The Medical Profession in Mid–Victorian London* (Berkeley: University of California Press, 1978).

14. For example, Jex-Blake's recent biographer makes no mention of her colonial interests or concerns about the zenana: see Shirley Roberts, *Sophia Jex-Blake: A Woman Pioneer in Nineteenth-Century Medical Reform* (London: Routledge, 1993). Catriona Blake's *The Charge of the Parasols* is an excellent study, though it does not refer to India at all, except to talk briefly about Mary Scharlieb's experiences in Madras on pages 175–76. David Arnold, *Colonizing the Body: State Medicine and Epidemic Disease in Nineteenth-Century India* (Berkeley: University of California Press, 1993), 260–68, devotes a small section to "Women Doctors in India" and focuses chiefly on the Dufferin Fund, as does Mark Harrison, "The Veil of the

'Zenana,'" *Public Health and Anglo-Indian Preventive Medicine, 1859–1914* (Cambridge: Cambridge University Press, 1994), 90–97.

15. The next year the university overturned this ruling, thereby preventing graduation from Edinburgh. See Blake, *The Charge of the Parasols*, part 3, esp. 218–19.

16. Jex-Blake, *Medical Women*, 154.

17. Ibid.

18. Hoggan, "Medical Work for Women in India," 150.

19. See Carpenter, *Six Months in India*, vol. 2; "Miss Carpenter and Her Work for India," *Our Magazine* (North London Collegiate School for Girls), July 1876, 182–84.

20. Josephine Butler, ed., *Woman's Work and Woman's Culture* (London: Macmillan, 1869); Jane Rendall, *The Origins of Modern Feminism: Women in Britain, France and the United States, 1780–1860* (New York: Macmillan, 1985); Philippa Levine, *Victorian Feminism, 1850–1900* (Gainesville: University Press of Florida, 1994); Antoinette Burton, "The White Woman's Burden: British Feminists and 'the Indian Woman,' 1865–1915," *Western Women and Imperialism: Complicity and Resistance*, ed. Nupur Chaudhuri and Margaret Strobel (Bloomington: Indiana University Press, 1992), 137–57.

21. The quote is in the *Calcutta Englishman*, 8 July 1878, Newspaper Cuttings Collection, Royal Free Hospital Archives, London. See also Geraldine Forbes, "Medical Careers and Health Care for Indian Women: Patterns of Control," *Women's History Review* 3, no. 4 (December 1994), 515–30; Nair, "Uncovering the Zenana," esp. 17–19; and Burton, "The White Woman's Burden," 146–47.

22. Vron Ware, *Beyond the Pale: White Women, Racism, and History* (London: Verso, 1992), parts 2–3; Burton, *Burdens of History*, chaps. 4, 6.

23. For a discussion of female doctors active in the suffrage movement, see Blake, *The Charge of the Parasols*, 193–94; Roberts, *Sophia Jex-Blake*, 167–68, 190.

24. *The Countess of Dufferin's Fund, 1885–1935: Fifty Years' Retrospect* (London: Women's Printing Society, 1935), 3. See also Maneesha Lal, "The Politics of Gender and Medicine in Colonial India: The Countess of Dufferin's Fund, 1885–1888," *Bulletin of the History of Medicine* 68 (March 1994), 5–6.

25. See Collin C. Davies, "India and Queen Victoria," *Asiatic Review* 33 (1937), 493.

26. According to W. W. Hunter, "The first object of the Association founded in 1885 . . . was to obtain from England, and to train up in India, a body of nurses and lady doctors, who should form the nucleus of a Female Medical Profession for India": W. W. Hunter, "A Female Medical Profession for India," *Contemporary Review* 56 (August 1889), 211. Margaret Balfour's and Ruth Young's characterization is equally revealing. They remembered the fund as having been organized to "bring women doctors to open women's hospitals and wards" and "to train Indian women to follow in their footsteps": see Margaret Balfour and Ruth Young, *The Medical Work of Women in India* (London: Humphrey, 1929), 33. See also Frances Hoggan, "Medical Work for Women in India," *Englishwomen's Review*, 15 May 1885, 200. For other accounts of the Dufferin Fund, see Arnold, *Colonizing the Body*, 260–68; Geraldine Forbes, "Managing Midwifery in India,"

Contesting Colonial Hegemony: State and Society in Africa and India, ed. Dagmar Engels and Shula Marks (New York: I. B. Tauris, 1994), 159–61.

27. Lal, "The Politics of Gender and Medicine in Colonial India," 7–8, 29.

28. See the *Fourteenth Annual Report of the National Association for Supplying Female Medical Aid to the Women of India* (for 1898) (Calcutta: Office of the Superintendent of Government Printing, 1899), 13.

29. Although not trained by the fund, Ganguli was appointed in 1888 to the Lady Dufferin Women's Hospital with a monthly salary of 300 rupees: see Forbes, "Managing Midwifery," 161. However, she felt that the fund discriminated against her countrywomen in hiring European-trained Western women.

30. Racism was undoubtedly combined with sexism in the Indian Medical Service, where all members had to be of military rank, thus ensuring the exclusion of many "native" men and all women. Although the Indian Medical Service had been opened up to competitive examination in 1855, by 1905 only 5 percent of the service was of Indian origin, and those were all men: see Harrison, "The Veil of the 'Zenana,'" 15, 31.

31. See Blake, *The Charge of the Parasols*, 154–55. The margin of defeat was, significantly, slim: seven of twelve voted against.

32. Garrett Anderson studied in Paris, and Blackwell studied in Geneva, New York: ibid., 215–17.

33. Isabel Thorne, *Sketch of the Foundation and Development of the London School of Medicine for Women* (London: G. Milford, 1906), 17.

34. Ibid., 18–19.

35. Ibid., 20–21.

36. S. Muthu Chidambaram, "Sex Stereotypes in Women Doctors' Contribution to Medicine: India," *Gender, Work and Medicine: Women and the Medical Division of Labour*, ed. Elianne Riska and Katarina Wegar, Sage Studies in International Sociology no. 44 (London: Sage Publications, 1993), 16. I am grateful to Philippa Levine for this reference.

37. E. M. Tonge, *Fanny Jane Butler: Pioneer Medical Missionary* (London: Church of England Zenana Missionary Society, 1930), 9. As one columnist wrote about Elizabeth Blackwell, "It is impossible that a woman whose hands reek of gore can be possessed of the same nature or feelings as the generality of women": quoted in Jo Manton, *Elizabeth Garrett Anderson* (New York: Dutton, 1965), 47.

38. Bell, *Storming the Citadel*, 113.

39. Tonge, *Fanny Jane Butler*, 50.

40. Balfour and Young, *The Medical Work of Women in India*, 18.

41. Executive Council Minutes, London School of Medicine, 1893, Royal Free Hospital Archives, London; E. B. Meakin, "Medical Work among the Women of 'Little' Indur (Nizam), India," *Magazine of the London School of Medicine for Women and the Royal Free Hospital* 5 (May 1903), 180.

42. Tonge, *Fanny Jane Butler*, p. 10.

43. Jex-Blake, *Medical Women*, 6, 52.

44. Huntley, *The Study and Practice of Medicine by Women*, 42–43.

45. Edith Pechey, *Inaugural Address, 1878* (London: McGowan"s Steam Printing, 1878), 27, Wellcome Institute, SA / MWF / C. 4.

46. Ibid., 28.

47. Charles West, *Medical Women: A Statement and an Argument* (London: J. A. Churchill, 1878), 17.

48. Blake, *The Charge of the Parasols*, 155.

49. Bell, *Storming the Citadel*, 115.

50. Ibid., 115–16.

51. Ibid. See also "Women Doctors in India," *Times* (London), 27 October 1881, where Beilby's account was excerpted from the *Indian Female Evangelist*, Newspaper Cuttings Collection, Royal Free Hospital Archives, London.

52. Lal, "The Politics of Gender and Medicine in Colonial India," 10. The National Indian Association had endeavored to project the same sense of woman-to-woman bond several years earlier when it printed an extensive account of Carpenter's personal meeting with the begum of Bhopal: see Ellen Etherington, "A Visit to the Present Begum of Bhopal," *Journal of the National Indian Association* 8 (May 1878), 215–19.

53. *The Countess of Dufferin's Fund, 1885–1935*, 3.

54. Balfour and Young, *The Medical Work of Women in India*, 33.

55. Elizabeth Beilby, "Women Doctors in India," reprinted in *Journal of the National Indian Association* (June 1882), 342.

56. Ibid.

57. This was an issue debated at some length in the pages of the *Journal of the National Indian Association*: see, e.g., Ellen Etherington, "Education in the North-west of India," *Journal of the National Institute Association* 5 (December 1875): 267–73; Arabella Shore, "English Indifference toward India," *Journal of the National Indian Association* 11 (September 1882): 506–15.

58. Elizabeth Garrett Anderson, "Medical Women for India," letter to the editor, *Times* (London) 31 October 1881, Newspaper Cuttings Collection, Royal Free Hospital Archives, London.

59. Isabel Thorne, "Medical Women for India," letter to the editor, *Times* (London), 31 October 1881, Newspaper Cuttings Collection, Royal Free Hospital Archives, London.

60. Garrett Anderson's rejection of royal benevolence was quite unusual in an era when many, if not most, women's reform and feminist organizations sought out public figureheads. I am grateful to Philippa Levine for this observation.

61. See "Women Doctors in India," *Journal of the National Indian Association* (December 1881), 718–22. Sarah Heckford was the wife of Nathaniel Heckford, the resident accoucheur for instruction at the London Hospital: see Manton, *Elizabeth Garrett Anderson*, 152.

62. "Medical Women for India," *Journal of the National Indian Association* (December 1882), 681–84.

63. See *Journal of the National Indian Association* 12 (January 1883), 11–18. See also

Hoggan, "Medical Work for Women in India," 15 April 1885, 145–58, and 15 May 1885, 193–200.

64. *Journal of the National Indian Association* 12 (January 1883), 12.

65. Ibid., 19. For accounts of the Indian Women's Medical Service, see Balfour and Young, *The Medical Work of Women in India*, chap. 4; Arnold, *Colonizing the Body*, 267–68.

66. "Medical Women for India," *Journal of the National Indian Association* 12 (January 1883), 25. Blackwell was also less agonized over the schism between the medical missionary and the lady doctor than some of her contemporaries, believing that "the arbitrary distinction between the physician of the body and the physician of the soul . . . tends to disappear as science advances": quoted in Regina Markell Morant, "Feminism, Professionalism and Germs: The Thought of Mary Putnam Jacobi and Elizabeth Blackwell," *American Quarterly* 34 (Winter 1982), 465.

67. For a general discussion of the loneliness and emotional hardships the first generation of female doctors faced, see Regina M. Morant-Sanchez, "The Many Faces of Intimacy: Professional Options and Personal Choices among Nineteenth- and Twentieth-Century Women Physicians," *Uneasy Careers and Intimate Lives: Women in Science, 1789–1979*, ed. Pnina G. Abir-Am and Dorinda Outram (New Brunswick: Rutgers University Press, 1989), 45–59.

68. "Medical Women for India," *Journal of the National Indian Association* 12 (January 1883), 28. The quote is from Anderson, "Medical Women for India."

69. "Medical Women for India," *Journal of the National Indian Association* 12 (January 1883), 31. For a full account of Kittredge's involvement and the establishment of medical aid for women in Bombay, see Lutzker, *Edith Pechey-Phipson, M.D.*, 67–68.

70. "Medical Women for India," *Journal of the National Indian Association* 12 (January 1883), 11. Dufferin, for her part, was not unwilling to admit that women of the zenana medical mission had the best opportunities to know Indian women most "intimately": see Harriot Dufferin, "The Women of India," *Nineteenth Century* 169 (March 1891), 359.

71. In addition to the alleged impropriety of working in laboratories and taking lecture courses on anatomy, women's physical unfitness for medical work had always been one of the arguments against removing the legal disabilities that aspiring female doctors faced. The harsh conditions in India, particularly the ill effects of its "burning sun" and "banishment from all that makes life worth living," were mustered with even more force in the debate about colonial women doctors: West, *Medical Women*, 19.

72. Huntley, *The Study and Practice of Medicine by Women*, 43.

73. Ibid., 32.

74. Elizabeth Beilby, "Medical Women for India," *Journal of the National Indian Association* (August 1883), 358. Beilby qualified in the summer of 1885 by passing her examinations at the Kings and Queens College of Physicians, Ireland. She then went to Lahore, where she headed the Lady Aitchison Hospital: see Balfour and Young, *The Medical Work of Women in India*, 21–22.

75. Lal, "The Politics of Gender and Medicine in Colonial India," 11. By the same

token, many women who went to hospitals for treatment were taken there by husbands and fathers or by police who picked up indigent women suspected of having the plague or other "contagious" diseases. I am grateful to an anonymous reviewer for pressing this point.

76. Sharpe, *Allegories of Empire*, 12.

77. Hoggan, "Medical Work for Women in India," 200.

78. Susan Thorne, "Missionary-Imperial Feminism," paper presented at the Annual Meetings of the American Anthropological Association, Washington, November 1993, 5, provided by the author.

79. Some medical missionary men, however, saw the fund as a direct threat to their proselytizing efforts: "Shall the Queen-Empress, or Lady Dufferin, or the National Association stand between you and the most blessed of all your privileges as a servant of Christ?" See J. L. Maxwell, "Lady Dufferin's Scheme: Its Bearing on Christian Freedom," *Medical Missionary Record* 2 (1887), 231, quoted in Lal, "The Politics of Gender and Medicine in Colonial India," 26.

80. The NIA, for example, initiated the John Stuart Mill Scholarship, under whose auspices a number of women attended the LSMW. It stipulated, as did the Fanny Butler Scholarship, that the winner would devote a specified numbers of years to medical service in India: see Isabel Thorne, "The London (R.F.H.) School of Medicine, Its Foundation and Development," *Magazine of the LSMW* (May 1896), 742–43.

81. *Fourteenth Annual Report of the National Association for Supplying Female Medical Aid to the Women of India*, 15. After 1886, Edinburgh was another site: see Thorne, "The London (R.F.H.) School of Medicine," 741.

82. Mangan, *Making Imperial Mentalities*.

83. "Sketches at the London School of Medicine for Women," *Daily Graphic* (London), 28 June 1890, Newspaper Cuttings Collections, Royal Free Hospital, London.

84. "How Can I Earn My Living?" *Young Women*, November 1893, 63, Newspaper Cuttings Collection, Royal Free Hospital Archives, London.

85. See the mimeographed copy of the ledger, "Entry of Students, 1874–1927," Royal Free Hospital Archives, London. See Lutzker, *Edith Pechey-Phipson, M.D.*; Helen Hanson, "From East to West: Women's Suffrage in Relation to Foreign Missions" (London: Francis, 1913), 1–21; Lilian Trewby to the secretary of the Association for Registered Medical Women, Bombay, letter, 19 April 1912, Wellcome Institute, SA/MFW/c. 148. See also D. Y., "A Chat about India," *Magazine of the LSMW and RFH* (October 1900), 688–95; Mary Pailthorpe, "A Letter from India," *Our Magazine* (July 1886), 74–81.

86. See the reports of the Executive Committee, 1884–1899, Royal Free Hospital Archives, London.

87. Of these, apparently only Vakil did not complete the training course at the LSMW.

88. I am grateful to an anonymous reviewer for urging a distinction between trained and untrained *dhais*, since the British in India continued to use the word *"dhai"* for women (not of the *dhai* caste) whom they trained in their hospitals. Significantly perhaps, the horror of the traditional *dhai* was shared by male and female Indian doctors who had been trained in Western medicine.

89. See Executive Committee Minutes, London School of Medicine for Women, 1895, Royal Free Hospital Archives. As the school continued to expand, calls for better midwifery and gynecology instruction multiplied. The charge was led by Garrett Anderson. She hired Scharlieb, who had practiced in India, to teach the course in gynecology: see Thorne, "The London (R.F.H.) School of Medicine," 741–45, *Echo*, 17 March 1891; "Women and the Medical Profession," *Times* (London), 11 December 1896; Huntley, *The Study and Practice of Medicine by Women*, 37–45; Elizabeth Blackwell, "The Influence of Women in the Profession of Medicine," *Essays in Medical Sociology* (London: Ernest Bell, 1902), 2:29; Manton, *Elizabeth Garrett Anderson*, 269–70, 287–90.

90. Nancy M. Theriot, "Women's Voices in Nineteenth-Century Medical Discourse: A Step toward Deconstructing Science," *Signs* 19, no. 1 (Fall 1993), 6.

91. Mary Scharlieb, "How to Become a Lady Doctor," *Queen*, 15 December 1888, Newspaper Cuttings Collection, Royal Free Hospital Archives, London.

92. Sophia Jex-Blake, *Medical Women: A Ten Years' Retrospect* (Edinburgh: National Association for Promoting the Medical Education of Women, 1888), 15–16.

93. Ibid., 23.

94. London School of Medicine, "Annual Report," 1894, Royal Free Hospital Archives, London, 23.

95. "North India School for Medicine for Christian Women, Ludhiana," *Magazine of the LSMW and RFH* (May 1895), 40–44.

96. I am indebted to Angela Woollacott for pressing this line of argument. She deals with some of these same issues in "From Moral to Professional Authority: Secularism, Social Work, and Middle-Class Women"s Self-Construction in World War I," *Journal of Women's History* 10, no. 2 (Summer 1998), 85–111.

97. I am grateful to DeWitt Ellinwood for encouraging me to consider this point during a panel discussion at the South Asia Conference at the University of Wisconsin, Madison, November 1994.

98. For an excellent example of the linkages made between women's medicine and scientific progress, see Elizabeth Garrett Anderson, "On the Progress of Medicine in the Victoria Era," *Magazine of the RFHSMW* 2 (October 1897), 290–305.

99. Lal, "The Politics of Gender and Medicine in Colonial India," 12–15.

100. Ganguli faced accusations of being a prostitute simply because she was an Indian woman who had gone to Britain for higher medical training and practiced medicine "in public": Karlekar, *Voices from Within*, 178.

101. Chidambaram, "Sex Stereotypes in Women Doctors Contribution to Medicine," 13.

102. The verse is, of course, from Rudyard Kipling's poem "The White Man's Burden" (1899). See Mary Scharlieb, "Preface," in Balfour and Young, *The Medical Work of Women in India*, 11–12.

103. For an insightful set of reflections on the challenges of narrating British women's and feminist histories, see Laura E. Nym Mayhall, "Creating the 'Suffragette Spirit': British Feminism and the Historical Imagination," *Women's History Review* 4, no. 3 (1995), 319–44.

10. Recapturing *Jane Eyre*

This essay was initially inspired by Firdous Azim's and Jenny Sharpe's provocative readings of *Jane Eyre*. I thank Belinda Edmondson, Darlene Hantzis, Madhavi Kale, Ann Klotz, Philippa Levine, Maria Lima, Hannah Rosen, Susan Thorne, and members of Lynn Lees's Delaware Valley British Historians group for reading and commenting on drafts of this essay. I am also grateful to students at Indiana State and Johns Hopkins University for reading Charlotte Brontë's novel with me. Devoney Looser's insights and support were invaluable from start to finish. The comments of anonymous reviewers, and especially of Ellen DuBois, have made all the difference.

My use of the term "recapturing" is a critical echo of Richard G. Fox, ed., *Recapturing Anthropology: Working in the Present* (Santa Fe: School of American Research Press, 1991). I am grateful to Laury Oaks for sharing this reference with me.

Epigraph: Firdous Azim, *The Colonial Rise of the Novel* (New York: Routledge, 1993).

1. Gayatri Spivak, "Three Women's Texts and a Critique of Imperialism," *Critical Inquiry* 12 (Fall 1985), 243–61; May Ellis Gibson, "The Seraglio or Suttee: Brontë's *Jane Eyre*," *Postscript* 4 (1987), 1–8; Susan L. Meyer, "Colonialism and the Figurative Strategy of *Jane Eyre*," *Victorian Studies* 33, no. 2 (Winter 1990), 247–68; Laura Donaldson, *Decolonizing Feminisms: Race, Gender and Empire Building* (Chapel Hill: University of North Carolina Press, 1992); Firdous Azim, *The Colonial Rise of the Novel* (New York: Routledge, 1993); Jenny Sharpe, *Allegories of Empire: The Figure of Woman in the Colonial Text* (Minneapolis: University of Minnesota Press, 1993); Joyce Zonana, "The Sultan and the Slave: Feminist Orientalism and the Structure of *Jane Eyre*," *Signs* 18, no. 3 (1993), 592–617; Carl Plasa, " 'Silent Revolt': Slavery and the Politics of Metaphor in *Jane Eyre*," *The Discourse of Slavery: Aphra Behn to Toni Morrison*, ed. Carl Plasa and Berry J. Ring (New York: Routledge, 1994), 64–93.

2. Moira Ferguson, *Subject to Others: British Women Writers and Colonial Slavery 1670–1834* (New York: Routledge, 1992), which, as the dates in the title suggest, does not deal with *Jane Eyre*. See also Clare Midgley, *Women against Slavery: The British Campaigns, 1780–1870* (London: Routledge, 1992).

3. Zonana, "The Sultan and the Slave," esp. 593–95. I thank Susan Thorne for helping me clarify this point. Carl Plasa interprets the master–slave metaphor somewhat differently; see his "Silent Revolt," 64–93.

4. Spivak, "Three Women's Texts and a Critique of Imperialism," 243–45.

5. Midgley, *Women against Slavery*.

6. Spivak, "Three Women's Texts and a Critique of Imperialism," 244.

7. Cora Kaplan, *Sea Changes: Culture and Feminism* (London: Verso, 1986), 172. Woolf's critique of Brontë, for all its intemperance, might in turn be read back as something of a template for feminists seeking to historicize their origins. Gerda Lerner, for example, showed some of the same attitudes toward Mary Ritter Beard's pioneering work, as Judith P. Zissner relates in *History and Feminism, A Glass Half Full: The Impact of Feminism on the Arts and Social Sciences* (New York: Twayne, 1993), 34.

8. Margaret J. M. Ezell, *Writing Women's Literary History* (Baltimore: Johns Hopkins University Press, 1993), 42. I thank Devoney Looser for sharing this reference with me.

9. Virginia Woolf, *A Room of One's Own* (New York: Harcourt Brace Jovanovich, 1981 [1929]), chap. 4.

10. Sandra M. Gilbert and Susan Gubar, *The Madwoman in the Attic: The Woman Writer and the Nineteenth-Century Literary Imagination* (New Haven: Yale University Press, 1979), 50. For a somewhat differently situated review of the literature on *Jane Eyre*, see Sharon Marcus, "The Profession of the Author: Abstraction, Advertising, and *Jane Eyre*," *Publications of the Modern Language Association* 110, 2 (March 1995), 208. I thank Maria Lima for this reference.

11. See Sonya Rose et al., "Dialogue: Women's History / Gender History: Is Feminist History Losing Its Critical Edge?," *Journal of Women's History* 5, no. 1 (Spring 1993), 89–128; Susie Tharu and K. Lalita, *Women Writing in India, Volume 1: 600 B.C. to the Early Twentieth Century* (New York: Feminist Press, 1991), esp. 1–37.

12. Azim, *The Colonial Rise of the Novel*, 28. See also Adrienne Rich, "Notes towards a Politics of Location," *Blood, Bread and Poetry: Selected Prose, 1979–1985* (New York: Norton, 1986), 210–31; Chandra Talpade Mohanty, " 'Under Western Eyes': Feminist Scholarship and Colonial Discourse," *Feminist Review* 30 (Fall 1988), 61–88; bell hooks, "Choosing the Margin as a Space of Radical Openness," *Yearnings: Race, Gender and Cultural Politics* (Boston: South End Press, 1990), 145–54; Zakia Pathak, Saswati Sengupta, and Sharmila Purkayastha, "The Prisonhouse of Orientalism," *Textual Practice* 5, no. 2 (1991), 195–218.

13. Sara Suleri, *The Rhetoric of English India* (Chicago: University of Chicago Press, 1992), 2.

14. Sharpe, *Allegories of Empire*, 11. Yet Sharpe warns us at the same time not to superimpose the system of gender on to that of race, or vice versa: "Race cannot be theorized from the functioning of gender hierarchies." For an elaboration of this crucial point, see Stuart Hall, "Signification, Representation, Ideology: Althusser and the Post-Structuralist Debates," *Critical Studies in Mass Communication* 2, no. 2 (June 1985), 91–114.

15. "It is one of the great advantages of being a woman that one can pass even a very fine negress without wanting to make an Englishwoman of her": Woolf, *A Room of One's Own*, 50. See also ibid., 25. Ezell reads Woolf as "not a great historian" and argues that "it is unfair to demand that she act in such a role": Ezell, *Writing Women's Literary History*, 4. Yet for me, Woolf enacts a mode of historical recovery that has been echoed down the century by feminists who, while not (perhaps significantly) historians by training, have demonstrated a keen historical sensibility. See, e.g., Rich, "Notes towards a Politics of Location," 214, where she asks us, in a reprise of Woolf, to demand "when, where and under what conditions has the statement been true?," and Michele Barrett, "Introduction," *Virginia Woolf on Women and Writing* (London: Womens Press, 1992 [1977]), 1–39, where Barrett valorizes the materialism of Woolf's historical approaches.

16. Azim, *The Colonial Rise of the Novel*, introduction and chap. 1. See also Rajeswari

Sunder Rajan, *The Lie of the Land: English Literary Studies in India* (Delhi: Oxford University Press, 1992).

17. Gauri Viswanathan, *Masks of Conquest: Literary Study and British Rule in India* (New York: Columbia University Press, 1989); Suvendrini Perera, *Reaches of Empire: the English Novel from Edgeworth to Dickens* (New York: Columbia University Press, 1991).

18. Shula Marks, "History, the Nation, and Empire: Sniping from the Periphery," *History Workshop Journal* 29 (1990), 111–19. See also Catherine Hall, *White, Male, and Middle Class: Explorations in Feminism and History* (New York: Routledge, 1992); Vron Ware, *Beyond the Pale: White Women, Racism and History* (London: Verso, 1991); Antoinette Burton, "Rules of Thumb: British History and 'Imperial Culture' in Nineteenth- and Twentieth-Century Britain," *Women's History Review* 3, no. 4 (1994), 483–500; idem, "Imperialism: A Useful Category of Analysis?," *Radical History Review* 57 (Fall 1993), 1–85.

19. Carolyn Steedman, "La theorie qui n'est pas une, or, Why Clio Doesn't Care," *History and Theory* 31, no. 4 (1992), 38.

20. This point was impressed upon me by Devoney Looser. See also Christina Crosby, *The Ends of History: Victorians and "the Woman Question"* (New York: Routledge, 1991).

21. The literature on the Afro-Asiatic presence in Britain is vast. What follow are a few prominent titles for the period before 1945: Folarin Shyllon, *Black People in Britain, 1555–1833* (New York: Oxford University Press, 1977); Peter Fryer, *Staying Power: Black People in Britain* (London: Pluto Press, 1987); Rozina Visram, *Ayahs, Lascars, and Princes: Indians in Britain, 1700–1947* (London: Pluto Press, 1986); Jagdish S. Gundara and Ian Duffield, eds., *Essays on the History of Blacks in Britain from Roman Times to the Mid-Twentieth Century* (Aldershot: Avebury, 1992); David Killingray, ed., *Africans in Britain* (London: Frank Cass, 1994). Statistics are hard to come by, and categories are even more slippery. Fryer (*Staying Power*, 235) estimates that there were 10,000 "black people" in Britain at the beginning of the nineteenth century; Killingray (*Africans in Britain*, 2) puts the number of "Africans" at 4,540 in 1911 and 11,000 in 1951; Visram, *Ayahs, Lascars, and Princes*, 53, quotes sources testifying that there were almost 4,000 "lascars" alone in London in 1873–74, a figure that included Indians, Africans, Malaysians, Chinese, Arabs, Turks, and South Sea Islanders. Nor do these kinds of numbers necessarily account for diasporic movement: see Paul Gilroy, *The Black Atlantic: Modernity and Double Consciousness* (Cambridge: Harvard University Press, 1993).

22. Three important exceptions are M. Dorothy George, *London Life in the Eighteenth Century* (New York: Capricorn Books, 1965); Douglas Lorimer, *Colour, Class and the Victorians* (New York: Holmes and Meier, 1978); Christine Bolt, *Victorian Attitudes towards Race* (London: Routledge and Kegan Paul, 1971).

23. See Meyer, "Colonialism and the Figurative Strategy of *Jane Eyre*," 247–68; Sharpe, *Allegories of Empire*, 45; John Kuchich, "*Jane Eyre* and Imperialism," *Approaches to Teaching Brontë's* Jane Eyre, ed. Diane Long Hoeveler and Beth Lau (New York: Modern Language Association of America, 1993), 105, where Kuchich names Bertha a "white Jamaican Creole"); Plasa, "Silent Revolt," 65.

24. For a discussion of the impact of "reading women for color," see Elizabeth Abel, "Black Writing, White Reading: Race and the Politics of Feminist Interpretation," *Critical Inquiry* 19 (Spring 1993), 470–98. I thank Hannah Rosen for bringing this reference to my attention.

25. Ziggi Alexander, "'Let It Lie upon the Table': The Status of Black Women's Biography in the United Kingdom," *Women's Studies International Forum* 2, no. 1 (Spring 1990), 22–33.

26. Lorimer, *Colour, Class and the Victorians*; Fryer, *Staying Power*; Visram, *Ayahs, Lascars and Princes*.

27. Midgley, *Women against Slavery*. See also Ware, *Beyond the Pale*.

28. Lata Mani, "Contentious Traditions: The Debate on Sati in Colonial India," *Recasting Women: Essays in Colonial History*, ed. Kumkum Sangari and Sudesh Vaid (New Delhi: Kali for Women, 1989), 88–126. Laura Chrisman offers an interesting critique of the notion that sati would have an "imperial resonance" in Bertha's Caribbean context: Laura Chrisman, "The Imperial Unconscious? Representations of Imperial Discourse," *Critical Inquiry* 32, no. 3 (1990), 39.

29. Susan Z. Andrade, "White Skin, Black Masks: Colonialism and the Sexual Politics of Oroonoko," *Cultural Critique* (Spring 1994), 189–214. I thank Maria Lima for this reference.

30. Plasa, "Silent Revolt," 64–93.

31. Hall, *White, Male, and Middle-Class*. John M. MacKenzie, ed., *Popular Imperialism and the Military, 1850–1950* (Manchester: Manchester University Press, 1992). The series includes over eighty volumes to date.

32. Ware, *Beyond the Pale*; Antoinette Burton, *Burdens of History: British Feminists, Indian Women, and Imperial Culture, 1865–1915* (Chapel Hill: University of North Carolina Press, 1994); Ferguson, *Subject to Others*.

33. The phrase is Toni Morrison's in *Playing in the Dark: Whiteness and the Literary Imagination* (New York: Vintage Books, 1993), 5. See also Moira Ferguson, ed., *The History of Mary Prince* (Ann Arbor: University of Michigan Press, 1993); Ziggi Alexander and Audrey Dewjee, eds., *Wonderful Adventures of Mrs. Seacole in Many Lands* (Bristol: Falling Wall Press, 1987); Paul Edwards and David Dabydeen, eds., *Black Writers in Britain, 1760–1890* (Edinburgh: Edinburgh University Press, 1991).

34. See Barnor Hesse, "Black to Front and Black Again," *Place and the Politics of Identity*, ed. Michael Keith and Steve Pile (New York: Routledge, 1993), 177.

35. Joan Scott, "The Evidence of Experience," *Critical Inquiry* 17 (Summer 1991), 773–97; Elsa Barkley Brown, "Polyrhythms and Improvisation: Lessons for Women's History," *History Workshop Journal* 31 (Spring 1991), 85–90.

11. Child Bride to "Hindoo Lady"

This essay originally went to press before the publication of Sudhir Chandra's book *Enslaved Daughters: Colonialism, Law and Women's Rights* (Delhi: Oxford University Press, 1998). My efforts have benefited from careful, critical readings by Gary Daily, Shelly Eversley, Geraldine Forbes, Kali Israel, Madhavi Kale, Philippa Levine, Jennifer

Morgan, Barbara Ramusack, George Robb, Mrinalini Sinha, and Amy Smiley. Doug Peer's help was invaluable in the final stages. Participants in the symposium on European Women's History at Monash University, Australia, in the summer of 1996 were also enormously generous in helping me to clarify some of these issues. I especially thank Barbara Caine, Dorothy Helly, and Jim Hammerton.

1. Rukhmabai, letter to the editor, *Times* (London), 9 April 1887, 8, and idem, *Rukhmabai's Reply to Dadajee's "Exposition" Bombay Gazette*, 29 June 1887. See also Sudhir Chandra, "Whose Laws? Notes on a Legitimising Myth of the Colonial Indian State," *Studies in History* 8, no. 2 (1992), 187–211, reprinted in Vasudha Dalmia and Heinrich von Stietencrom, eds., *Representing Hinduism: The Construction of Religious Traditions and National Identity* (New Delhi: Sage Publications, 1995), 154–75; Padma Anagol-McGinn, "The Age of Consent Act (1891) Reconsidered: Women's Perspectives and Participation in the Child-Marriage Controversy in India," *South Asia Research* 12 (November 1992), 100–18.

2. A review of the law columns in the Anglo-Indian *Bombay Gazette* reveals that this was by no means the first such case: see, e.g., *Bombay Gazette*, 6 January 1884, 3; ibid., 3 October 1884, 3. In the latter case, *Jeewa Jussa v. Jalloo et al.*, Telang, who defended Rukhmabai, was also the defendant's counsel: ibid., 6 October 1884, 3. Perhaps significantly, the *Bombay Gazette* began by headlining Rukhmabai's case as "A Novel Suit for the Institution of Conjugal Rights": ibid., 4 March 1887, 3. Only after this was her case referred to as a *restitution* of rights. For a full discussion of Indian newspapers' responses to the trial, see Sudhir Chandra, "Rukhmabai: Debate over Woman's Right to Her Person," *Economic and Political Weekly*, 2 November 1996, 2937–47.

3. *Indian Law Reports*, Bombay series, 9:529–35. Also quoted in Chandra, "Whose Laws?," 188. According to Meera Kosambi, " 'Hindu law' as understood by the British state meant the British codifications which were commonly used in law suits, but which did not enjoy unchallenged authority. The obvious effect of this codification was rigidification and fossilization through the omission of customary law, which was constantly evolving," as well as the introduction of British common law "almost by the back door": Meera Kosambi, "Gender, Reform, and Competing State Controls over Women: The Rukhmabai Case (1884–1888)," *Contributions to Indian Sociology* 29, nos. 1–2 (1995), 270, reprinted in Patricia Uberoi, ed., *Social Reform, Sexuality, and the State* (New Delhi: Sage Publications, 1996), 265–90.

4. See Chandra, "Rukhmabai," 2937.

5. Idem, "Whose Laws?," 189. The Law Member was assigned to the executive branch of the government of India to draft legislation.

6. Kosambi, "Gender, Reform, and Competing State Controls over Women," 274.

7. Jim Masselos, "Sexual Property / Sexual Violence: Wives in Nineteenth Century Bombay," *South Asia Research* 12 (November 1992), 85. See also Edythe Lutzker, *Edith Pechey-Phipson, M.D.: The Story of England's Foremost Pioneering Woman Doctor* (New York: Exposition Press, 1973), 207–9; "Dr. Rukhmabai," *World Medical*

Journal (January 1964), 35–36; Meera Kosambi, "The Meeting of the Twain: The Cultural Confrontation of Three Women in Nineteenth Century Maharashtra," *Indian Journal of Gender Studies* 1, no. 1 (1995), 1–22.

8. This included the consummation of child marriages when the bride was younger than twelve. According to Dagmar Engels, "Such illegal sex was defined as rape and was punishable by a maximum of ten years imprisonment or transportation for life": Dagmar Engels, "The Age of Consent Act of 1891: Colonial Ideology in Bengal," *South Asia Research* 3 (1983), 107.

9. See Behramji Malabari, *An Appeal from the Daughters of India* (London: Farmer and Sons, 1890); Dayaram Gidumal, *The Life and Life-Work of Behramji M. Malabari* (Bombay: Educ. Society's Press, 1888); Mrinalini Sinha, *Colonial Masculinity: The "Manly Englishman" and the "Effeminate Bengali" in the Late Nineteenth Century* (Manchester: Manchester University Press, 1995); Antoinette Burton, *At the Heart of the Empire: Indians and the Colonial Encounter in Late–Victorian Britain* (Berkeley: University of California Press, 1998), chap. 4.

10. Anagol-McGinn, "The Age of Consent Act (1891) Reconsidered," 100–18; Charles Heimsath, "The Origin and Enactment of the Indian Age of Consent Bill, 1891," *Journal of Asian Studies* 21, no. 4 (1962), 499–500; Jim Masselos, *A History of Indian Nationalism* (New Delhi: Sterling, 1991), 95–103; Sumit Sarkar, *Modern India, 1885–1947* (Delhi: Macmillan, 1983), 71–72; Stanley Wolpert, *Tilak and Gokhale: Revolution and Reform in the Making of Modern India* (Berkeley: University of California Press, 1962), 45–56; Radha Kumar, *The History of Doing: An Illustrated Account of the Movements for Women's Rights and Feminism in India, 1800–1990* (London: Verso, 1993), 27; Engels, "The Age of Consent Act of 1891," 107; Uma Chakravarti, "The Myth of 'Patriots' and 'Traitors': Pandita Ramabai, Brahmanical Patriarchy, and Militant Hindu Nationalism," *Embodied Violence: Communalising Women's Sexuality in South Asia*, ed. Kumari Jayawardena and Malathi de Alwis (London: Zed Books, 1996), 190–239.

11. Mrinalini Sinha, "Nationalism and Respectable Sexuality in India," *Genders* 21 (1995), 34.

12. See Lata Mani, "Contentious Traditions: The Debate on Sati in Colonial India," *Recasting Women: Essays in Colonial History*, ed. Kumkum Sangari and Sudesh Vaid (New Delhi: Kali for Women, 1989), 88–126; Lucy Carroll, "Law, Custom and Social Reform: The Hindu Widows' Remarriages Act of 1856," *Women in Colonial India: Essays on Survival, Work, and the State*, ed. J. Krishnamurty (Delhi: Oxford University Press, 1989), 1–26; Tanika Sarkar, "Rhetoric against Age of Consent: Resisting Colonial Reason and the Death of a Child-Wife," *Economic and Political Weekly*, 24 September 1993, 1869–78.

13. Sarkar, "Rhetoric against Age of Consent," 1873.

14. See Vinay Lal, "The 'Rule of Law' and Modalities of Governance in Colonial India: The Trials of King Bahadur Shah (1858) and Mahatma Gandhi (1922)," paper presented at the Workshop on State Formation in Comparative Historical and Cultural Perspective, Oxford, 1997, provided by the author. For another example of Lal's point, see Usha Thakkur, "Puppets on the Periphery: Women and Social

Reform in 19th Century Gujerati Society," *Economic and Political Weekly*, 4–11 January 1997, 46–52. Here I am also self-consciously echoing John D. Kelly, *A Politics of Virtue: Hinduism, Sexuality, and Countercolonial Discourse in Fiji* (Chicago: University of Chicago Press, 1991), x.

15. The Indian National Congress was the culmination of decades of local and regional social-reform activity, as well as the beginning of the organized pursuit of "national" representations: see Anil Seal, *The Emergence of Indian Nationalism: Competition and Collaboration in the Later Nineteenth Century* (London: Cambridge University Press, 1968); John Gallagher, Gordon Johnson, and Anil Seal, eds., *Locality, Province, and Nation: Essays on Indian Politics, 1870 to 1940* (Cambridge: Cambridge University Press, 1973); Partha Chatterjee, *The Nation and Its Fragments: Colonial and Postcolonial Histories* (Princeton: Princeton University Press, 1993).

16. I draw here in part from Kali Israel's conclusion in "French Vices and British Liberties: Gender, Class and Narrative Competition in a Late Victorian Sex Scandal," *Social History* 22 (January 1997), esp. 26.

17. Sinha, *Colonial Masculinity*, esp. chap. 1.

18. See Bernard S. Cohn, *Colonialism and Its Forms of Knowledge: The British in India*, ed. Nicholas B. Dirks (Princeton: Princeton University Press, 1996).

19. I am indebted to Tanika Sarkar's rich and thoughtful essay "Talking about Scandal: Religion, Law and Love in Late Nineteenth Century Bengal," *Studies in History* 13, no. 1 (1997), esp. 63–66.

20. I thank Eamon Dyas, Dorothy Helly, and Mrinalini Sinha for helping me track down the identity of the Calcutta correspondent. See also *Reis and Reyyet*, 28 April 1883, 195.

21. A. James Hammerton, *Cruelty and Companionship: Conflict in Nineteenth-Century Married Life* (London: Routledge, 1992), 1–2.

22. Israel, "French Vices and British Liberties," 1–26; Judith R. Walkowitz, *City of Dreadful Delight: Narratives of Sexual Danger in Late–Victorian London* (Chicago: University of Chicago Press, 1992), 82, 103–4; Frank Mort, *Dangerous Sexualities: Medico-Moral Politics in England since 1830* (London: Routledge and Kegan Paul, 1987). The fact that Rukhmabai was a "child" bride may have also resonated with a metropolitan public immersed in the sentimentalization of children, and especially those of the urban poor, by the mid-1880s: see Hugh Cunningham, *The Children of the Poor: Representations of Childhood since the Seventeenth Century* (Oxford: Blackwell, 1992), chaps. 5–6.

23. *Times* (London), 22 March 1886, 5.

24. Ibid., 12 April 1886, 5.

25. See Gayatri Spivak, "The Rani of Sirmur: An Essay in Reading the Archives," *History and Theory* 23 (1985), 247–80; idem, "Can the Subaltern Speak?," *Marxism and the Interpretation of Culture*, ed. Cary Nelson and Lawrence Grossberg (Urbana: University of Illinois Press, 1988), 271–313.

26. Tanika Sarkar, "Bankimchandra and the Impossibility of a Political Agenda," *Oxford Literary Review* 16 (1994), 183.

27. See Geraldine Forbes, "Women and Modernity: The Issue of Child Marriage in India," *Women's Studies International Quarterly* 2 (1979), 408–9; Wolpert, *Tilak and Gokhale,* 46; T. V. Parvate, *Mahadev Govind Ranade* (Bombay: Asian Publishing House, 1963), 152; Barbara Ramusack, "Women's Organizations and Social Change: The Age-of-Marriage Issue in India," *Women and World Change: Equity Issues in Development,* ed. Naomi Black and Ann Baker (Beverly Hills: Sage Publications, 1981), 198–216; Sinha, "Nationalism and Respectable Sexuality in India," 30–57.

28. Rassundari Devi, *Amar Jiban (My Life),* excerpted in Susie Tharu and K. Lalita, eds., *Women Writing in India, Volume 1: 600 B.C. to the Early Twentieth Century* (New York: Feminist Press, 1991), 193. For an astute analysis of the whole autobiography, see Tanika Sarkar, "A Book of Her Own, a Life of Her Own: Autobiography of a Nineteenth Century Woman," *History Workshop Journal* 36 (1993), 35–65. On women's writings in Bengal on girlhood, see Shivani Banerjee Chakravorty, "The Girl Child as the Site for Gender Construction: Women's Writings in Colonial Bengal," Women's Research Working Papers, University of Hawaii, Manoa, vol. 3 (1994), 8–19.

29. Tanika Sarkar, "The Hindu Wife and the Hindu Nation: Domesticity and Nationalism in Nineteenth Century Bengal," *Studies in History* 8, no. 2 (1992), 231. Bengali women were not alone in these critiques: see Anagol-McGinn, "The Age of Consent Act"; Rosalind O'Hanlon, *A Comparison between Men and Women: Tarabai Shinde and the Critique of Gender Relations in Colonial India* (Madras: Oxford University Press, 1994); idem, "Issues of Widowhood: Gender and Resistance in Colonial Western India," *Contesting Power: Resistance and Everyday Social Relations in South Asia,* ed. Douglas Haynes and Gyan Prakash (Oxford: Oxford University Press, 1991).

30. As with Max Müller, Clairsse Spader, and other Western observers: see Uma Chakravarti, "Whatever Happened to the Vedic *Dasi?:* Orientalism, Nationalism, and a Script for the Past," in Sangari and Vaid, *Recasting Women,* 46.

31. Mani, "Contentious Traditions," 88–126; Antoinette Burton, *Burdens of History: British Feminists, Indian Women, and Imperial Culture, 1865–1915* (Chapel Hill: University of North Carolina Press, 1994).

32. Mary Carpenter, *Six Months in India,* vol. 1 (London: Longmans, Green, 1868), 77–78; Antoinette Burton, "Fearful Bodies into Disciplined Subjects: Pleasure, Romance and the Family Drama of Colonial Reform in Mary Carpenter's *Six Months in India,*" *Signs* 20 (Spring 1995), 545–74.

33. For accounts of some of these Indian influences, see Meredith Borthwick, *Keshub Chunder Sen: A Search for Cultural Synthesis* (Calcutta: Minerva, 1977); Burton, "Fearful Bodies into Disciplined Subjects."

34. A Brahmo, "The Evils of Early Marriage," *Journal of the National Indian Association* (February 1879), 81–83.

35. See *Journal of the National Indian Association* (January 1873), 245. After 1886, the *Journal of the National Indian Association* became *Indian Magazine and Review.* See also A. R., "Hindu Domestic Reform," *Journal of the National Indian Association* (June 1880), 342–50.

36. *Times* (London), 22 March 1886, 5.

37. Ibid., 14 March 1887, 5.

38. Ibid.

39. Mani, "Contentious Traditions," 88–126.

40. *Times* (London), 14 March 1887, 5.

41. Judge, letter to the editor, *Times* (London), 18 March 1887, 12.

42. Ibid., 13.

43. For an account of the relationship between Hindu, Muslim, and English law in India until 1864, see Bernard S. Cohn, "Law and the Colonial State in India," in *History and Power in the Study of Law: New Directions in Legal Anthropology*, ed. June Starr and Jane F. Collier (Ithaca: Cornell University Press, 1989), 131–52.

44. Upendra Baxi, " 'The State's Emissary': The Place of Law in Subaltern Studies," *Subaltern Studies VII: Writings on South Asian History and Society*, ed. Partha Chatterjee and Gyanendra Pandey (Delhi: Oxford University Press, 1993), 249–50.

45. F. L. Latham, letter to the editor, *Times* (London), 18 March 1887, 13.

46. Max Müller, letter to the editor, *Times* (London), 21 April 1887), 9. See also idem, "The Story of an Indian Child Wife," *Contemporary Review* 60 (August 1891), 180–92. For a discussion of Müller's Orientalism, especially with regard to Indian women, see Chakravarti, "Whatever Happened to the Vedic *Dasi*?," 27–87. As Chakravarti's evidence suggests, Müller's sympathy for early marriages did not contradict his Orientalism but was constitutive of it.

47. Hunter is quoted in Thomas R. Metcalf, *Ideologies of the Raj* (Cambridge: Cambridge University Press, 1994), 207. See also ibid., 35.

48. If any of these men were aware that several Indian women had used the courts in the 1840s to petition for the restitution of conjugal rights from their husbands, they did not indicate it: see Masselos, "Sexual Property / Sexual Violence," 83.

49. R. H. P., letter to the editor, *Times* (London), 27 April 1887, 15.

50. Müller, letter to the editor, *Times* (London), 22 August 1887, 3.

51. Nor can Müller be said to be representative of metropolitan opinion on the Rukhmabai trial. As Mrinalini Sinha found in the public debates about the Age of Consent Act before it passed in 1891, English views were quite heterogeneous—though possibly more so than here, because it was a much larger legislative question: See Sinha, *Colonial Masculinity*, esp. chap. 4.

52. Müller, letter to the editor (22 August 1887). It was precisely this that clinched the Hindu middle-class case against her, as Uma Chakrayarti argues in "Myth of 'Patriots' and 'Traitors,' " 208.

53. J. Scott, letter to the editor, *Times* (London), 24 August 1887, 12.

54. Müller, letter to the editor (21 April 1887), 9.

55. Ibid., (22 August 1887), 3.

56. Ibid.

57. Pandita Ramabai, letter to the editor, *Times* (London), 27 September 1887, 14.

58. Idem, *The High-Caste Hindu Woman*, repr. edn. (Westport, Conn.: Hyperion Press, 1976 [1877]), 36.

59. See "Obituary: Frances Power Cobbe," *Englishwoman's Review* (April 1904), 133; Frances Power Cobbe, letter to the editor, *Times* (London), 1 October 1887, 6.

60. For coverage of the "domestic" Contagious Diseases Acts crusade, see Judith R. Walkowitz, *Prostitution and Victorian Society: Women, Class, and the State* (Cambridge: Cambridge University Press, 1980). For examination of the imperial dimension, see Burton, *Burdens of History*, chap. 4; Philippa Levine, "Venereal Disease, Prostitution, and the Politics of Empire: The Case of British India," *Journal of the History of Sexuality* 4, no. 4 (1994), 579–602; idem, "Re-reading the 1890s: Venereal Disease as 'Constitutional Crisis' in Britain and British India," *Journal of Asian Studies* 55 (August 1996), 585–612.

61. See *Times* (London): 11 April 1887, 3; 25 April 1887, 7; 2 May 1887, 5; 4 July 1887, 5; 25 July 1887, 5; 5 August 1887, 5; 8 February 1888, 4; 9 July 1888, 5; 16 July 1888, 5; 30 July 1888, 5; 13 August 1888, 5; 17 September 1888, 5; 8 November 1888, 9.

62. Ibid., 11 April 1887, 3.

63. Ibid., 27 April 1887, 15.

64. "The Rukhmabai Case," *Indian Magazine and Review* (September 1888), 449–51.

65. *Pall Mall Gazette*: 22 March 1886, 7; 12 April 1886, 10; 9 July 1888, 10.

66. Stephen Koss, *The Rise and Fall of the Political Press in Britain, Volume 1: The Nineteenth Century* (Chapel Hill: University of North Carolina Press, 1981), 22; Marilyn Strathern, "The Nice Thing about Culture Is That Everyone Has It," *Shifting Contexts: Transformations in Anthropological Knowledge*, ed. Marilyn Strathern (London: Routledge, 1995), 154.

67. *Pall Mall Gazette*, 12 April 1886, 10.

68. Pandit Sivanath Sastri, "Marriage Reform in India," *Pall Mall Gazette*, 17 August 1888, 11.

69. *Pall Mall Gazette*, 8 December 1888, 6, 12 December 1888, 4. For a discussion of the "Maiden Tribute" scandal and the role of the *Pall Mall Gazette* in shaping narratives of sexual danger in London, see Walkowitz, *City of Dreadful Delight*, chaps. 3–4.

70. *Pall Mall Gazette*, 13 December 1888, 4.

71. Quoted in Chandra, "Whose Laws?," 199–201.

72. *Englishwoman's Review* lacked the staff to do its own stories on India, except where the Dufferin Fund and the emergence of the medical women for India movement was concerned. Even in these cases, it relied heavily on *Indian Magazine and Review* for its information: see Burton, *Burdens of History*.

73. "The Hindoo Marriage Law," *Englishwoman's Review*, 15 April 1887, 182.

74. Ibid., 181.

75. *Women's Penny Paper*, 10 November 1888, 5; *Englishwoman's Review*, 15 January 1889, 47. Millicent Garrett Fawcett, a leading English suffragist, took up the question later, contributing to debates about the Age of Consent Act in "Infant Marriage in India," *Contemporary Review* 58 (November 1890), 714–20, in which she referred to Rukhmabai's trial.

76. See Mona Caird, "Marriage," *Westminster Review* 130 (August 1888), 186–201; idem, "Ideal Marriage," *Westminster Review* 130 (November 1888), 617–36; Harry

Quilter, ed., *Is Marriage a Failure?* (London: Swan Sonnenschein, 1888), which reprints many of the *Daily Telegraph* letters; Mary Lyndon Shanley, *Feminism, Marriage and the Law in Victorian England, 1850–1895* (Princeton: Princeton University Press, 1989), chap. 4; Hammerton, *Cruelty and Companionship*, 159.

77. Weldon's case was covered in the *Bombay Gazette*: see, e.g., *Bombay Gazette*, 24 March 1884, 3; 11 April 1884, 5. On Dilke, see Kali Israel, "Writing inside the Kaleidoscope: Re-presenting Victorian Women Public Figures," *Gender and History* 2 (Spring 1990), 42; idem, "French Vices and British Liberties," 1–26. On Campbell, see Gordon H. Fleming, *Victorian "Sex Goddess": Lady Colin Campbell and the Sensational Divorce Case of 1886* (Oxford: Oxford University Press, 1990). Her trial was one of the most drawn out of the century, taking eighteen full court days.

78. Lala Baijnath, *England and India: Being Impressions of Persons and Things English and Indian, and Brief Notes of Visits to France, Switzerland, Italy and Ceylon* (Bombay: Jehangir B. Karani, 1893), 118.

79. Quoted in Y. N. Ranade, ed., *England Opinion on India* 1, no. 5 (June 1887), 201, 205.

80. Ibid., 203, 206, 196.

81. I thank Kali Israel for this insight.

82. Dadaji Bhikaji, *An Exposition of Some of the Facts of the Case of Dadaji vs. Rakhmabai* (Bombay, 1887); Rukhmabai, *Rukhmabai's Reply to Dadajee's "Exposition."*

83. Bhikaji, *Exposition of Some of the Facts of the Case of Dadaji vs. Rakhmabai*, 7–10.

84. Rukhmabai, *Rukhmabai's Reply to Dadajee's "Exposition,"* 8–10.

85. See, e.g., *Mahratta* (Poona; in English), 24 July 1887, 8.

86. For a discussion of these maneuvers, see Anagol-McGinn, "The Age of Consent Act," 100–18; Sinha, *Colonial Masculinity*, chap. 4.

87. See *Times* (London), 6 July 1885, 5, 28 September 1885, 6.

88. A Hindoo Lady, "Child Marriage in India," *Journal of the Indian National Association* (September 1885), 416.

89. For a more complete discussion of the material locations of the "speaking" Indian woman, see Mrinalini Sinha, "Gender in the Critiques of Colonialism and Nationalism: Locating the 'Indian Woman,'" *Feminists Revision History*, ed. Ann-Louise Shapiro (New Brunswick: Rutgers University Press, 1994), 246–75; Mrinalini Sinha, "Reading Mother India: Empire, Nation, and the Female Voice," *Journal of Women's History* 6 (Summer 1994), 6–44.

90. A Hindoo Lady, "Child Marriage in India," 416.

91. Ibid., 417.

92. Ibid., 420.

93. Ibid., 423.

94. Idem, "Widow Marriage," *Journal of the National Indian Association* (December 1885), 586–89.

95. Ibid., 588–89.

96. This was also a moment when critiques of British marriage law could be directly linked to claims for women's suffrage: see "The Law in Relation to Women," *Westminster Review* 128 (1887), 698–710. Frances Power Cobbe had also advanced

this connection a decade earlier in "Wife-Torture in England," *Contemporary Review* 32 (1878), 55–87.

97. Meera Kosambi, "Anandibai Joshee: Retrieving a Fragmented Feminist Image," *Economic and Political Weekly* 31, no. 49 (7 December 1996), 3193.

98. Anagol-McGinn, "The Age of Consent Act," esp. 103–5.

99. Gauri Viswanathan, "Coping with (Civil) Death: The Christian Convert's Rights of Passage in Colonial India," *After Colonialism: Imperial Histories and Postcolonial Displacements*, ed. Gyan Prakash (Princeton: Princeton University Press, 1995), 183–210.

100. Rukhmabai, letter to the editor (9 April 1887), 8.

101. It may also have occluded her non–Brahman status from British readers, who might have been unaware that her eligibility to remarry differed from that of high-caste women in Bombay, Bengal, and Madras.

102. Nora Scott, *An Indian Journal*, ed. John Radford (London: I. B. Tauris, 1994), 43.

103. Ibid., 43.

104. Rukhmabai, letter to the editor (9 April 1887), 43.

105. For an insightful analysis of how the speech of Indian women historically has been managed, see Sinha, "Gender in the Critiques of Colonialism and Nationalism," 246–75.

106. So concerned were "native" Indian papers about the misrepresentation of Indian news in the English press at home (especially over the case of Rukhmabai) that Y. N. Ranade created *English Opinion on India*, a monthly journal that culled excerpts from the English press on Indian affairs. It was published from 1887 to 1894 and touched on high politics as well as social-reform issues. Ranade was explicitly politically motivated, his purpose being to guarantee that "the native press should be an important factor in the administration of this country": Ranade, *English Opinion on India* 1, no. 1 (February 1887), 3; "English Opinion on Rukhmabai's Case," *Mahratta*, 19 June 1887, 1.

107. *Times* (London), 13 September 1886, 5.

108. Ibid., 22 November 1887, 5; 19 August 1885, 8.

109. Ibid., 20 December 1886, 5.

110. Ibid., 22 March 1886, 5.

111. It should be noted that Indian nationalists and "social" reformers also distinguished between the political and the social: see, e.g., M. J. Ranade, "The Sixth Social Conference" (1892), *The Miscellaneous Writings of the Late Honourable Mr. Justice Ranade* (New Delhi: Sahitya Akademi, 1992), 116.

112. Rudyard Kipling, "In the Case of Rukhmibhaio," *Early Verse by Rudyard Kipling, 1879–1889: Unpublished, Uncollected, and Rarely Collected Poems*, ed. Andrew Rutherford (Oxford: Clarendon Press, 1986), 374–75.

113. Metcalf, *Ideologies of the Raj*, 166.

114. See Sinha, *Colonial Masculinity*; Baxi, "The State's Emissary," 250.

115. Gyan Prakash, "Introduction: After Colonialism," in Prakash, *After Colonialism*, 7.

116. See the exchange between J. D., letter to the editor, *Times* (London), 6 January 1888, 14, and F. M. M. [Max Müller], letter to the editor, *Times* (London), 14

January 1888, 4. For a discussion of this tendency by both Müller and colonial officials, see Chakravarti, "Whatever Happened to the Vedic *Dasi*?," 27–86; Mani, "Contentious Traditions," 88–126. See also Chandra, "Whose Laws?," 200.

117. See Jean Comaroff and John L. Comaroff, "Home-Made Hegemony: Modernity, Domesticity, and Colonialism in South Africa," *African Encounters with Domesticity*, ed. Karen Tranberg Hansen, 37–74 (New Brunswick: Rutgers University Press, 1992), 39.

118. See Kamala Visweswaran, "Small Speeches, Subaltern Gender: Nationalist Ideology and Its Historiography," in *Subaltern Studies IX*, ed. Shahid Amin and Dipesh Chakrabarty (Delhi: Oxford University Press, 1996). For critiques of Britain's presumptive originality and discussions of its dialectical relationship with empire, see Catherine Hall, "Competing Masculinities: Thomas Carlyle, John Stuart Mill and the Case of Governor Eyre," in idem, *White, Male, and Middle Class: Explorations in History and Feminism* (London: Routledge, 1992), 255–95; idem, "Rethinking Imperial Histories: The Reform Act of 1867," *New Left Review* 208 (1994), 3–29; Frederick Cooper and Ann Laura Stoler, "Between Metropole and Colony: Rethinking a Research Agenda," in *Tensions of Empire: Colonial Cultures in a Bourgeois World*, ed. Frederick Cooper and Ann Laura Stoler (Berkeley: University of California Press, 1996), 1–58; Anne McClintock, *Imperial Leather: Race, Gender and Sexuality in the Colonial Conquest* (New York: Routledge, 1995); Antoinette Burton, "Who Needs the Nation? Interrogating 'British' History," *Journal of Historical Sociology* 10, no. 3 (1997), 227–48.

119. Sarkar, "Rhetoric against Age of Consent," 1873; see also *Times* (London): 28 July 1890, 5; 7 August 1890, 3; 29 January 1891, 5.

120. See Behramji Malabari, letter to the editor, *Times* (London): 22 August 1890, 8; 13 September 1890, 8; "Child Marriage and Enforced Widowhood in India," *Times* (London), 13 September 1890, 8 (part 1), 15 September 1890, 3 (part 2). See also *Times* (London): 6 October 1890, 3; 9 October 1890, 3; 17 October 1890, 3; 22 October 1890, 5; 9 November 1890, 5; 18 November 1890, 5; 20 November 1890, 8; 28 November 1890, 5; 1 December 1890, 5; 8 December 1890, 5; 22 December 1890, 5; 25 December 1890, 3; 13 January 1891, 3, 5; 19 January 1891, 5; 24 January 1891, 5; 5 February 1891, 5; 9 February 1891, 5; 11 February 1891, 4; 16 February 1891, 5; 18 February 1891, 5; 23 February 1891, 5; 24 February 1891, 9; 28 February 1891, 7; 2 March 1891, 5; 26 March 1891, 3; 27 March 1891, 6; 15 May 1891, 13. See also Rukhmabai, "Indian Child Marriages," *New Review* 3, no. 16 (September 1890), 263–69; Henry Manning, "Indian Child Marriages: I," *New Review* 3, no. 18 (September 1890), 447–49; Millicent Garrett Fawcett, "Indian Child Marriages: II," *New Review* 3, no. 18 (September 1890), 450–54; J. D. Rees, "Meddling with Hindu Marriages," *Nineteenth Century* 28 (October 1890), 660–75; Millicent Garrett Fawcett, "Infant Marriage in India," *Contemporary Review* 58 (November 1890), 712–20; Müller, "The Story of an Indian Child-Wife"; idem, "The Indian Woman and Her Wrongs," *Saturday Review*, 20 September 1890, 341–42; "The Indian Renaissance," *Englishwoman's Review* (February 1890), 55–60.

121. See Meera Kosambi, "Girl-Brides and Socio-Legal Change: The Age of Consent

Bill (1891) Controversy," *At the Intersection of Gender Reform and Religious Belief* (Bombay: Research Centre for Women's Studies, Shreemati Nathibai Damodar Thackersey Women's University, 1993), 105–50; idem, "Gender, Reform, and Competing State Controls over Women."

122. Geraldine Forbes, "Child Marriage Reform in India," unpublished ms. provided by the author; Heimsath, "The Origin and Enactment of the Indian Age of Consent Bill, 1891," 502.

123. Rukhmabai, "Indian Child Marriages," 263.

12. Tongues Untied

The title of this chapter owes its origins to the late Marlon T. Riggs and his film *Tongues Untied* (1989).

1. R. P. Masani, *Dadhabai Naoroji: The Grand Old Man of India* (London: George Allen and Unwin, 1939), 247.

2. Rozina Visram, *Ayahs, Lascars, and Princes: Indians in Britain, 1700–1947* (London: Pluto Press, 1986), 78. See also S. R. Mehrotra, *The Emergence of the Indian National Congress* (New York: Barnes and Noble, 1971), 405. Dyce Sombre (1808–51) was a person of mixed Indian and European ancestry who did sit and vote on several bills, even though his election was "controverted" the next year. I am indebted to Michael Fisher for this information. See Michael Fisher, *The Inordinately Strange Life of Dyce Sombre: Victorian Anglo Indian MP and Chancery "Lunatic"* (New York: Columbia University Press, 2010).

3. Although he ran for a London constituency and was its official representative, Naoroji was also, and consistently, viewed as "the representative for India" to the House of Commons.

4. See, e.g. Jonathan Schneer, *London 1900: The Imperial Metropolis* (New Haven: Yale University Press, 1999), which devotes an entire chapter to Naoroji but only briefly mentions the "black man" incident.

5. The *Finsbury and Holborn Guardian* remarked of Central Finsbury, "or, as it still prefers to be called, Clerkenwell," 23 May 1891, 5.

6. Masani, *Dadhabai Naoroji*, 263.

7. Ibid., 263–64.

8. As Lala Lajpat Rai put it in 1920, "The Indian nation, such as it is or such as we intend to build [it], neither is nor will be exclusively Hindu, Muslim, Sikh or Christian. *It will be each and all.* That is my goal of nationhood," quoted in Gyanendra Pandey, *The Construction of Communalism in Colonial North India* (Delhi: Oxford University Press, 1992), 213; emphasis added. The period during which Naoroji attempted to secure a seat in Parliament overlapped with the general historical moment during which "the Muslim" was being constructed as a different kind of dark, abiding, signing presence by Hindus and British reformers: see Mushirul Hasan, "The Myth of Unity: Colonial and National Narratives," *Contesting the Nation: Religion, Community, and the Politics of Democracy in India,* ed. David Ludden (Philadelphia: University of Pennsylvania Press, 1996), 185–210.

9. In fact, work for the Indian National Congress and the work of electoral politics in Britain went hand in glove in Naoroji's mind: see Anil Seal, *The Emergence of Indian Nationalism: Competition and Collaboration in the Later Nineteenth Century* (Cambridge: Cambridge University Press, 1968), 282–85; Hira Lal Singh, *Problems and Policies of the British in India, 1885–1898* (New York: Asia Publishing House, 1963), 219.

10. Judith Butler, *Excitable Speech: A Politics of the Performative* (New York: Routledge, 1997), 10, 93.

11. Ibid., 89.

12. Charles Dickens's essay "The Black Man" is instructive here. Written in 1875, it routinely refers to the black man as coming from "Asia or Africa," suggesting that the distinctions between Indians and Africans (or "West Indians") was either a product of the 1880s or, more likely, was continually in flux. The essay may have been written by Dickens or by one of his colleagues: see *Household Words* 13 (6 March 1875), 489–93; George F. Rehin, "Blackface Street Minstrels in Victorian London and its Resorts: Popular Culture and its Racial Connotations as Revealed in Polite Opinion," *Journal of Popular Culture* 15 (1981), 19–38.

13. For discussions of the "new journalism," see Allen J. Lee, *The Origins of the Popular Press in England, 1855–1914* (London: Croom Helm, 1976), esp. 117–30; Stephen Koss, *The Rise and Fall of the Political Press in Britain: The Nineteenth Century*, vol. 1 (Chapel Hill: University of North Carolina Press, 1981); Judith R. Walkowitz, *City of Dreadful Delight: Narratives of Sexual Danger in Late–Victorian London* (Chicago: University of Chicago Press, 1992).

14. Lata Mani, *Contentious Traditions: The Debate on Sati in Colonial India* (Berkeley: University of California Press, 1998), 4.

15. Quoted in *Lord Salisbury's Blackman* (Lucknow: G. P. Varma and Brothers, 1889), 21.

16. Ibid., 30.

17. Ibid., 3.

18. Ibid., 10–11.

19. Ibid., 3.

20. Ibid., 26.

21. Ibid., 18–19.

22. Ibid., 6–7.

23. Ibid., 29–30.

24. Ibid., 15.

25. Ibid., 17.

26. Ibid., 4.

27. Ibid., 18.

28. Ibid., 34.

29. Ibid., 16.

30. Ibid.

31. Ibid., 12.

32. Thomas Trautmann, *Aryans and British India* (Berkeley: University of California Press, 1997). See also J. R. Seeley, *The Expansion of England* (Chicago: University of Chicago Press, 1971), 190.

33. *Lord Salisbury's Blackman*, 17.

34. Martin Bernal, *Black Athena: The Afroasiatic Roots of Classical Civilization* (New Brunswick: Rutgers University Press, 1987).

35. Quoted in Douglas Lorimer, "Bibles, Banjoes, and Bones: Images of the Negro in the Popular Literature of Victorian Culture," *In Search of the Visible Past: History Lectures at Wilfred Laurier University*, ed. Barry M. Gough (Waterloo, Ontario: Wilfrid Laurier, 1975), 44. See also James Walvin, *The Black Presence: A Documentary History of the Negro in England, 1555–1860* (New York: Schocken Books, 1972).

36. John Beddoe, *The Races of Britain: A Contribution to the Anthropology of Western Europe* (Bristol: J. W. Arrowsmith, 1885), iv. See also idem, "On the Testimony of Local Phenomena in the West of England to the Permanence of Anthropological Types," *Memoirs Read before the Anthropological Society of London* 2 (1865–67), 37–45; L. Owen Pike, "On the Psychical Characteristics of the English People," *Memoirs Read before the Anthropological Society of London* 2 (1865–67), 153–88. For a brief discussion of Beddoe, see Robert Young, *Colonial Desire: Hybridity in Theory, Culture, and Race* (London: Routledge, 1995), 72, 76, 81.

37. Trautmann, *Aryans and British India*.

38. *Lord Salisbury's Blackman*, 2.

39. Ibid., 24–25.

40. Ibid., 44.

41. See, e.g., Mokshodayani Mukhopadhyay (sister of W. C. Bonnerjee), from "Bangalir Babu (The Bengali Babu)," *Women Writing in India, Volume 1: 600 B.C. to the Early Twentieth Century*, ed. Susie Tharu and K. Lalita (New York: Feminist Press, 1991), 220–21.

42. *Lord Salisbury's Blackman*, 14. See also *English Opinion on India* 3 (October 1888), 441–42.

43. See Mrinalini Sinha, *Colonial Masculinity: The "Manly Englishman" and the "Effeminate Bengali" in the Late Nineteenth Century* (Manchester: Manchester University Press, 1995).

44. *Lord Salisbury's Blackman*, 1–3, 10, 26, 48.

45. Ibid., 25.

46. Ibid., 9, 18.

47. Ibid., 26.

48. Ibid., 1–2, 5, 10, 28.

49. Ibid., 11, 40.

50. Ibid., 4.

51. Ibid., 10–11.

52. Ibid., 22.

53. Ibid., 24.

54. Ibid., 32–33. Actually, what was on Salisbury's mind in the fall of 1888 was not

Africa but India and, more specifically, proposals for the reform of the Indian councils: see Gwendolyn Cecil, *Life of Robert Marquis of Salisbury, Volume 4 (1887–1892)* (London: Hodder and Stoughton, 1932), 193–202.

55. On Suakin, see Ronald Robinson, John Gallagher, and Alice Denny, *Africa and the Victorians: The Climax of Imperialism* (New York: Anchor Books, 1968), 133, 139–40, 346, 357; J. A. S. Grenville, *Lord Salisbury and Foreign Policy at the Close of the Nineteenth Century* (London: Althone Press, 1964), 117–18.

56. See Homi Bhabha, "The Other Question: Difference, Discrimination, and the Discourse of Colonialism," *Black British Cultural Studies: A Reader*, ed. Houston A. Baker Jr., Manthia Diawara, and Ruth H. Lindeborg (Chicago: University of Chicago Press, 1996), 101; George Birdwood on the photograph of Naoroji as evidence of the inaccuracy of Salisbury's remarks, quoted in Christopher Pinney, *Camera Indica: The Social Life of Indian Photographs* (Chicago: University of Chicago Press, 1997), 97–98. As Frantz Fanon put it, "If I am black, it is not the result of a curse, but it is because, having offered my skin, I have been able to absorb all the cosmic *effluvia*": Frantz Fanon, *Black Skin, White Masks* (New York: Grove Press, 1967), 45.

57. I draw here from Etienne Balibar, "Ambiguous Universality," *Differences* 7 (Spring 1995), 63.

58. Peter Marsh, *The Discipline of Popular Government: Lord Salisbury's Domestic Statecraft, 1881–1902* (Sussex: Harvester Press, 1978). On the tradition of flawed speech among aristocrats, see Edward Bulwer Lytton, *England and the English*, ed. Standish Meacham (Chicago: University of Chicago Press, 1970 [1833]).

59. Marsh, *The Discipline of Popular Government*, 145. This remark was much criticized in India: see Iqbal Singh, *The Indian National Congress: A Reconstruction, Volume 1: 1885–1918* (Riverdale, Md.: Riverdale, 1988), 35. See also L. P. Curtis, *Apes and Angels: The Irishman in Victorian Caricature* (Washington: Smithsonian Institution Press, 1971).

60. Both are quoted in G. N. Uzoigwe, *Britain and the Conquest of Africa: The Age of Salisbury* (Ann Arbor: University of Michigan Press, 1974), 8. See also Gwendolyn Cecil, "Lord Salisbury in Private Life," *Salisbury: The Man and His Policies*, ed. Lord Blake and Hugh Cecil (London: Macmillan, 1987), 30–59.

61. See Uzoigwe, *Britain and the Conquest of Africa*, esp. preface, chap. 1; Viscountess Milner, *My Picture Gallery, 1886–1901* (London: John Murray, 1951), 78–83; Arthur D. Elliot, *The Life of Lord George Joachim Goschen, First Viscount Goschen*, vol. 1 (London: Longmans, Green, 1911), 61–62; Percy Colson, ed., *Lord Goschen and His Friends* (London: Hutchinson, 1946). Colson writes that the young Lord Cecil "had all the contempt of a Cecil for a 'Jew Adventurer,' a contempt he expressed with cynical frankness": Colson, *Lord Goschen and His Friends*, 22, 99. It is not surprising, although it remains little commented on, that Salisbury introduced a private member's bill in 1894 to restrict the entry of anarchists and destitute aliens into Britain: see Bill Schwarz, "Conservatism, Nationalism and Imperialism," *Politics and Ideology: A Reader*, ed. James Donald and Stuart Hall (Milton Keynes: Open University Press, 1986), 167.

62. Quoted in March, *The Discipline of Popular Government*, 26. See also Lord Rose-berry, *Miscellanies Literary and Historical*, vol. 1 (London: Hodder and Stoughton, 1921), 274; D. Steele, "Lord Salisbury at the India Office," 117, and A. N. Porter, "Lord Salisbury, Foreign Policy and Domestic Finance, 1860–1900," 149, both in Blake and Cecil, *Salisbury*; R. J. Moore, "The Twilight of the Whigs and the Reform of the Indian Councils, 1886–1892," *Historical Journal* 10 (1967), 414.

63. Marc Jason Gilbert, "Insurmountable Distinctions: Racism and the British Re-sponse to the Emergence of Indian Nationalism," *The Man on the Spot: Essays in British Empire History*, ed. Roger D. Long (Westport, Conn.: Greenwood Press, 1995), 162–63.

64. Uzoigwe, *Britain and the Conquest of Africa*, 8.

65. Marsh, *The Discipline of Popular Government*, 5.

66. Quoted in ibid., 12. This is from Salisbury's essay "Disintegration," which is also known under its original title, "Speeches of the Right Hon. W. E. Forster, M.P., at Devonport and Stonehouse," *Quarterly Review* 156 (1883), 571. See also Jonathan Parry, *The Rise and Fall of Liberal Government in Victorian Britain* (New Haven: Yale University Press, 1993), 305.

67. *Lord Salisbury's Blackman*, 37.

68. Ibid., 47.

69. Ibid., 66.

70. Ibid., 54.

71. Ibid., 26.

72. Ibid., 2.

73. Ibid., 9; emphasis added. To quote J. R. Seeley's precise formula, "The English are those who speak English": Seeley, *The Expansion of England*, 174. For recent work on the English language and colonialism, see N. Krishnaswamy and Archana S. Durde, *The Politics of Indians' English* (Calcutta: Oxford University Press, 1998); Alastair Pennycock, *English and the Discourses of Colonialism* (London: Routledge, 1998).

74. *Lord Salisbury's Blackman*, 19.

75. Ibid.

76. Ibid., 63.

77. See Antoinette Burton, *At the Heart of the Empire: Indians and the Colonial Encoun-ter in Late–Victorian Britain* (Berkeley: University of California Press, 1998), esp. chap. 2; W. T. Webb, *English Etiquette for Indian Gentlemen*, 5th edn. (Calcutta: S. K. Lahiri, 1915), 6.

78. A character in Salman Rushdie's novel echoes and continues this tradition, refer-ring to the twentieth-century Indian National Congress as "a talk-shop for wogs": see Salman Rushdie, *The Moor's Last Sigh* (New York: Pantheon Books, 1995), 19.

79. Quoted in *English Opinion on India* 4 (February 1890), 3 and *passim*. See also ibid. 1 March 1887, 70; Singh, *The Indian National Congress*, 31. Because the INC sessions met on Boxing Day, "A newspaper wit in England [took to calling it] . . . the Great Indian Pantomime": Singh, *The Indian National Congress*, 91.

80. See Gerald Sider, "When Parrots Learn to Talk, and Why They Can't: Domination, Deception, and Self-Deception in Indian–White Relations," *Comparative Studies in Society and History* 27 (1987), 3–23. For earlier Indian contexts, see Parama Roy, *Indian Traffic: Identities in Question in Colonial and Postcolonial India* (Berkeley: University of California Press, 1998), 36; T. M. Lurhmann, *The Good Parsi* (Cambridge: Harvard University Press, 1996), 87.

81. See, e.g., "Our Future," *Calcutta Review* 30 (June 1858), 449.

82. Patrick Joyce, *Visions of the People: Industrial England and the Question of Class, 1848–1914* (Cambridge: Cambridge University Press, 1991), esp. chap. 8; Eugenio F. Biagini, *Liberty, Retrenchment, and Reform: Popular Liberalism in the Age of Gladstone, 1860–1880* (Cambridge: Cambridge University Press, 1992), 417, in which a commentator in 1886 describes a villager using "his homely Doric" dialect to address Gladstone on the hustings.

83. See Burton, *At the Heart of the Empire*, chap. 2; Thomas Babington Macaulay, "On the Athenian Orators," *Critical and Miscellaneous Essays*, vol. 3 (Philadelphia: Carey and Hart, 1843), 413.

84. *Lord Salisbury's Blackman*, 18.

85. Masani, *Dadhabai Naoroji*, 279.

86. *Lord Salisbury's Blackman*, 54.

87. Dadhabia Naroji, *The European and Asiatic Races: Observations on the Paper Read by John Crawfurd before the Ethnographical Society* (London: Trubner, 1866). He was responding specifically to John Crawfurd, "On the Physical and Mental Characteristics of the European and Asiatic Races of Man," *Transactions of the Ethnological Society of London* (London: John Murray, 1867). The paper was presented on 13 February 1866. For Catherine Hall's work, see her "Competing Masculinities: Thomas Carlyle, John Stuart Mill and the Case of Governor Eyre," *White, Male, and Middle Class: Explorations in History and Feminism* (London: Routledge, 1992), 255–95; idem, "Rethinking Imperial Histories: The Reform Act of 1867," *New Left Review* 208 (1994), 3–29; idem, "Imperial Man: Edward Eyre in Australasia and the West Indies, 1833–66," *The Expansion of England: Race, Ethnicity, and Cultural History*, ed. Bill Schwarz (London: Routledge, 1996), 130–70.

88. John Vincent, *The Formation of the Liberal Party, 1857–1868* (London: Constable, 1966), xxiv.

89. Henry Louis Gates Jr., *Figures in Black: Words, Signs and the "Racial" Self* (Oxford: Oxford University Press, 1987); David Dabydeen, "On Not Being Milton: Nigger Talk in England Today," *The State of the Language*, ed. Christopher Ricks and Leonard Michaels (Berkeley: University of California Press, 1990), 7; Lorimer, "Bibles, Banjoes, and Bones," 31–49; Rehin, "Blackface Street Minstrels," 19–38.

90. *Lord Salisbury's Blackman*, 71.

91. The persistence of this nomenclature is remarkable, as Fred Leventhal notes in his biography of George Howell, who was defeated by Mancherjee Bhownaggree for the seat for Bethnal Green North East in 1895. Ten years after the fact, Howell recalled bitterly, "I was kicked out by a black man, a stranger from India, not one known in the constituency or in public life": quoted in Fred Leventhal,

Respectable Radical: George Howell and Victorian Working Class Politics (Cambridge: Harvard University Press, 1971), 212.

92. Ibid., 81.

93. I am indebted to Gary Wilder for seeing this point so clearly and for offering such an articulate rendition of it.

94. I thank Sudipta Sen for this point.

95. See Koss, *The Rise and Fall of the Political Press in Britain*; Lee, *The Origins of the Popular Press in England, 1855–1914*; Biagini, *Liberty, Retrenchment, and Reform*.

96. See Hall, "Rethinking Imperial Histories," 3–29.

97. See Sinha, *Colonial Masculinity*; Eugenio F. Biagini, ed., *Citizenship and Community: Liberals, Radicals, and Collective Identities in the British Isles, 1865–1931* (Cambridge: Cambridge University Press, 1996), esp. 2. The Naoroji case is evidence that empire was one of the things that gave liberalism its ideological coherence "at all levels" and would thereby strengthen Biagini's argument against John Vincent and D. A. Hamer. But empire remains almost completely occluded in Biagini's work: see Biagini, *Liberty, Retrenchment, and Reform*, 2–4.

98. Butler, *Excitable Speech*, 87–88.

99. I am borrowing here from Rajeswari Sunder Rajan, "Fixing English: Nation, Language, Subject," *The Lie of the Land: English Literary Studies in India*, ed. Rajeswari Sunder Rajan (Delhi: Oxford University Press, 1992), 14.

100. Sanjay Joshi, "Empowerment and Identity: The Middle Class and Hindu Communalism in Colonial Lucknow, 1880–1930," Ph.D. diss., University of Pennsylvania, 1995, 35–36, provided by the author. See idem, *Fractured Modernity: The Making of a Middle Class in Colonial North India* (Delhi: Oxford University Press, 2001).

101. *Lord Salisbury's Blackman*, i; Antoinette Burton, "A Pilgrim Reformer at the Heart of the Empire: Behramji Malabari in Late–Victorian London," *Gender and History* 8 (1996), 190. Interestingly, Mancherjee Bhownaggree's visit to India in 1896–97 (he had been elected to Parliament in 1895 as a Conservative) prompted harsh criticism from the nationalist press and the publication of the book *The Indian Political Estimate of Mr. Bhavnagri*, which reprinted more than one hundred negative articles about him from Indian newspapers. I thank John McLeod both for this information and for the opportunity to read his unpublished paper, "Sir Mancherjee Bhownaggree and the Transvaal Question."

102. *Lord Salisbury's Blackman*, ii.

103. See Koss, *The Rise and Fall of the Political Press in Britain*, 306. A propos of this, see W. T. Stead, "Government by Journalism," *Contemporary Review* 49 (1886), 653–74.

104. See Koss, *The Rise and Fall of the Political Press in Britain*, 22. Koss remarks, "The press, a ravenous animal, has always fed on itself, not always with appropriate acknowledgment."

105. See S. B. Cook, *Imperial Affinities: Nineteenth Century Analogies and Exchanges between India and Ireland* (New Delhi: Sage Publications, 1993); Curtis, *Apes and Angels*; Daniel T. Dorrity, "Monkeys in a Menagerie: The Imagery of Unionist Opposition to Home Rule, 1886–1893," *Eire-Ireland* 7 (Fall 1997), 5–22.

106. Cited in Visram, *Ayahs, Lascars, and Princes*, 85. For further discussion of how

Jewishness unsettles facile imperial–metropolitan dichotomies, see Judith R. Walkowitz, "The Indian Woman, the Flower Girl, and the Jew: Photojournalism in Edwardian London," *Victorian Studies* 42 (Fall 1998–99), 3–46.

107. I am exceedingly grateful to Sidney Lemelle, Dan Segal, and Gary Wilder for urging me to take this point seriously during discussions of my paper at Pomona College in December 1999.

108. Stanley Trapido, "African Divisional Politics in the Cape Colony, 1884–1910," *Journal of African History* 9 (1968), 79–98; James Hunt, *Gandhi in London*, rev. ed. (New Delhi: Promilla & Co., 1993); Mohandas K. Gandhi, *An Autobiography; or, The Story of My Experiments with Truth* (Ahmedhabad: Navajivan Publishing House, 1990 [1927]).

109. See Belinda Edmondson, *Making Men: Gender, Literary Authority, and Women's Writing in Caribbean Narrative* (Durham: Duke University Press, 1999), esp. chap. 1.

110. Quoted in Faith Smith, "Gentlemen, not Savages: Negotiating Respectability in Nineteenth Century Trinidad," paper presented at the Mapping African America Conference, Collegium of African American Research, Liverpool, April 1997, and at the Twenty-Second Annual Conference of the Caribbean Studies Association, Barranquilla, May 1997, 2, provided by the author.

111. Ibid., 6–8.

112. I borrow here from Gayatri Chakravarty Spivak, "The Burden of English," *Orientalism and the Postcolonial Predicament*, ed. Carol Breckenridge and Peter Van der Veers (Philadelphia: University of Pennsylvania Press, 1993), 145.

113. Madhavi, Kale, *Fragments of Empire: Capital, Anti-slavery, and Indian Indenture Migration* (Philadelphia: University of Pennsylvania Press, 1998), 6.

114. Ibid., 5.

13. India Inc.?

This essay is dedicated to the memory of Doreen Hantzis, whose courage was quiet and inspirational. Thanks also to Paul Arroyo, Gary Daily, Lara Kriegel, Laura Mayhall, Barbara Ramusack, Maura O'Connor, George Robb, Mrinalini Sinha, and Hsu-Ming Teo, all of whom offered comments and lively engagement that undoubtedly have improved the outcome. Heidi Holder gave me crucial references, for which I thank her. Members of the Social History Workshop at the University of Illinois also provided valuable feedback and suggestions for further reading. Without Stuart Ward, this essay might have had quite a different incarnation. I appreciate his encouragement and persistence. I am especially grateful to Darlene Hantzis, who alone knows how much of it belongs to her.

1. Ackbar Abbas, *Hong Kong: Culture and the Politics of Disappearance* (Minneapolis: University of Minnesota Press, 1997), 23.

2. As Tom Stoppard himself admits, both the radio and the stage plays remain unclear about whether a relationship was literally consummated between Das and Flora: see Tom Stoppard, "I Retain Quite a Nostalgia for the Heat and the Smells and the Sounds of India," *Conversations with Stoppard*, ed. Mel Gussow

(New York: Grove Press, 1995), 121–22. But I maintain that it is both a "love affair" and a "sexual encounter," if only in the metaphorical senses of those terms.

3. Quoted in Onyekachi Wambu, ed., *Empire Windrush: Fifty Years of Writing about Black Britain* (London: Victor Gollancz, 1998), 397.

4. See Laurie Kaplan, *"In the Native State / Indian Ink:* Footnoting the Footnotes on Empire," *Modern Drama* 41, no 3 (Fall 1998), 337–46.

5. For a contrast to some other Raj fiction, see Tana Woolen, "Over Our Shoulders: Nostalgic Screen Fictions for the 1980s," *Enterprise and Heritage: Crosscurrents of National Culture,* ed. John Corner and Sylvia Harvey (London: Routledge, 1991), 187.

6. Tom Stoppard, *Indian Ink* (London: Faber and Faber, 1995).

7. Roger Hudson, Catherine Itzin, and Simon Trussler, "Ambushes for the Audience: Towards a High Comedy of Ideas," *Theatre Quarterly* 4, no. 14 (May 1974), reprinted in Paul Delaney, ed., *Tom Stoppard in Conversation* (Ann Arbor, University of Michigan Press, 1994), 52.

8. Gussow, *Conversations with Stoppard,* 131; Tom Stoppard, "On Turning Out to Be Jewish," *Talk* (September 1999).

9. Paul Allen, *Third Ear,* BBC Radio 3, 16 April 1991, in Delaney, *Tom Stoppard in Conversation,* 239–47.

10. Ibid., 241; see also Stoppard, "On Turning Out to Be Jewish," 241.

11. Thomas O'Connor, "Welcome to the World of Tom Stoppard," *Orange County Register,* 2 April 1989, reprinted in Delaney, *Tom Stoppard in Conversation,* p. 229.

12. See Allen, *Third Ear,* 242; Gussow, *Conversations with Stoppard,* 123–34.

13. Allen, *Third Ear,* 241.

14. Stoppard, *Indian Ink,* 1.

15. Tim Barringer and Tom Flynn, eds., *Colonialism and the Object: Empire, Material Culture and the Museum* (London: Routledge, 1998).

16. Arjun Appadurai, ed., *The Social Life of Things: Commodities in Cultural Perspective* (Cambridge: Cambridge University Press, 1986).

17. The placement of the scene where Nell shows Anish the painting rolled up in the suitcase varied from the text of the play to the performance on stage: see Gussow, *Conversations with Stoppard,* 137.

18. Ibid., 122

19. Stoppard, *Indian Ink,* 24.

20. Ibid., 25.

21. See Stoppard, "I Retain Quite a Nostalgia for the Heat and the Smells and the Sounds of India."

22. Allen, *Third Ear,* 239–47.

23. Gillian Reynolds, "Tom's Sound Effects," *Daily Telegraph,* 20 April 1991, reprinted in Delaney, *Tom Stoppard in Conversation,* 249.

24. Stoppard, *Indian Ink,* 43.

25. Ibid., 44.

26. *Hobson–Jobson* was a glossary of colloquial Anglo-Indian words and phrases indispensable to India *wallahs* in the twentieth century.

27. Stoppard, *Indian Ink*, 44–45.

28. Ibid., 45.

29. Ibid., 82.

30. Quoted in Gussow, *Conversations with Stoppard*, 132; John Taylor, "Our Changing Theatre, No. 3: Changes in Writing," in Delaney, *Tom Stoppard in Conversation*, 26.

31. Pike's role was amplified in the transition from radio to stage: see Gussow, *Conversations with Stoppard*, 118.

32. Hudson et al., "Ambushes for the Audience," 61.

33. See Vron Ware, *Beyond the Pale: White Women, Racism and History* (London: Verso, 1992); Antoinette Burton, *Burdens of History: British Feminists, Indian Women, and Imperial Culture, 1865–1915* (Chapel Hill: University of North Carolina Press, 1994).

34. See Gussow, *Conversations with Stoppard*, 128–29.

35. See Clare Midgley, *Women against Slavery: The British Campaign, 1780–1870* (London: Routledge, 1992); Ware, *Beyond the Pale*; Burton, *Burdens of History*.

36. Stoppard, *Indian Ink*, 83.

37. See Annette B. Weiner, *Inalienable Possessions: The Paradox of Keeping-while-Giving* (Berkeley: University of California Press, 1992), 48.

38. Michael Billington, "No Stoppard Fireworks, Just Meditations on Love and Empire," *Guardian* (London), 28 February 1995, 28.

39. For evidence of Indian women's contributions to nationalism, see Vinay Lal, "The Incident of the Crawling Lane: Women in the Punjab Disturbances of 1919," *Genders* 16 (Spring 1993), 80–120; Kamala Visweswaran, "Small Speeches, Subaltern Gender: Nationalist Ideology and Its Historiography," *Subaltern Studies IX*, ed. Shahid Amin and Dipesh Chakrabarty (Delhi: Oxford University Press, 1996).

40. Peter Kemp, "Flinging Mangos at the Resident's Daimler," *Guardian Weekly* (London), 17 March 1995.

41. Gussow, *Conversations with Stoppard*, 124–25.

42. Playbill, *Indian Ink*, Aldwych Theatre, Summer 1995.

43. See Susan Stewart, *On Longing: Narratives of the Miniature, the Gigantic, the Souvenir, the Collection* (Baltimore: Johns Hopkins University Press, 1984), 138.

44. Gussow, *Conversations with Stoppard*, 126. Stoppard's Anglo-American prestige has no doubt increased since the movie *Shakespeare in Love*, for which he co-wrote the screenplay, which won several Oscars in 1999.

45. Jyotirmoy Datta, "Unprecedented Extension for 'Indian Ink' Is Announced," *India Today*, 3 December 1999, 46. The opening of his play about A. E. Housman, *The Invention of Love*, in February 2000 brought *Indian Ink* back into public discourse: see Bernard Weintraub, "When Stoppard Sends His 'Love,' San Francisco Reciprocates," *New York Times*, 2 February 2000; Carlin Romano, "High-Flying Love Story," *Philadelphia Inquirer*, 8 February 2000.

46. Gussow, *Conversations with Stoppard*, 141. Russell Twisk wrote that, if the play were ever made into a movie, "at least a third of the dialogue [would] be lost": Russell Twisk, "Stoppard Basks in a Late Indian Summer," *Observer* (London), 21 April 1991, reprinted in Delaney, *Tom Stoppard in Conversation*, 254.

47. The 1980s were by no means the first decade in which people of color appeared in

British films or television: see Stephen Bourne, *Black in the British Frame: Black People in British Film and Television, 1896–1996* (London: Cassell, 1998).

48. See Anna Marie Smith, *New Right Discourse on Race and Sexuality: Britain, 1968–1990* (Cambridge: Cambridge University Press, 1993).

49. See Yasmin Ali, "Echoes of Empire: Towards a Politics of Representation," in Corner and Harvey, *Enterprise and Heritage*, 194–211.

50. Quoted in Paul Delaney's introduction to Gillian Reynold's article in Delaney, *Tom Stoppard in Conversation*, 248.

51. As Laurie Kaplan has noted, the radio play was dedicated to Felicity: see Kaplan, "*In the Native State / Indian Ink*," 346, fn. 14.

52. Gussow, *Conversations with Tom Stoppard*, 119.

53. For details and photographs, see Felicity Kendal, *White Cargo* (London: Michael Joseph, 1998).

54. Ali, "Echoes of Empire," 194.

55. The quote is from Kathleen Paul, *Whitewashing Britain: Race and Citizenship in the Postwar Era* (Ithaca: Cornell University Press, 1997), 190.

56. See Bernard S. Cohn, *Colonialism and Its Forms of Knowledge*, ed. Nicholas B. Dirks (Princeton: Princeton University Press, 1996).

57. Declan Kiberd, "The Universal Borders of Brian Friel's Ireland," *New York Times*, 14 July 1999, 14.

58. See Eric Santner, *Stranded Objects: Mourning, Memory, and Film in Postwar Germany* (Ithaca: Cornell University Press, 1991).

59. See Stewart, *On Longing*; Renato Rosaldo, "Imperialist Nostalgia," *Representations* 26 (Spring 1989), 107–22.

14. New Narrative

Epigraphs: John Bright, quoted in Mary Cumpston, "Some Early Indian Nationalists and Their Allies in the British Parliament, 1851–1906," *English Historical Review* 76 (1961), 280; William Ewart Gladstone, "England's Mission," *Nineteenth Century* 4 (1878), 560–84; Salman Rushdie, quoted in Homi K.Bhabha, "Dissemination: Time, Narrative, and the Margins of the Modern State," *Nation and Narration*, ed. Homi K. Bhabha (New York: Routledge, 1990), 317.

1. For the latter, see Richard Oastler, "Slavery in Yorkshire," *Victorian Prose: An Anthology*, ed. Rosemary Mundhenk and Luann Fletcher (New York: Columbia University Press, 1999), 9–11.

2. See Clare Midgley, *Women against Slavery: The British Feminists, Indian Women, and Imperial Culture, 1865–1915* (Chapel Hill: University of North Carolina Press, 1994).

3. Catherine Hall, "The Rule of Difference: Gender, Class, and Empire in the Making of the 1832 Reform Act," in *Gendered Nations: Nationalisms and Gender Order in the Long Nineteenth Century*, ed. Ida Blom, Karen Hagemann, and Catherine Hall (Oxford: Berg Publishers, 2000), 107–35.

4. Ibid., 112. See also Stephen Howe, *Ireland and Empire: Colonial Legacies in Irish History and Culture* (Oxford: Berg Publishers, 2000).

5. See Lord Durham, "Report on the Affairs of British North America (1839)," *Selected Speeches and Documents in British Colonial Policy, 1763–1917*, ed. Arthur Berridale Keith (Oxford: Oxford University Press, 1929).

6. Hall, "The Rule of Difference," 118–19; Tom Holt, *The Problem of Freedom: Race, Labor, and Politics in Jamaica and Britain, 1832–1938* (Baltimore: Johns Hopkins University Press, 1992).

7. Eric Williams, *Capitalism and Slavery* (Chapel Hill: University of North Carolina Press, 1994 [1944]).

8. Thomas Babington Macaulay, "A Speech Delivered to the House of Commons on the 2nd of March, 1831," *The Works of Lord Macaulay: Speeches, Poems, and Miscellaneous Writings* (London: Longmans Green, 1898), 407–26.

9. Thomas Babington Macaulay, *Macaulay's Minutes of Education in India in the Years 1835, 1836, and 1837 and Now First Collected from Records in the Department of Public Instruction* (London: C.B. Lewis, 1862).

10. Richard Cobden, *Russia and the Eastern Question* (Cleveland: Jewett, Proctor and Worthington, 1854).

11. William Greg, "Shall We Retain Our Colonies?," *Edinburgh Review*, April 1851, 475–98.

12. Karl Marx and Friedrich Engels, *The First Indian War of Independence, 1857–59* (Moscow: Foreign Languages Publishing House, 1975), 82.

13. Available online at http://www.adam-matthew-publications.co.uk (Cultural Contacts: Mutiny Writings).

14. See Catherine Hall, Keith McClelland, and Jane Rendall, *Defining the Victorian Nation: Class, Race, Gender and the British Reform Act of 1867* (Cambridge: Cambridge University Press, 2000).

15. See John Newsinger, *Fenianism in Mid–Victorian Britain* (London: Pluto Press, 1994).

16. Auberon Herbert, "The Canadian Confederation," *Fortnightly Review* 7 (April 1867), 480–90.

17. See Hall et al., *Defining the Victorian Nation*, chap. 3.

18. Millicent Garrett Fawcett, "The Women's Suffrage Bill," *Fornightly Review* 51 (March 1889), 555–67; Burton, *Burdens of History: British Feminists, Indian Women, and Imperial Culture, 1865–1915* (Chapel Hill: University of North Carolina Press 1994).

19. Benjamin Disraeli, "Conversative and Liberal Principles," *Selected Speeches of the Right Honourable the Earl of Beaconsfield*, vol. 2. ed. T. E. Kebbel (London: Longmans, 1882), 523–35; Gladstone, "England's Mission."

20. For an excellent account of this thorough document, see Barbara Harlow and Mia Carter, eds., *Imperialism and Orientalism: A Documentary Sourcebook* (Oxford: Blackwell, 1999), chap. 8.

21. William Gladstone, *The Irish Question* (New York: Charles Scribner's Sons, 1886).

22. W. C. Bonnerjee, ed., *Indian Politics* (Madras: G.A. Natesan, 1898).

23. See Antoinette Burton, "Tongues Untied: Lord Salisbury's 'Black Man' and the

Boundaries of Imperial Democracy," *Comparative Studies in Society and History* 43, no. 2 (2000), 632–59.

24. Bernard Semmel, *Imperialism and Social Reform: English Social-Imperial Thought, 1895–1914* (New York: G. Allen & Unwin, 1960), 2.

25. For more on the Boer War, see Andrew N. Porter, *The Origins of the South African War: Joseph Chamberlain and the Diplomacy of Imperialism 1895–99* (Manchester: Manchester University Press, 1980).

26. The formal beginnings of the Australian nation were also very much a white-supremacist masculine affair, despite the role of women in its creation: see Patricia Grimshaw, Marilyn Lake, Ann McGrath, and Marian Quartly, *Creating a Nation* (Ringwood, Vic., Australia: McPhee Gribble, 1994).

27. J. A. Hobson, *Imperialism: A Study* (London: A. Constable, 1905).

28. See, e.g., Pamela Scully, *Liberating the Family?: Gender and British Slave Emancipation in the Rural Western Cape, South Africa, 1823–1854* (Portsmouth: Heinemann, 1997); Adele Perry, *On the Edge of Empire: Gender, Race, and the Making of British Columbia, 1849–1871* (Toronto: University of Toronto Press, 2000); Cecilia Morgan, " 'A Wigwam to Westminister': Performing Mohawk Identities in Imperial Britain, 1890s–1900s," *Gender and History* 15, no. 2 (2003), 319–41; Angela Woollacott, *To Try Her Fortune in London: Australian Women, Colonialism, and Modernity* (Oxford: Oxford University Press, 2001).

29. See, e.g., the Merseyside Maritime Museum's collections on slavery, available online at http://www.liverpoolmuseums.org.uk/maritime/collections/slavery/. See also Durba Ghosh, "Exhibiting Asia in Britain: Commerce, Consumption, and Globalization," *Contested Histories in Public Space: Memory, Race, and Nation*, ed. Daniel J. Walkowitz and Lisa Maya Knauer (Durham: Duke University Press, 2009), 101–21. For two rather different narratives of imperial culture at home that I have tried to work out, see Antoinette Burton, "Women and 'Domestic' Imperial Culture: The Case of Victorian Britain," *Connecting Spheres: Women in a Globalizing World, 1500 to the Present*, 2d edn., ed. Marilyn J. Boxer and Jean H. Quataert (Oxford: Oxford University Press, 2000), 174–84; idem, "The Visible Empire at Home, 1832–1905," available online at www.adam-matthew-publications.co.uk.

30. Antoinette Burton, ed., *Politics and Empire in Victorian Britain: A Reader* (New York: Palgrave, 2001).

31. *Pace* Michael Davitt's boyhood recollection of hawking newspapers that featured coverage of the Maori Wars and the U.S. Civil War: Michael Davitt, *Life and Progress in Australasia* (London: Methuen, 1898), 344.

32. Mary Seacole, *Wonderful Adventures of Mrs. Seacole in Many Lands* (London: James Blackwood, 1858).

33. This is true despite the proliferation of imaginative new work on both events: see Jenny Sharpe, *Allegories of Empire: The Figure of Woman in the Colonial Text* (Minneapolis: University of Minnesota Press, 1993); Nancy Paxton, *Writing under the Raj: Gender, Race, and Rape in the British Imagination, 1830–1857* (New Brunswick: Rutgers University Press, 1999); Jeffery Auerbach, *The Great Exhibition of 1851: A*

Nation on Display (New Haven: Yale University Press, 1999); Peter Hoffenberg, *An Empire on Display: English, Indian, and Australian Exhibitions from the Crystal Palace to the Great War* (Berkeley: University of California Press, 2001); Louise Purbrick, ed., *The Great Exhibition of 1851: New Interdisciplinary Essays* (Manchester: Manchester University Press, 2002); Lara Kriegel, "The Pudding and the Palace: Labor, Print Cultures and Imperial Britain in 1851," *After the Imperial Turn: Thinking with and through the Nation*, ed. Antoinette Burton (Durham: Duke University Press, 2003), 230–34.

34. See Rajnarayan Chandavarkar, *The Origins of Industrial Capitalism in India: Business Strategies and the Working Classes in Bombay, 1900–1940* (Cambridge: Cambridge University Press, 1994).

35. Anna Davin, "Imperialism and Motherhood," *Tensions of Empire: Colonial Cultures in a Bourgeois World*, ed. Frederick Cooper and Ann Laura Stoler (Berkeley: University of California Press, 1997), 87–151.

36. See Richard Price, *An Imperial War and the British Working Class: Working-Class Attitudes and Reactions to the Boer War, 1899–1902* (London: Routledge and Kegan Paul, 1972); Henry Pelling, *Popular Politics and Society in Late Victorian Britain: Essays* (London: Macmillan, 1968), chap. 5; Paul Ward, *Red Flag and Union Jack: Englishness, Patriotism, and the British Left, 1881–1924*, Royal Historical Society Studies in History (Rochester, N.Y.: Boydell Press, 1998), chap. 4.

37. See Burton, *After the Imperial Turn*.

38. Susan Pedersen, *Family, Dependence, and the Origins of the Welfare State: Britain and France, 1914–1945* (Cambridge: Cambridge University Press, 1993); Seth Koven and Sonya Michel, eds., *Mothers of a New World: Maternalist Politics and the Origins of Welfare States* (New York: Routledge, 1993).

39. Ian Tyrell, *Woman's World, Woman's Empire: The Woman's Christian Temperance Union in International Perspective, 1880–1930* (Chapel Hill: University of North Carolina Press, 1991); Daniel T. Rodgers, *Atlantic Crossings: Social Politics in a Progressive Age* (Cambridge: Harvard University Press, 1998); Paul Kramer, "Empires, Exceptions, and Anglo-Saxons: Race and Rule between the British and United States Empires, 1880–1910," *Journal of American History* 88, no. 4 (2002), 1315–53.

40. Patricia Grimshaw, *Women's Suffrage in New Zealand* (Auckland: Auckland University Press, 1972). On the long life of this phenomenon in feminist circles, see Fiona Paisley, "Performing 'New Zealand': Maori and Pakeha Delegates at the Pan–Pacific Women's Conference, Hawai'i, 1934," *New Zealand Journal of History* 38, no. 1 (2004), 22–38.

41. For a full account of this phenomenon, see Michael Bassett, *The State in New Zealand, 1840–1984: Socialism without Doctrines?* (Auckland: Auckland University Press, 1998). esp. 9–11.

42. Quoted in John Rickard, "The Anti-Sweating Movement in Britain and Victoria: The Politics of Empire and Social Reform," *Historical Studies: Australia and New Zealand* 18 (1979), 596.

43. This phrase was coined by Andre Métin in *Le socialisme sans doctrines: La question agraire et la question ouvrière en Australie et Nouvelle-Zélande* (Paris: F. Alcan, 1901).

44. Davitt, *Life and Progress in Australasia*, 366, 373.

45. Quoted in A. G. Austin, ed., *The Webbs' Australian Diary* (Melbourne: I. Pitman and Sons, 1965), 113.

46. Ibid., 114–15.

47. Quoted in Bassett, *The State in New Zealand, 1840–184*, 9, 93.

48. See Keith Sinclair, *William Pember Reeves, New Zealand Fabian* (Oxford: Clarendon Press, 1965).

49. Ibid., 270.

50. Ibid., 249.

51. Ibid., chap. 21.

52. Sally Alexander, ed., *Women's Fabian Tracts* (London: Routledge, 1988), 5–7. See also Ruth Fry, *Maud and Amber: A New Zealand Mother and Daughter and the Women's Cause, 1865 to 1981* (Christchurch: Canterbury University Press, 1992); Patricia Pugh, *Educate, Agitate, Organize: One Hundred Years of Fabian Socialism* (London: Methuen, 1984), chap. 10; Ruth Brandon, *The New Women and the Old Men: Love, Sex, and the Woman Question* (New York: W. W. Norton, 1990).

53. Brandon, *The New Women and the Old Men*, 200–23. See also Sally Alexander, "Introduction," in Maud Pember Reeves, *Round about a Pound a Week* (New York: Garland, 1979), ix–xxi.

54. David Vincent, *Poor Citizens: The State and the Poor in Twentieth-Century Britain* (London: Longman, 1991), 10.

55. Reprinted in Alexander, *Women's Fabian Tracts*, 33–52.

56. Lady Emilia Dilke, "Trades Unionism for Women," in Burton, *Politics and Empire in Victorian Britain*, 265.

57. Alan Lester, *Imperial Networks: Creating Identities in Nineteenth Century South Africa and Britain* (London and New York: Routledge, 2001). The Reeves are still probably best known for being the parents of Amber Reeves, who had a liaison and a daughter with H. G. Wells: see Brandon, *The New Women and the Old Men*, 181; Andrea Lynn, *Shadow Lovers: The Last Affairs of H. G. Wells* (Boulder: Westview Press, 2001).

58. Bassett, *The State in New Zealand, 1840–1984*, 99.

59. See "Report of the Department Committee on Old-Age Pensions," British Parliamentary papers (Aged Poor), 1898. I am most grateful to Danielle Kinsey for tracking down this reference for me.

60. Vaughan Nash, "The Old-Age Pension Movement," *Contemporary Review* (April 1899), 503.

61. See Anne Freemantle, *This Little Band of Prophets: The British Fabians* (New York: New American Library, 1959), 149; William Pember Reeves, "The New Zealand Old-Age Pension Act," *National Review* 32 (February 1899), 818–25. This was part of the larger Fabian influence on the development of old-age pensions and, of course, the reform of the Poor Law. The former was heavily influenced by the New Zealand case: see A. M. McBriar, *Fabian Socialism and English Politics, 1884–1918* (Cambridge: Cambridge University Press, 1962), 128–29.

62. See Nash, "The Old-Age Pension Movement," 495–504; Vincent, *Poor Citizens*, 27.

63. See Peter J. Coleman, *Progressivism and the World of Reform: New Zealand and the*

Origins of the American Welfare State (Lawrence: University Press of Kansas, 1987), 82.

64. Samuel Barnett referred to the views of Sir Harry Johnson, the African colonial administrator and botanist, as grounds for the kind of remedies he thought Poor Law reform could accomplish. Johnston, "who speaks with rare authority, has told us how negroes with a reputation for idleness respond to treatment which, showing them respect, calls out their hope and their manhood. Treat them, he implies, as children, drive them as cattle, and you are justified in your belief in their idleness. Treat them as men, give them wages and money, open to them the hope of better things, and they work as men": Canon [Samuel] Barnett, "Poor Law Reform," *Contemporary Review* 94 (1908), 565. See also Sidney Low, "Old Age Pensions and Military Service: A Suggestion," *Fortnightly Review* 73 (April 1903), 606–16.

65. Coleman, *Progressivism and the World of Reform.*

66. See Royden Harrison, *The Life and Times of Sidney and Beatrice Webb, 1858–1905: The Formative Years* (London: Palgrave, 2000), esp. chap. 8.

67. As Rickard has shown, Reeves was not a one-off example. Charles Dilke credited Alfred Deakin, whose practical discussions with him about a wages board scheme resulted in the Trades Board Act of 1909 (which Rickard says was derivative of the earlier Victorian model in Australia, as well). This was part of a larger cross-relay between Britain and the white settler colonies over wages and sweating more generally: see Rickard, "The Anti-Sweating Movement in Britain and Victoria," 585.

68. Bassett, *The State in New Zealand, 1840–1984*, 97; Sinclair, *William Pember Reeves*, 209–10.

69. The phrase is Ian Fletcher's. See his "Double Meanings: Nation and Empire in the Edwardian Era," in Burton, *After the Imperial Turn*, 254.

70. Sanjay Sharma, *Famine, Philanthropy, and the Colonial State: North India in the Early Nineteenth Century* (New Delhi: Oxford University Press, 2001).

71. See Mine Ener, *Managing Egypt's Poor and the Politics of Benevolence, 1800–1952* (Princeton: Princeton University Press, 2003).

72. For the persistence of this view in contemporary analyses, see Gore Vidal, "Requiem for the American Empire" (1986), *Perspectives on the Nation, 1865–2000* (New York: The Nation, 2004), 115; Martin Walker, "America's Virtual Empire," *World Policy Journal* 19, no. 2 (2002), 149.

73. See Tim Pratt and James Vernon, " 'Appeal from This Fiery Bed . . .': The Colonial Politics of Gandhi's Fasts and Their Metropolitan Reception," *Journal of British Studies* 44, no. 1 (2005), 92. See also Michael Fisher, *Counterflows to Colonialism: Indian Travellers and Settlers in Britain, 1600–1857* (Delhi: Permanent Black, 2004).

74. Jed Esty, *A Shrinking Island: Modernism and National Culture in England* (Princeton: Princeton University Press, 2004), 6.

15. Getting Outside of the Global

This essay owes much to conversation and reading with Tony Ballantyne, Tani Barlow, Anna Bateman, Nathan Chio, Ian Hartman, Ashley Howard, Deborah Hughes, Dane Kennedy, Danielle Kinsey, Chris Lintecum, Joel Miyasaki, Becky Nickerson, Jin Park, Dana Rabin, Jeff Sahadeo, Dave Stramecky, Edwin Vega, and Jamie Warren. I am grateful and indebted to each of them in ways I hope they recognize. Thanks, too, to the History Workshop at the University of Illinois, which gave me invaluable feedback and much food for thought.

1. Philippa Levine, *The British Empire: Sunrise to Sunset* (Harlow, U.K.: Pearson Longman, 2007); Barbara Bush, *Imperialism and Postcolonialism* (Harlow, U.K.: Pearson Longman 2006); Andrew S. Thompson, *The Empire Strikes Back? The Impact of Imperialism on Britain from the Mid-Nineteenth Century* (Harlow, U.K.: Pearson Longman, 2005); Dane Kennedy, *Britain and Empire, 1880–1945* (Harlow, U.K.: Pearson Longman 2002); Stephen Howe, *Empire: A Very Short Introduction* (Oxford: Oxford University Press, 2002).

2. Dane Kennedy, "On the American Empire from a British Imperial Perspective," *International History Review* 29, no. 1 (March 2007), 83–108.

3. Niall Ferguson, *Empire: The Rise and Demise of the British World Order and the Lessons for Global Power* (New York: Basic Books, 2003); Linda Colley, *Captives: Britain, Empire, and the World, 1600–1850* (New York: Anchor Books, 2004); idem, *The Ordeal of Elizabeth Marsh: A Woman in World History* (New York: Pantheon Books, 2007).

4. Antoinette M. Burton, *Burdens of History: British Feminists, Indian Women, and Imperial Culture, 1865–1915* (Chapel Hill: University of North Carolina Press, 1994), chap. 5.

5. "Defining the British World" is the name of an annual conference (see http:// www.uwe.ac.uk / hlss / history / britishworld2007 / index.shtml) and has begun to make its way into historiography, as well: see Carl Bridge and Kent Fedorowich, eds., *The British World: Diaspora, Culture, and Identity* (London: Frank Cass, 2003).

6. This is one way to read contemporary theorists' understanding of empire's relationship to globalization: see Kennedy, "On the American Empire from a British Imperial Perspective," 86–87.

7. Kevin Grant, Philippa Levine, and Frank Trentmann, eds., *Beyond Sovereignty: Britain, Empire and Transnationalism c. 1880–1950* (Houndmills: Palgrave Macmillan, 2007), 2.

8. Durba Ghosh and Dane Kennedy, eds., *Decentring Empire: Britain, India, and the Transcolonial World* (Hyderabad, India: Orient Longman, 2006), p. 1.

9. David Lambert and Alan Lester, eds., *Colonial Lives across the British Empire: Imperial Careering in the Long Nineteenth Century* (Cambridge: Cambridge University Press, 2006), 2, 27.

10. Alan Lester, *Imperial Networks: Creating Identities in Nineteenth-Century South Africa and Britain* (London: Routledge, 2001); Tony Ballantyne, *Orientalism and Race: Aryanism in the British Empire* (Houndmills: Palgrave, 2002).

11. Lambert and Lester, *Colonial Lives across the British Empire*, 2, 27.

12. This is a counterpoint, perhaps, to Partha Chatterjee's rule of colonial difference: see Partha Chatterjee, *The Nation and Its Fragments: Colonial and Postcolonial Histories* (Princeton: Princeton University Press, 1993).

13. Bernard Porter sees Britain's ability to "persuade its own people, at least, that it was so much more civilized when it came to shedding colonies than for example, France in Algeria (despite Kenya) and less obstinate than Portugal (in spite of Rhodesia) as its 'major success' ": Bernard Porter, "Trying to Make Decolonisation Look Good," *London Review of Books*, 2 August 2007, 9.

14. In this respect, Philippa Levine, "What's British about Gender and Empire? The Problem of Exceptionalism," *Comparative Studies of South Asia, Africa and the Middle East* 27, no. 2 (2007), 273–82, makes an interesting read against Asfaneh Najmabadi, *Women with Mustaches and Men without Beards: Gender and Sexual Anxieties of Iranian Modernity* (Berkeley: University of California Press, 2005).

15. See Kenneth Pomeranz, *The Great Divergence: China, Europe, and the Making of the Word Economy* (Princeton: Princeton University Press, 2001). I thank Tony Ballantyne, Clare Crowston, and Dana Rabin for helping me refine this point.

16. Eric J. Hobsbawm, *The Age of Empire, 1875–1914* (New York: Vintage, 1989), 56.

17. Ferguson, *Empire*.

18. Duncan Bell, *The Idea of Greater Britain: Empire and the Future of World Order, 1860–1900* (Princeton: Princeton University Press, 2007), 92.

19. Ania Loomba, "Periodization, Race, and Global Contact," *Journal of Medieval and Early Modern Studies* 37, no. 3 (2007), 604.

20. Rebecca Karl, *Staging the World: Chinese Nationalism at the Turn of the Twentieth Century* (Durham: Duke University Press, 2002).

21. See Jonathan Culler and Pheng Cheah, eds., *Grounds of Comparison around the Work of Benedict Anderson* (New York: Routledge, 2005), 13. I am aware of the critiques of this metaphor (see esp. the essay in *Grounds of Comparison* by H. D. Haratoonian, who discusses his own critiques, as well as those of some subaltern studies critics, and Elleke Boehmer and Bart Moore-Gilbert, eds., "Introduction to Special Issue: Postcolonial Studies and Transnational Resistance," *Interventions* 4, no. 1 [2002], 13–14), but I hold to it here for its heuristic value in this context, for this argument, even as I realize its limitations—especially with respect to the question of how shadows fall, where time is set, and what "ghostly effects" can result.

22. Jeff Sahadeo, *Russian Colonial Society in Tashkent, 1865–1923* (Bloomington: Indiana University Press, 2007), 90.

23. For one angle on this question, see Matti Bunzl, "Between Anti–Semitism and Islamophobia: Some Thoughts on the New Europe," *American Ethnologist* 32, no. 4 (2005), 499–508.

24. The literature here is vast. For an early take, see Jane Burbank and David L. Ransel, eds., *Imperial Russia: New Histories for the Empire* (Bloomington: Indiana University Press, 1998). For a more recent perspective, see I. Gerasimov, S. Gle-

bov, A. Kaplunovski, M. Mogilner, and A. Semyonov, "In Search of a New Imperial History," *Ab Imperio* 1 (2005), 33–56.

25. See Mark R. Beissinger, "Soviet Empire as Family Resemblance," *Slavic Review* 65, no. 2 (2006), 294–303. I thank Jane Hedges and Mark Steinberg for putting this in my hands. Significantly, his invocation of the metaphor "family resemblance" derives from Wittgenstein; see also Christopher A. Bayly, *The Birth of the Modern World, 1780–1914: Global Connections and Comparisons* (Malden, Mass.: Blackwell, 2004).

26. I am grateful to Anna Bateman for enabling me to calcify this point.

27. Dina Rizk Khoury and Dane Kennedy, "Comparing Empires: The Ottoman Domains and the British Raj in the Long Nineteenth Century," *Comparative Studies of South Asia, Africa, and the Middle East* 27, no. 2 (2007), 233–44. For a useful discussion of imperial "variation," see Joseph W. Esherick, Hasan Kayali, and Eric Van Young, "Introduction," *Empire to Nation: Historical Perspectives on the Making of the Modern World* (Lanham, Md.: Rowman and Littlefield, 2006), 1–31.

28. Khoury and Kennedy, "Comparing Empires," 237.

29. "Proclamation on Imperialism by the German Conservative Party, 1906," in Louis L. Snyder, ed., *The Imperialism Reader: Documents and Readings on Modern Expansionism* (Princeton: D. Van Nostrand, 1962), 89.

30. In this sense, imperial "anxiety" was not produced only by the precarious hold of colonizer over colonized but also by the fragile hegemony that empires exercised over one another, especially when they were cheek by jowl. For a powerful example of this, see Ross G. Forman, "Randy on the Rand: Portuguese African Labor and the Discourse on 'Unnatural Vice' in the Transvaal in the Early Twentieth Century," *Journal of the History of Sexuality* 11, no. 4 (2002), 570–609.

31. Edward Ross Dickinson, "The German Empire: An Empire?" *History Workshop Journal* 66 (2008), 129–62.

32. Stefan Tanaka, *Japan's Orient: Rendering Pasts into History* (Berkeley: University of California Press, 1993).

33. Lambert and Lester, *Colonial Lives across the British Empire*, 30.

34. Cited in Bush, *Imperialism and Postcolonialism*, 6.

35. S. B. Cook, *Imperial Affinities: Nineteenth Century Analogies and Exchanges Between India and Ireland* (Newbury Park, Calif.: Sage Publications, 1993); David Gilmartin, "Imperial Rivers: Irrigation and British Visions of Empire," in Ghosh and Kennedy, *Decentring Empire*, 104–29; James Hevia, *English Lessons: The Pedagogy of Imperialism in Nineteenth-Century China* (Durham: Duke University Press, 2003), 2 (the latter on soldiers of the Raj seconded to China during the Boxer Rebellion).

36. Robert J. Blyth, *The Empire of the Raj: India, Eastern Africa, and the Middle East, 1858–1947* (Houndmills: Palgrave Macmillan, 2003). For a different but related take on this subject, see Tani E. Barlow, "Eugenic Woman, Semicolonialism, and Colonial Modernity as Problems for Postcolonial Theory," *Postcolonial Studies and Beyond*, ed. Ania Loomba, Suvir Kaul, Antoinette Burton, Jed Esty, and Matti Bunzl (Durham: Duke University Press, 2005), 359–84.

37. Ghosh and Kennedy, *Decentring Empire*.

38. Peter Duus, *The Abacus and the Sword: The Japanese Penetration of Korea, 1895–1910* (Berkeley: University of California Press, 1995), 92. By this they meant intervening economically and militarily rather than simply trying to bring about internal reform from afar.

39. Joe Cleary, "Amongst Empires: A Short History of Ireland and Empire Studies in International Context," *Eire-Ireland* 42, nos. 1–2 (2007), 17.

40. Manu Goswami, *Producing India: From Colonial Economy to National Space* (Chicago: University of Chicago Press, 2004); Mrinalini Sinha, *Specters of Mother India: The Global Restructuring of an Empire* (Durham: Duke University Press, 2006).

41. Lydia H. Liu, *The Clash of Empires: The Invention of China in Modern World Making* (Cambridge: Harvard University Press, 2004); Karl, *Staging the World*; Hevia, *English Lessons*; Ruth Rogaski, *Hygienic Modernity: Meanings of Health and Disease in Treaty-Port China* (Berkeley: University of California Press, 2004).

42. Monica Burguera and Christopher Schmidt-Nowara, "Backwardness and Its Discontents," *Social History* 29, no. 3 (2004), 279–83.

43. Nor is this view limited to scholars of the Qing empire per se. As Peter Duus has argued, "If any East Asian country was 'imperialist' during these years, it was Ch'ing China, whose armies marched and countermarched across the Inner Asian frontier, shoring up old areas of domination on the steppes of Mongolia and establishing new ones in the highlands of Tibet": Duus, *The Abacus and the Sword*, 2. Interestingly, Peer Vries, who is determined to juxtapose China and Britain with respect to their comparative industrial revolutions, reads the Qing as a regime that "sank into semi-colonialism" from the 1840s onward: Peer Vries, *Via Peking Back to Manchester: Britain, the Industrial Revolution, and China* (Leiden: Research School of Asian, African, and Amerindian Studies, Leiden University, 2003), 31.

44. Hevia, *English Lessons*, chap. 10. As Ruth Rogaski has pointed out, Hevia represses Qing imperial ambition over other Asians, an unfortunate omission if we are to historicize fully Chinese imperial ambition or apply the term "semi-colonial" to all nineteenth-century and twentieth-century imperial powers: see 1547 n. 30: Ruth Rogaski, "Review of *English Lessons: The Pedagogy of Imperialism in Nineteenth-Century China*, by James Hevia," *American Historical Review* 109, no. 5 (December 2004), 1546–57. I thank Becky Nickerson for this reference.

45. See Peter C. Perdue, *China Marches West: The Qing Conquest of Central Asia* (Cambridge: Harvard University Press, 2005), esp. chap. 16. I am grateful to both Tani Barlow and Dave Stramecky for helping me to grasp this point.

46. Bush, *Imperialism and Postcolonialism*, 6.

47. Sarah Ahmed, *Queer Phenomenology: Orientations, Objects, Others* (Durham: Duke University Press, 2006), 3, 137.

48. See Antoinette M. Burton, *The Postcolonial Careers of Santha Rama Rau* (Durham: Duke University Press, 2007), esp. "Introduction."

49. Shu-Mei Shih, *The Lure of the Modern: Writing Modernism in Semi-Colonial China, 1917–1937* (Durham: Duke University Press, 2001), 31.

50. Ibid., 34.

51. Sugata Bose, *A Hundred Horizons: The Indian Ocean in an Age of Global Empire* (Cambridge: Harvard University Press, 2006); Thomas Metcalf, *Imperial Connections: India and the Indian Ocean Arena, 1860–1920* (Berkeley: University of California Press, 2007). For a different though related approach to the question of regional connection and global comparison, see Leila Fawaz and Christoper A. Bayly, eds., *Modernity and Culture: From the Mediterranean to the Indian Ocean* (New York: Columbia University Press, 2002).

52. I am drawing here on William W. Fitzhugh and Aron Crowell, eds., *Crossroads of Continents: Cultures of Siberia and Alaska* (Washington: Smithsonian Institution Press, 1988); Esherick et al., "Introduction," 15–16; Roberto González Echevarria, "Introduction," *José Martí: Selected Writings* (New York: Penguin Books, 2002). One important exception here is the work of Adele Perry: see *On the Edge of Empire: Gender, Race, and the Making of British Columbia, 1849–1871* (Toronto: University of Toronto Press, 2001). See also Adrienne Edgar, "Bolshevism, Patriarchy, and the Nation: The Soviet 'Emancipation' of Muslim Women in Pan–Islamic Perspective," *Slavic Review* 65, no. 2 (2006), 252–72.

53. Ann Laura Stoler, "Intimidations of Empire: Predicaments of the Tactile and Unseen," *Haunted by Empire: Geographies of Intimacy in North American History*, ed. Ann Laura Stoler (Durham: Duke University Press, 2006), 19.

54. See Suchetana Chattopadhyay, "War, Migration, and Alienation in Colonial Calcutta: the Remaking of Muzaffar Ahmad," *History Workshop Journal* 64 (2007), 212–39.

55. That is, perhaps, "subaltern" in the sense of "extra-imperial," beyond the reach of empire in all times and places.

56. Sanjay Krishnan, *Reading the Global: Troubling Perspectives on Britain's Empire in Asia* (New York: Columbia University Press, 2007), 2.

57. Tanaka, *Japan's Orient*, 24.

58. Ibid., 6.

59. I draw here on both Liu, *Clash of Empires*, and Radhika Mongia, "Historicizing State Sovereignty: Inequality and the Form of Equivalence," *Comparative Studies in Society and History* 49, no. 2 (2007), 384–41. Mongia understands this maneuver as making comparison still possible, if differently so.

60. Boehmer and Moore-Gilbert, "Introduction to Special Issue," 11, 16.

61. Benedict Anderson, *Under Three Flags: Anarchism and the Anti-colonial Imagination* (London: Verso, 2005), 4.

62. Stephen Howe, "Afterword: Transnationalism Good, Bad, Real, Imagined, Thick and Thin," *Interventions* 4, no. 1 (2002), 79–88.

63. See Duus, *The Abacus and the Sword*; Rogaski, *Hygienic Modernity*.

64. The phrase is Damon Salesa's: Damon Salesa, "Samoa's Half-Castes and Frontiers of Comparison" in Stoler, *Haunted by Empire*, 73.

65. Here I borrow from Kumkum Sangari, "Love's Repertoire: Qurratulain Hyder's *River of Fire*," *Love in South Asia: A Cultural History*, ed. Francesca Orsini (Cambridge: Cambridge University Press, 2006), p. 259.

66. Neil Smith, "After the American Lebensraum: 'Empire,' Empire, and Globalization," *Interventions* 5, no. 2 (2003), 259.

67. See , e.g., Amrijit Singh and Peter Schmidt, eds., *Postcolonial Theory and the United States: Race, Ethnicity, and Literature* (Jackson: University Press of Mississippi, 2000).

68. Warwick Anderson, *Colonial Pathologies: American Tropical Medicine, Race and Hygiene in the Philippines* (Durham: Duke University Press, 2006), 10.

69. Duus, *The Abacus and the Sword*, 23. In many ways, this is another version of Sanjay Subrahmanyam's idea of "connected histories": see Sanjay Subrahmanyam, *Explorations in Connected History: Mughals and Franks* (New Delhi: Oxford University Press, 2005).

70. The phrase is Ania Loomba's: see Loomba, "Periodization, Race, and Global Contact," 596.

71. I am grateful to Clare Crowston for this observation.

72. For an especially trenchant account of the latter point in the context of Chinese history, see William T. Rowe, "Owen Lattimore, Asia and Comparative History," *Journal of Asian Studies* 66, no. 3 (2007), 758–86. Of course, English hardly corners the market on linguistic imperialism, but its gargantuan global power also cannot be gainsaid.

73. For one diagnosis of this structural situation, see Tejaswini Niranjana, *Mobilizing India: Women, Music and Migration between India and Trinidad* (Durham: Duke University Press, 2006), esp. "Introduction," chap. 1. I thank Shefali Chandra for helping me move this reference to the forefront.

74. Erez Manela, *The Wilsonian Moment: Self-Determination and the International Origins of Anticolonial Nationalism* (Oxford: Oxford University Press, 2007).

Afterword

1. Rammohan Roy, "Brief Remarks Regarding Modern Encroachments on the Ancient Rights of Females," *The Essential Writings of Raja Rammohan Ray*, ed. B. C. Robertson (Delhi: Oxford University Press, 1999), 147–55.

2. Dadabhai Naoroji, "The Parsee Religion," in *The Grand Little Man of India: Speeches and Writings of Dadabhai Naoroji*, ed. A. M. Zaidi (New Delhi: S. Chand, 1984). 28. "The Parsee Religion" was presented to the Liverpool Philomathic Society on 18 March 1861.

3. Idem, "The European and Asiatic Races," in Zaidi, *The Grand Little Man of India*, 405. "The European and Asiatic Races" was presented before the Ethnological Society of London on 27 March 1866.

4. Radhakamal Mukerjee, "The Colonial Wave and Subject Races," *Hindustan Review*, March 1936, 724.

Index

Colley, Linda, 275–76

Colonial Lexicon, A (Hunt), 102

Colonial Rise of the Novel, The (Azim), 175

"Components of the National Culture" (Anderson), 42

Congregational Missions and the Making of an Imperial Culture in Nineteenth-Century England (Thorne), 61

Contagious Diseases Act, 36, 155, 199

Cooper, Robert, 92

Corrigan, Philip, 51

Cotton mills, 262

Countess of Dufferin Fund, 155–56, 162, 164, 168–70

Cowper-Temple, William, 153–54

Crewe, Flora (fictional character), 242–51, 254. See also *India Ink*

Crimean War, 259, 262

Cultural vs. social history and categories, 57–67; anthropology and, 62; archive vs. linguistic turn in, 61–62; author's training in, 63; colonialism and, 59, 63; definitions of, 58; epistemological domains vs. historigraphical practices in, 65–66; as least theorized concept, 58; others in Victorian England and, 65; postmodern studies in, 61; poststructuralism and, 63; "savage slot" in, 59; E. P. Thompson and, 63; Victorian social reform and, 65

Culture and Imperialism (Said), 57

"Culture of disappearance," 241

Currency, 77

Daily News (English newspaper), 225

Damon, Eamon, 81

Dancing at Lughnasa (Friel), 255–56

Das, Anish (fictional character), 242, 245–47. See also *India Ink*

Das, Nirad (fictional character), 243, 245–47, 249–52. See also *India Ink*

Davin, Anna, 263

Davitt, Michael, 265

Decentering Empire (Ghosh and Kennedy), 283

Delusions and Discoveries (Parry), 57

"Destination Globalization: Women, Gender, and Comparative Colonial Histories in the New Millennium" (essay, *Journal of Colonialism and Colonial History*), 109

Diana, Lady, 79

Dilke, Charles, 264–65

Dilke, Lady Emilia, 268

Dirk, Nicholas, 59

Disraeli, Benjamin, 260

Doctors and medicine. *See* Lady Doctors for India; London School of Medicine for Women

Don Pacifico affair, 262

DuBois, W. E. B., 52

Dufferin, Harriot, 155–56

Dundee Advertiser (English newspaper), 227–28

Dutch East Indies, 46

Eakin, Emily, 92

East India Company, 94

Eden, Emily, 246, 248–49, 251

Egypt, 283–84

Eley, Geoff, 61

Eliot, T. S., 89

Elmy, Elizabeth Wolstenholme, 125

Empire, 31; discursive fields of, 35–37; historical amnesia and, 41–42; Said on Austen and, 80

Empire (Ferguson), 275

Empire and global history, 83–91, 275–78; Africa and, 282; "Anglo-globalization" and, 279–80; Asian Empires, 278, 281, 284–86; Boer War and, 280; fiction of British exceptionalism, 50–51, 282, 285–86, 287; gender and, 278; global perspective as reorienting device, 285–86; need for multi-axial approach to, 282–83; North American Conference of British Studies report

Gilroy, Paul, 44, 46, 59, 89

Gladstone, Herbert, 221–22

Gladstone, William, 257, 260

Glasgow Mail (Scottish newspaper), 221

Globalization. *See* Empire and global history

Globe (English newspaper), 232

Gordon, Deborah, 52

Gospel of Gentility, The (Hunter), 32

Governor Eyre, 59

Grant, Kevin, 276–77, 277

Great Arch, The (Corrigan and Sayer), 51

Greater Britain (Dilke), 264

Great Reform Act, 258

Gregg, Robert, 63

Griffin, Sir Lepel, 231

Hall, Catherine, 32, 52, 69, 150, 258; Governor Eyre work of, 59

Hamlet (Shakespeare), 231

Hanif Kureishi, 253, 255

Harvey, Robert, 165

Hawk (English newspaper), 225

Heckford, Sarah, 164

Hevia, James, 284–86

"Hindoo Lady, A" (Rukhmabai), 188, 203, 208. *See also* Rukhmabai

Hinduism, 142–45, 147

Hindu marriage and sexual respectability, 184–87, 189–95, 197–98, 210–12; child marriage and, 188–94, 204–9, 212–13; coverage of, in *Pall Mall Gazette*, 200; Mary Carpenter and, 191

"Hip deafeatism," 63

History writing, 27, 53–54; culture as least theorized concept in, 58; as "narrative contract" with nation, 54–55; as production of history, 65

Hobsbawm, Eric, 41–42

Hobson, J. A., 41, 261

Hoggan, Frances, 154, 164–66

Holt, Thomas, 35

Home Work and Sweating: The Causes and Remedies (Hutchins), 268

Homi Bhabha, 48, 65

Hong Kong, 77, 79

Hopkins, A. G., 283

Hulme, Peter, 43

Hunt, Lynn, 56, 60

Hunt, Rose Nancy, 102

Hunter, Jane, 32

Huntley, Edith A., 166–67, 171

Hutchins, B. L., 268

Imperial history and imperial culture, 28–30, 42, 45, 49–55, 65, 77, 88, 242, 265, 267; "area studies" approach to, 87; "betrayals" of, 44; as big business, 275; censure of studies on race pre-1945 and, 44; as constitutive of domestic culture, 43; as cultural commodity, 83, 86, 251–52, 255; disciplining action of boundaries of, 47, 52, 61; emphasis on racial connections with Anglo-Saxons and Teutons, 29; fiction of pre-existing England in, 42–43, 46, 55, 80, 82, 87; first modern historians of, 29; linkage with world history and, 83–84, 86–87; as local history, 89; media exports of, 78–81; "national culture" and, 42; need for multiperspective practices in, 50, 53, 55; performativity of, 51, 78; question of "need for nation" and, 48, 55; repackaging of, 90–91; spatial anxieties in, 47; "uncanny doubleness" in, 69; U.S. and, 78–81, 89–90; "Victorian Vision" art exhibit and, 70–76; whitewashed commodification of, 78–82, 89–91; white women in, 32. *See also* "New imperial history"

Imperialism (Hobson), 261

"Imperialism and Motherhood" (Davin), 263

Imperialism and Popular Culture (Mackenzie), 31

Imperialism and Postcolonialism (Bush), 285

Imperialism and Social Reform (Semmel), 31

Müller, Friedrich Max, 196–98, 211, 223–24

"Murder of Stephen Lawrence" (PBS series), 80–81; review of, 81

Music, ignoring of teen-age, 89

Muslims (British), 82

My Beautiful Launderette (Kureishi), 253

Nair, Janaki, 148

Naoroji, Dadhabai, 214–15, 230; "blackness" of, 219–20, 222, 224–27; Indian National Congress (INC) presidency of, 216; Indian representation in Parliament and, 216, 218; response to "Black Man" debate of, 232–33, 235; Lord Salisbury and, 215, 217–18; slavery vs. citizenship rhetoric of, 233; speech of, 233–35

National Indian Association, 127, 148–49, 164, 169, 192, 198; London School of Medicine for Women (LSMW) and, 164–66; Rukhamabai and, 203–5

Nell. *See* Swann, Eleanor

"New imperial history," 58, 62; controversy of, 56–57; feminist historiography and, 57–58, 64; imperial archives and, 64–65; insiderism in, 284; *Ornamentalism* and, 68–69; reverse-flow paradigm of, 267, 271, 276; "Victorian Vision" art exhibit and, 70–76. *See also* Imperial history and imperial culture

New Yorker (magazine), 82

New York Times (U.S. newspaper), 81, 92

New Zealand, 264–65; Arbitration Act of, 265, 267; Pensions Bill of, 269; reform travel to, 265–67; suffrage in, 268

NIA. *See* National Indian Association

Nield, Keith, 61

Nightingale, Florence, 262

North American Conference of British Studies report (1999), 83–90

Nostalgia for empire, 48, 241; American, 82, 86; Celtic, 256; critics of empire and, 42; cultural imports and, 255; for India, 241, 248, 251–52, 256; in *India Ink*, 245

Notts Daily Express (English newspaper), 219

O'Connell, Daniel, 258

O'Connor, Maura, 59

Old Age Pensions Act, 269

Oriental and India Office Collections, 94

Orientalism (Said), 47, 57; *Ornamentalism* and, 74

"Origins of the Present Crisis" (Perry), 41

Ornamentalism: How the British Saw Their Empire (Cannadine), 68–69, 73, 91; as companion to "Victorian Vision" exhibit at V&A, 70–71; exploration rhetoric in, 70–71; *Orientalism* and, 74

Ortner, Sherry, 53

Othello (Shakespeare), 81, 231

"Others," 43, 52, 65, 103

Oxford History of the British Empire (Louis), 56, 69, 262, 276; American editor of, 53

Oz (television program), 81

Pall Mall Gazette (English newspaper), 200, 227; Hindu marriage coverage in, 200

Parekh Report, 91

Parry, Benita, 57

Passage to India, A (Forster), 34

Paternalism, 130–31, 133, 135, 147, 204–5; of Mary Carpenter, 130–31, 135

PBS, 78–79, 81, 91, 255

Peasants into Frenchmen (Weber), 51

Pechey, Dr., 159–61, 169

Pederson, Susan, 49

Penny dreadfuls, 224

Pensions Bill (New Zealand), 269

Perera, Suvendrini, 32

Pike, Eldon (fictional character), 242, 245. *See also India Ink*

Pinhey, Robert Hill (British justice), 184, 189, 193, 197, 208

"Three Women's Texts and a Critique of Imperialism" (Spivak), 175

Tilak, B. G., 185

Times (London newspaper), 188–89, 193, 195–96, 199–202, 207, 212

Times of India (Indian newspaper), 203

Todd, Isabelle, 124

Transnationalism, 276–77, 283–84; insiderism and, 284; national exceptionalism in, 277, 279

"Transnationalizing Women's, Gender and Sexuality History: the View from the Journals" (AHA conference), 110

Trust, Runnymede, 74–75

United States, 284; American imperialism, 63, 276; anti-national subculture of, 51–52; British relationship post-9 / 11, 76, 92; consumption of "Britishness" in, 78–79, 252, 255; gender history, 110; nostalgia for empire in, 82, 86; political stagings with Britain, 78; Salman Rushdie and, 81–82; whitewashed commodified Britain for export and, 78–82, 89–91

University in Ruins, The (Readings), 88

Upstairs, Downstairs (television program), 81

Up the Country (Eden), 246, 248–49

"Victoria and Albert" (television program), 78–79

Victorian feminism and social reform, 123–26, 260; Fabians and, 267–68; Indian women and, 155; "marriage" with state and (Parliament), 125–26; pleasure of social reform, 124–28; presumptions in, 124; romantic love idiom and, 124–25, 127–28; traditional femininity and, 125–26, 140–41; utopian visions in, 124. *See also* Carpenter, Mary; Lady Doctors for India

Victorian imperial democracy, 217–19, 236–37, 258–63, 269–72; alternative dating suggestion and, 262; challenge of defining "Victorian" period and, 261–62; colonial influence on, 269–72; Khaki election of 1900, 261; public debate on, 258; reform travel to Australia and New Zealand and, 265–67; visionary politics of Australia and New Zealand and, 266–67. *See also* Naoroji, Dadhabai; Reform and Reform Acts

"Victorian Vision: Inventing New Britain" (art exhibit at V&A): exploration rhetoric in, 70–71; management of imperialism in, 72–73; *Ornamentalism* as companion to, 70

Victorian Vision: Inventing New Britain, The (ed. MacKenzie), 70

Viswanathan, Gauri, 143

Walkowitz, Judith R., 34

Webb, Beatrice, 265–67

Webb, Sidney, 265–67

Weber, Eugen, 51

Wedderburn, Sir William, 234–35

Weekly Despatch (English newspaper), 230

Welfare state. *See* Reform and Reform Acts

West, Charles, 160

Whiteness, 223, 277; of Lord Salisbury, 221–22

White women, 32, 150, 181, 249–50; Mary Carpenter in India, 128; in imperial archives, 96, 99–100; in *Prime Suspect*, 80

White Women in Fiji (Knapman), 32

Williams, Eric, 41

Women against Slavery: The British Campaigns, 1780–1870 (Midgley), 33, 181

Women's Penny Paper (magazine), 201

Women's periodicals, 200–201

Women's Work and Woman's Culture (Butler), 123

Women Writing Culture (Behar and Gordon), 52

Wood, Peter, 243
Woolf, Virginia, 166, 176–78
Worcestershire Echo (English newspaper), 231
Working classes, 41

Antoinette Burton is the Catherine C. and Bruce A. Bastian Professor of Global and
Transnational Studies at the University of Illinois, Urbana-Champaign. She is the
author of *The Postcolonial Careers of Santha Rama Rau* (2007); *Dwelling in the Archive:
Women Writing House, Home, and History in Colonial India* (2003); *At the Heart of the
Empire: Indians and the Colonial Encounter in Late-Victorian Britain* (1998); and *Burdens
of History: British Feminists, Indian Women, and Imperial Culture, 1865–1915* (1994). Her
edited books include *Archive Stories: Facts, Fiction, and the Writing of History* (2005);
(with Ania Loomba, Suvir Kaul, Matti Bunzl, and Jed Esty) *Postcolonial Studies and
Beyond* (2005); (with Tony Ballantyne) *Bodies in Contact: Rethinking Colonial
Encounters in World History* (2005); *After the Imperial Turn: Thinking with and through
the Nation* (2003); *Majumdar, Janaki Agnes Penelope, 1886–1963* (2003); *Politics and Empire
in Victorian Britain: A Reader* (2001); and *Gender, Sexuality, and Colonial Modernities*
(1999). In 2010–11, she was named a Simon Guggenheim Foundation Fellow.

Library of Congress Cataloging-in-Publication Data
Burton, Antoinette M.
Empire in question : reading, writing, and teaching British imperialism /
Antoinette Burton ; with a foreword by Mrinalini Sinha and an
afterword by C. A. Bayly.
p. cm.
Includes bibliographical references and index.
ISBN 978-0-8223-4880-1 (cloth : alk. paper)
ISBN 978-0-8223-4902-0 (pbk. : alk. paper)
1. Great Britain—Colonies—Historiography. 2. Imperialism—
Historiography. I. Title.
DA16.B86 2011
909'.0971241072—dc22   2010041584